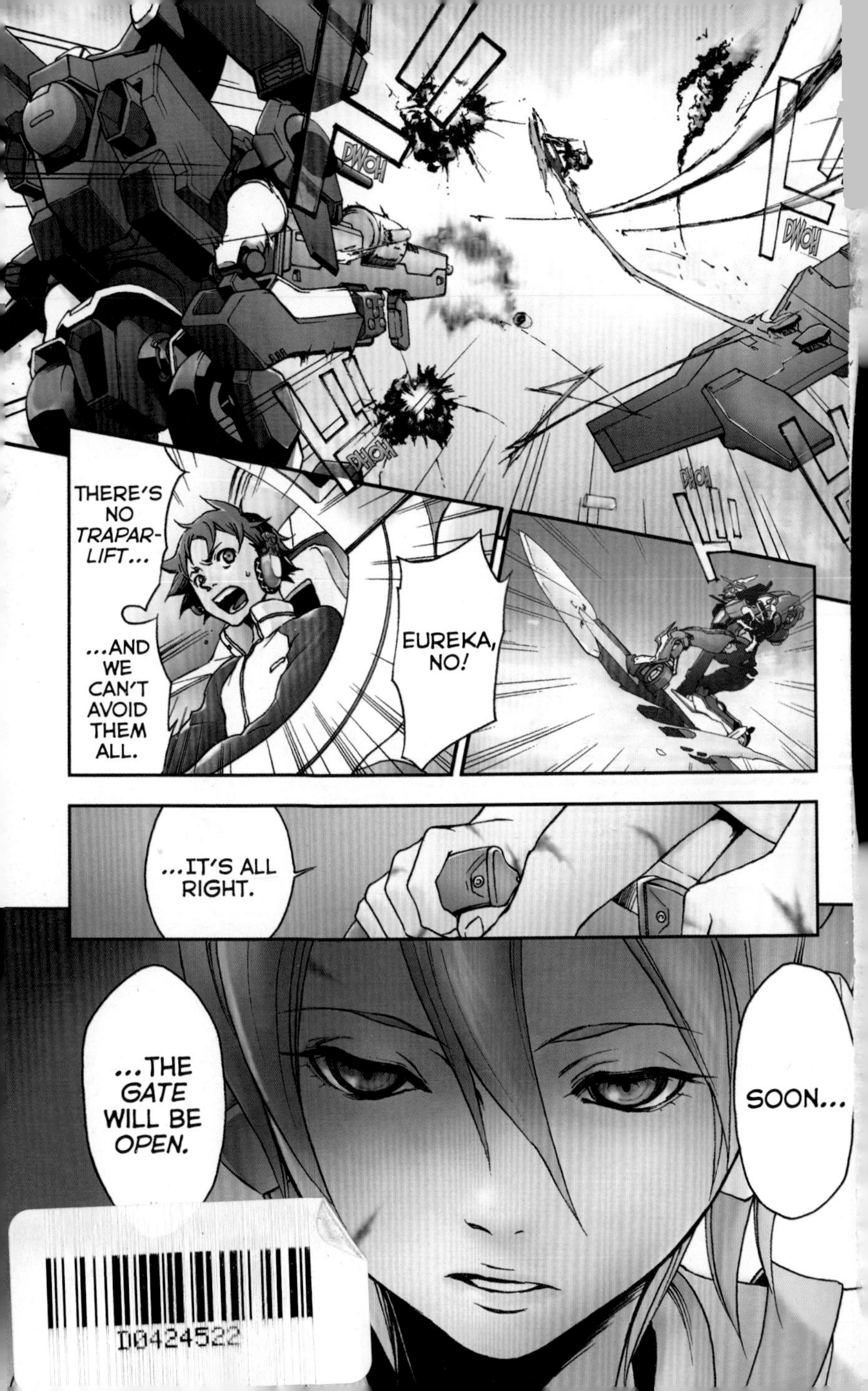
DWOH
DWOH
DWOH
DWOH
THERE'S NO *TRAPAR-LIFT*...
...AND WE CAN'T AVOID THEM ALL.
EUREKA, NO!
...IT'S ALL RIGHT.
SOON...
...THE *GATE* WILL BE *OPEN.*

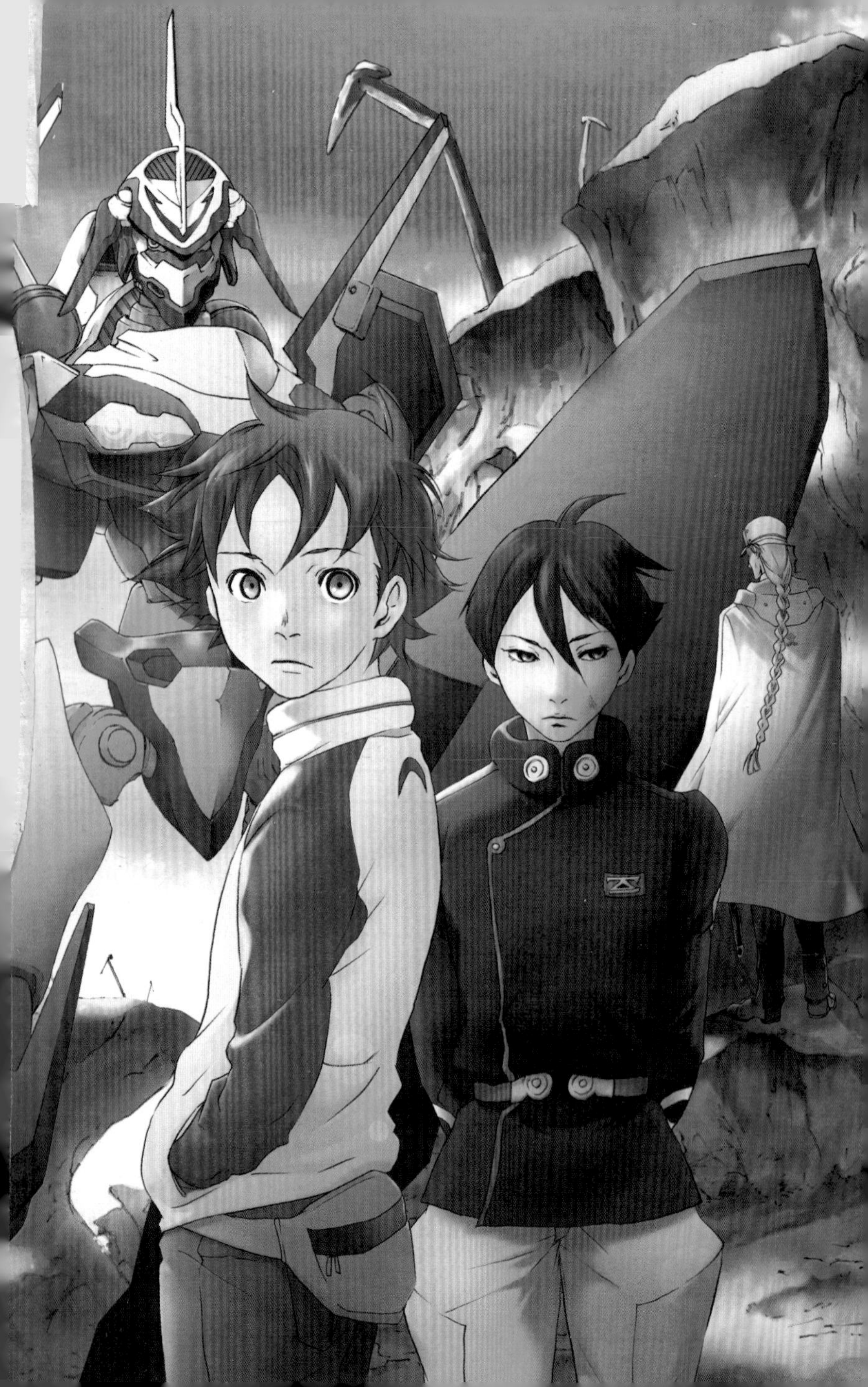

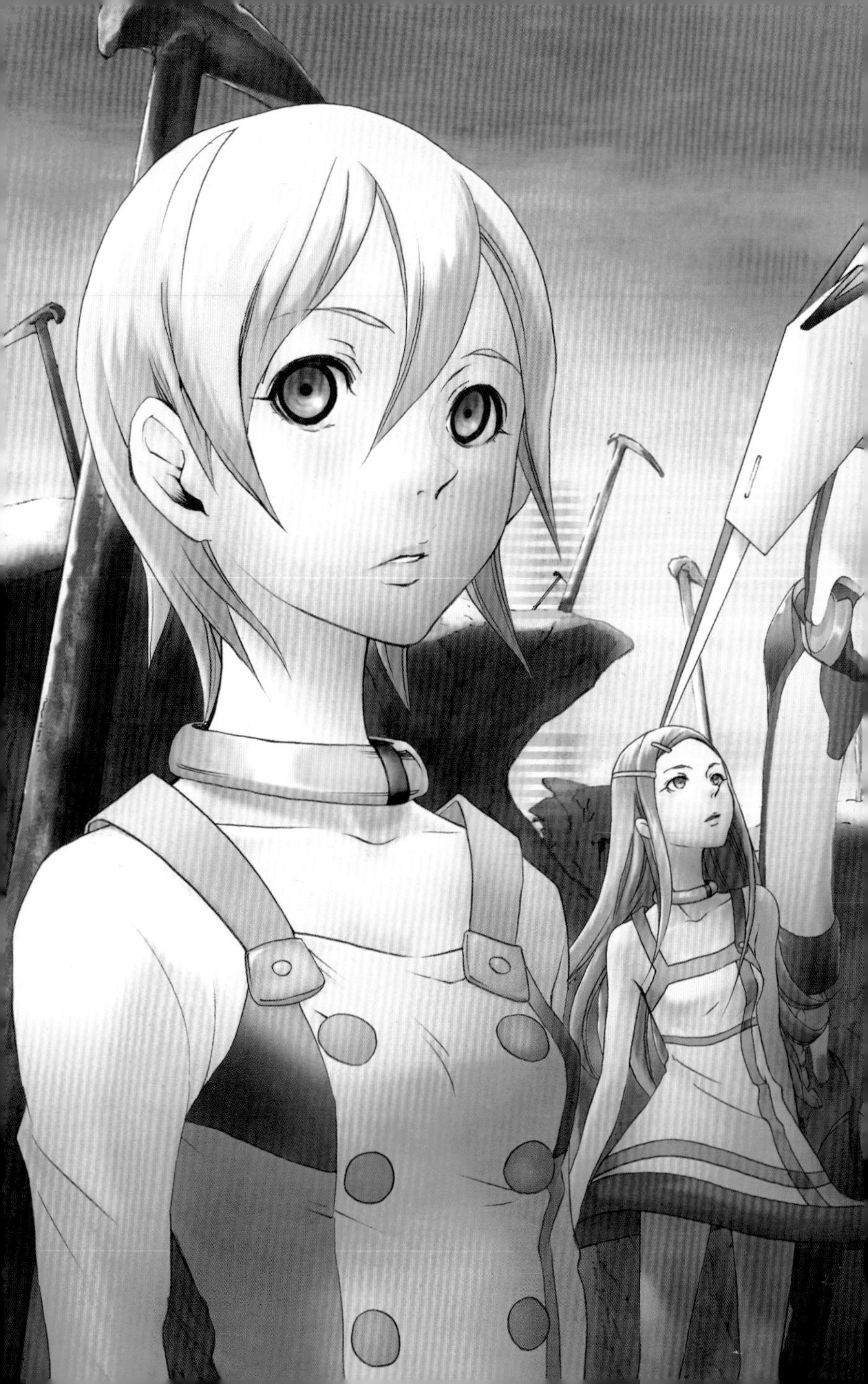

Psalms of Planets Eureka seveN

Volume 5

CONTENTS

ORIGINAL STORY

Bones

MANGA

Jinsei Kataoka & Kazuma Kondou

ORIGINAL BOOK DESIGN

Tsuyoshi Kusano

ENGLISH PRODUCTION CREDITS

TRANSLATION	Toshifumi Yoshida
ADAPTOR	T. Ledoux
LETTERING	Fawn Lau
COVER DESIGN	Kit Loose
EDITOR	Robert Place Napton
COORDINATOR	Rika Davis
PUBLISHER	Ken Iyadomi

Published in the United States
by Bandai Entertainment, Inc.

© Jinsei KATAOKA 2006
© Kazuma KONDOU 2006
© 2005 BONES/Project EUREKA-MBS
Originally published in Japan in 2006 by KADOKAWA SHOTEN PUBLISHING CO., LTD., Tokyo.
English translation rights arranged with KADOKAWA SHOTEN PUBLISHING CO., LTD., Tokyo.

ISBN-13: 978-1-59409-761-4

Printed in Canada
First Bandai printing: April 2007

10 9 8 7 6 5 4 3 2 1

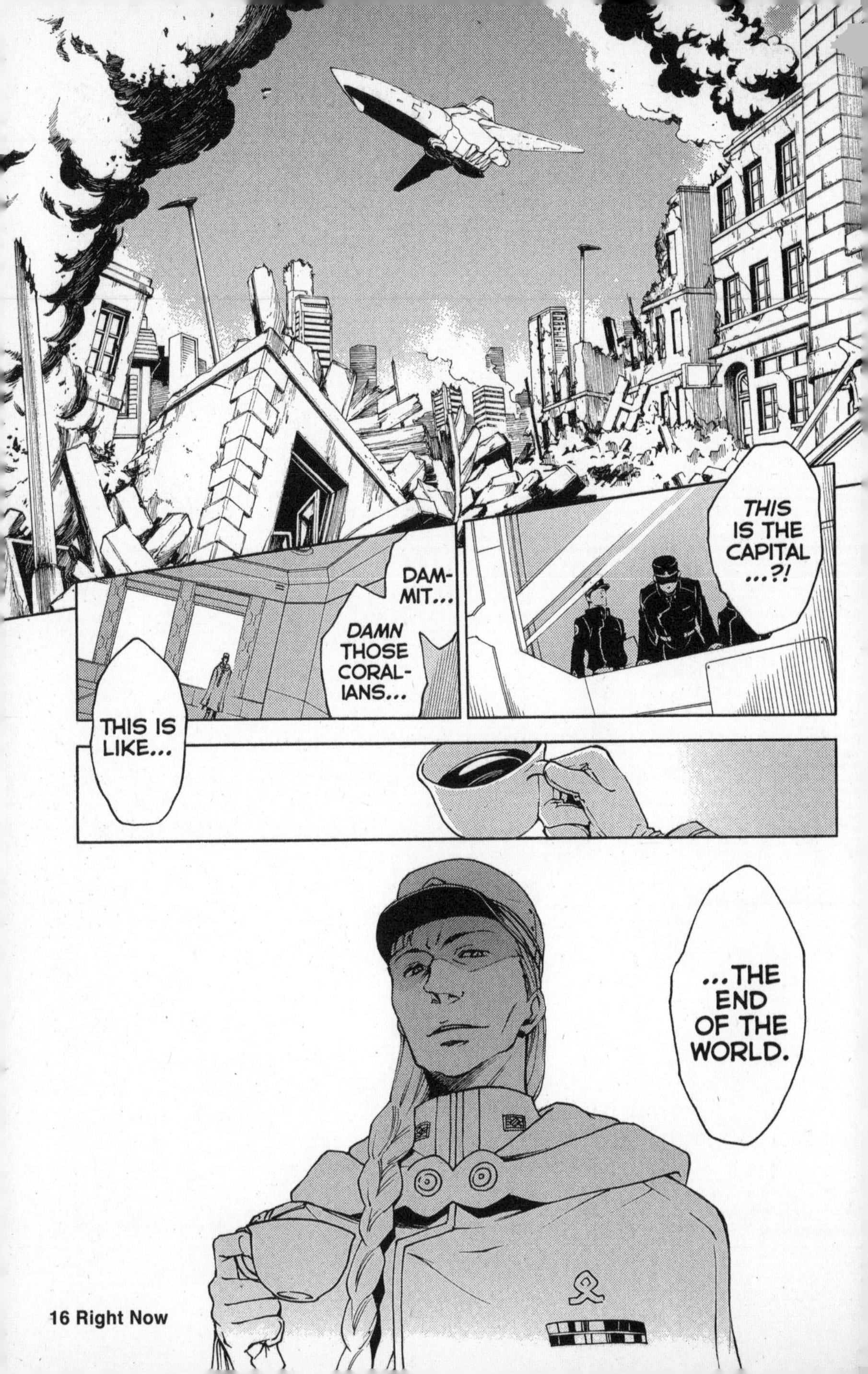
THIS IS THE CAPITAL ...?!
DAM-MIT... DAMN THOSE CORAL-IANS...
THIS IS LIKE...
...THE END OF THE WORLD.

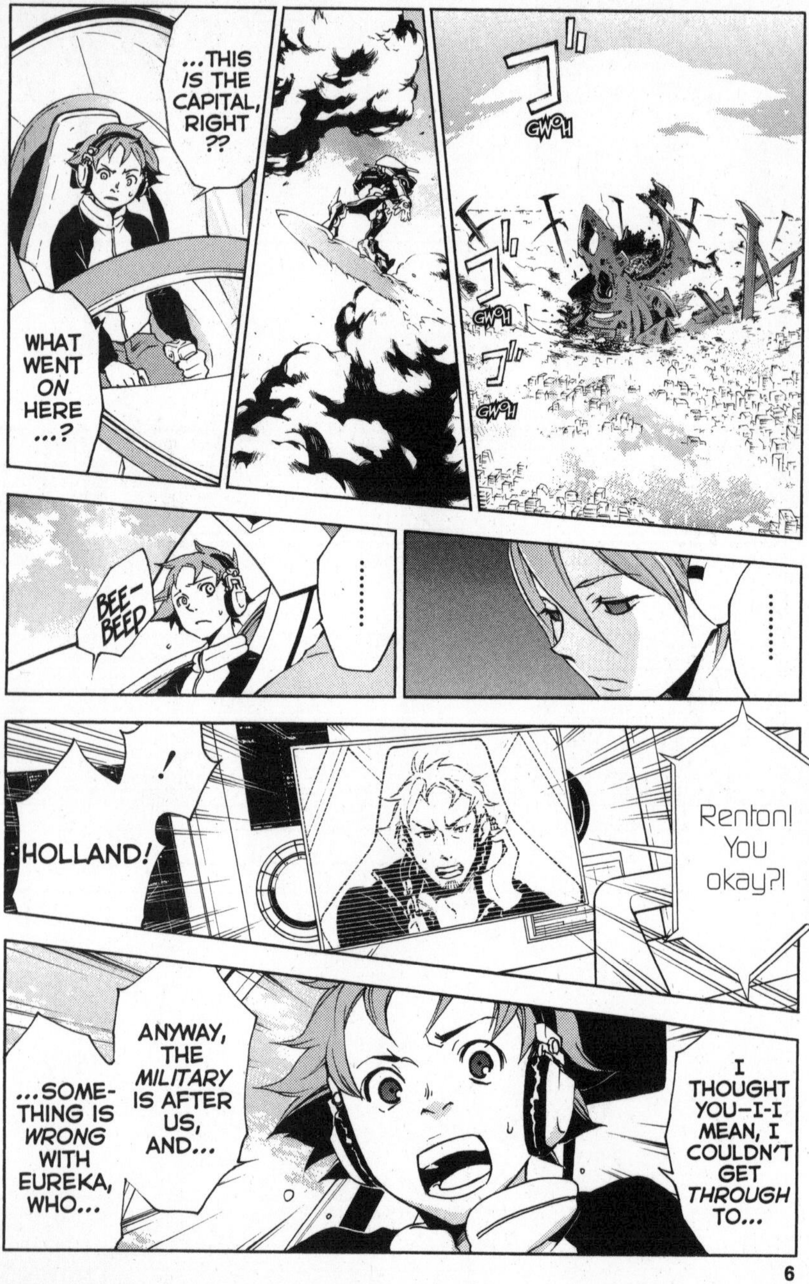
GWOH
GWOH
GWOH
...THIS IS THE CAPITAL, RIGHT??
WHAT WENT ON HERE...?
......
......
BEE-BEEP
Renton! You okay?!
!
HOLLAND!
I THOUGHT YOU—I-I MEAN, I COULDN'T GET THROUGH TO...
ANYWAY, THE MILITARY IS AFTER US, AND...
...SOME-THING IS WRONG WITH EUREKA, WHO...

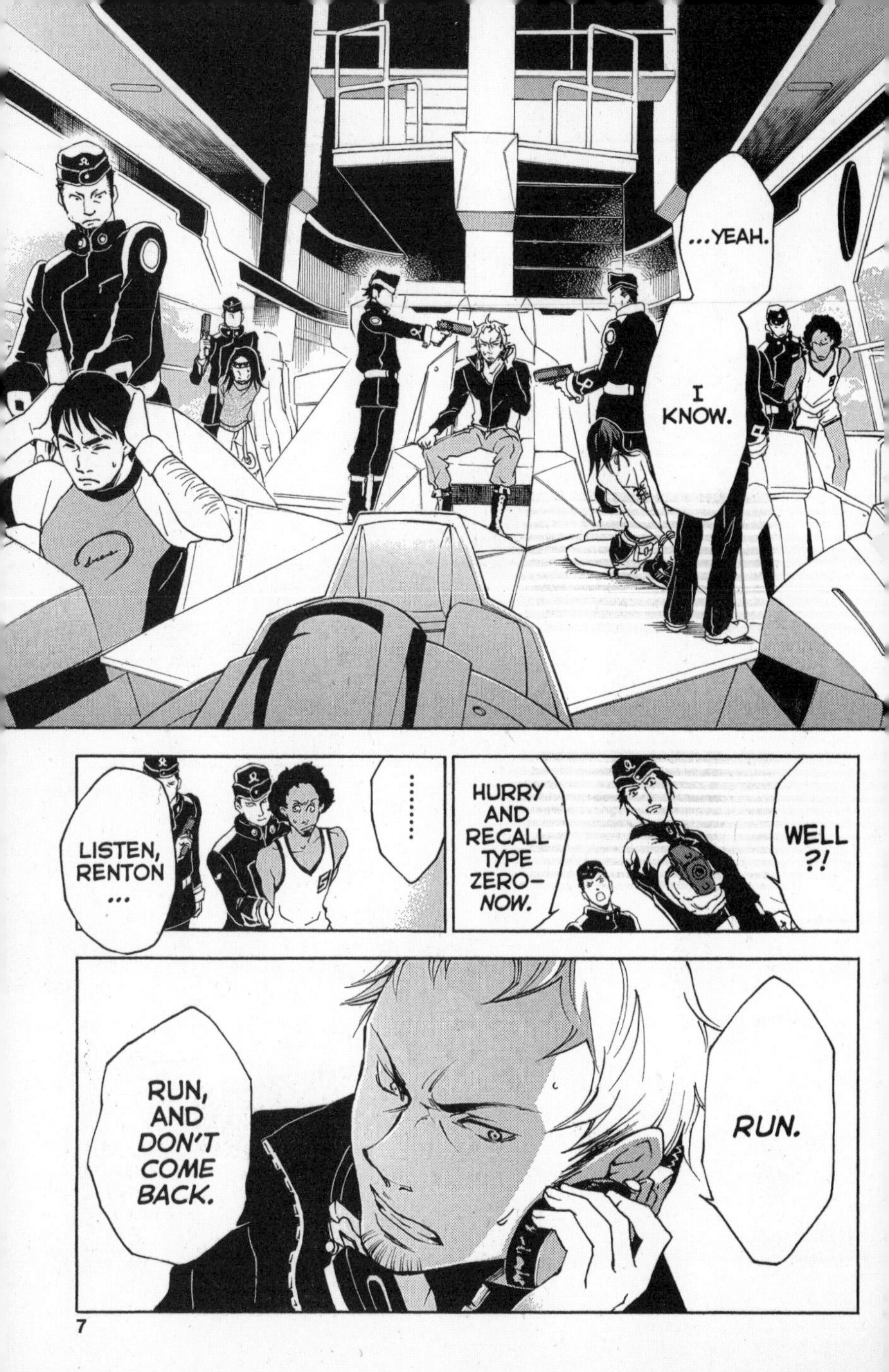
...YEAH.
I KNOW.
WELL ?!
HURRY AND RECALL TYPE ZERO— NOW.
....
LISTEN, RENTON ...
RUN.
RUN, AND DON'T COME BACK.

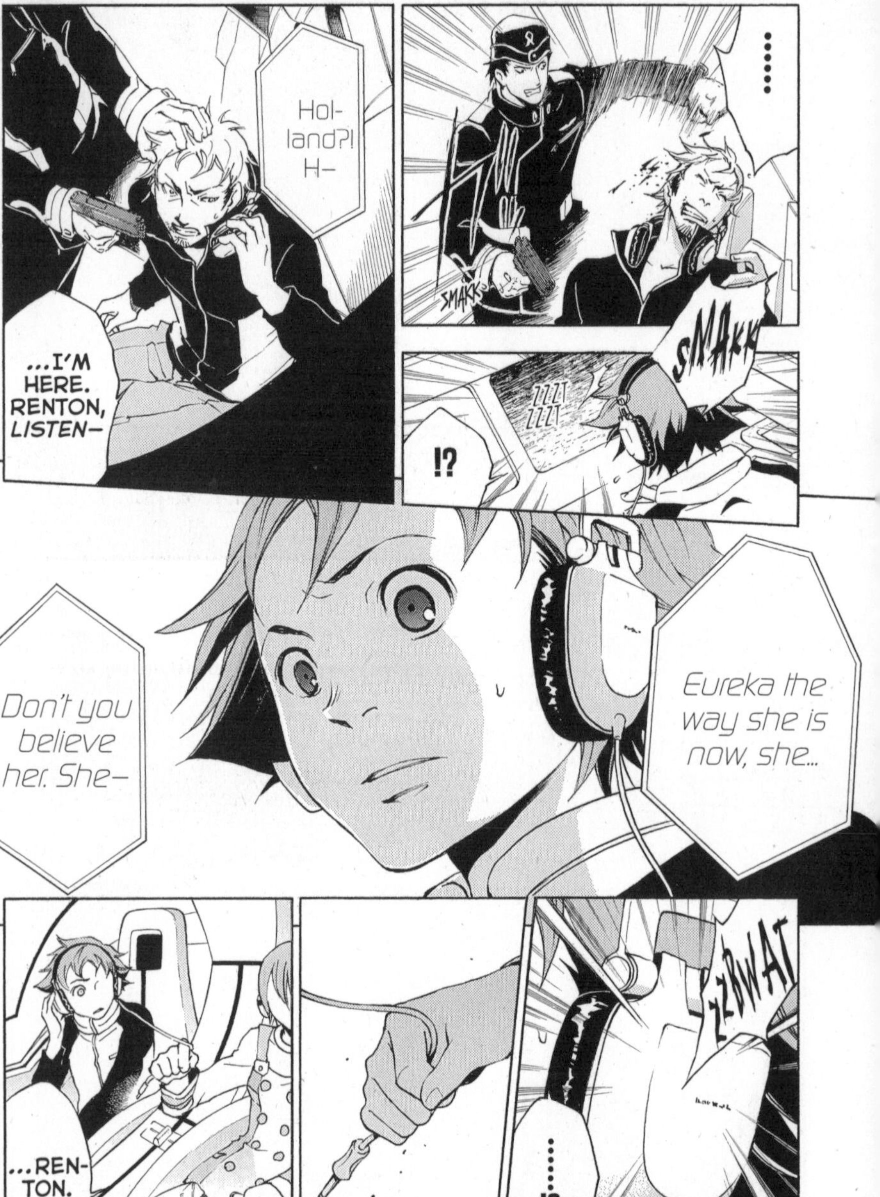
......
SMAKK
SMAKK
ZZZT ZZZT
!?
Hol-land?! H-
...I'M HERE. RENTON, LISTEN-
Eureka the way she is now, she...
Don't you believe her. She-
ZZBWAT
......
!?
...REN-TON.

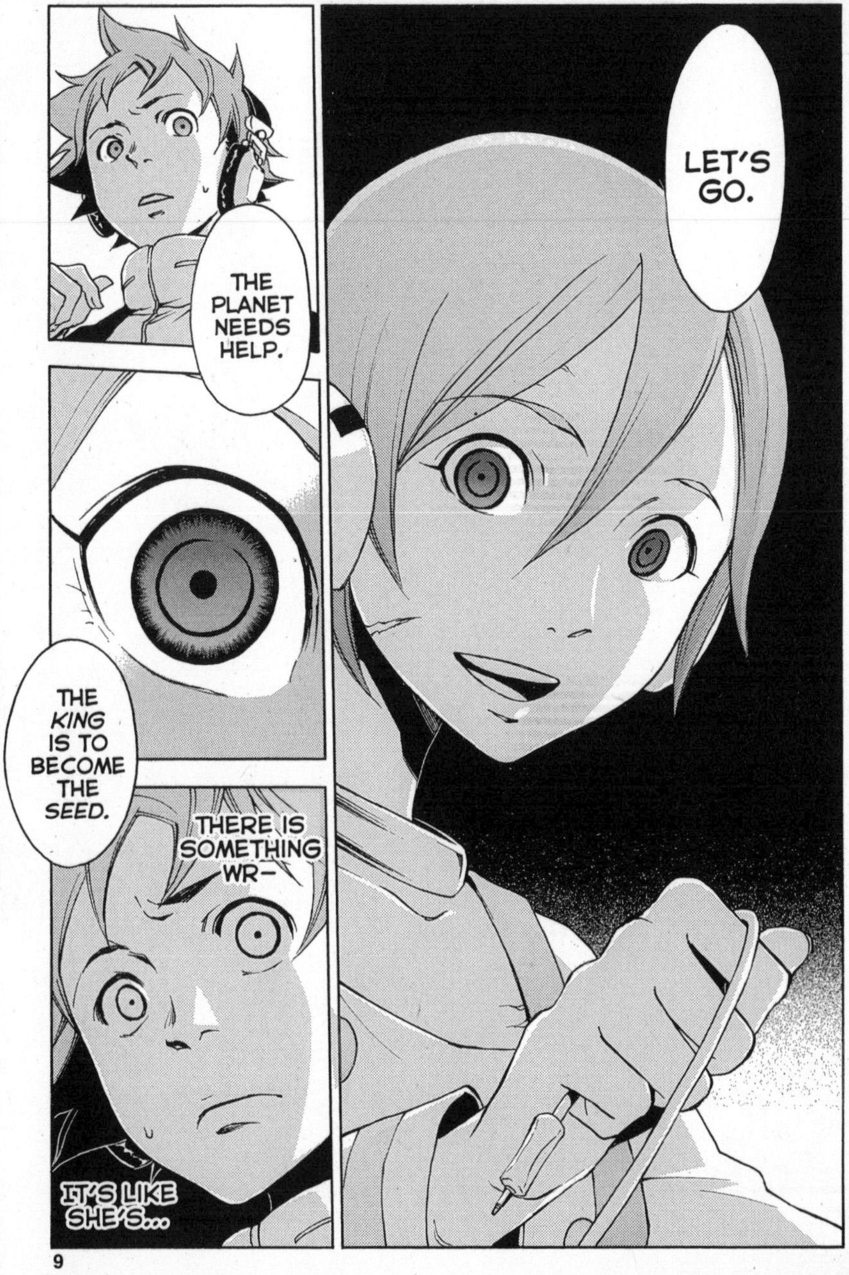
LET'S GO.
THE PLANET NEEDS HELP.
THE KING IS TO BECOME THE SEED.
THERE IS SOMETHING WR-
IT'S LIKE SHE'S...

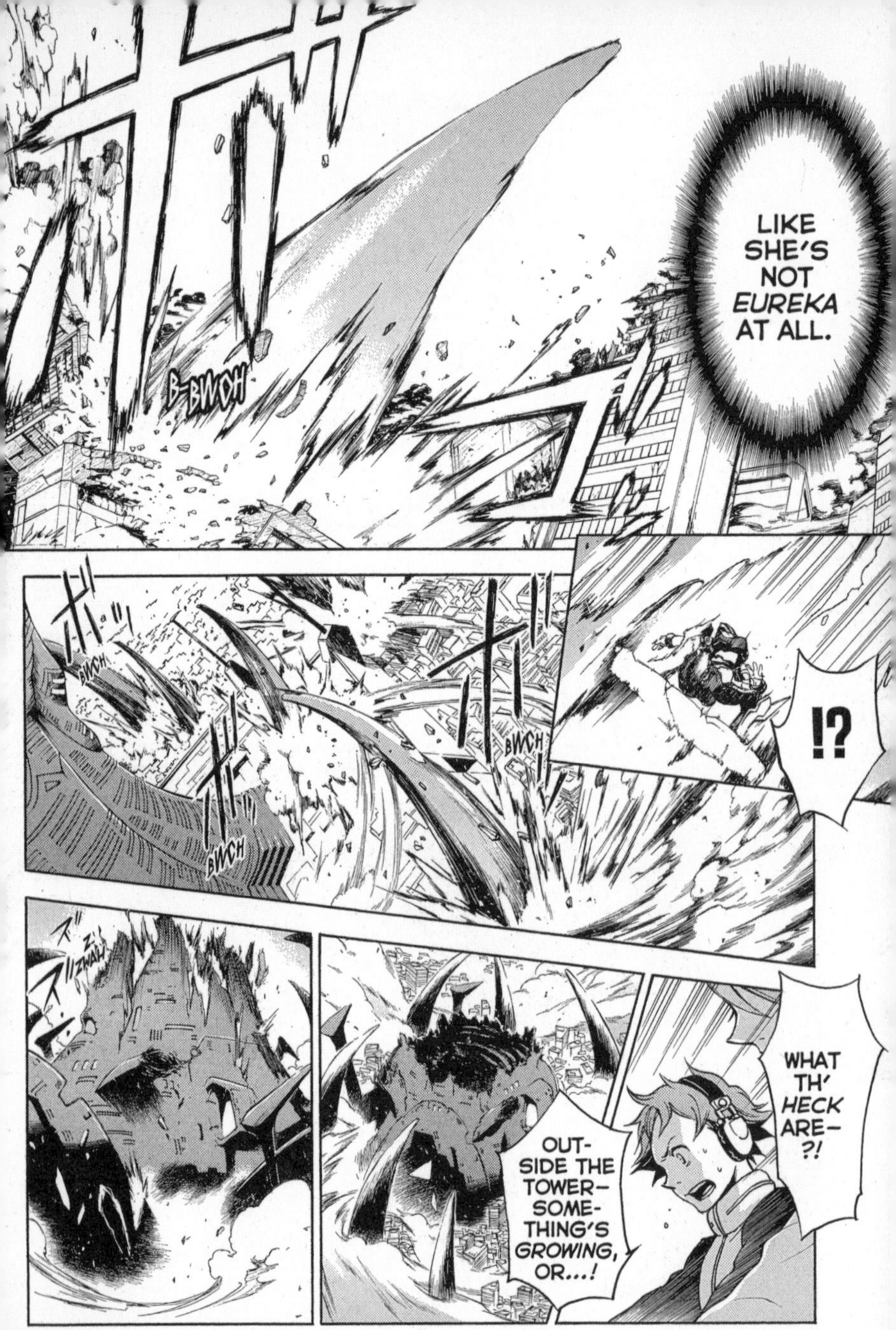
LIKE SHE'S NOT *EUREKA* AT ALL.
B-BWCH
!?
BWCH
BWCH
BWCH
WHAT TH' *HECK* ARE—?!
OUTSIDE THE TOWER—SOMETHING'S *GROWING*, OR...!
Z-ZWAH

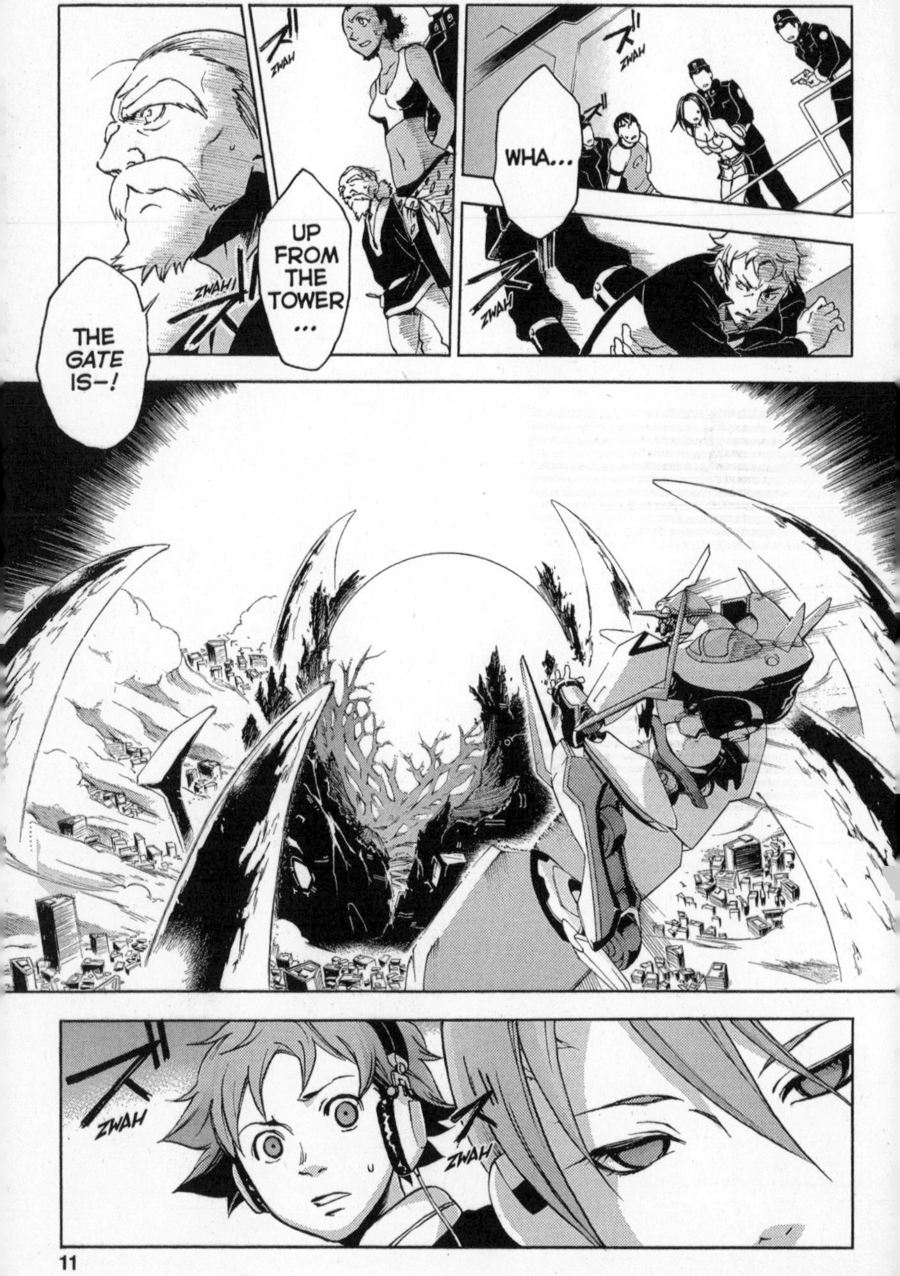
ZWAH
WHA...
ZWAH
ZWAH
UP FROM THE TOWER ...
ZWAH
THE GATE IS–!
ZWAH
ZWAH

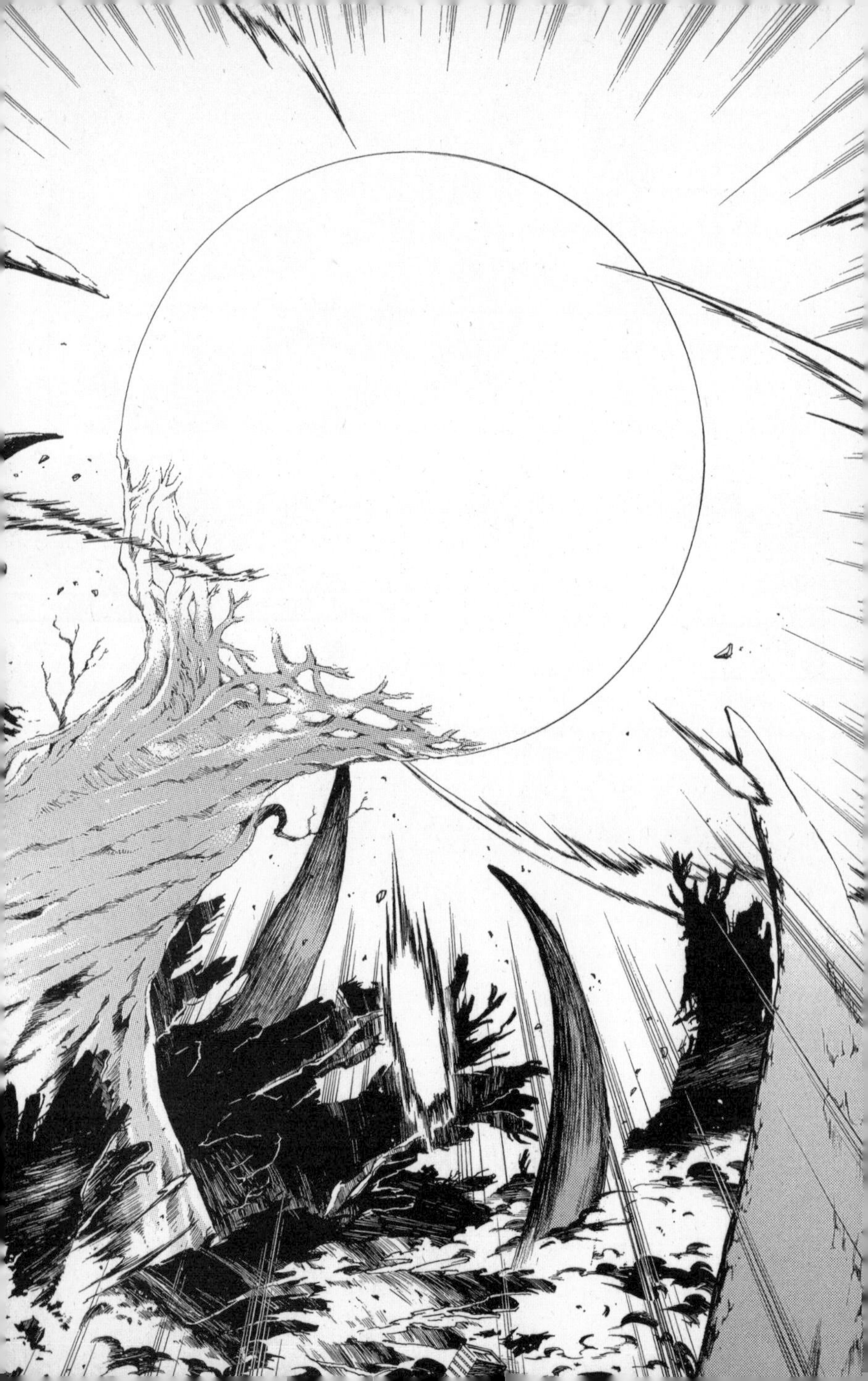

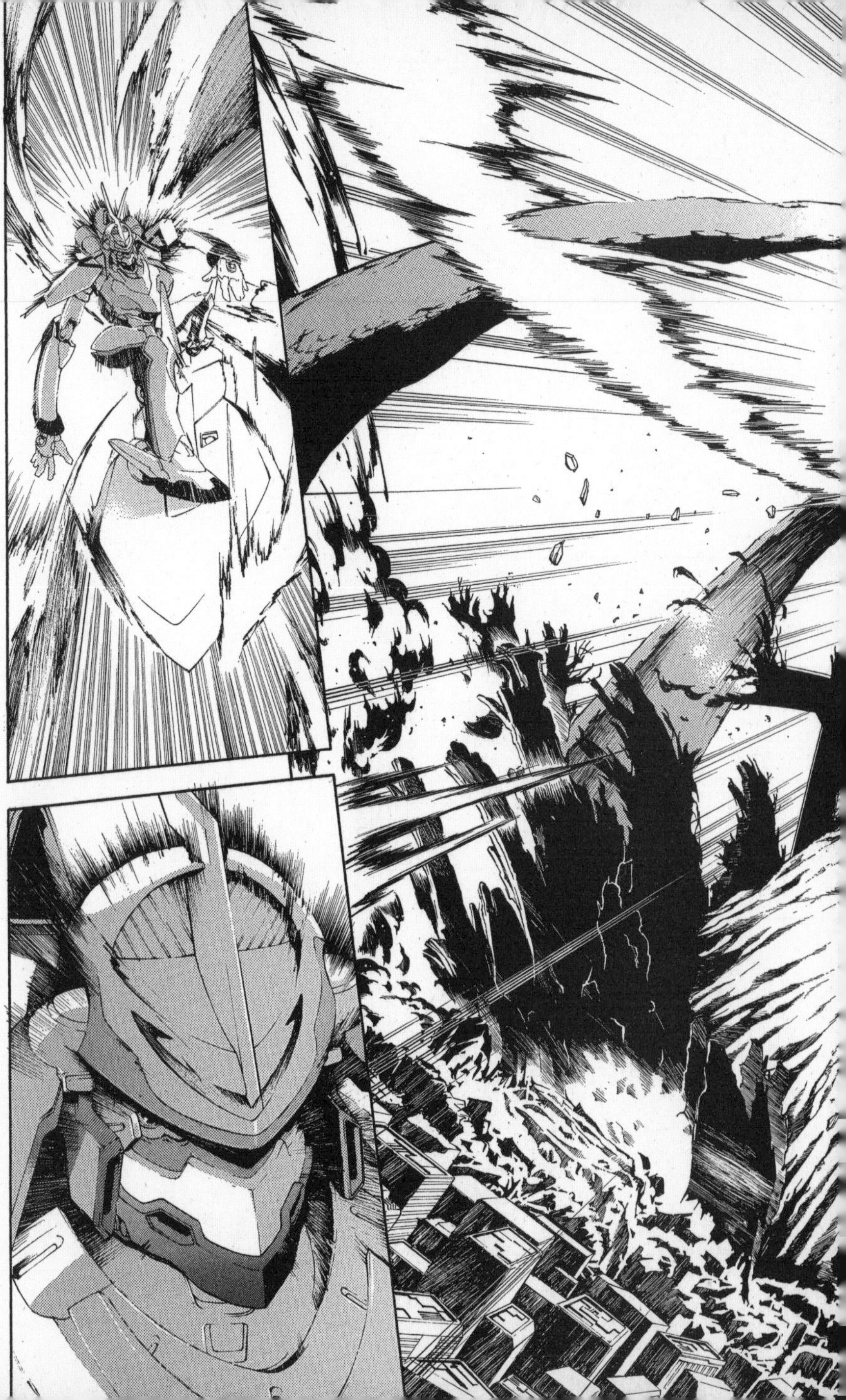

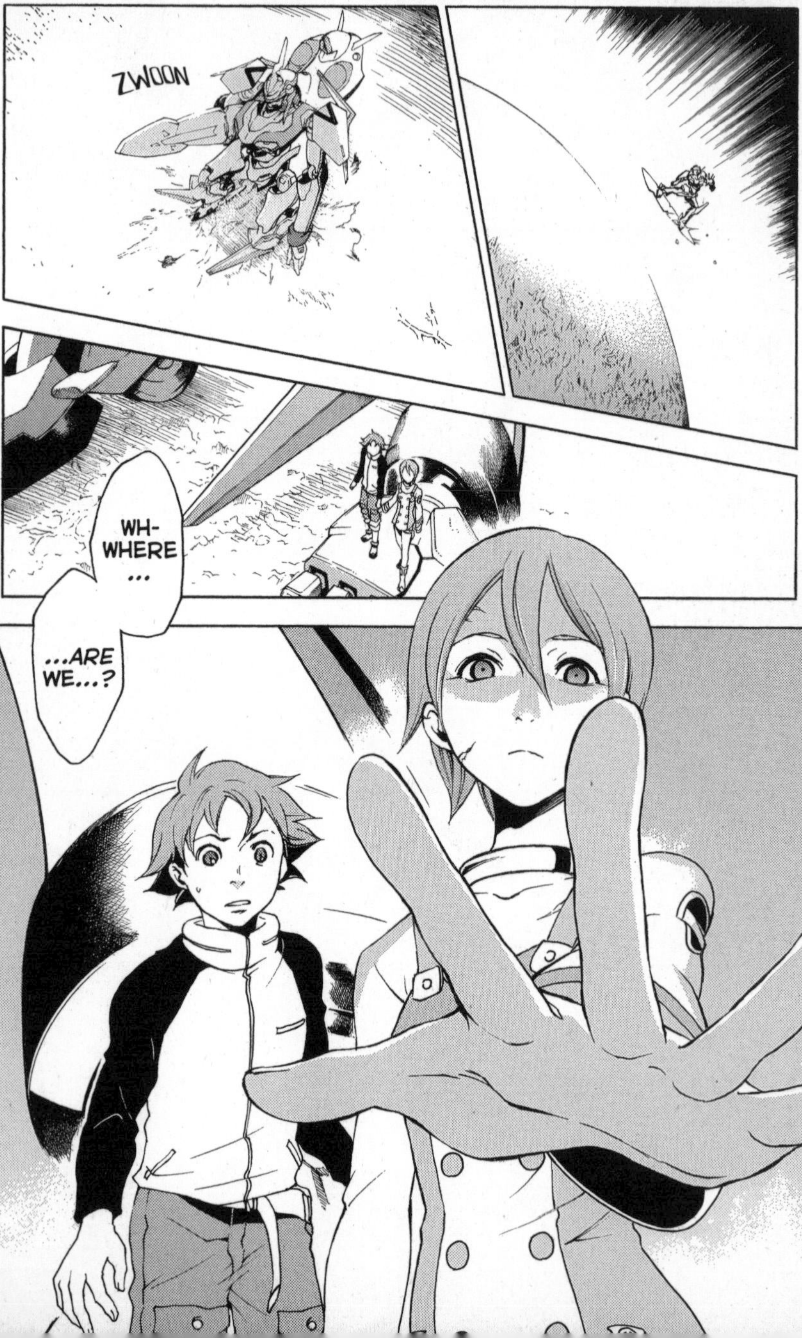
ZWOON
WH- WHERE ...
...ARE WE...?

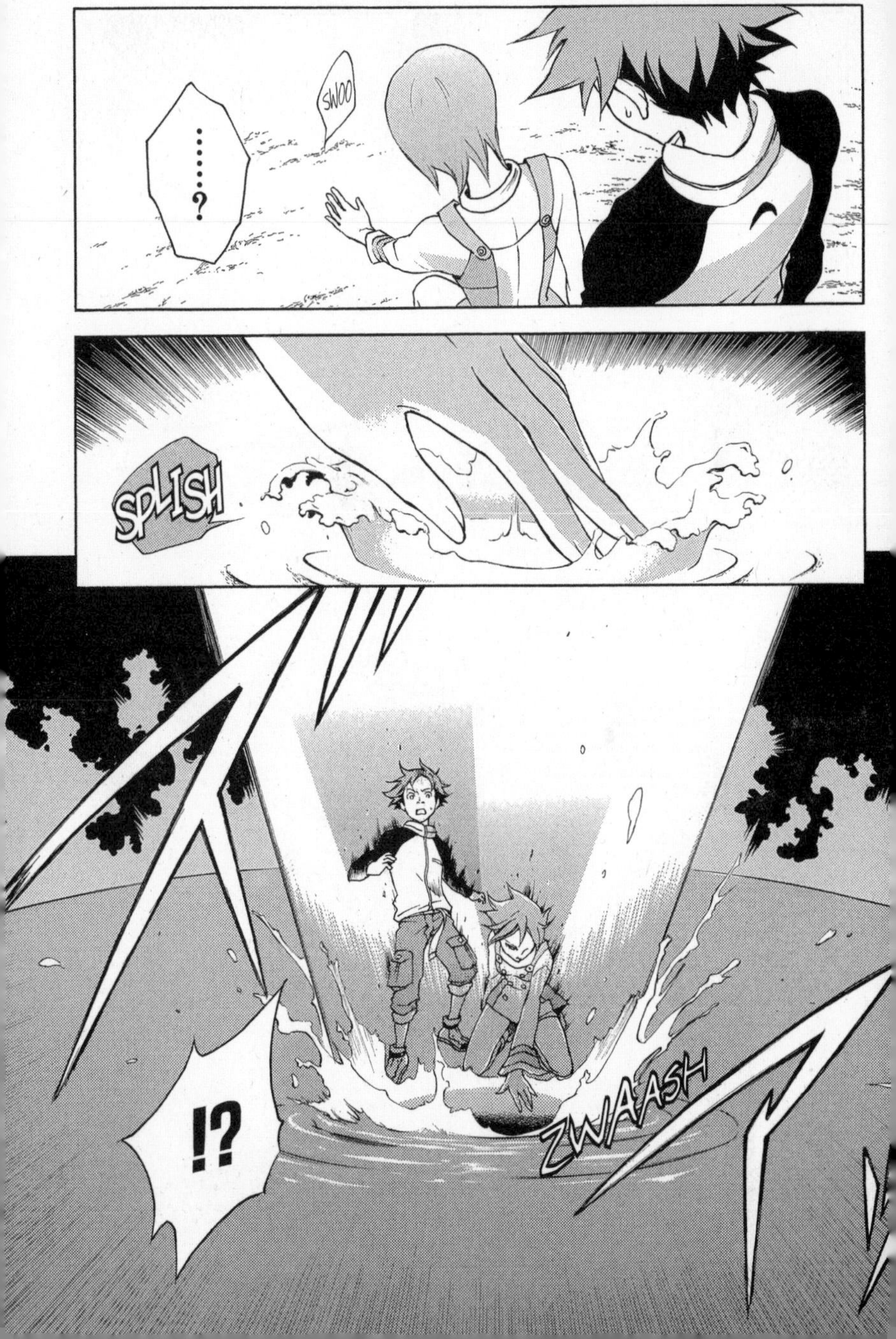
SWOO
......?
SPLISH
ZWAASH
!?

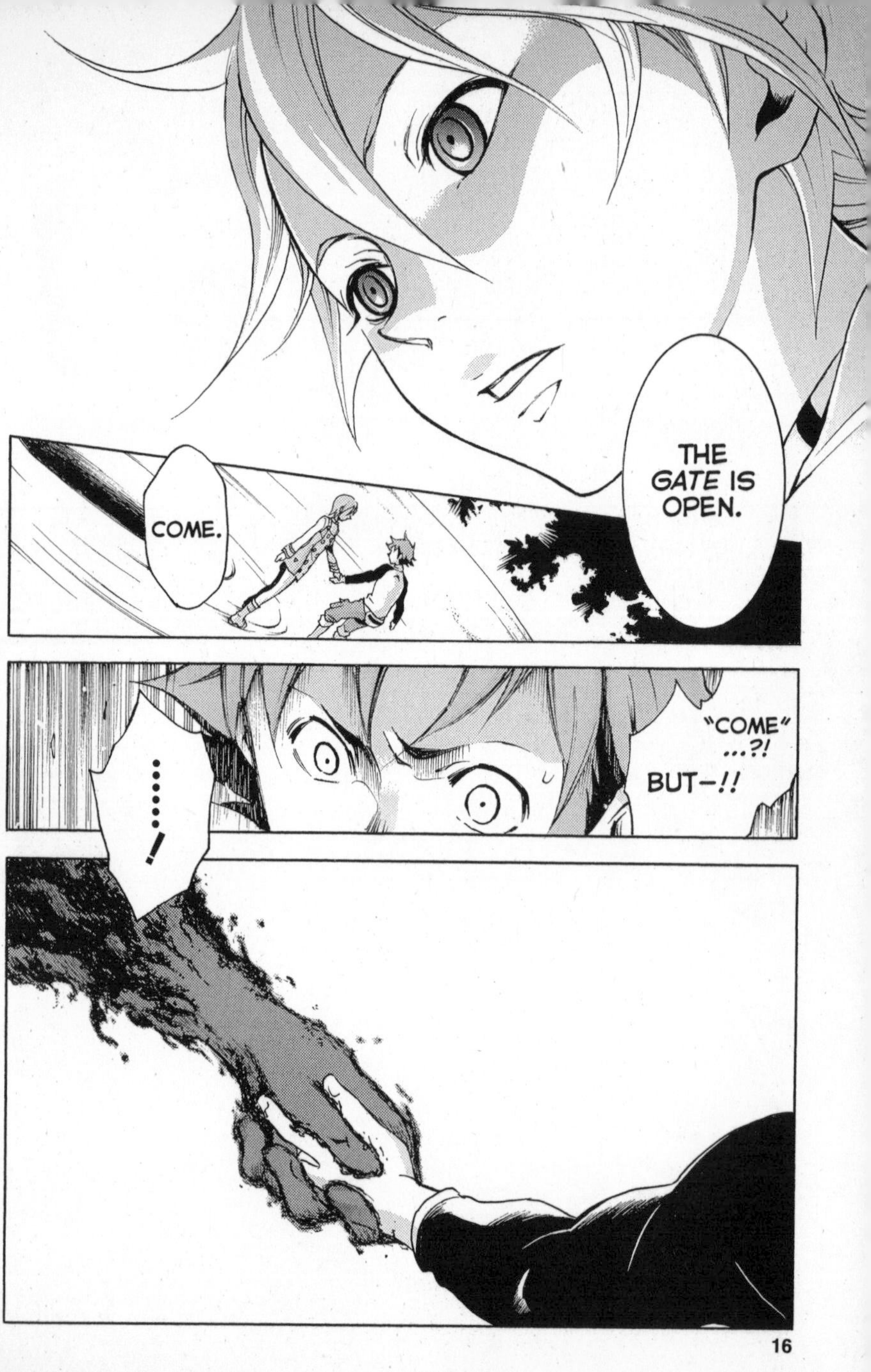
THE *GATE* IS OPEN.
COME.
"COME" ...?!
BUT–!!
......!

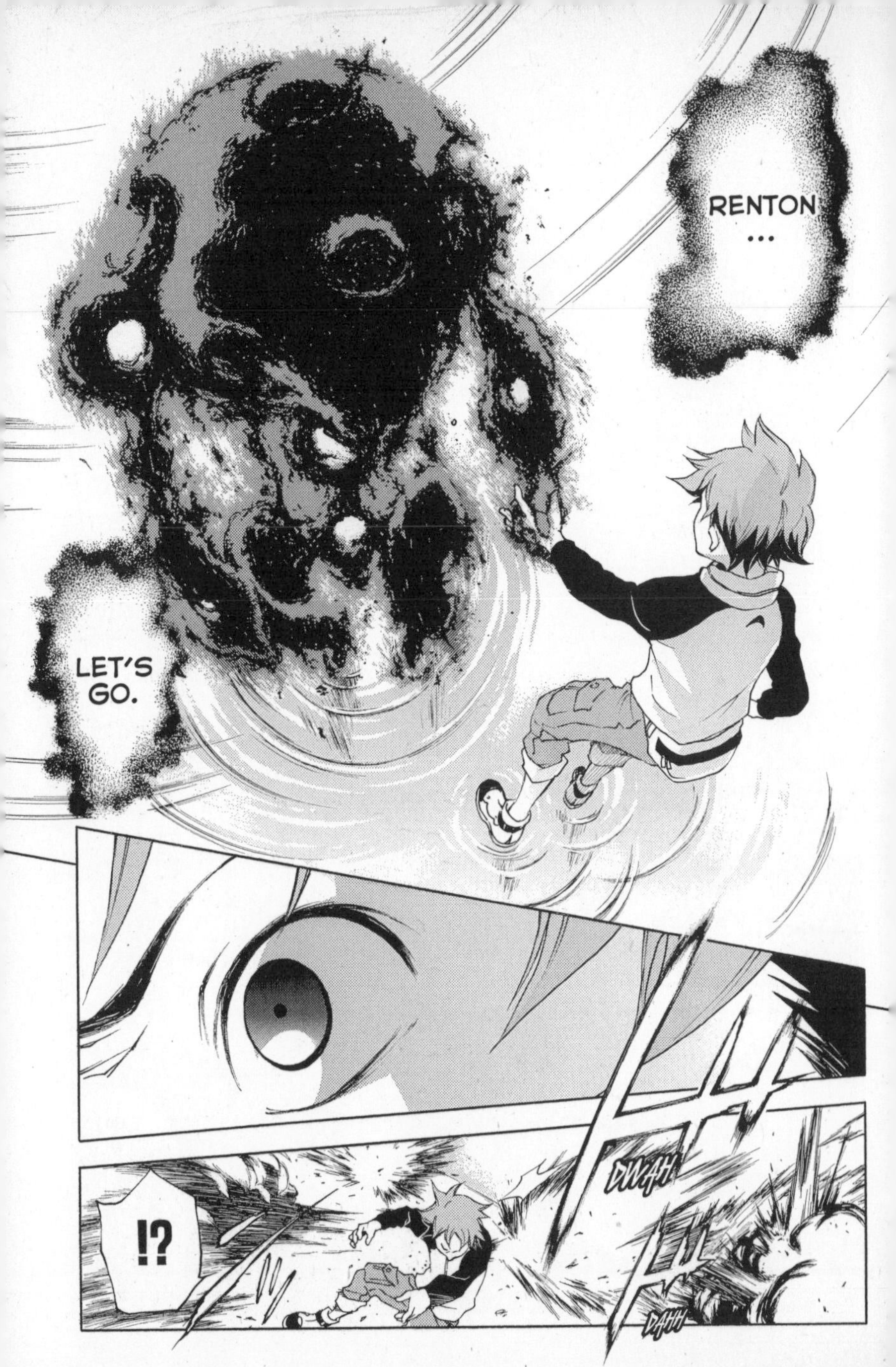
RENTON
...
LET'S GO.
DWAH
DAHH
!?

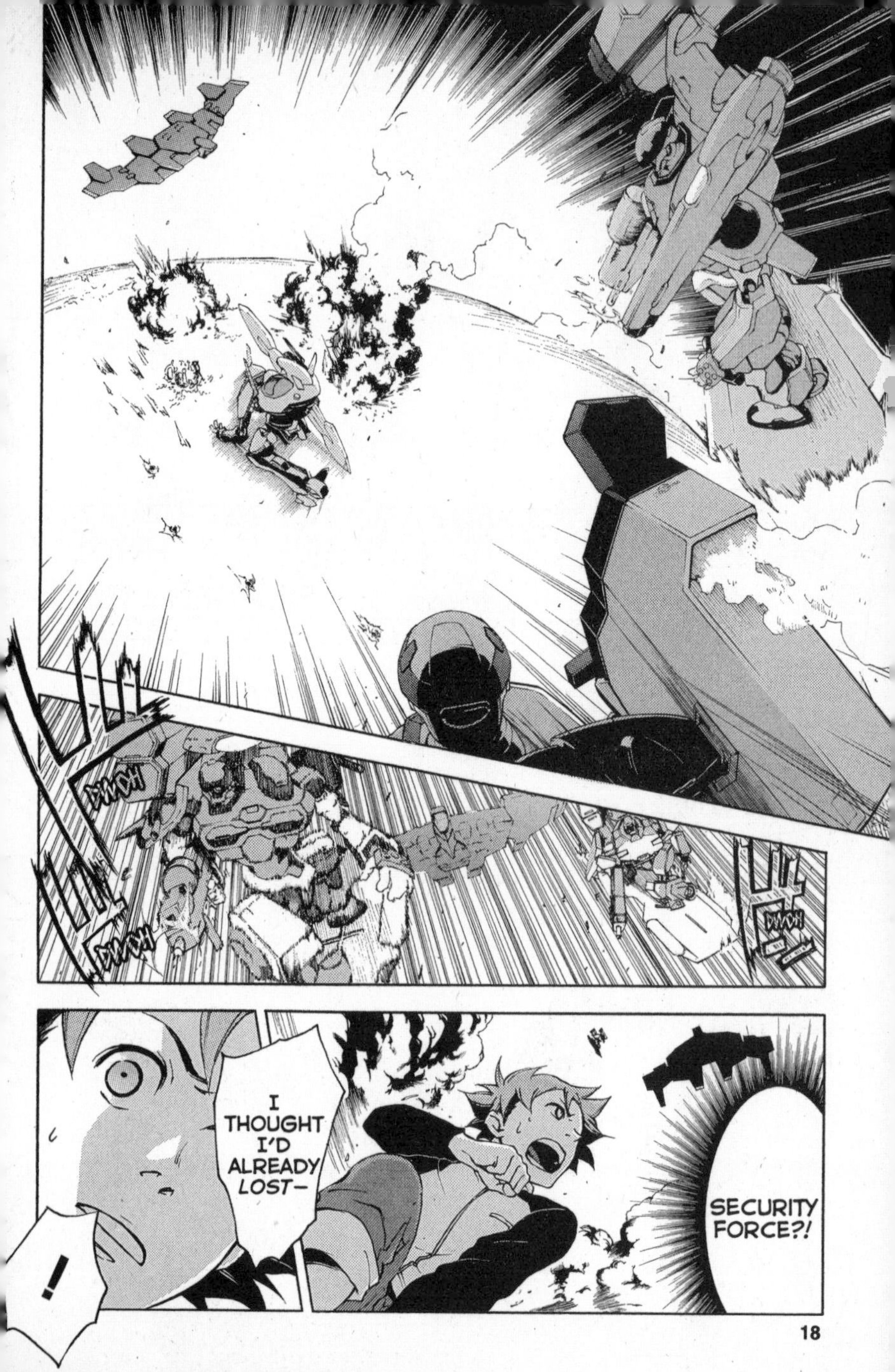
DWOOH
DWOOH
DWOOH
SECURITY FORCE?!
I THOUGHT I'D ALREADY *LOST*—
!

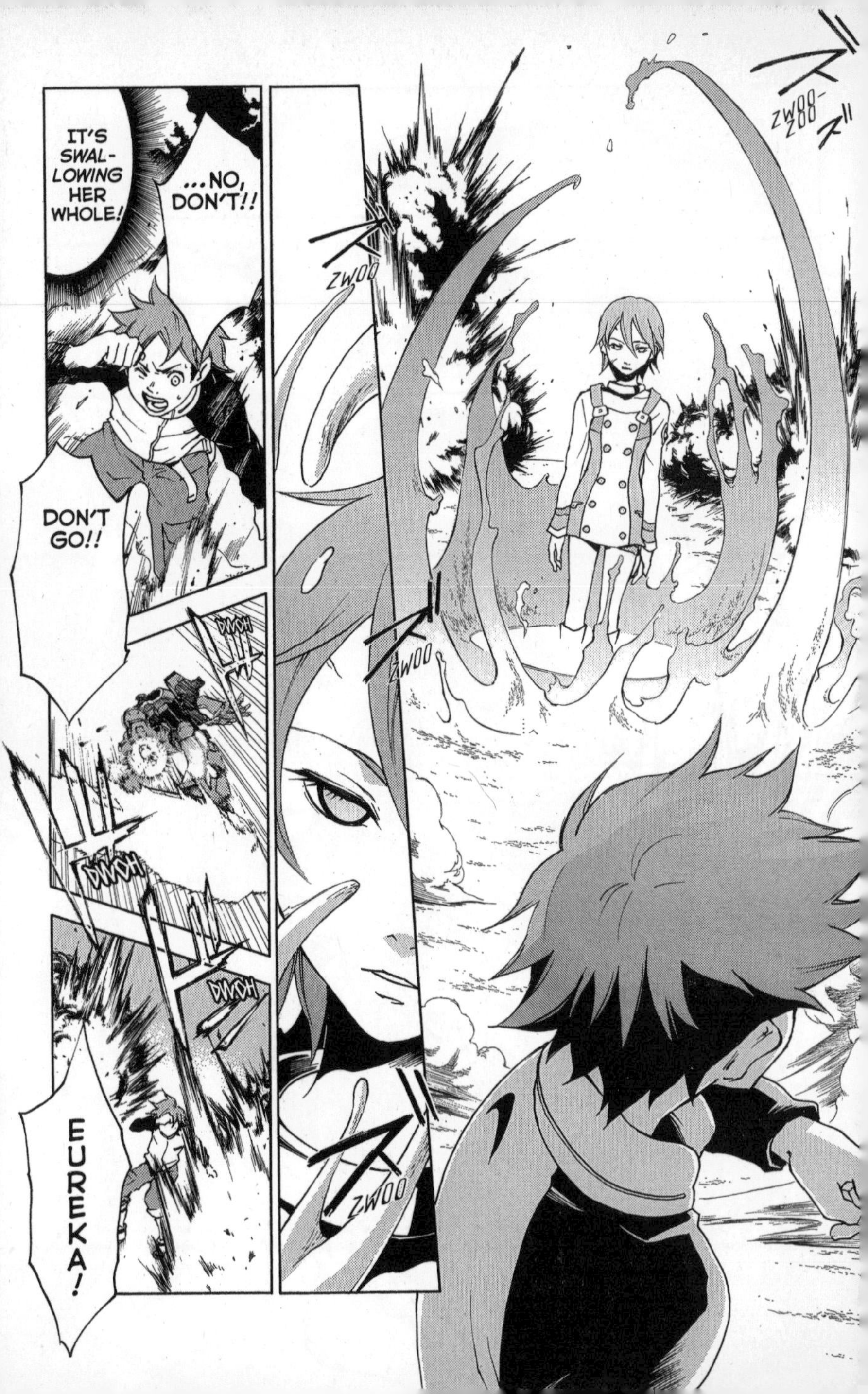
ZWOO-ZOO
ZWOO
ZWOO
ZWOO
IT'S SWALLOWING HER WHOLE!
...NO, DON'T!!
DON'T GO!!
DWOH
DWOH
DWOH
EUREKA!

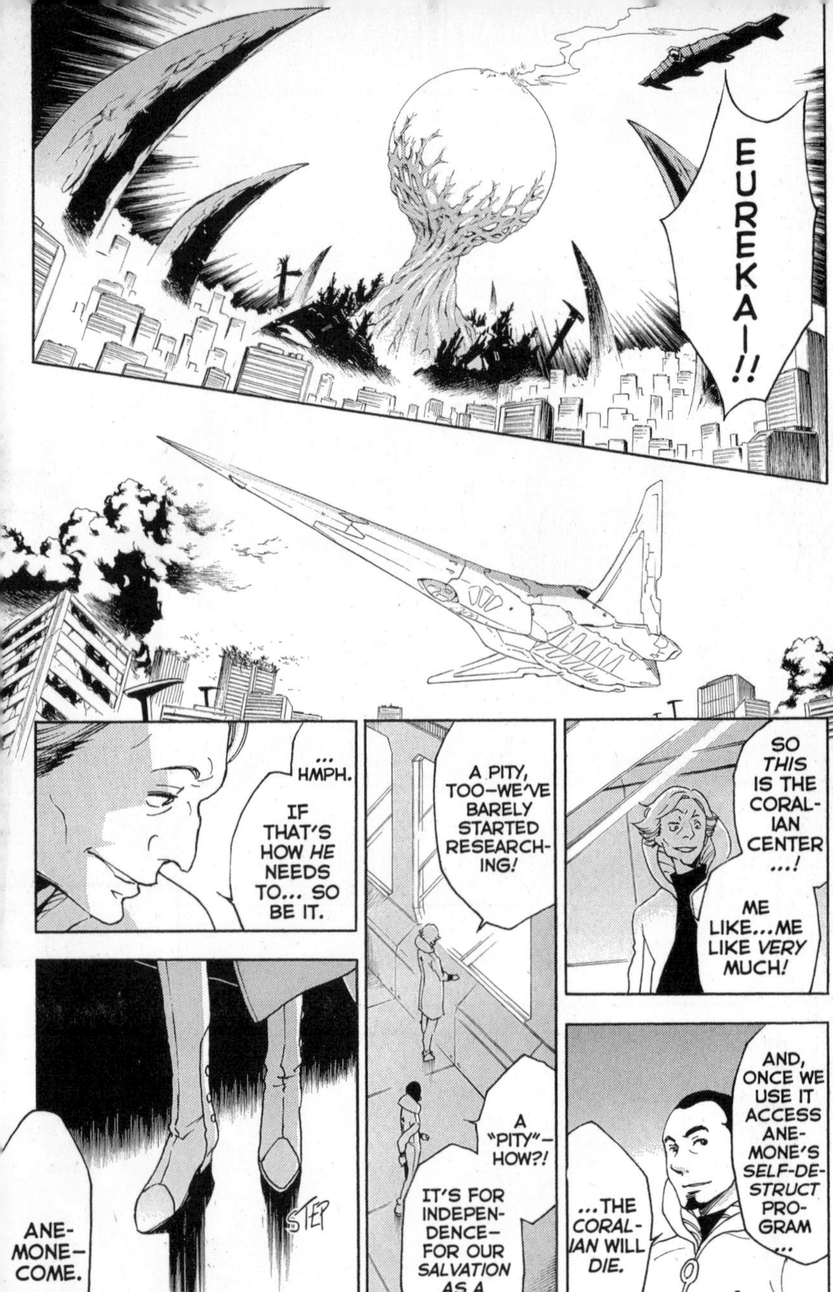
EUREKA!!
SO THIS IS THE CORALIAN CENTER...!
ME LIKE...ME LIKE VERY MUCH!
AND, ONCE WE USE IT ACCESS ANEMONE'S SELF-DESTRUCT PROGRAM...
...THE CORALIAN WILL DIE.
A PITY, TOO—WE'VE BARELY STARTED RESEARCHING!
A "PITY"—HOW?!
IT'S FOR INDEPENDENCE—FOR OUR SALVATION AS A PEOPLE!
...HMPH.
IF THAT'S HOW HE NEEDS TO... SO BE IT.
STEP
ANEMONE—COME.

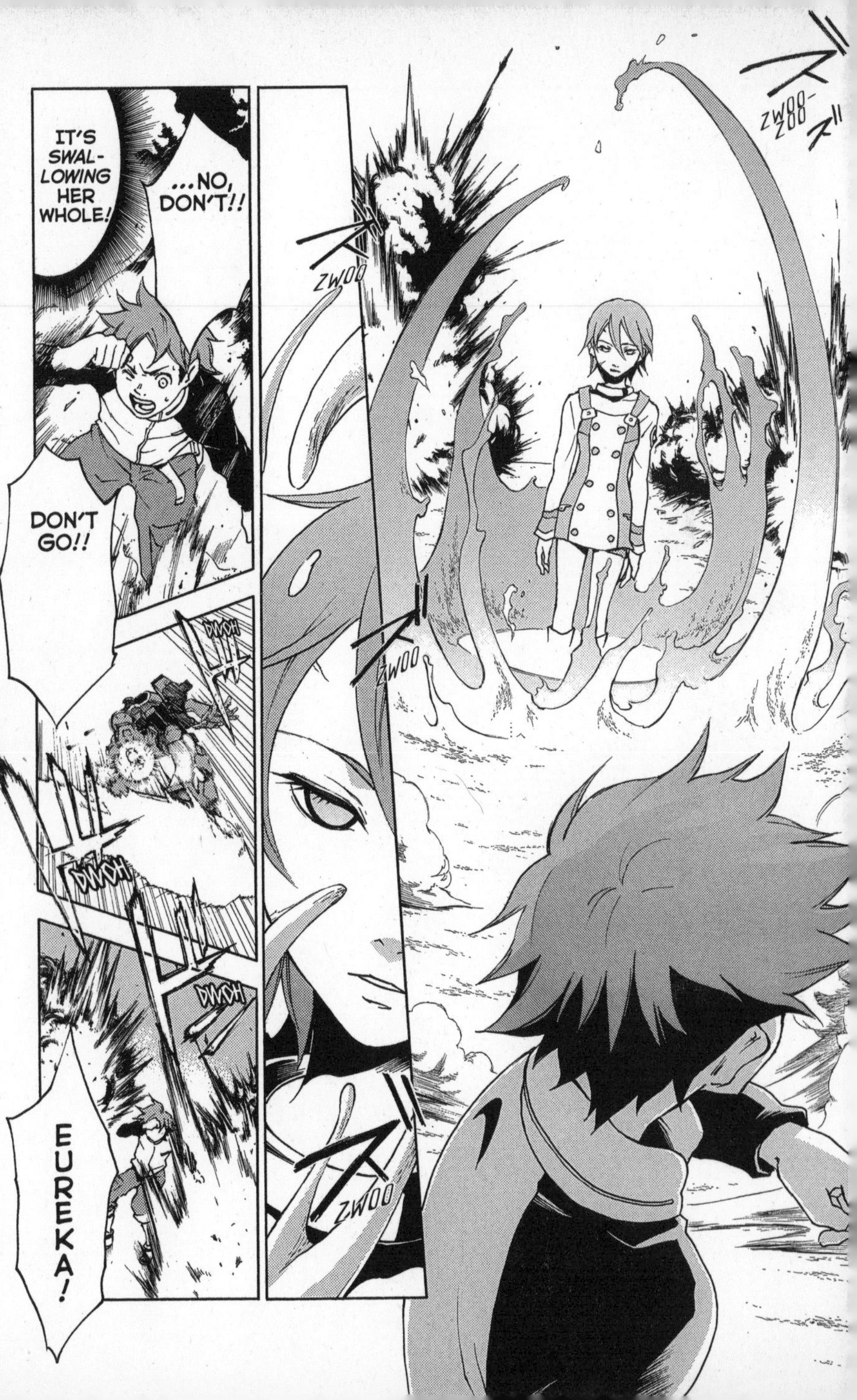
ZWOO-ZOO
ZWOO
ZWOO
ZWOO
...NO, DON'T!!
IT'S SWAL-LOWING HER WHOLE!
DON'T GO!!
DWOH
DWOH
DWOH
EUREKA!

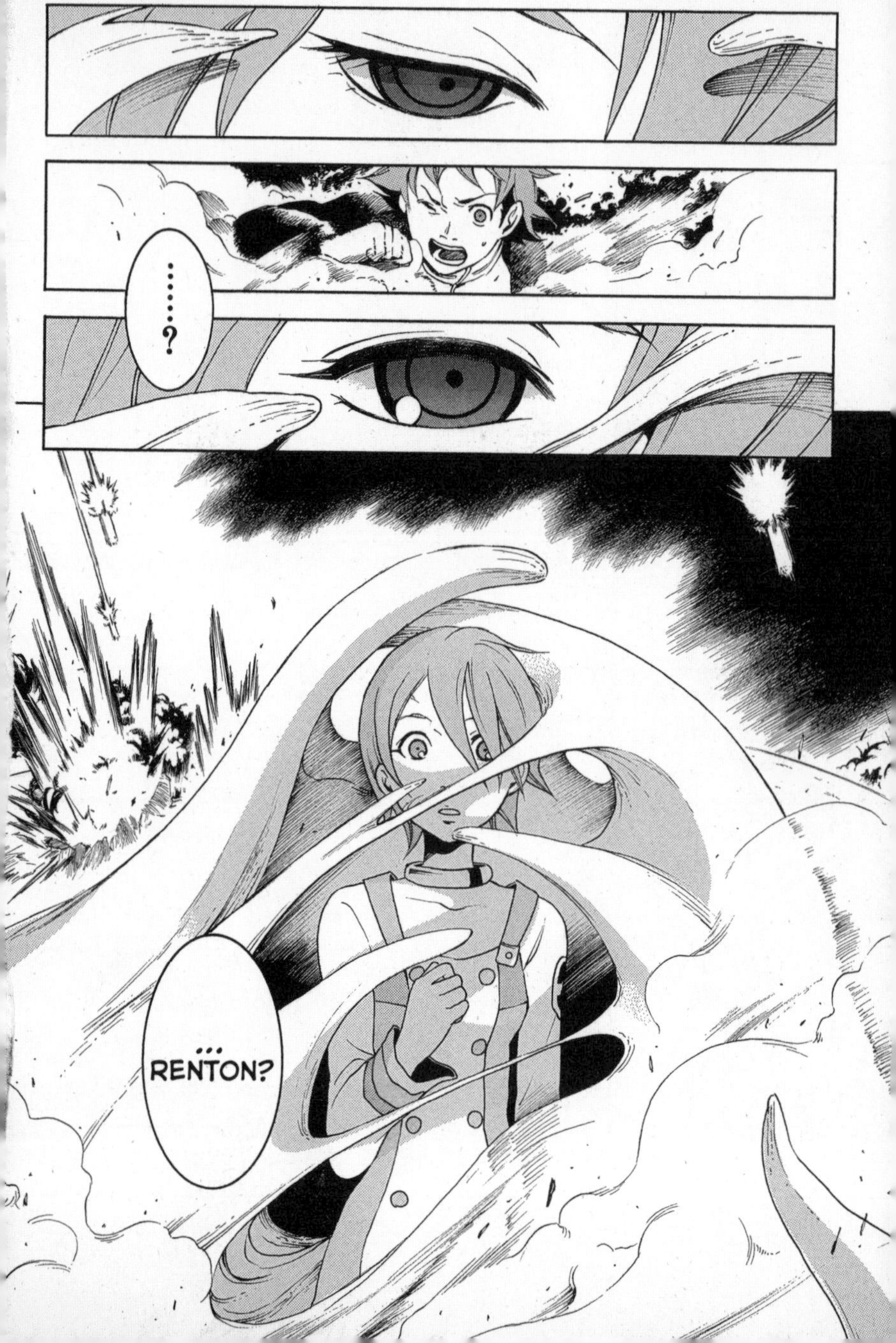
......?
...RENTON?

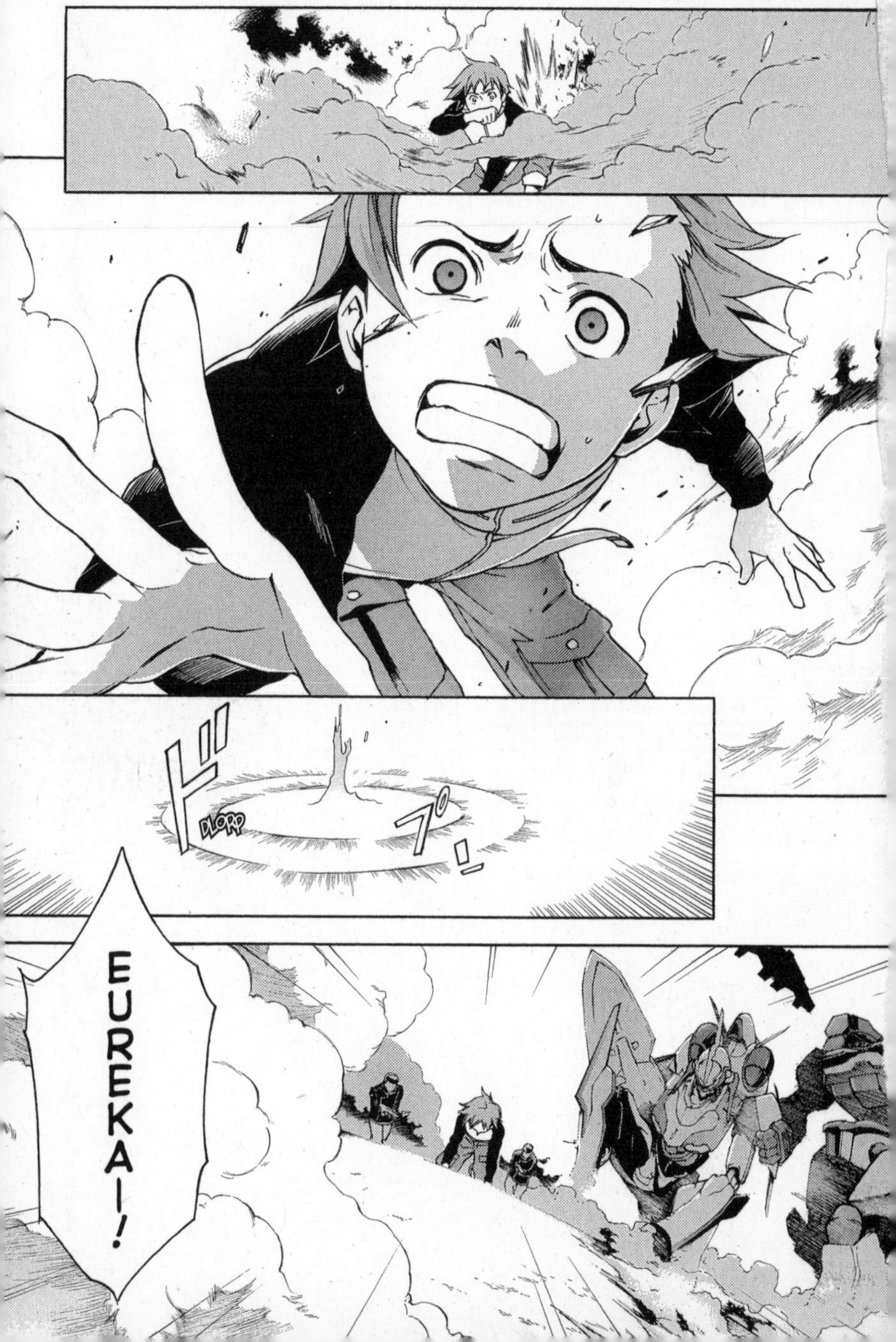

ドプッ
DLORP
EUREKA!!

EUREKA!!

...HMPH.

IF THAT'S HOW *HE* NEEDS TO... SO BE IT.

A PITY, TOO—WE'VE BARELY STARTED RESEARCH-ING!

SO *THIS* IS THE CORAL-IAN CENTER...!

ME LIKE...ME LIKE *VERY* MUCH!

A "PITY"—HOW?!

IT'S FOR INDEPEN-DENCE— FOR OUR *SALVATION* AS A PEOPLE!

ANE-MONE—COME.

STEP

AND, ONCE WE USE IT ACCESS ANE-MONE'S SELF-DE-STRUCT PRO-GRAM...

...THE CORAL-IAN WILL DIE.

22

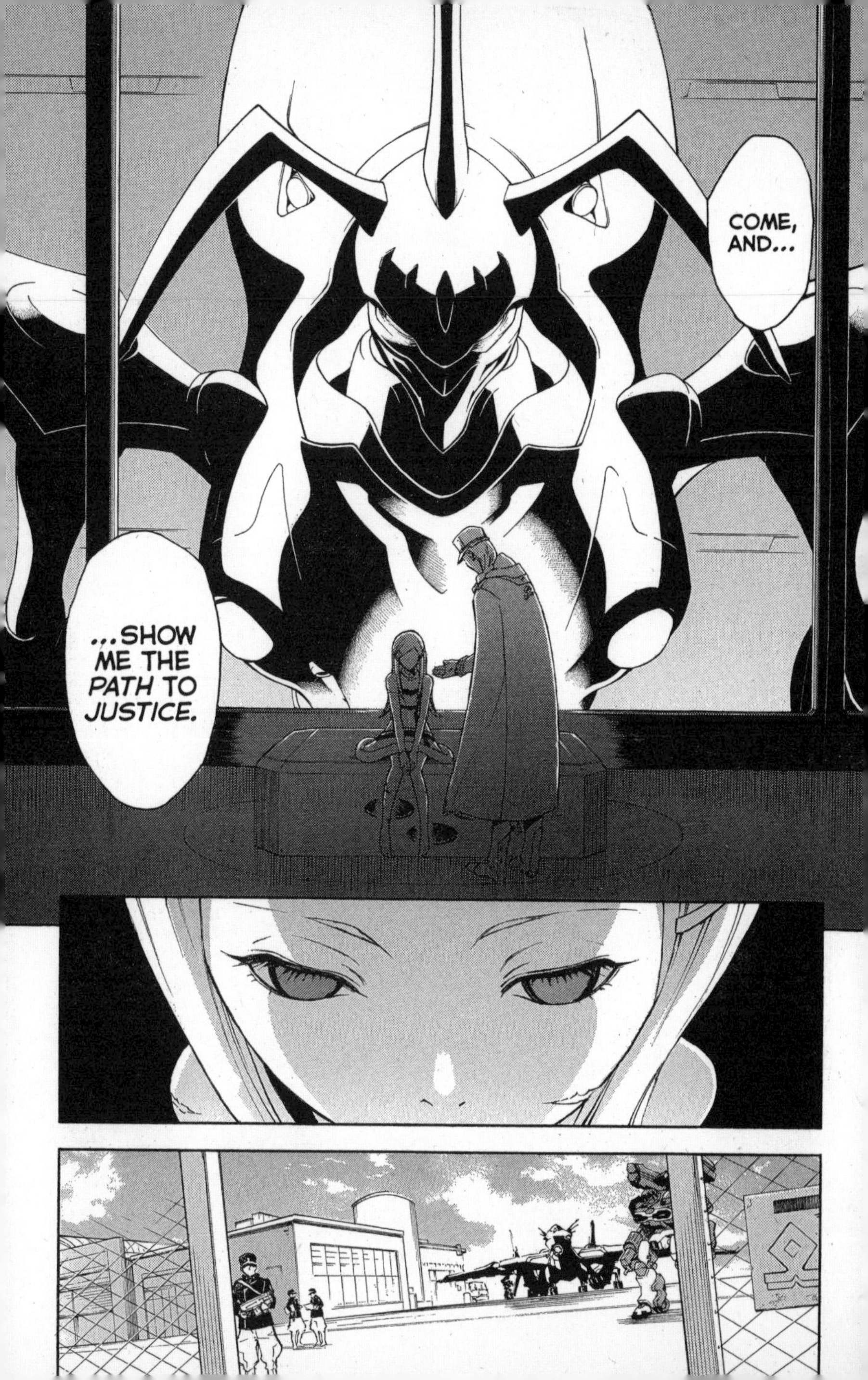
COME, AND...
...SHOW ME THE PATH TO JUSTICE.

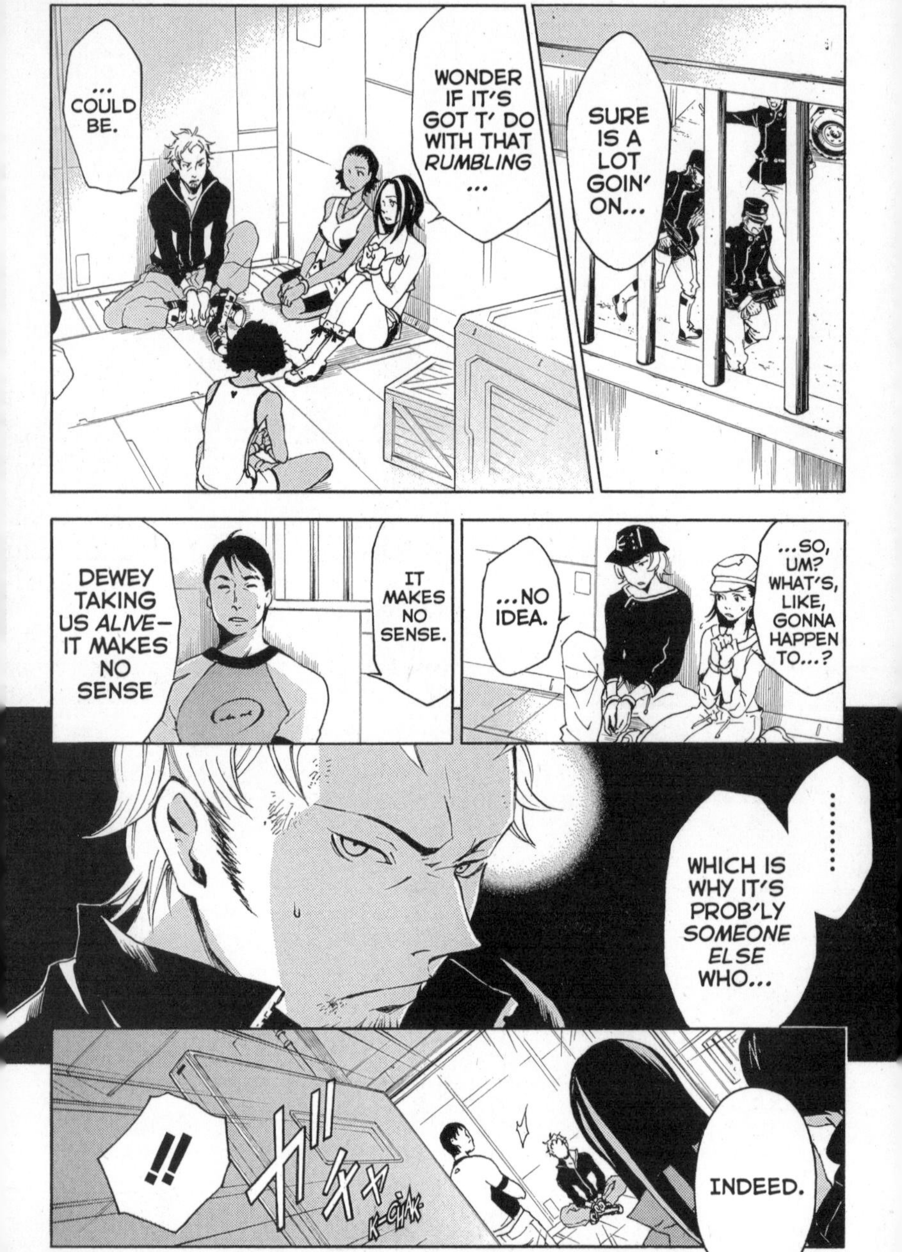
SURE IS A LOT GOIN' ON...
WONDER IF IT'S GOT T' DO WITH THAT *RUMBLING* ...
... COULD BE.
...SO, UM? WHAT'S, LIKE, GONNA HAPPEN TO...?
...NO IDEA.
IT MAKES NO SENSE.
DEWEY TAKING US *ALIVE*—IT MAKES NO SENSE
....
WHICH IS WHY IT'S PROB'LY *SOMEONE ELSE* WHO...
INDEED.
!!
K-CHAK

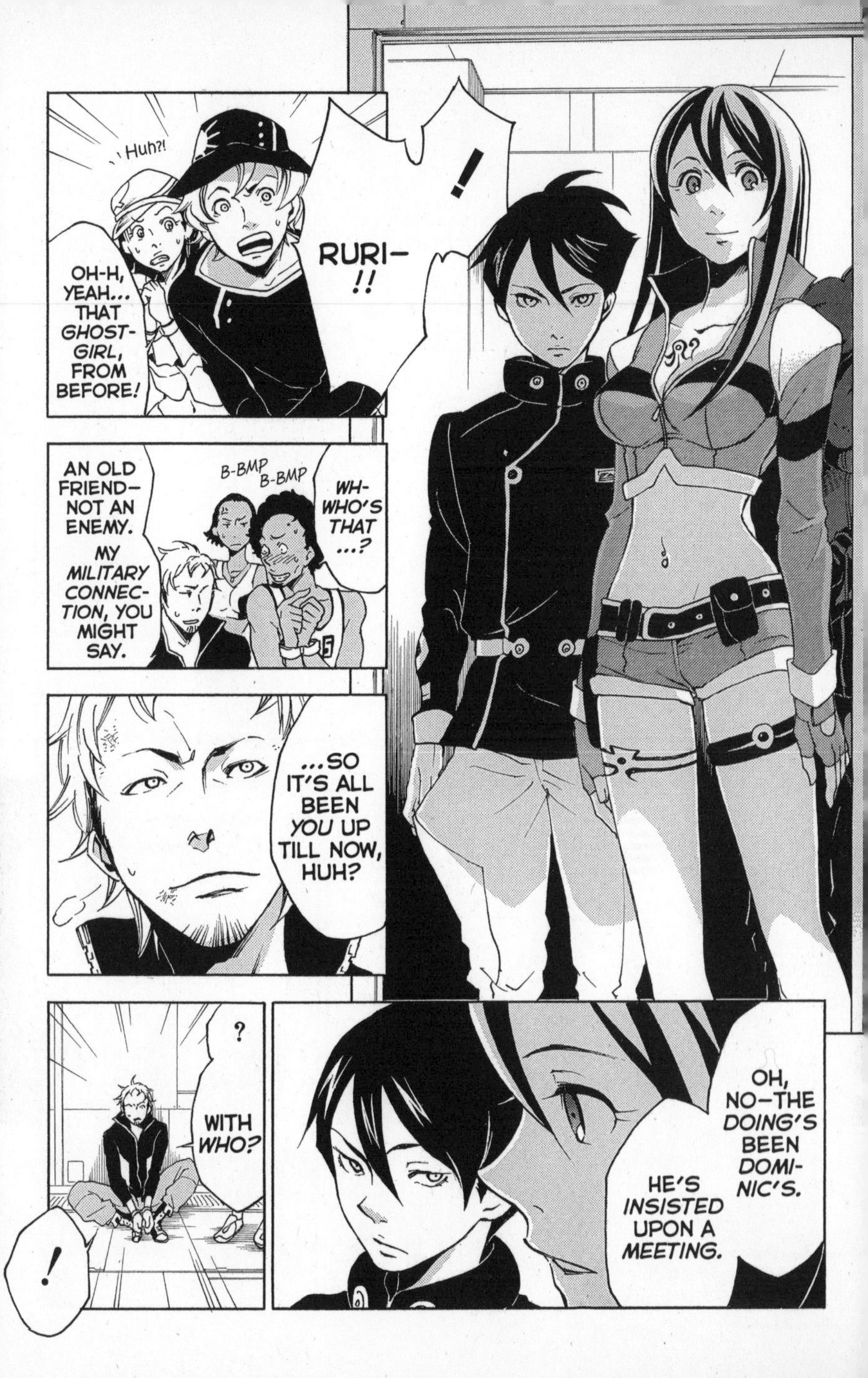
!
RURI—!!
Huh?!
OH-H, YEAH... THAT GHOST-GIRL, FROM BEFORE!
WH-WHO'S THAT ...?
B-BMP B-BMP
AN OLD FRIEND—NOT AN ENEMY.
MY MILITARY CONNECTION, YOU MIGHT SAY.
...SO IT'S ALL BEEN YOU UP TILL NOW, HUH?
OH, NO—THE DOING'S BEEN DOMINIC'S.
HE'S INSISTED UPON A MEETING.
?
WITH WHO?
!

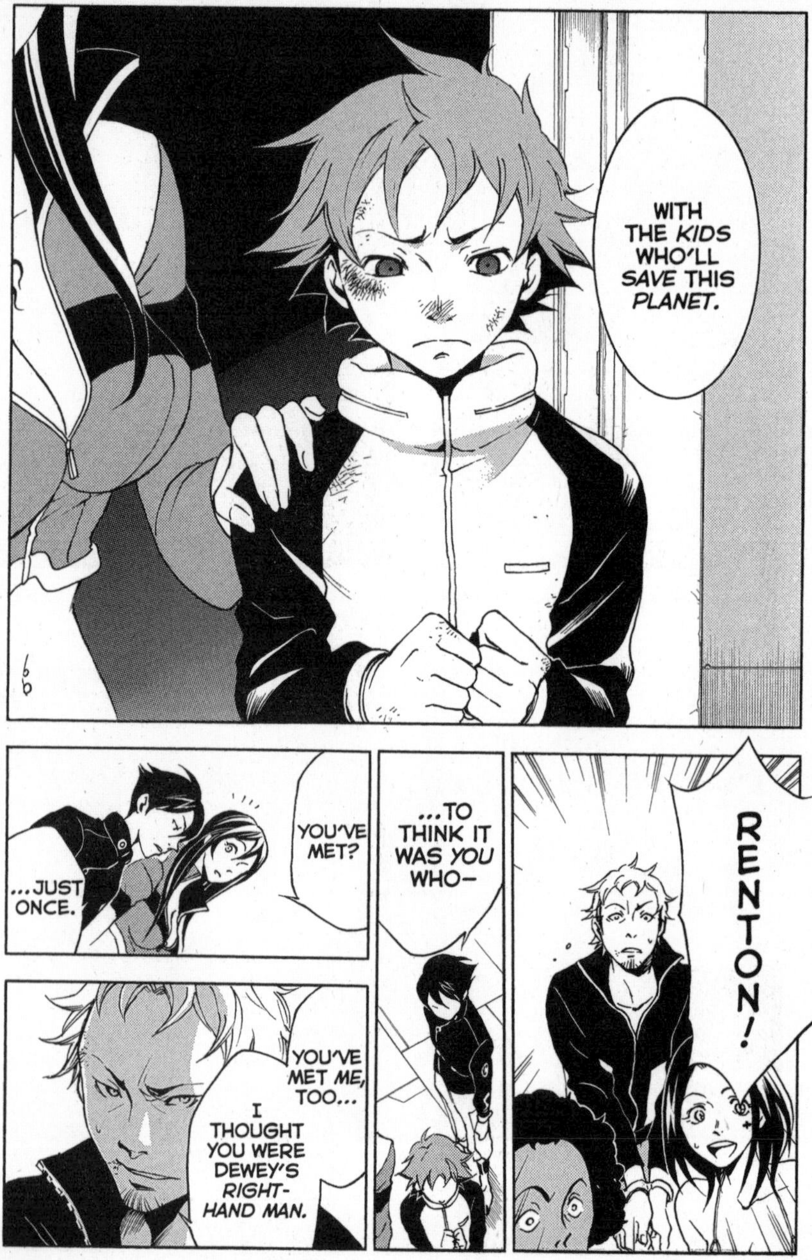

WITH THE KIDS WHO'LL SAVE THIS PLANET.
RENTON!
...TO THINK IT WAS YOU WHO–
YOU'VE MET?
...JUST ONCE.
YOU'VE MET ME, TOO...
I THOUGHT YOU WERE DEWEY'S RIGHT-HAND MAN.

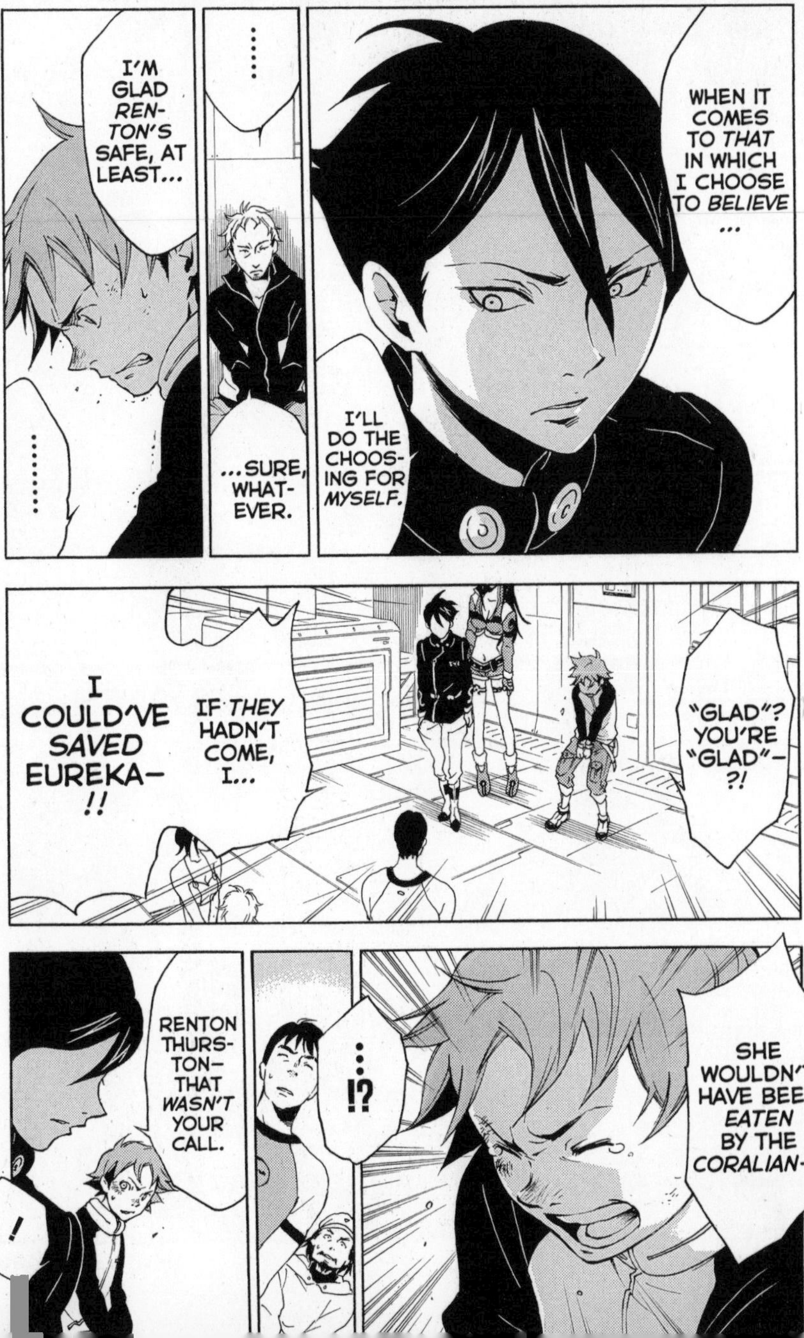
WHEN IT COMES TO *THAT* IN WHICH I CHOOSE TO *BELIEVE* ...
I'LL DO THE CHOOSING FOR *MYSELF*.
......
...SURE, WHATEVER.
I'M GLAD *RENTON'S* SAFE, AT LEAST...
....
"GLAD"? YOU'RE "GLAD"—?!
IF *THEY* HADN'T COME, I...
I COULD'VE *SAVED* EUREKA—!!
SHE WOULDN'T HAVE BEEN *EATEN* BY THE *CORALIAN*—!
...!?
RENTON THURSTON—THAT *WASN'T* YOUR CALL.
!

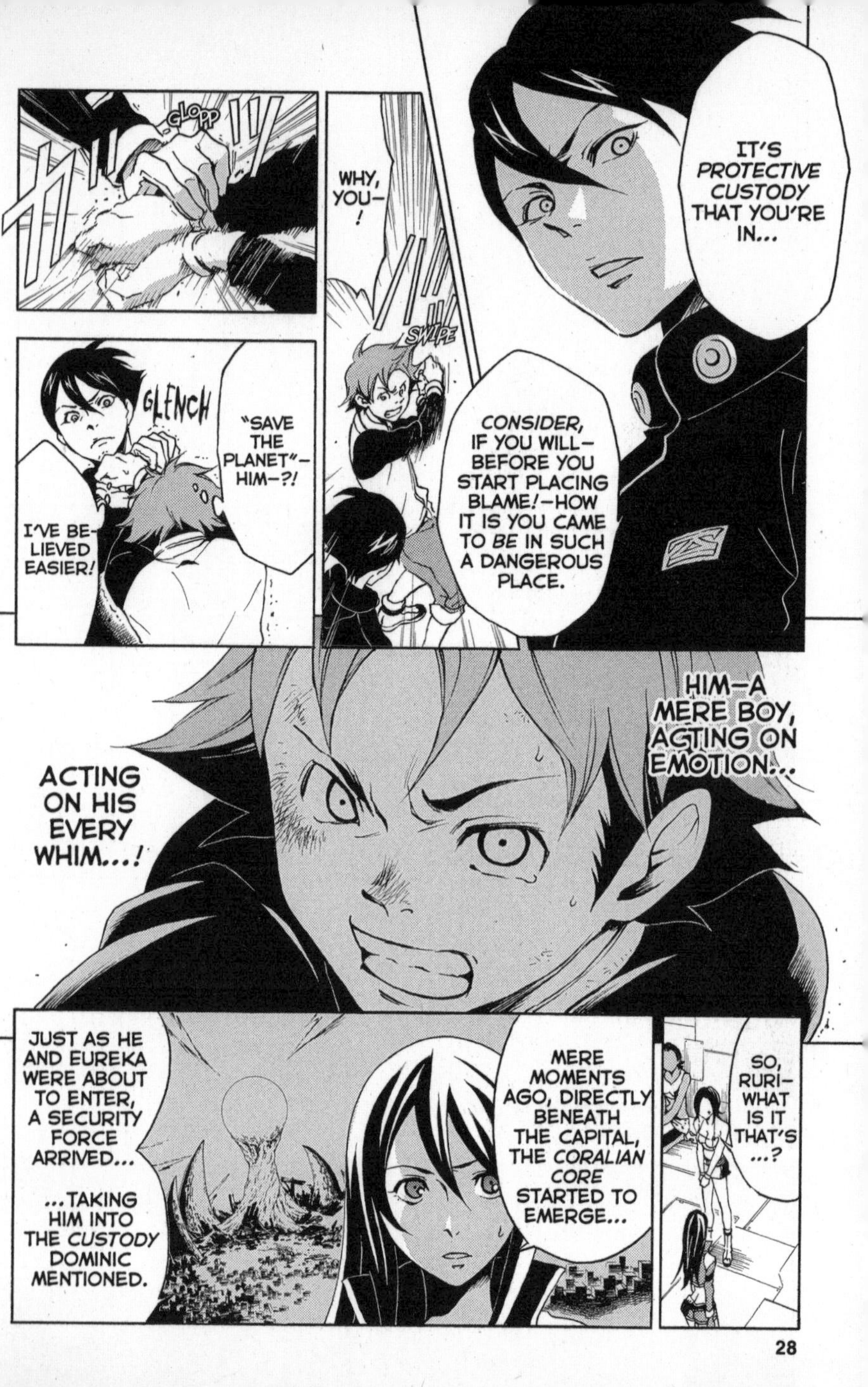
IT'S *PROTECTIVE CUSTODY* THAT YOU'RE IN...
CONSIDER, IF YOU WILL— BEFORE YOU START PLACING BLAME!—HOW IT IS YOU CAME TO *BE* IN SUCH A DANGEROUS PLACE.
WHY, YOU—!
SWIPE
GLOPP
"SAVE THE PLANET"— HIM—?!
CLENCH
I'VE BE- LIEVED EASIER!
HIM—A MERE BOY, ACTING ON EMOTION...
ACTING ON HIS EVERY WHIM...!
SO, RURI— WHAT IS IT THAT'S ...?
MERE MOMENTS AGO, DIRECTLY BENEATH THE CAPITAL, THE *CORALIAN CORE* STARTED TO EMERGE...
JUST AS HE AND EUREKA WERE ABOUT TO ENTER, A SECURITY FORCE ARRIVED...
...TAKING HIM INTO THE *CUSTODY* DOMINIC MENTIONED.

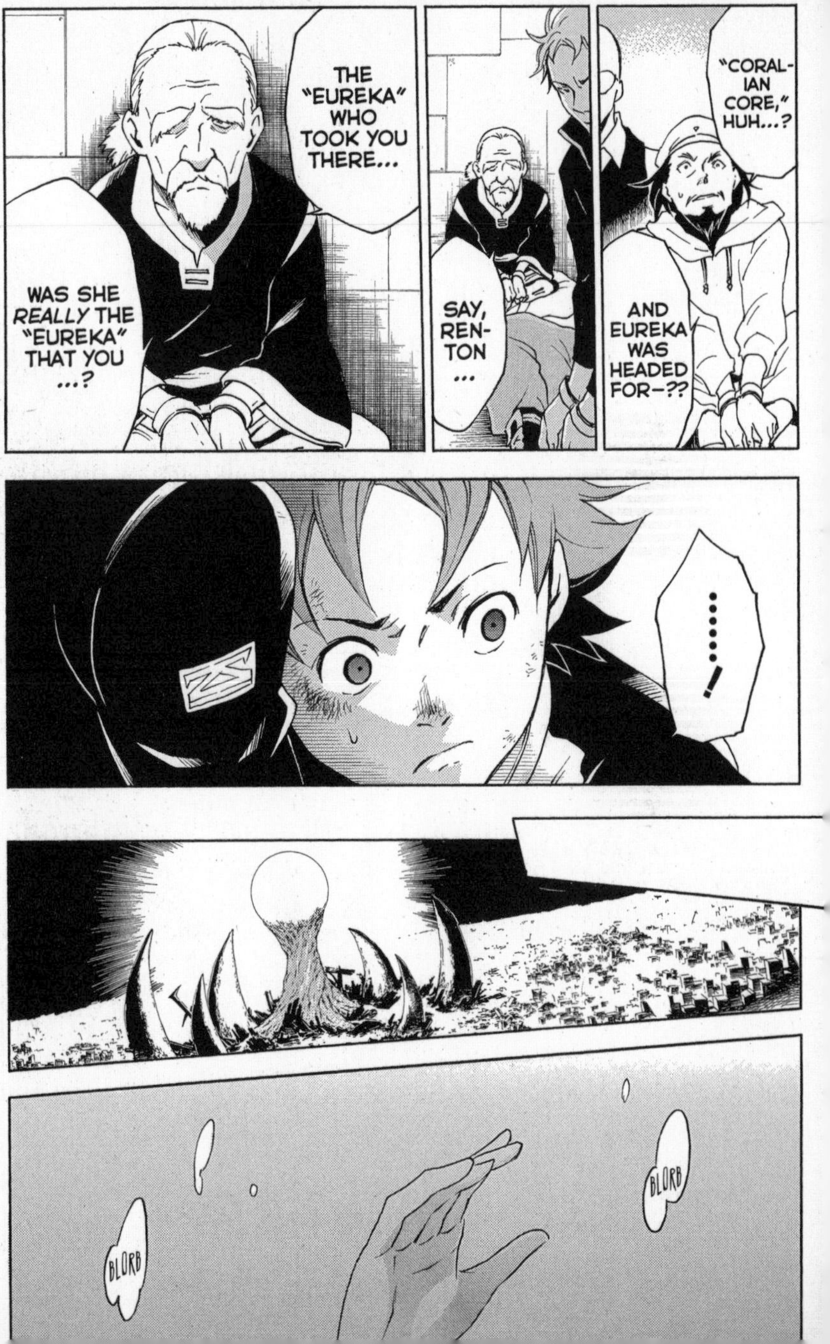
"CORAL-IAN CORE," HUH...?
AND EUREKA WAS HEADED FOR-??
SAY, REN-TON ...
THE "EUREKA" WHO TOOK YOU THERE...
WAS SHE *REALLY* THE "EUREKA" THAT YOU ...?
......!
BLORB
BLORB

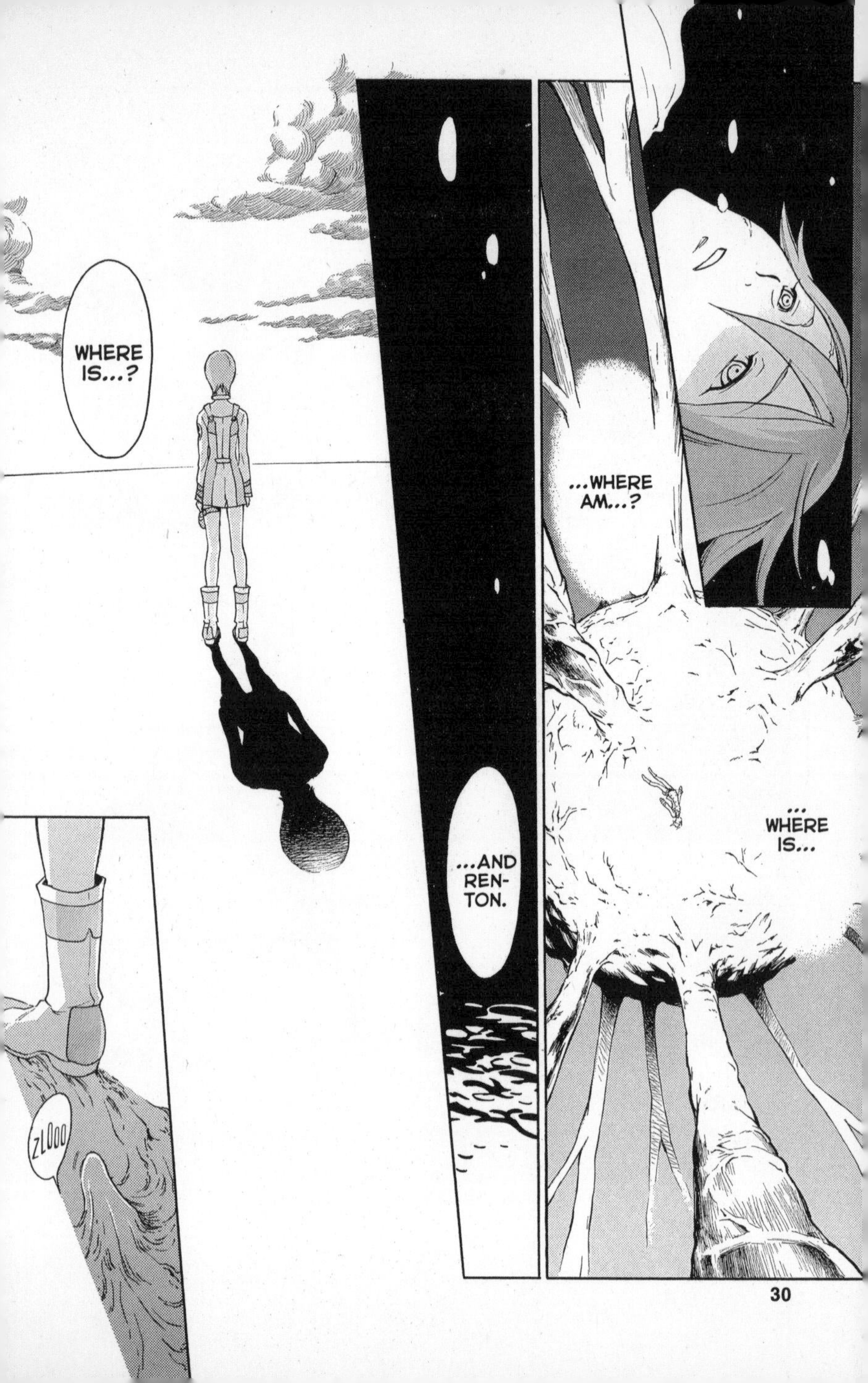
...WHERE AM...?
... WHERE IS...
...AND REN-TON.
WHERE IS...?
ZLOOO

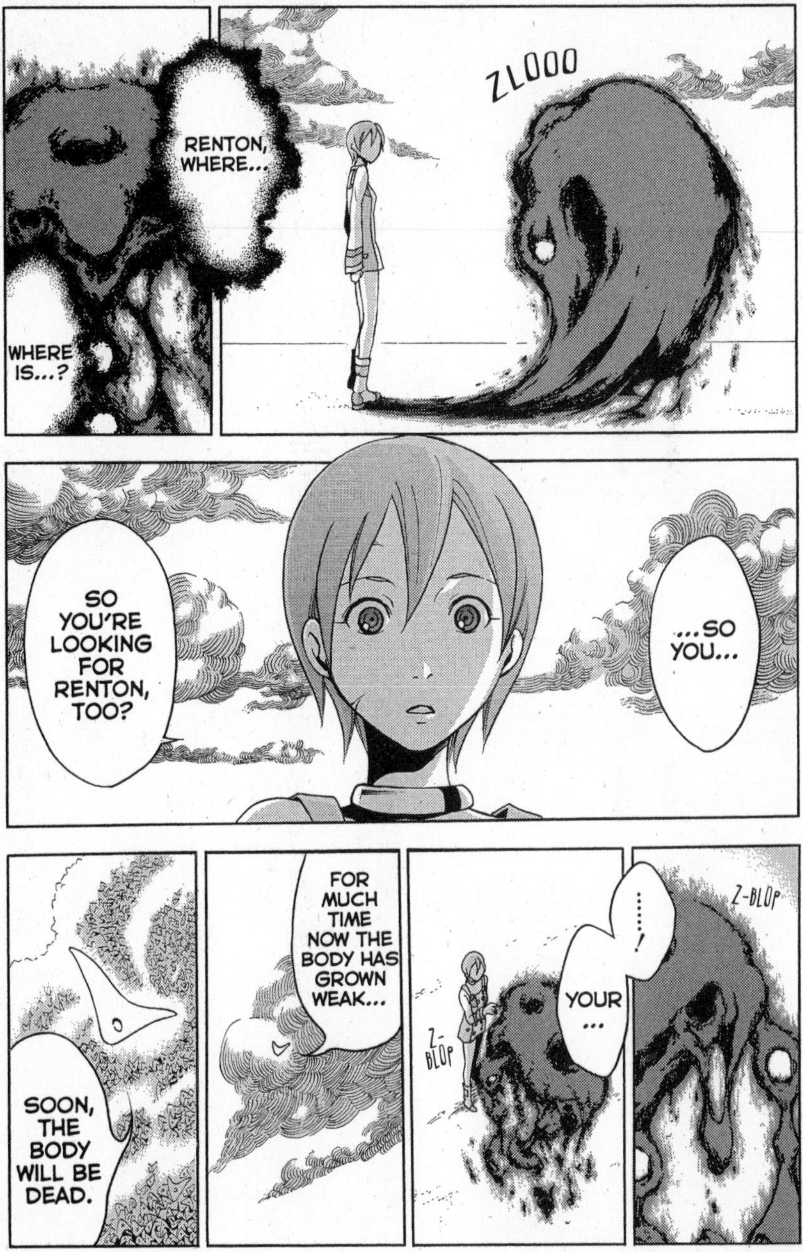
ZLOOO
RENTON, WHERE...
WHERE IS...?
...SO YOU...
SO YOU'RE LOOKING FOR RENTON, TOO?
Z-BLOP
......!
YOUR ...
Z-BLOP
FOR MUCH TIME NOW THE BODY HAS GROWN WEAK...
SOON, THE BODY WILL BE DEAD.

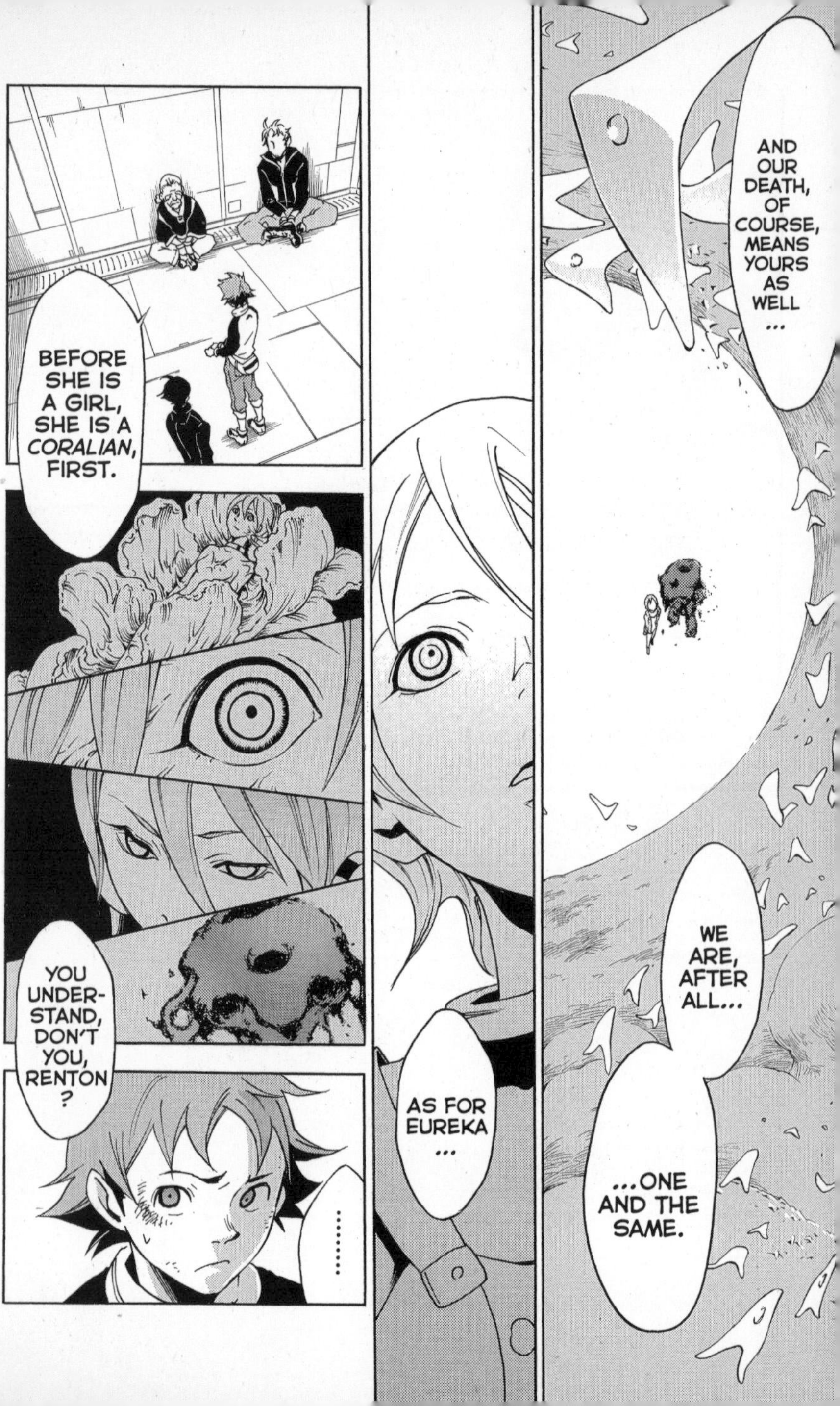
AND OUR DEATH, OF COURSE, MEANS YOURS AS WELL...
WE ARE, AFTER ALL...
...ONE AND THE SAME.
AS FOR EUREKA...
BEFORE SHE IS A GIRL, SHE IS A *CORALIAN*, FIRST.
YOU UNDER-STAND, DON'T YOU, RENTON?
....

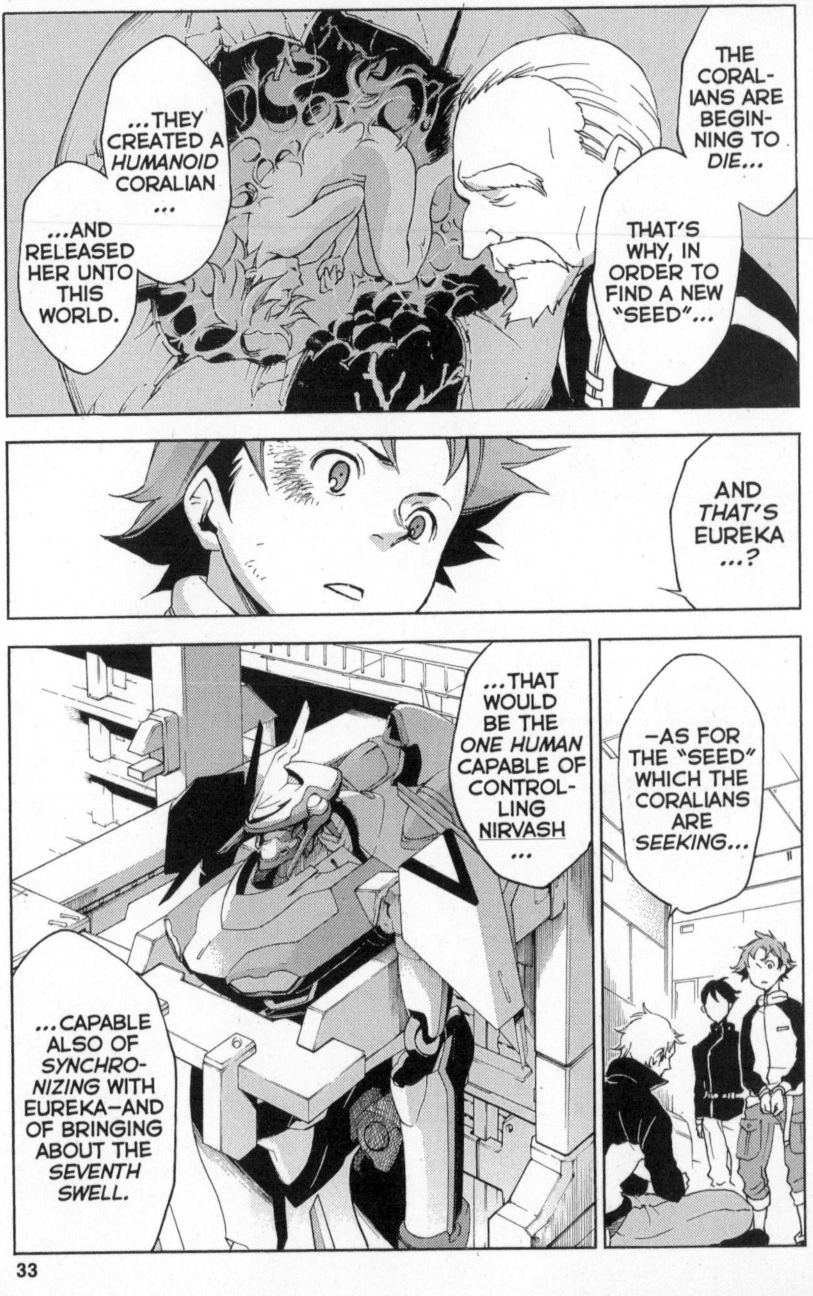
THE CORALIANS ARE BEGINNING TO DIE...
THAT'S WHY, IN ORDER TO FIND A NEW "SEED"...
...THEY CREATED A HUMANOID CORALIAN ...
...AND RELEASED HER UNTO THIS WORLD.
AND THAT'S EUREKA ...?
—AS FOR THE "SEED" WHICH THE CORALIANS ARE SEEKING...
...THAT WOULD BE THE ONE HUMAN CAPABLE OF CONTROLLING NIRVASH ...
...CAPABLE ALSO OF SYNCHRONIZING WITH EUREKA—AND OF BRINGING ABOUT THE SEVENTH SWELL.

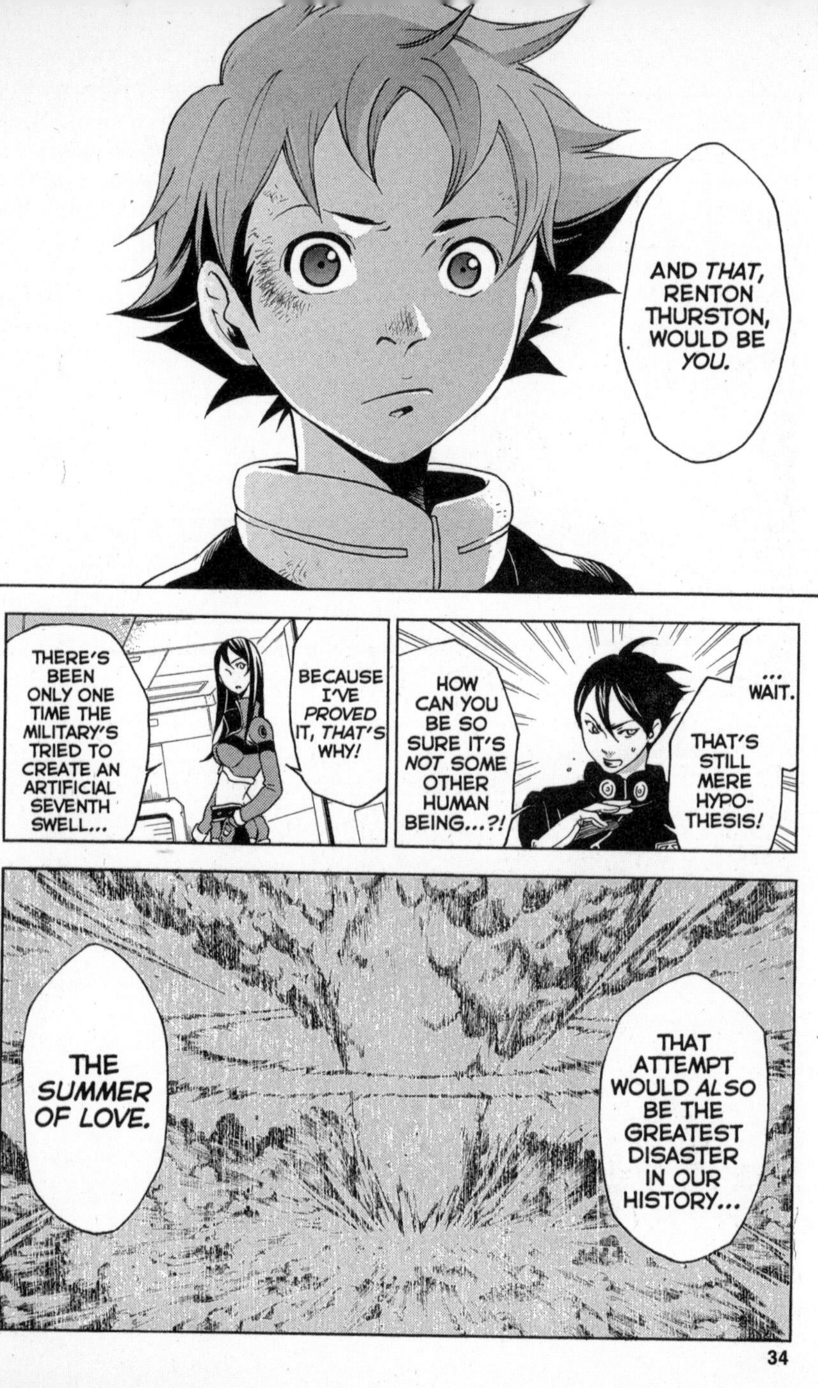
AND *THAT*, RENTON THURSTON, WOULD BE *YOU*.
... WAIT.
THAT'S STILL MERE HYPOTHESIS!
HOW CAN YOU BE SO SURE IT'S *NOT* SOME OTHER HUMAN BEING...?!
BECAUSE I'VE *PROVED* IT, *THAT'S* WHY!
THERE'S BEEN ONLY ONE TIME THE MILITARY'S TRIED TO CREATE AN ARTIFICIAL SEVENTH SWELL...
THAT ATTEMPT WOULD *AL*SO BE THE GREATEST DISASTER IN OUR HISTORY...
THE *SUMMER* OF LOVE.

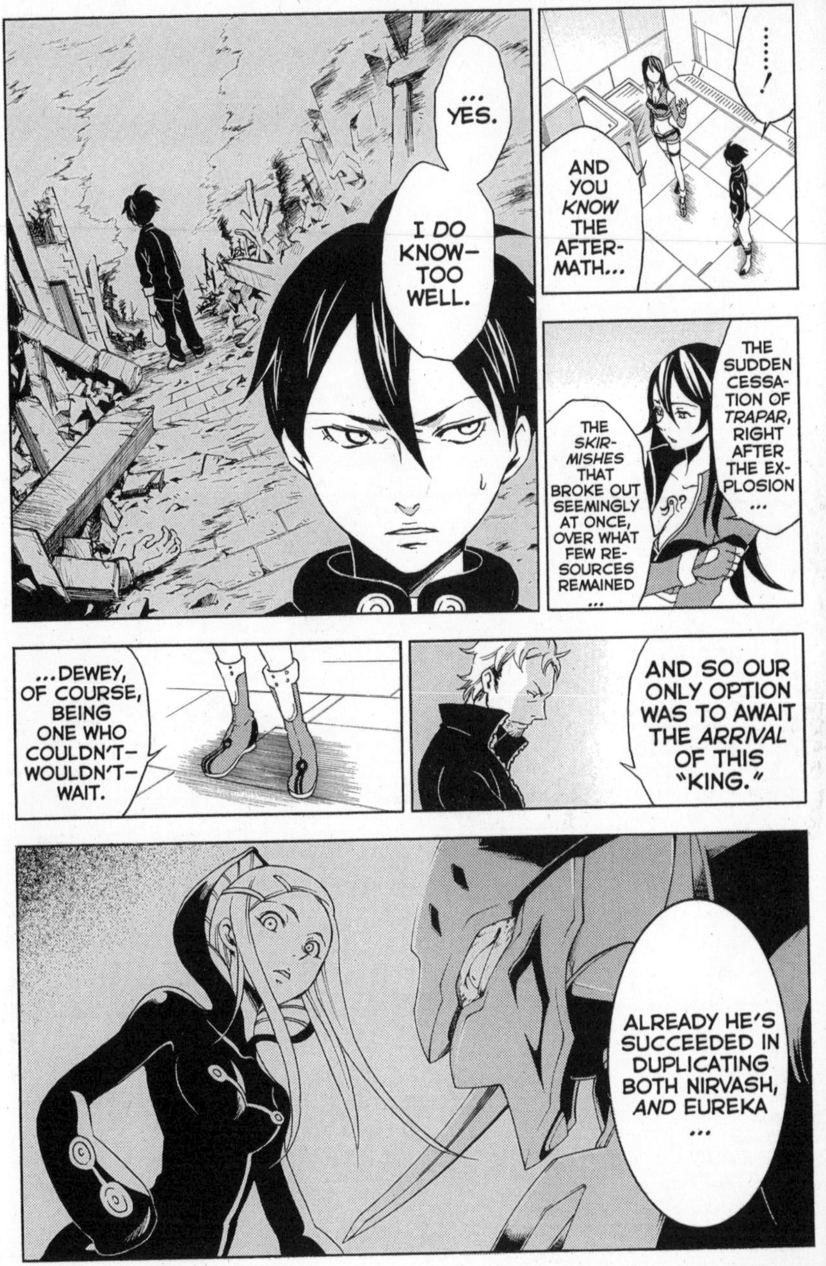
......!
AND YOU *KNOW* THE AFTERMATH...
THE SUDDEN CESSATION OF *TRAPAR*, RIGHT AFTER THE EXPLOSION...
THE *SKIRMISHES* THAT BROKE OUT SEEMINGLY AT ONCE, OVER WHAT FEW RESOURCES REMAINED...
...YES.
I *DO* KNOW—TOO WELL.
AND SO OUR ONLY OPTION WAS TO AWAIT THE *ARRIVAL* OF THIS "KING."
...DEWEY, OF COURSE, BEING ONE WHO COULDN'T—WOULDN'T—WAIT.
ALREADY HE'S SUCCEEDED IN DUPLICATING BOTH NIRVASH, *AND* EUREKA...

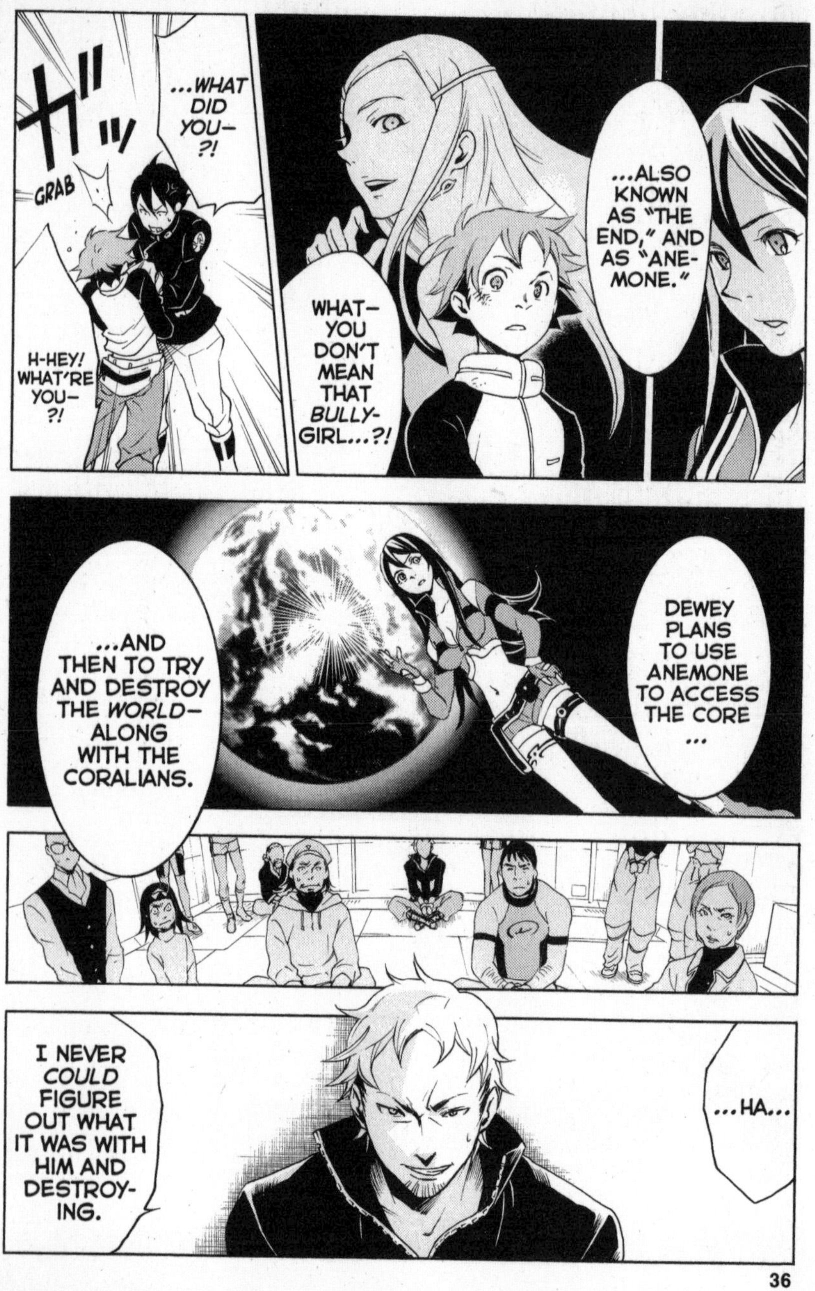
...ALSO KNOWN AS "THE END," AND AS "ANE-MONE."
WHAT— YOU DON'T MEAN THAT BULLY-GIRL...?!
...WHAT DID YOU— ?!
ガッ
GRAB
H-HEY! WHAT'RE YOU— ?!
DEWEY PLANS TO USE ANEMONE TO ACCESS THE CORE ...
...AND THEN TO TRY AND DESTROY THE WORLD— ALONG WITH THE CORALIANS.
...HA...
I NEVER COULD FIGURE OUT WHAT IT WAS WITH HIM AND DESTROY-ING.

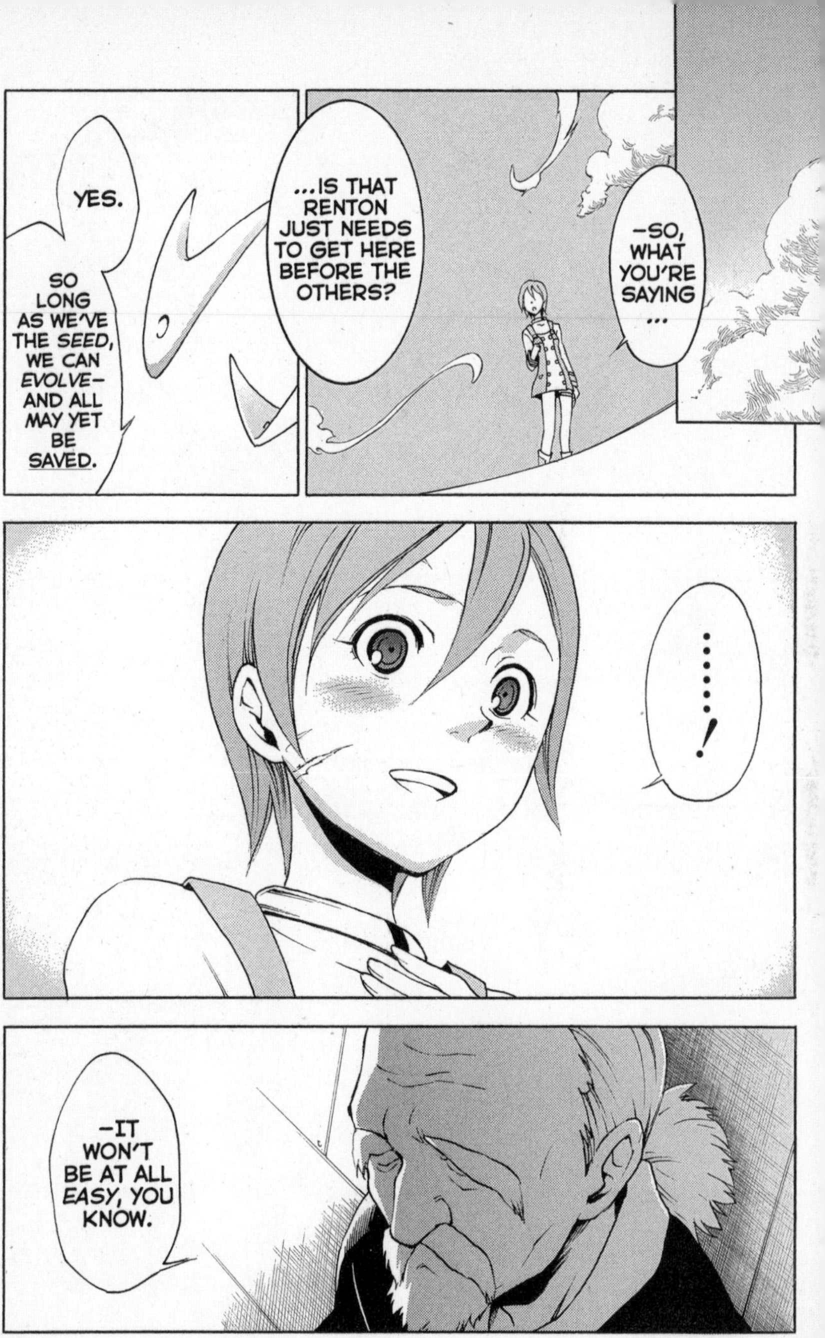
—SO, WHAT YOU'RE SAYING ...
...IS THAT RENTON JUST NEEDS TO GET HERE BEFORE THE OTHERS?
YES.
SO LONG AS WE'VE THE *SEED*, WE CAN *EVOLVE*—AND ALL MAY YET BE SAVED.
......!
—IT WON'T BE AT ALL *EASY*, YOU KNOW.

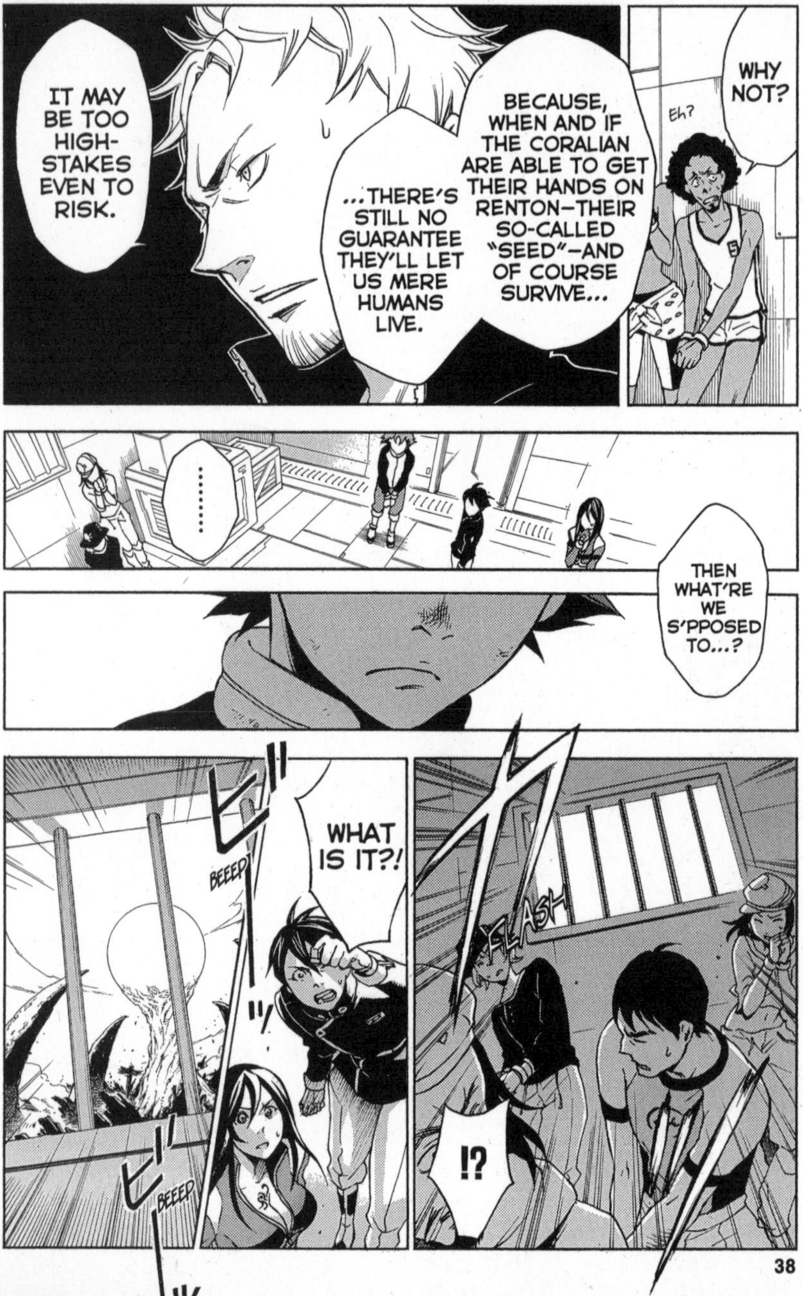
WHY NOT?
Eh?
BECAUSE, WHEN AND IF THE CORALIAN ARE ABLE TO GET THEIR HANDS ON RENTON—THEIR SO-CALLED "SEED"—AND OF COURSE SURVIVE...
...THERE'S STILL NO GUARANTEE THEY'LL LET US MERE HUMANS LIVE.
IT MAY BE TOO HIGH-STAKES EVEN TO RISK.
THEN WHAT'RE WE S'PPOSED TO...?
....
FLASH
!?
WHAT IS IT?!
BEEEP
BEEEP

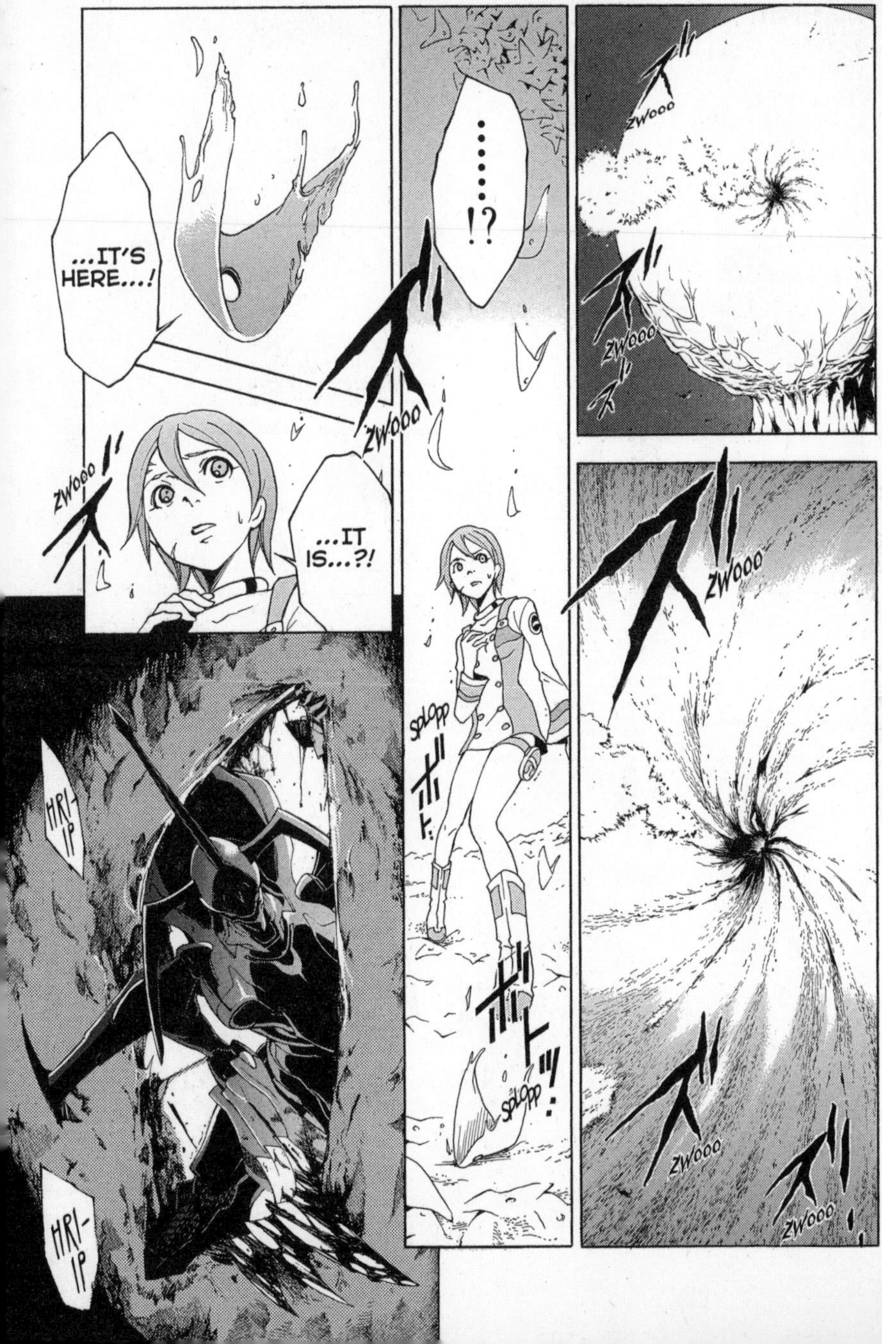
ZWOOO
ZWOOO
ZWOOO
ZWOOO
ZWOOO
......!?
ZWOOO
SPLOPP
SPLOPP!
...IT'S HERE...!
ZWOOO
...IT IS...?!
HRI-IP
HRI-IP

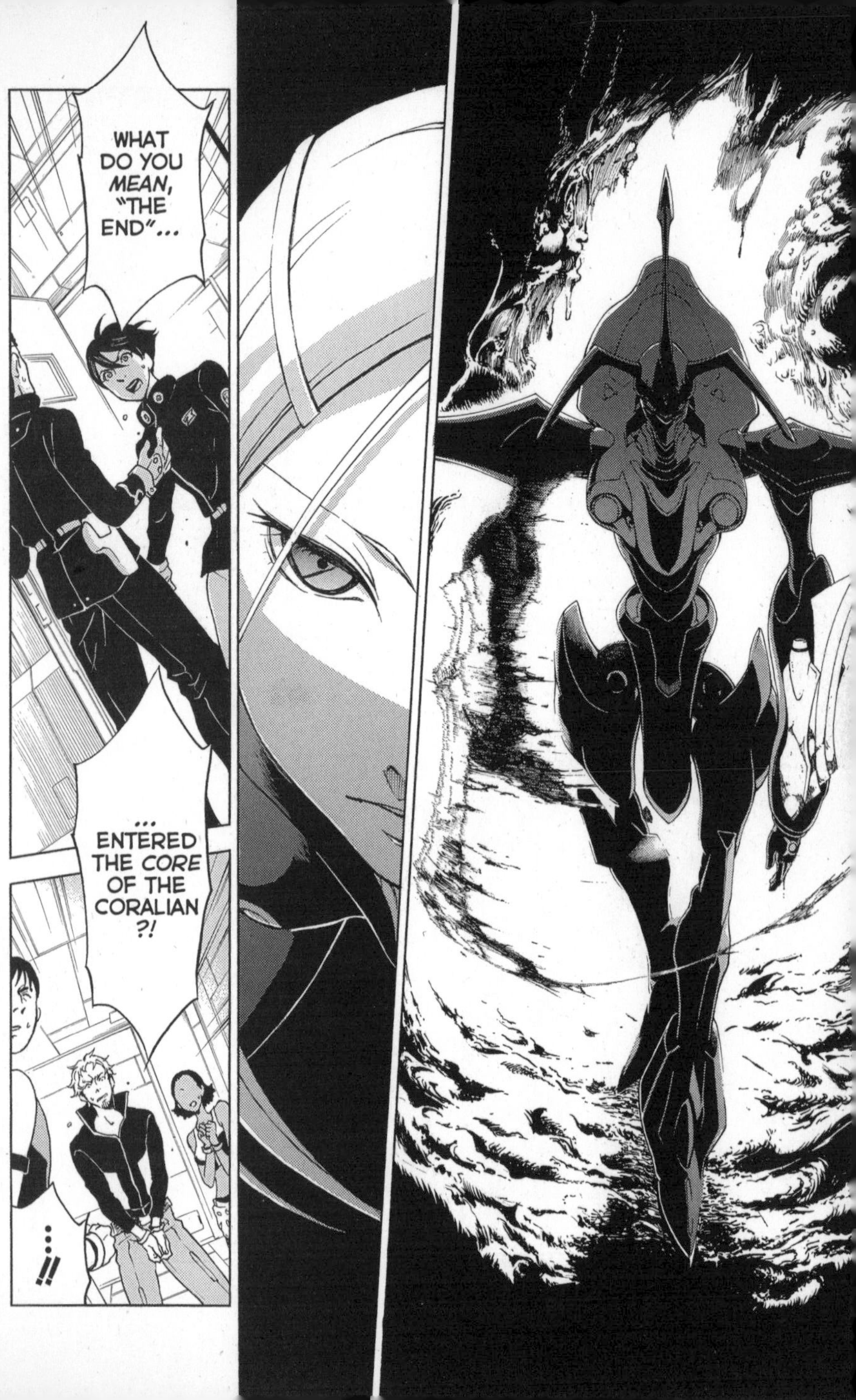
WHAT DO YOU MEAN, "THE END"...
... ENTERED THE CORE OF THE CORALIAN ?!
...!!

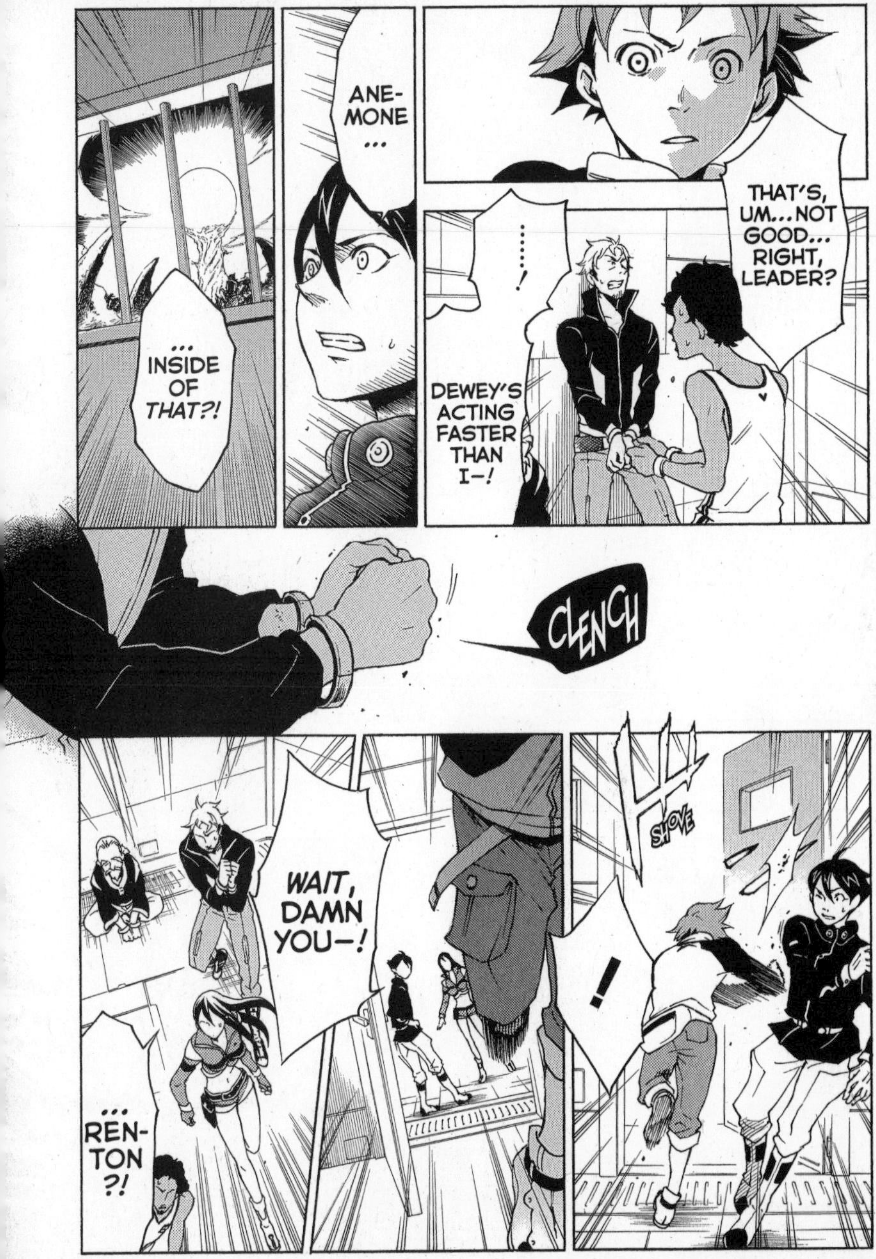
THAT'S, UM...NOT GOOD... RIGHT, LEADER?
......!
DEWEY'S ACTING FASTER THAN I—!
ANE-MONE ...
... INSIDE OF *THAT?!*
CLENCH
SHOVE
!
WAIT, DAMN YOU—!
... REN-TON ?!

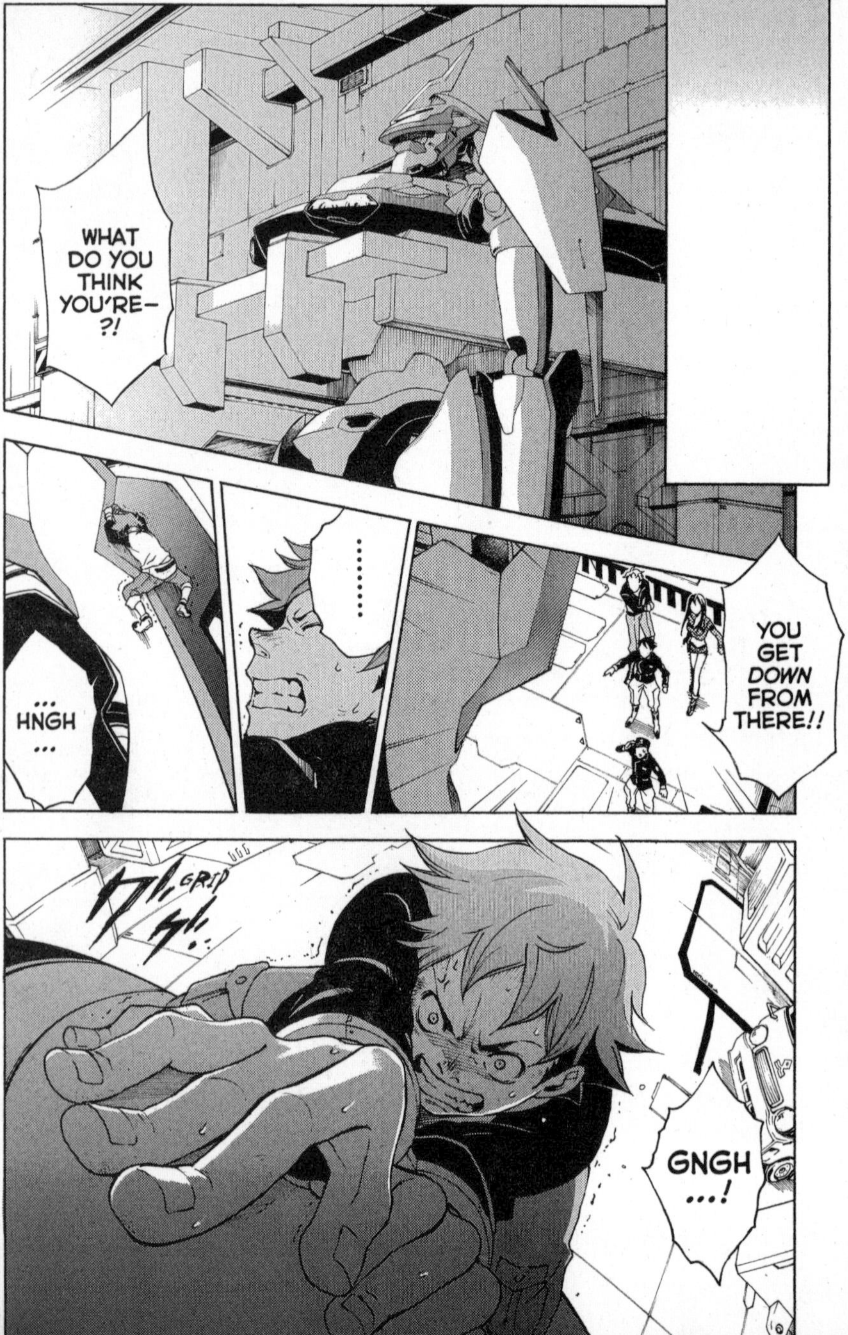
WHAT DO YOU THINK YOU'RE—?!
YOU GET DOWN FROM THERE!!
....
... HNGH ...
GRIP
GNGH ...!

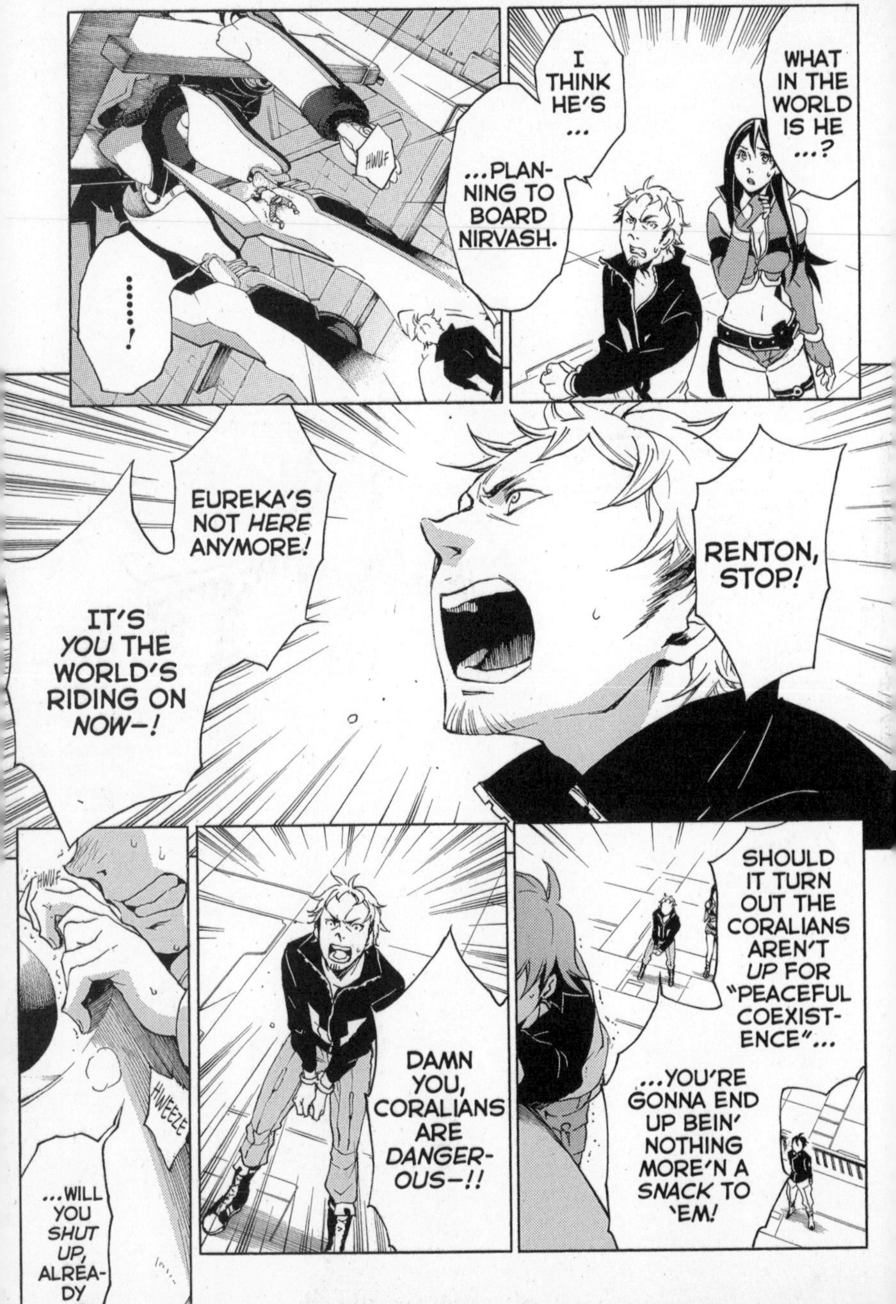
WHAT IN THE WORLD IS HE ...?
I THINK HE'S ...
...PLAN-NING TO BOARD NIRVASH.
HWUF
......!
RENTON, STOP!
EUREKA'S NOT HERE ANYMORE!
IT'S YOU THE WORLD'S RIDING ON NOW-!
SHOULD IT TURN OUT THE CORALIANS AREN'T UP FOR "PEACEFUL COEXIST-ENCE"...
...YOU'RE GONNA END UP BEIN' NOTHING MORE'N A SNACK TO 'EM!
DAMN YOU, CORALIANS ARE DANGER-OUS-!!
HWUF
HWEEZE
...WILL YOU SHUT UP, ALREA-DY ...?!

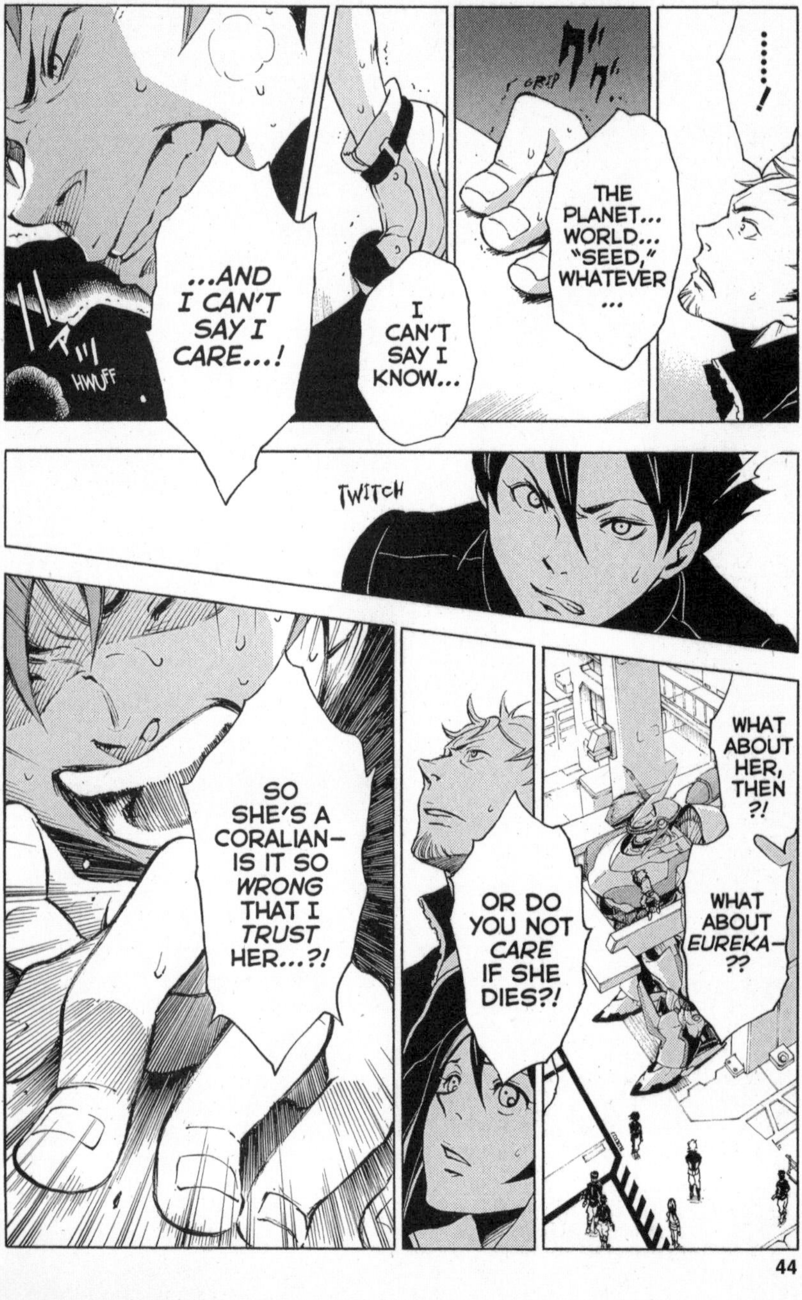
......!
GRIP
THE PLANET... WORLD... "SEED," WHATEVER ...
I CAN'T SAY I KNOW...
...AND I CAN'T SAY I CARE...!
HWUFF
TWITCH
WHAT ABOUT HER, THEN?!
WHAT ABOUT *EUREKA*-??
OR DO YOU NOT *CARE* IF SHE DIES?!
SO SHE'S A CORALIAN- IS IT SO *WRONG* THAT I *TRUST* HER...?!

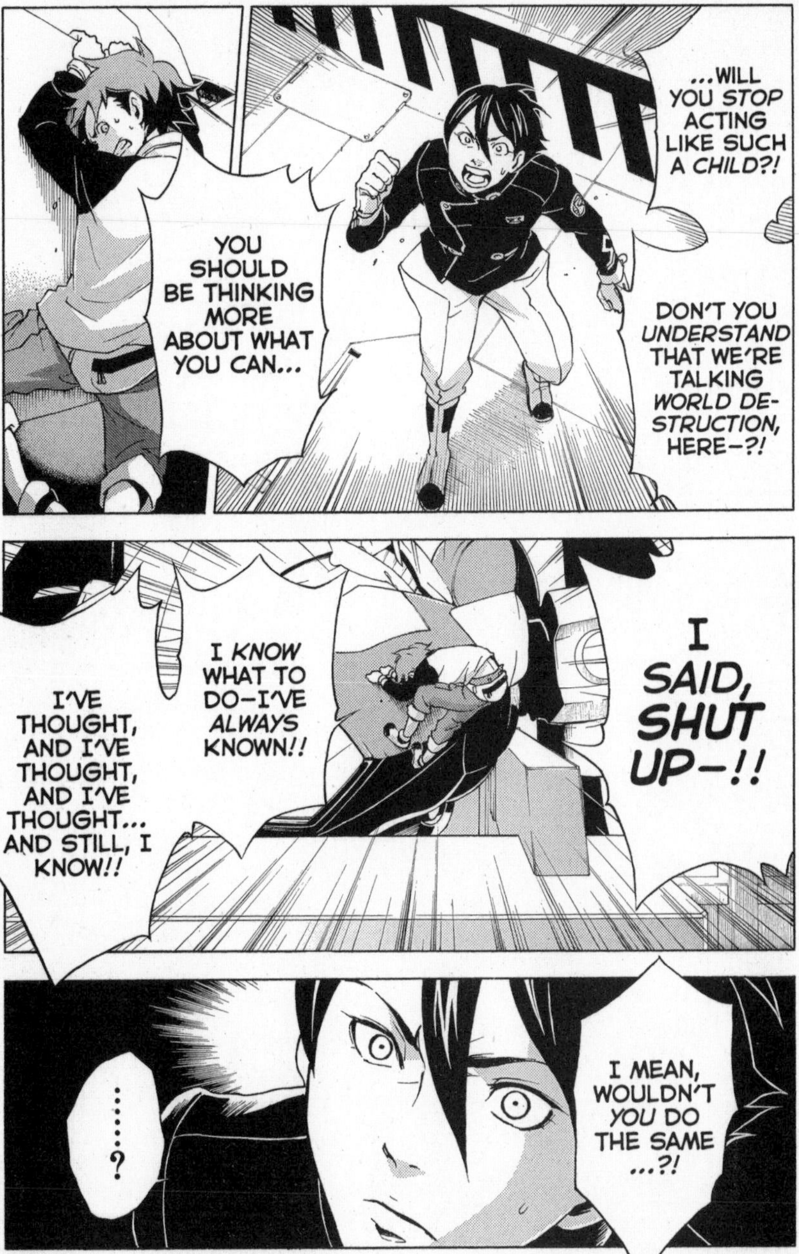
...WILL YOU STOP ACTING LIKE SUCH A CHILD?!
DON'T YOU UNDERSTAND THAT WE'RE TALKING WORLD DE- STRUCTION, HERE-?!
YOU SHOULD BE THINKING MORE ABOUT WHAT YOU CAN...
I SAID, SHUT UP-!!
I KNOW WHAT TO DO-I'VE ALWAYS KNOWN!!
I'VE THOUGHT, AND I'VE THOUGHT, AND I'VE THOUGHT... AND STILL, I KNOW!!
I MEAN, WOULDN'T YOU DO THE SAME ...?!
......?

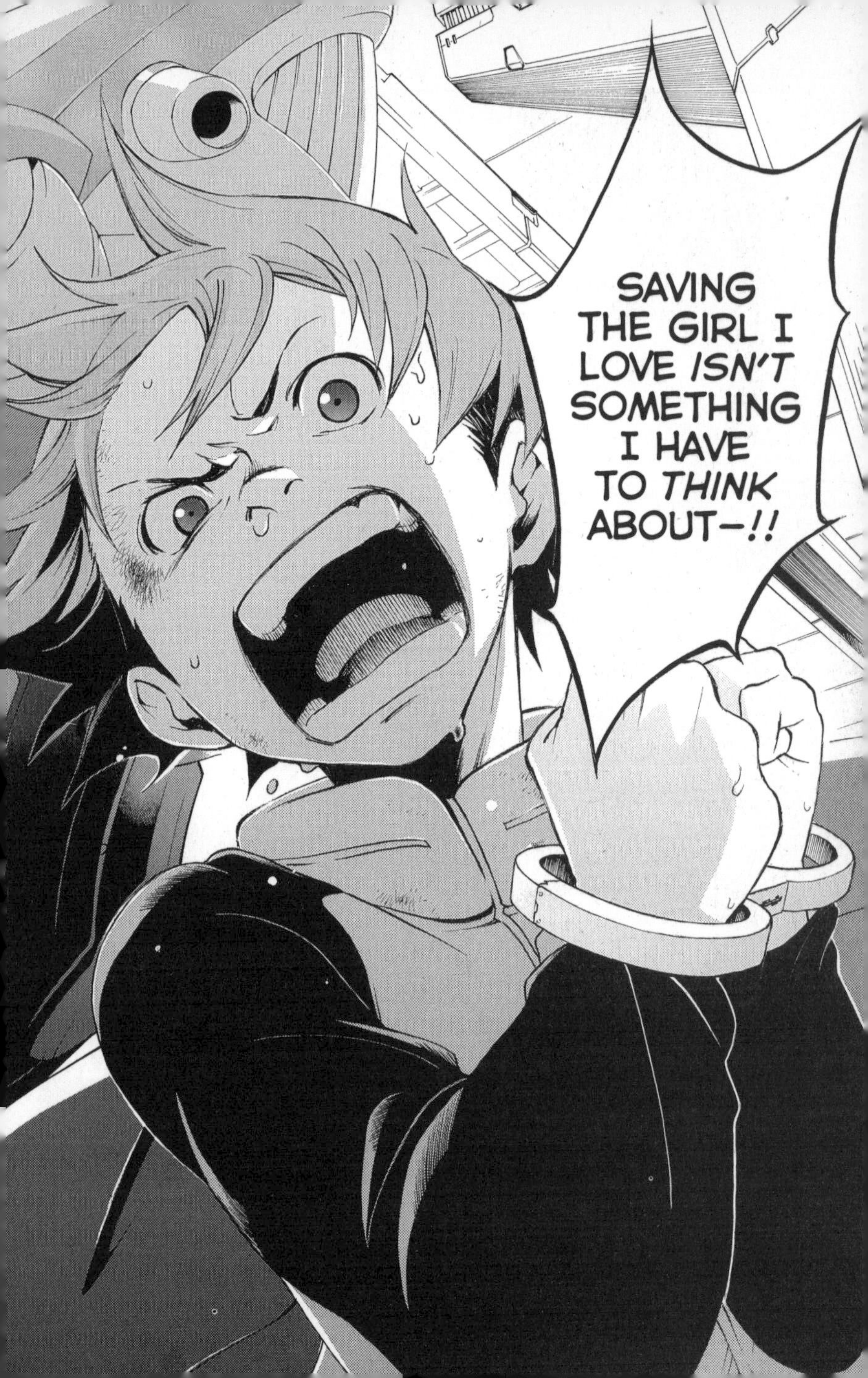
SAVING THE GIRL I LOVE *ISN'T* SOMETHING I HAVE TO *THINK* ABOUT–!!

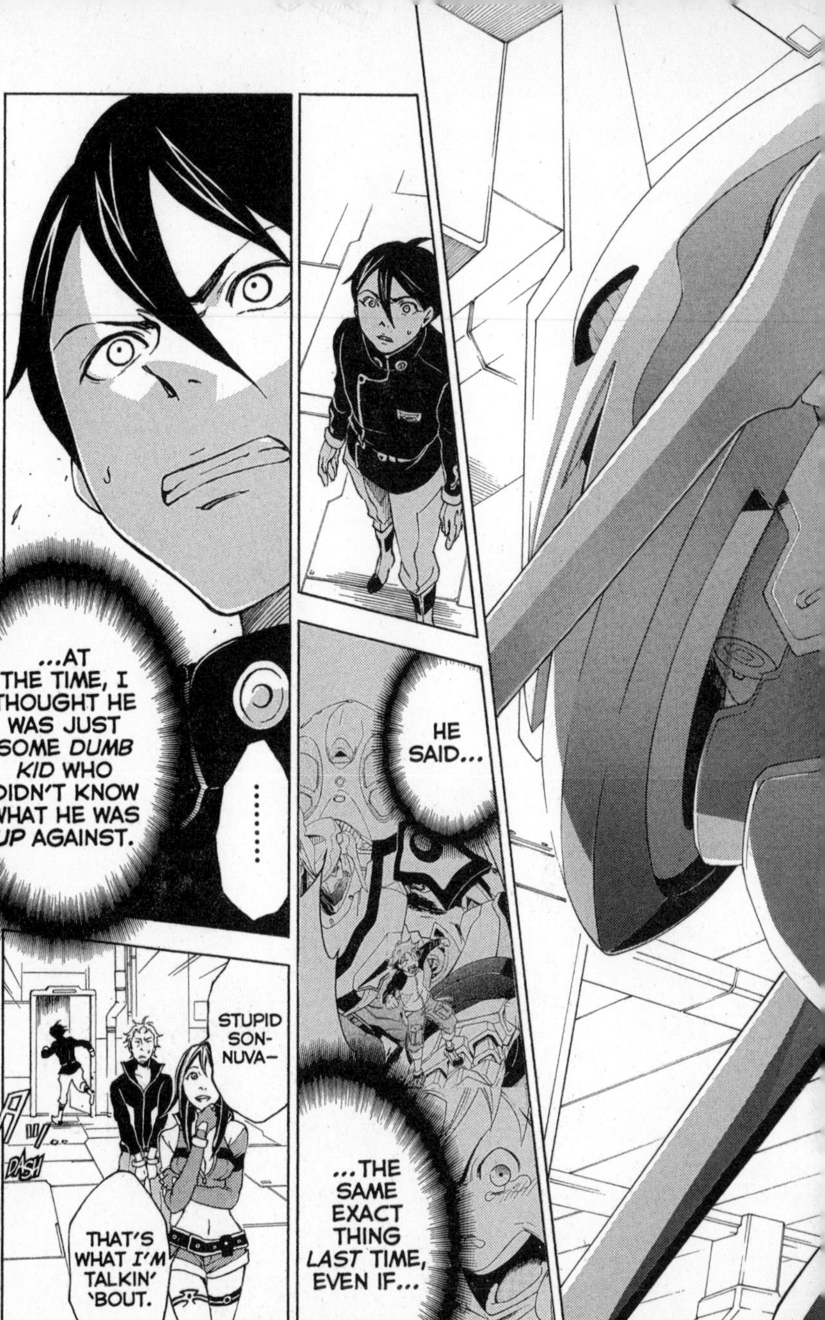
HE SAID...
...THE SAME EXACT THING LAST TIME, EVEN IF...
...AT THE TIME, I THOUGHT HE WAS JUST SOME *DUMB KID* WHO DIDN'T KNOW WHAT HE WAS *UP* AGAINST.
......
STUPID SON-NUVA—
DASH
THAT'S WHAT *I'M* TALKIN' 'BOUT.

HWUFF
HWUFF

—IF, KNOWING WHAT'S AHEAD, YOU *FEAR* IT AND *STILL* GO...

FWEEEN

...THEN YOU *ARE* JUST AN IDIOT—!!

!

...ME, ON THE OTHER HAND—!

BWA!

WHAT DID YOU—?!

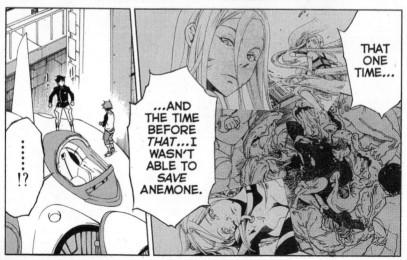

THAT ONE TIME...

...AND THE TIME BEFORE *THAT*...I WASN'T ABLE TO *SAVE* ANEMONE.

.....

!?

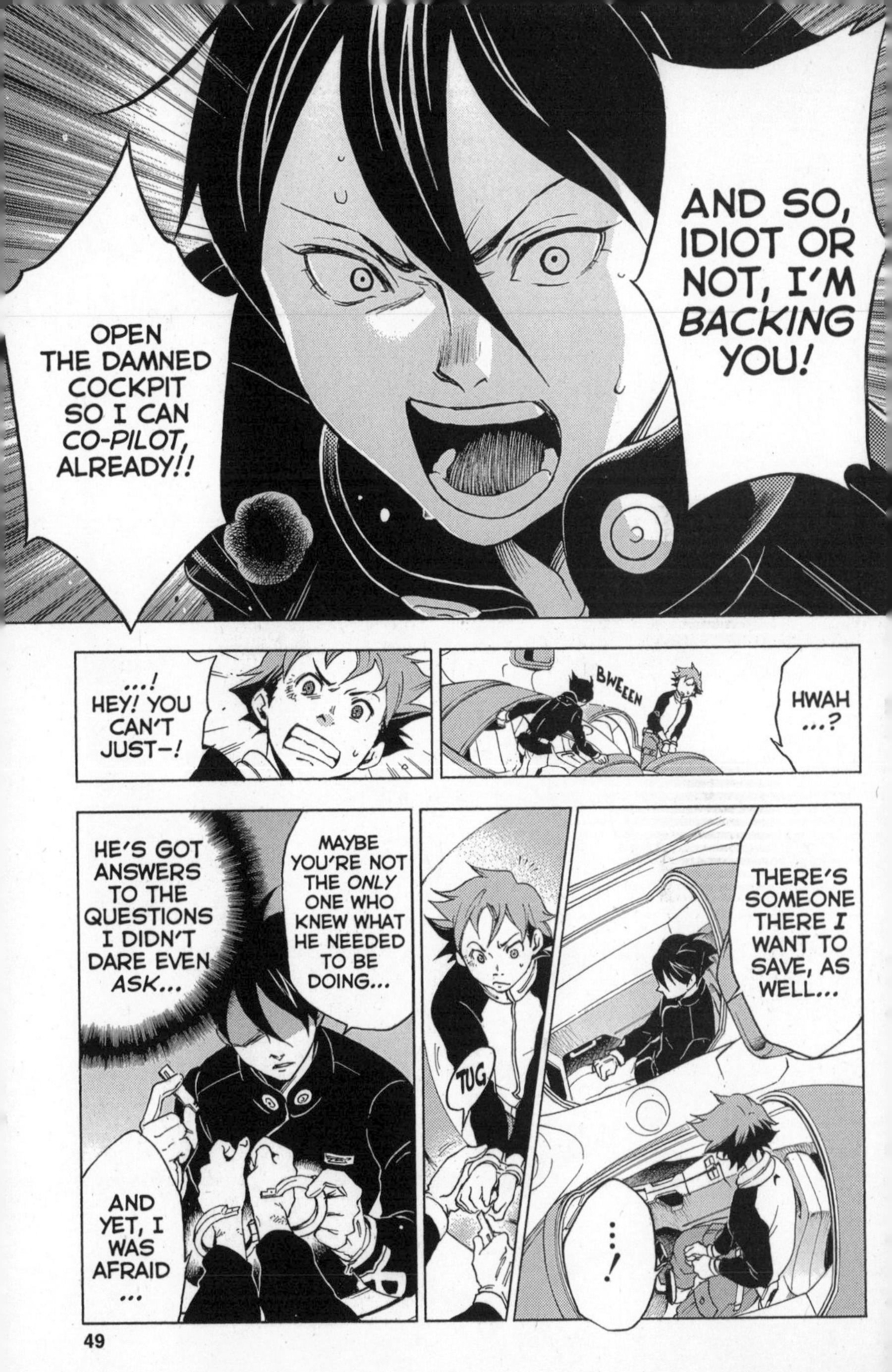
AND SO, IDIOT OR NOT, I'M *BACKING* YOU!
OPEN THE DAMNED COCKPIT SO I CAN *CO-PILOT*, ALREADY!!
HWAH ...?
BWEEEN
...! HEY! YOU CAN'T JUST-!
THERE'S SOMEONE THERE *I* WANT TO SAVE, AS WELL...
...!
MAYBE YOU'RE NOT THE *ONLY* ONE WHO KNEW WHAT HE NEEDED TO BE DOING...
TUG
HE'S GOT ANSWERS TO THE QUESTIONS I DIDN'T DARE EVEN *ASK*...
AND YET, I WAS AFRAID ...

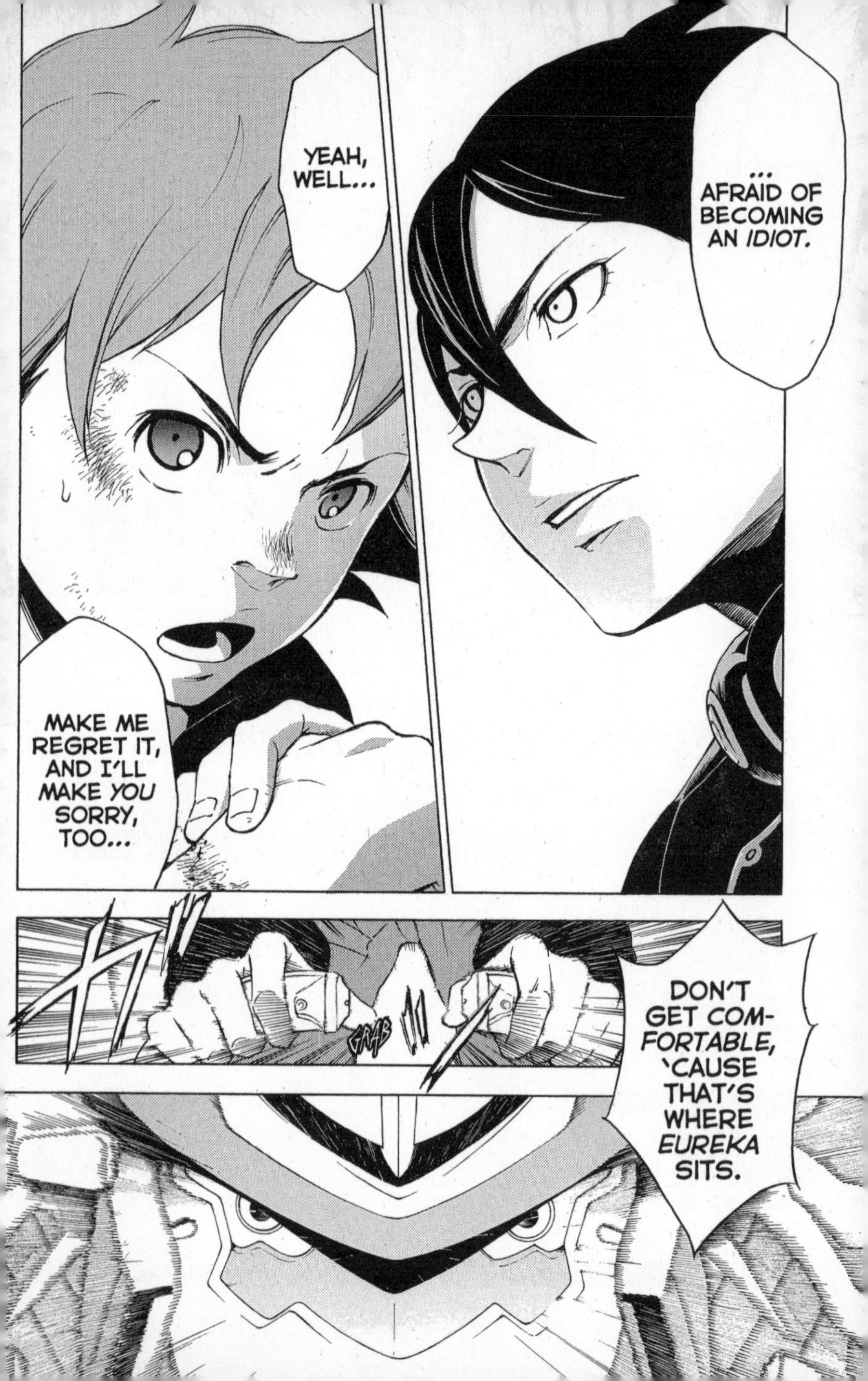
... AFRAID OF BECOMING AN *IDIOT*.
YEAH, WELL...
MAKE ME REGRET IT, AND I'LL MAKE *YOU* SORRY, TOO...
GRAB
DON'T GET *COM-FORTABLE*, 'CAUSE THAT'S WHERE *EUREKA* SITS.

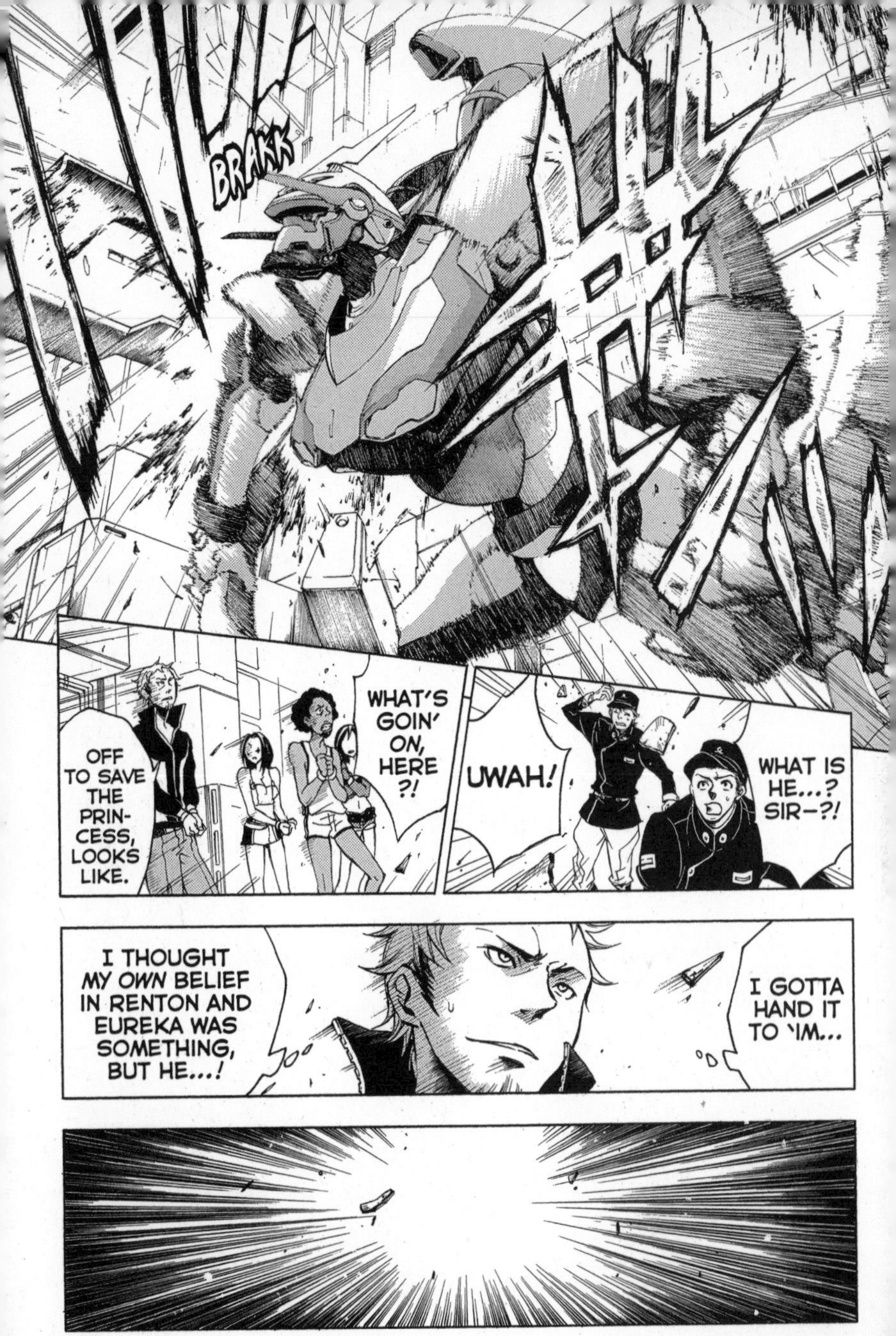
BRAKK
WHAT IS HE...? SIR–?!
UWAH!
WHAT'S GOIN' ON, HERE?!
OFF TO SAVE THE PRINCESS, LOOKS LIKE.
I GOTTA HAND IT TO 'IM...
I THOUGHT MY *OWN* BELIEF IN RENTON AND EUREKA WAS SOMETHING, BUT HE...!

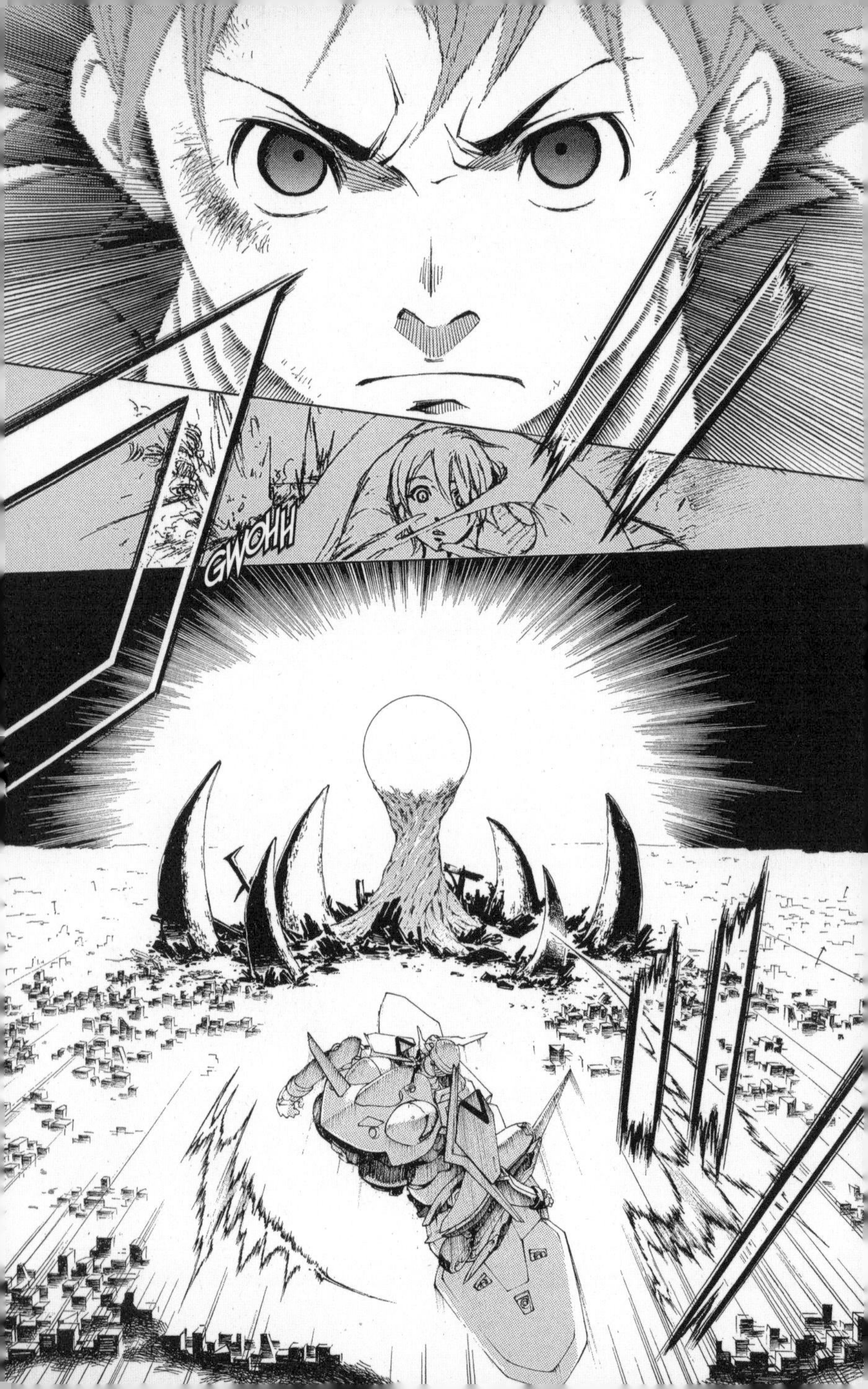
GWOHH

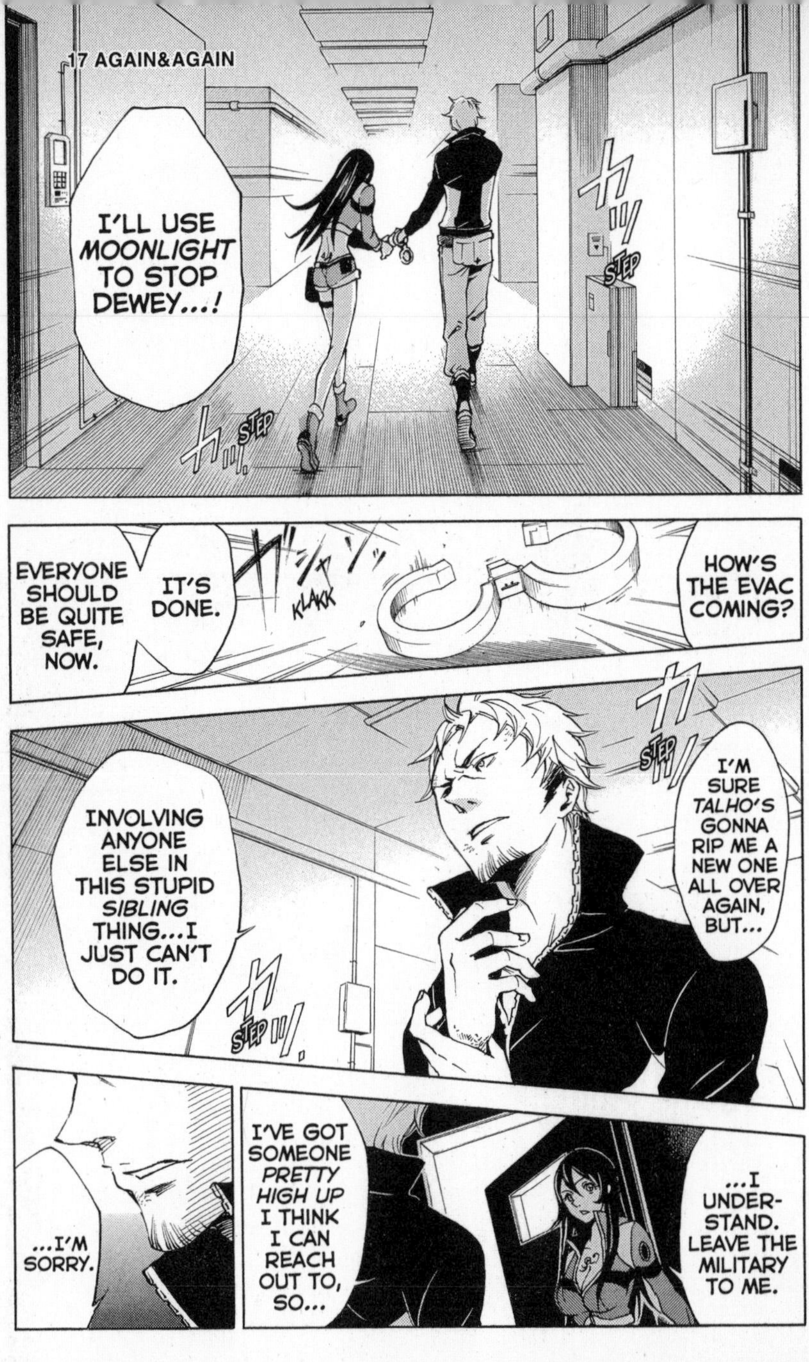
I'LL USE MOONLIGHT TO STOP DEWEY...!
STEP
STEP
HOW'S THE EVAC COMING?
KLAKK
IT'S DONE.
EVERYONE SHOULD BE QUITE SAFE, NOW.
STEP
I'M SURE TALHO'S GONNA RIP ME A NEW ONE ALL OVER AGAIN, BUT...
INVOLVING ANYONE ELSE IN THIS STUPID SIBLING THING...I JUST CAN'T DO IT.
STEP
...I UNDERSTAND. LEAVE THE MILITARY TO ME.
I'VE GOT SOMEONE PRETTY HIGH UP I THINK I CAN REACH OUT TO, SO...
...I'M SORRY.

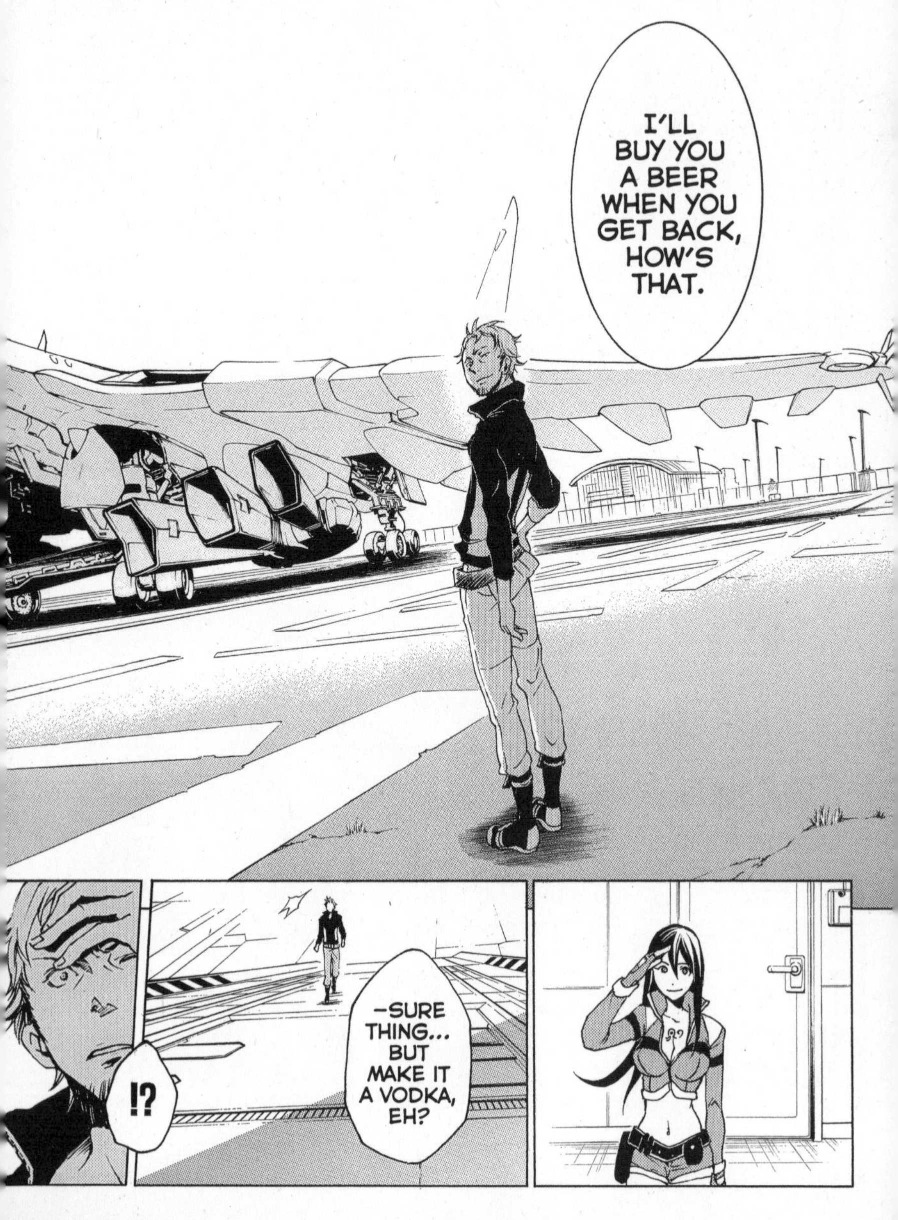
I'LL BUY YOU A BEER WHEN YOU GET BACK, HOW'S THAT.
—SURE THING... BUT MAKE IT A VODKA, EH?
!?

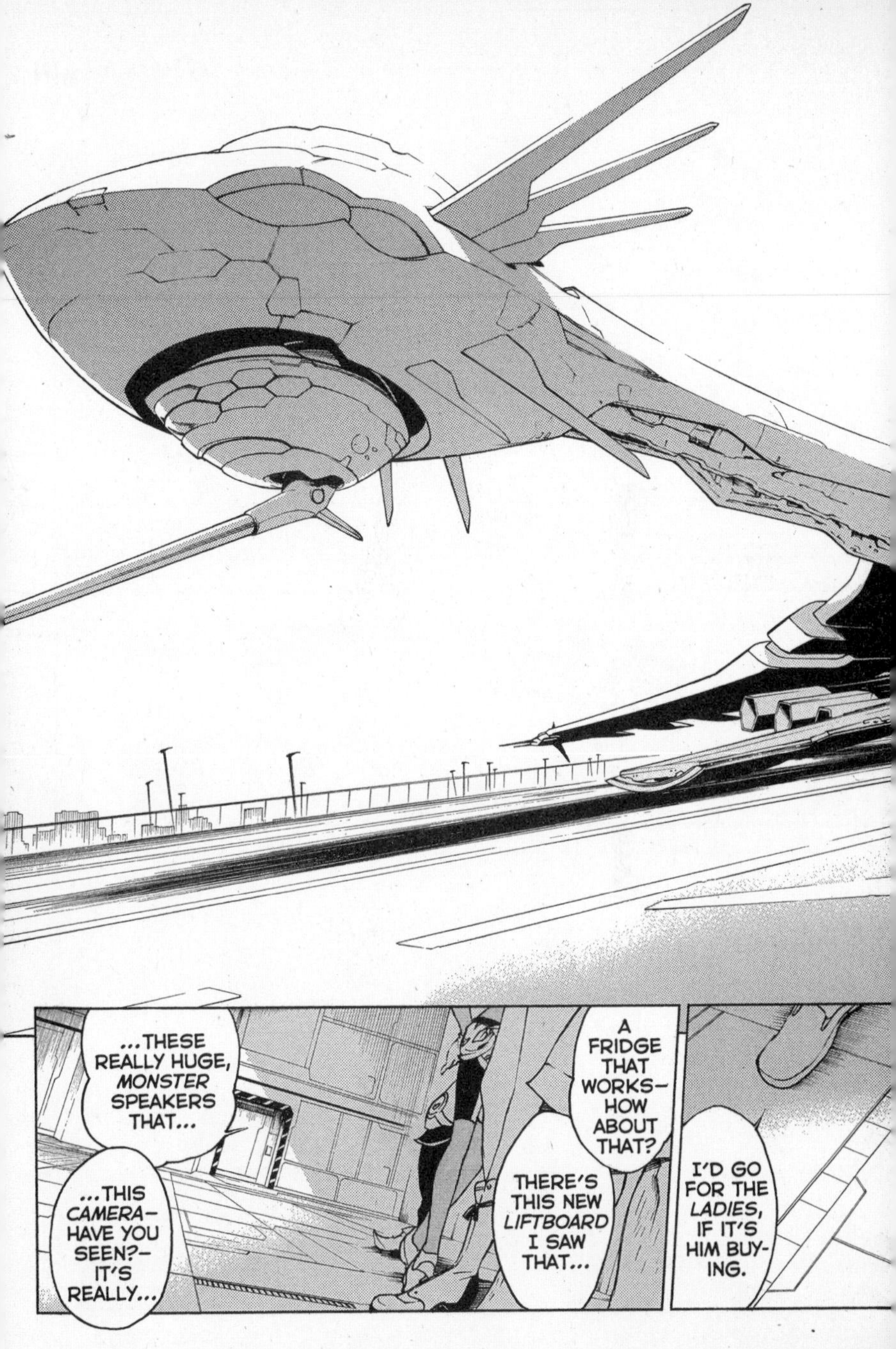
I'D GO FOR THE *LADIES,* IF IT'S HIM BUY-ING.
A FRIDGE THAT WORKS— HOW ABOUT THAT?
...THESE REALLY HUGE, *MONSTER* SPEAKERS THAT...
THERE'S THIS NEW *LIFTBOARD* I SAW THAT...
...THIS *CAMERA*— HAVE YOU SEEN?— IT'S REALLY...

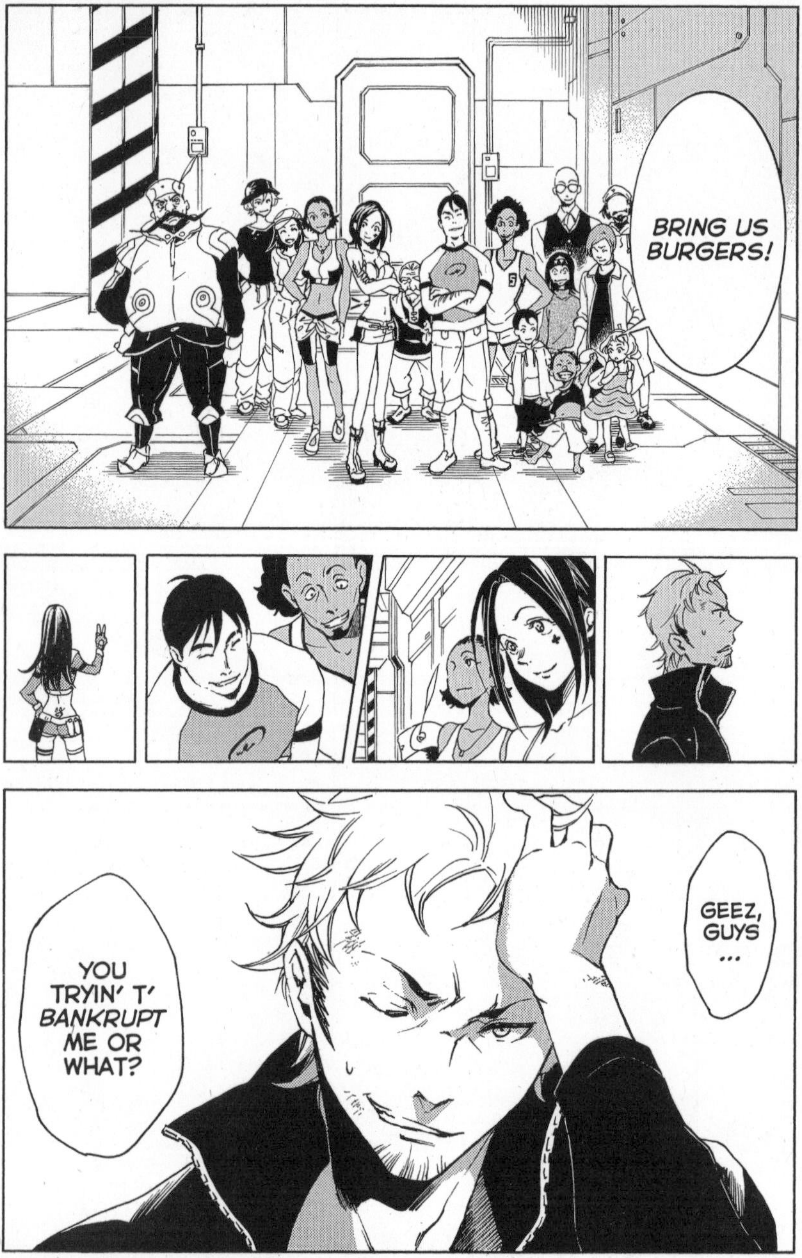
BRING US BURGERS!
GEEZ, GUYS ...
YOU TRYIN' T' BANKRUPT ME OR WHAT?

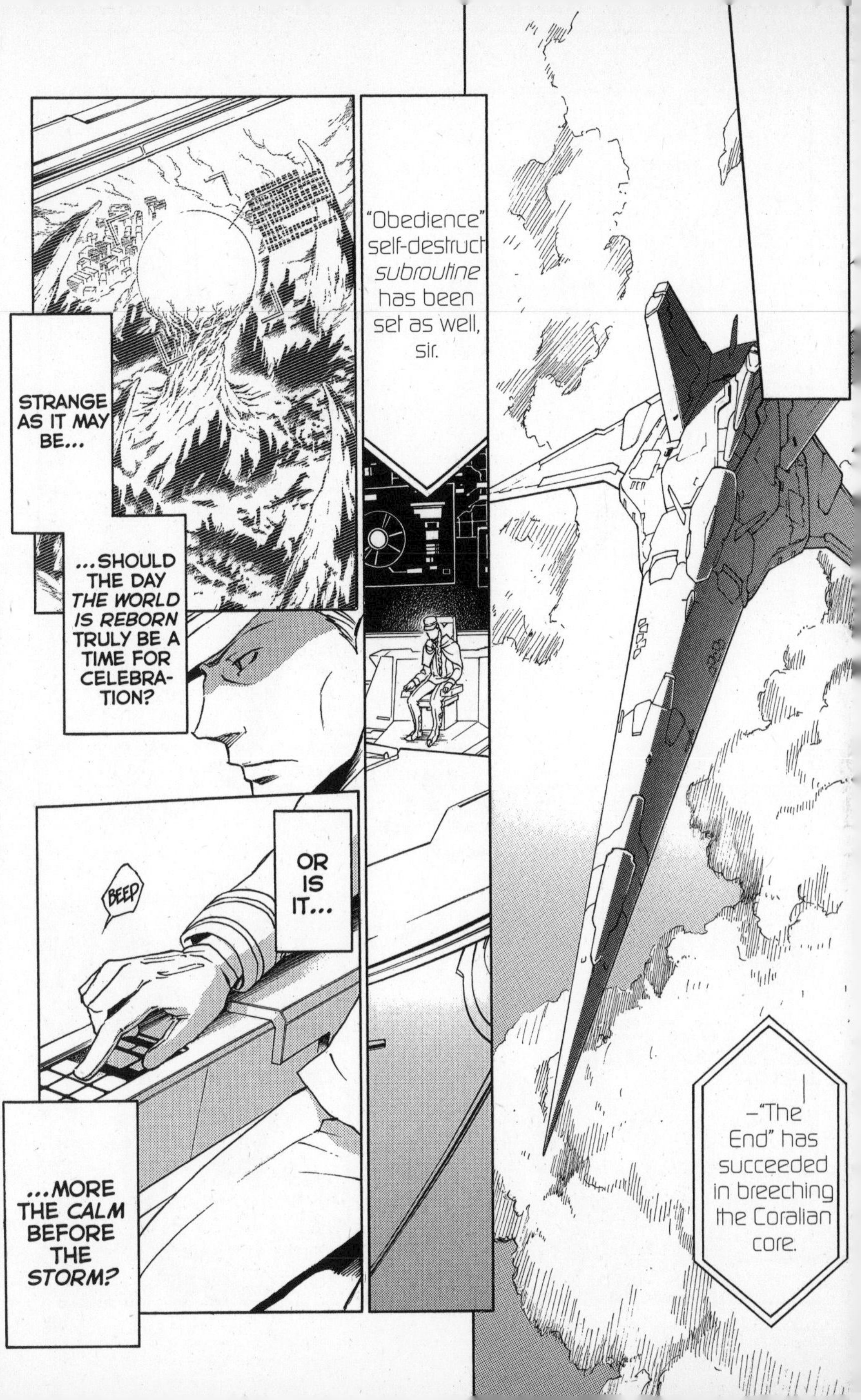

–"The End" has succeeded in breeching the Coralian core.
"Obedience" self-destruct *subroutine* has been set as well, sir.
STRANGE AS IT MAY BE...
...SHOULD THE DAY *THE WORLD IS REBORN* TRULY BE A TIME FOR CELEBRATION?
OR IS IT...
BEEP
...MORE THE *CALM* BEFORE THE *STORM?*

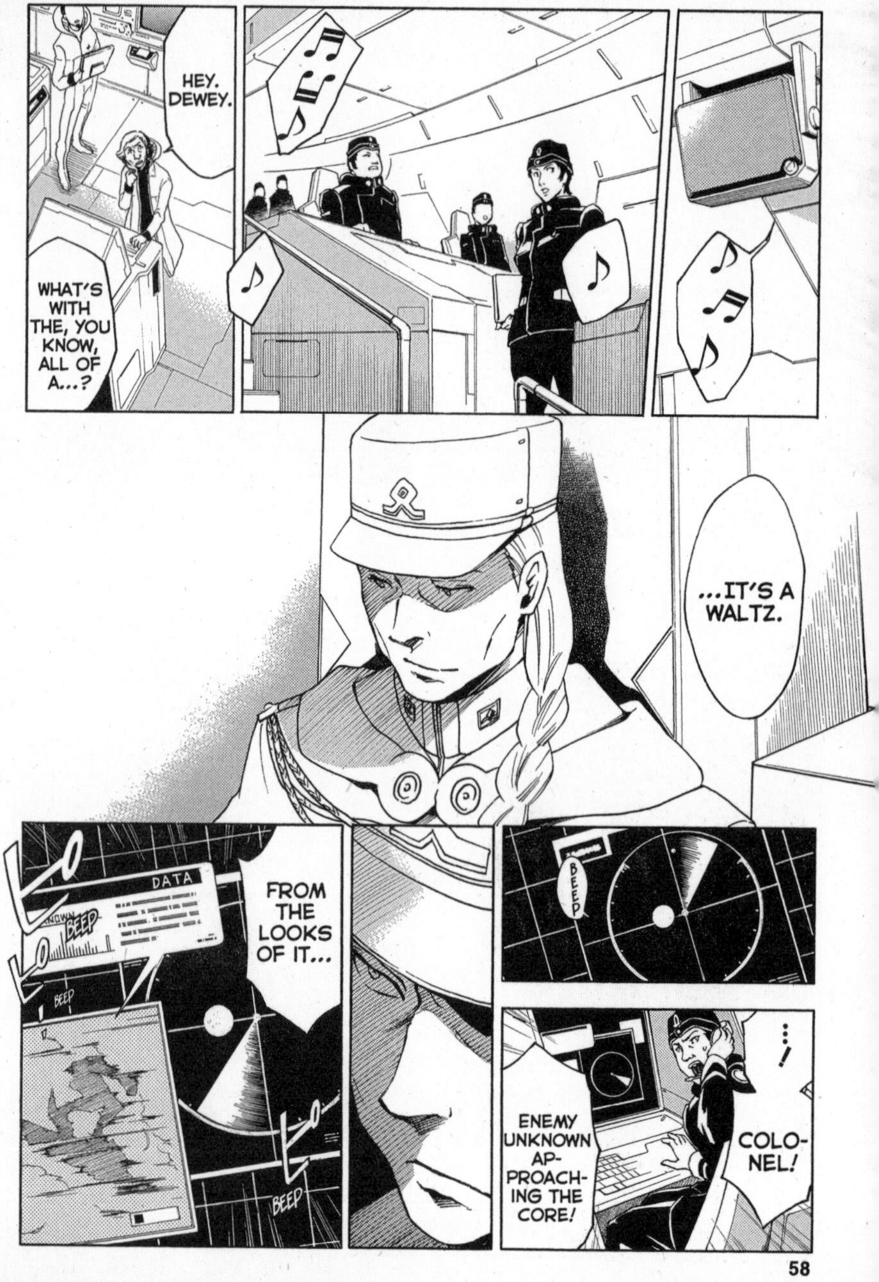
HEY. DEWEY.
WHAT'S WITH THE, YOU KNOW, ALL OF A...?
...IT'S A WALTZ.
BEEP
...!
COLO-NEL!
ENEMY UNKNOWN AP-PROACH-ING THE CORE!
FROM THE LOOKS OF IT...
DATA
BEEP
BEEP
BEEP

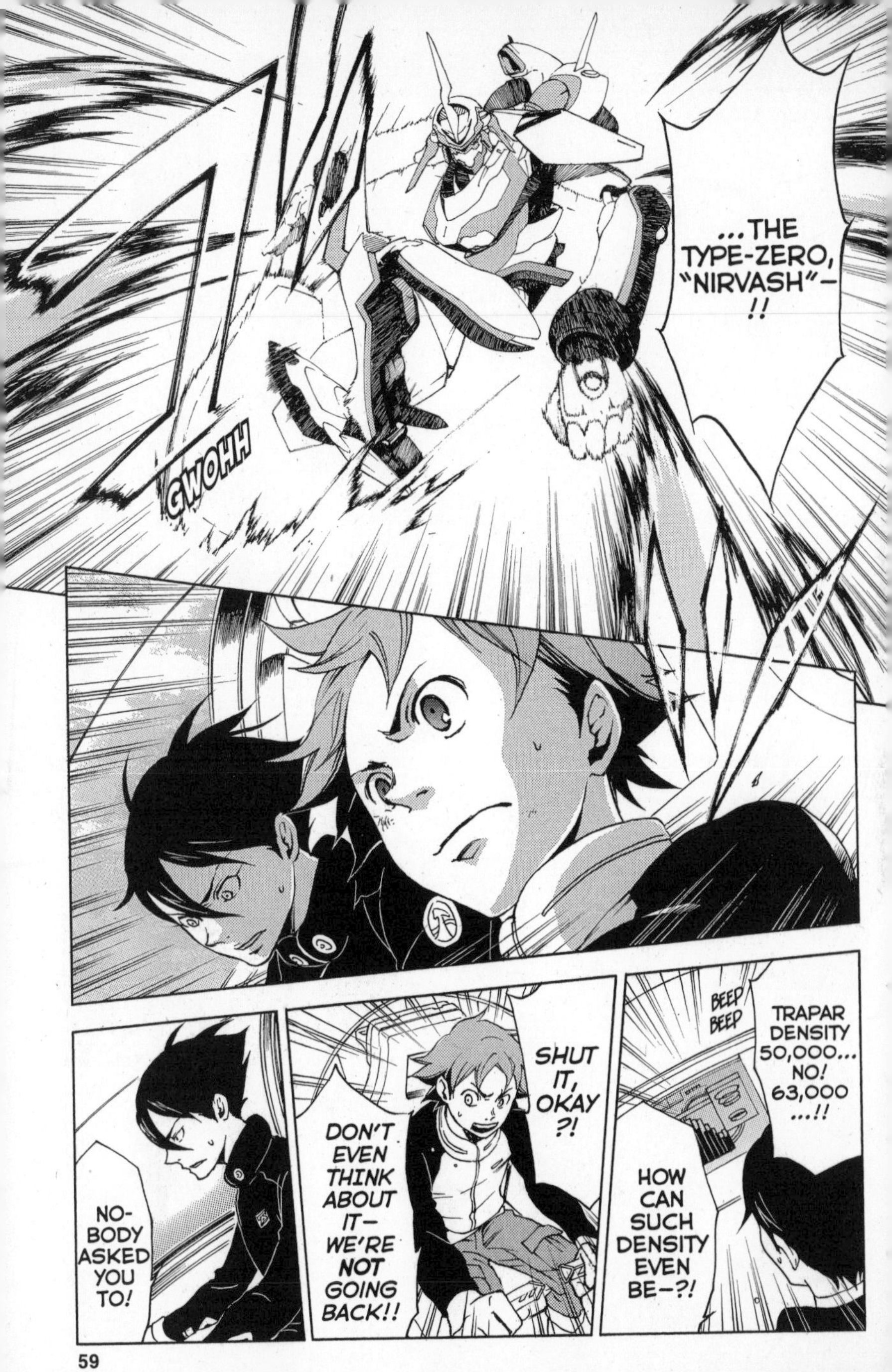
...THE TYPE-ZERO, "NIRVASH"—!!
GWOHH
BEEP BEEP
TRAPAR DENSITY 50,000... NO! 63,000 ...!!
HOW CAN SUCH DENSITY EVEN BE—?!
SHUT IT, OKAY?!
DON'T EVEN THINK ABOUT IT— WE'RE NOT GOING BACK!!
NO-BODY ASKED YOU TO!

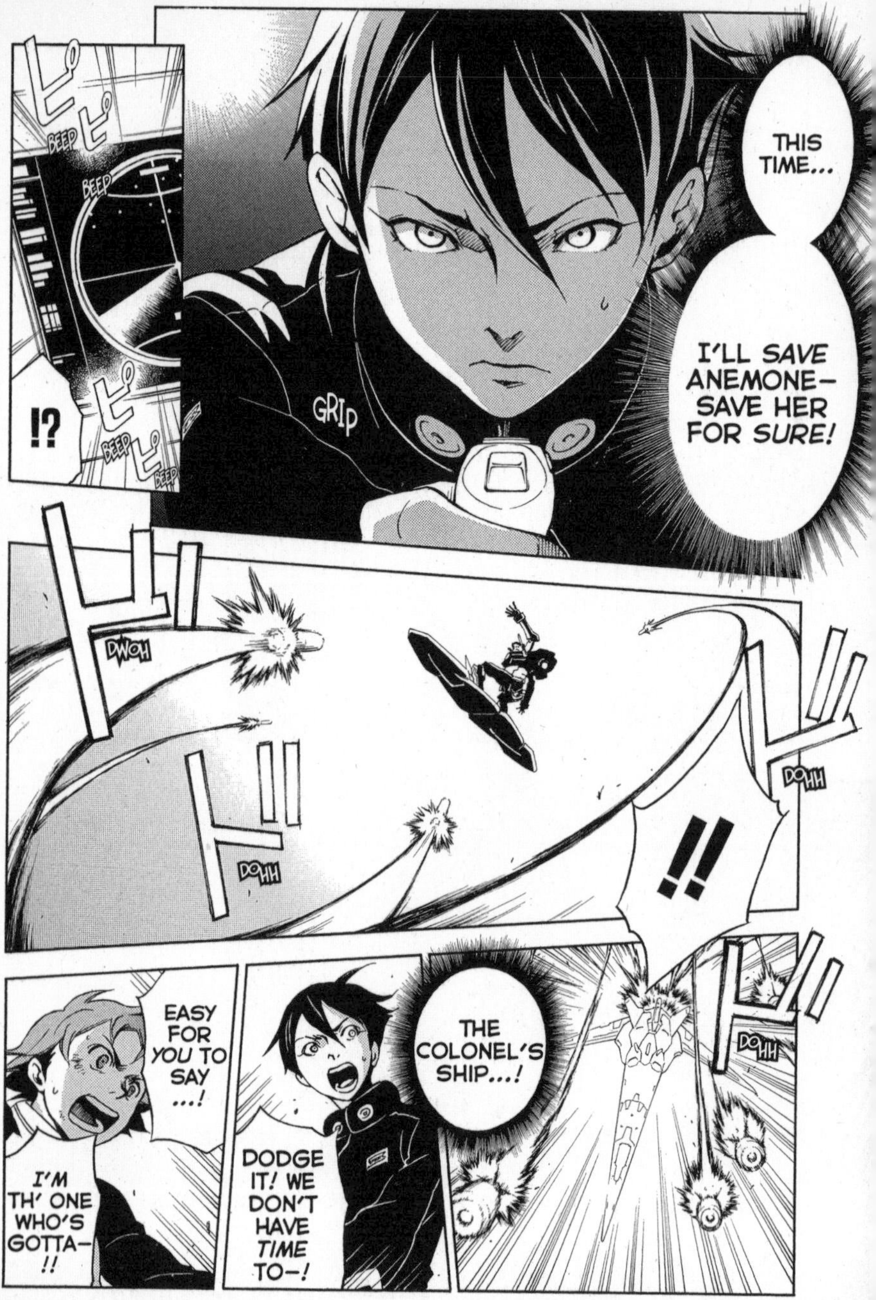
THIS TIME...
I'LL SAVE ANEMONE—SAVE HER FOR SURE!
GRIP
BEEP
BEEP
!?
BEEP
BEEP
DOHH
!!
DWOH
DOHH
DOHH
THE COLONEL'S SHIP...!
DODGE IT! WE DON'T HAVE TIME TO—!
EASY FOR YOU TO SAY...!
I'M TH' ONE WHO'S GOTTA—!!

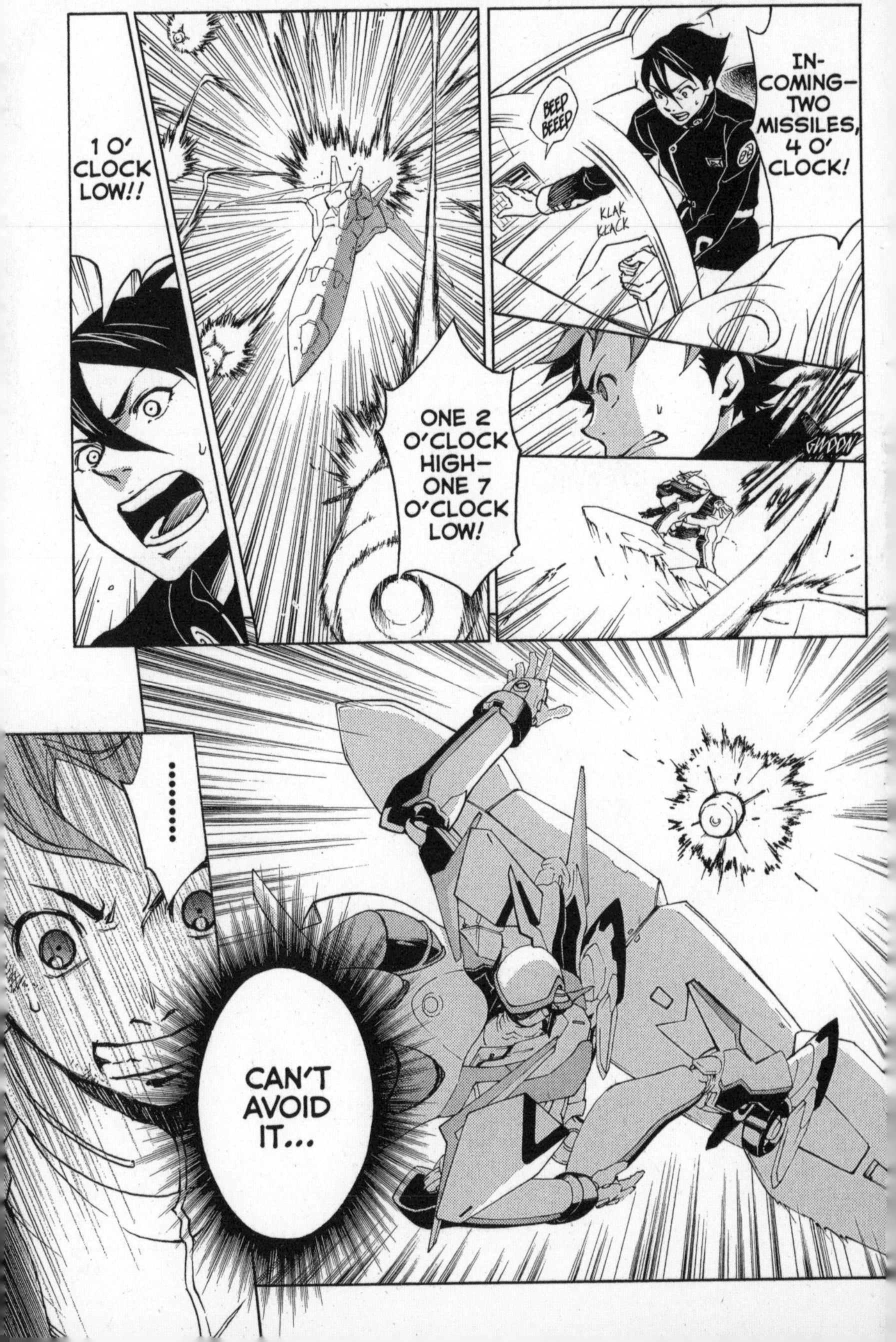
BEEP BEEEP
IN-COMING—TWO MISSILES, 4 O' CLOCK!
KLAK KLACK
GADOON
ONE 2 O'CLOCK HIGH—ONE 7 O'CLOCK LOW!
1 O' CLOCK LOW!!
....
CAN'T AVOID IT...

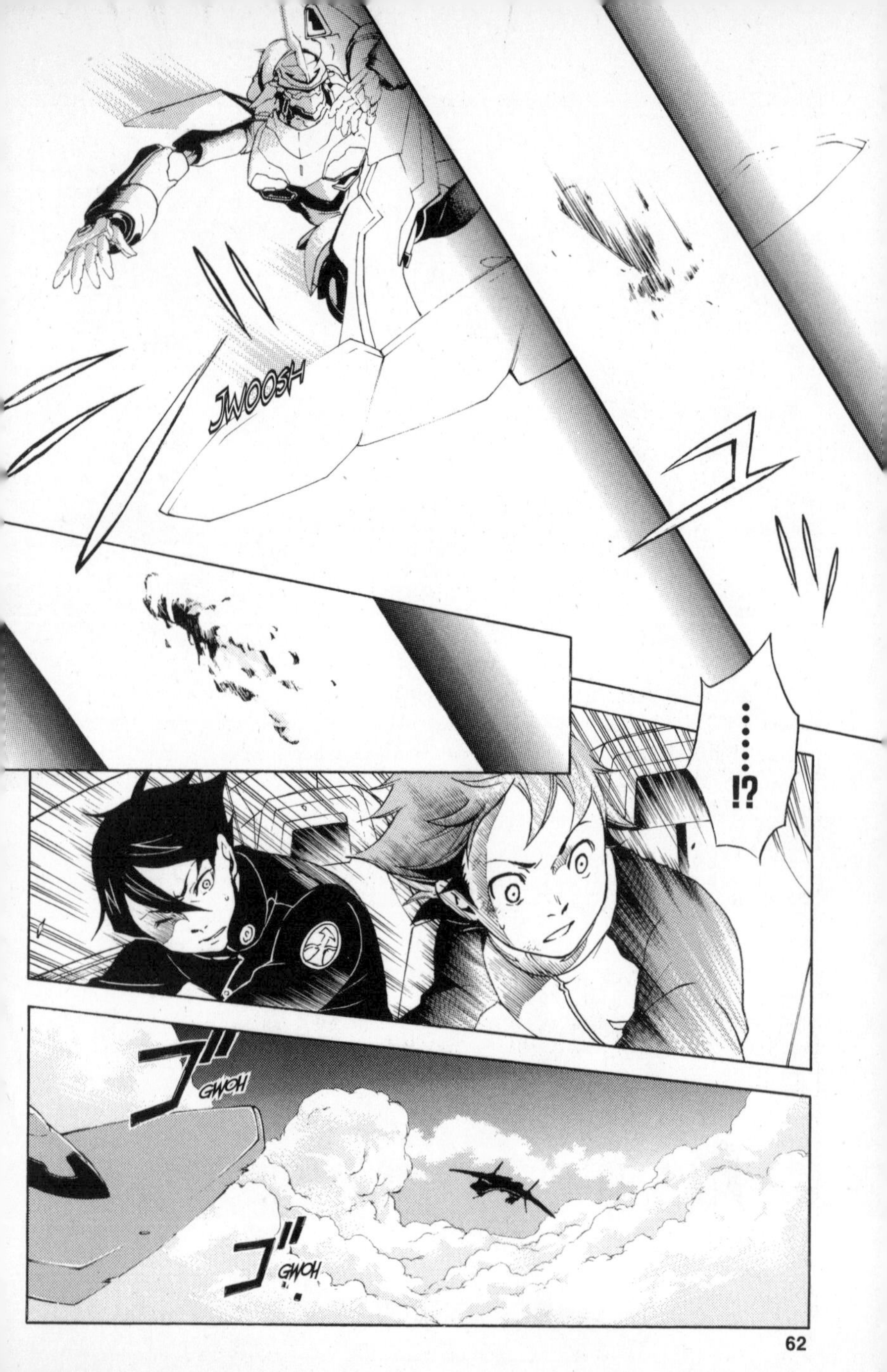
JWOOSH
......!?
GWOH
GWOH

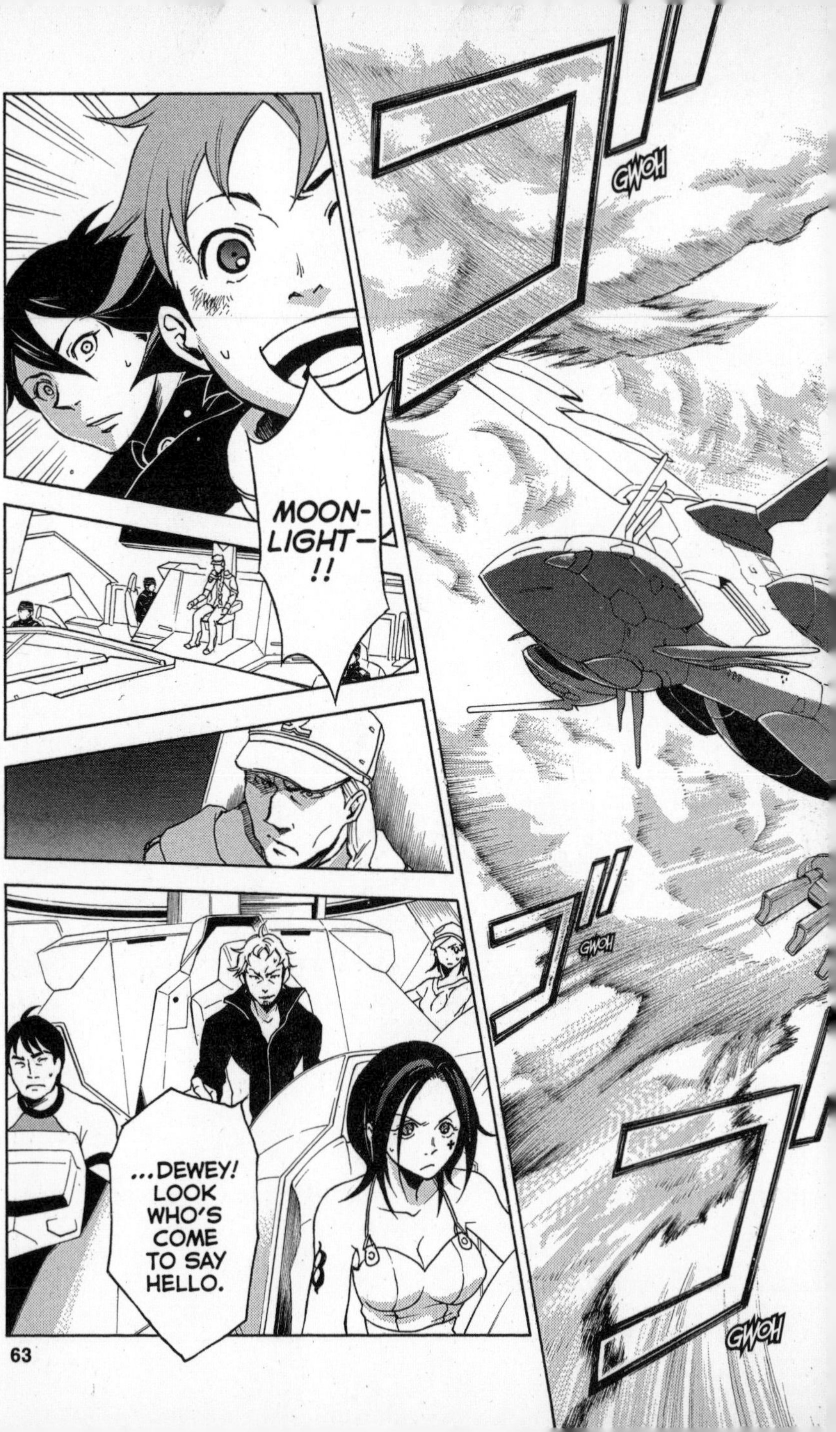
GWOH
MOON-LIGHT—!!
GWOH
GWOH
...DEWEY! LOOK WHO'S COME TO SAY HELLO.

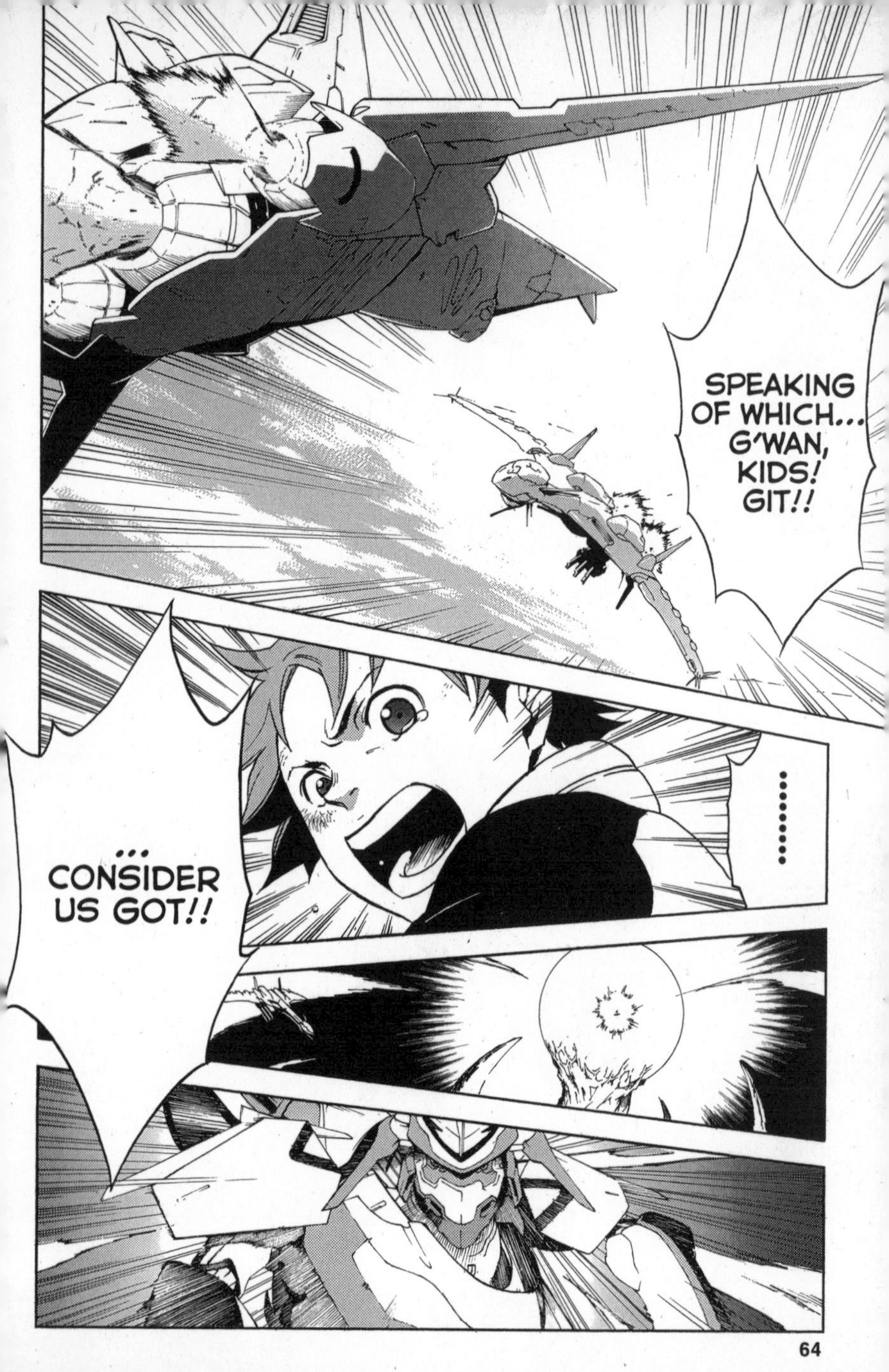
SPEAKING OF WHICH... G'WAN, KIDS! GIT!!
....
...CONSIDER US GOT!!

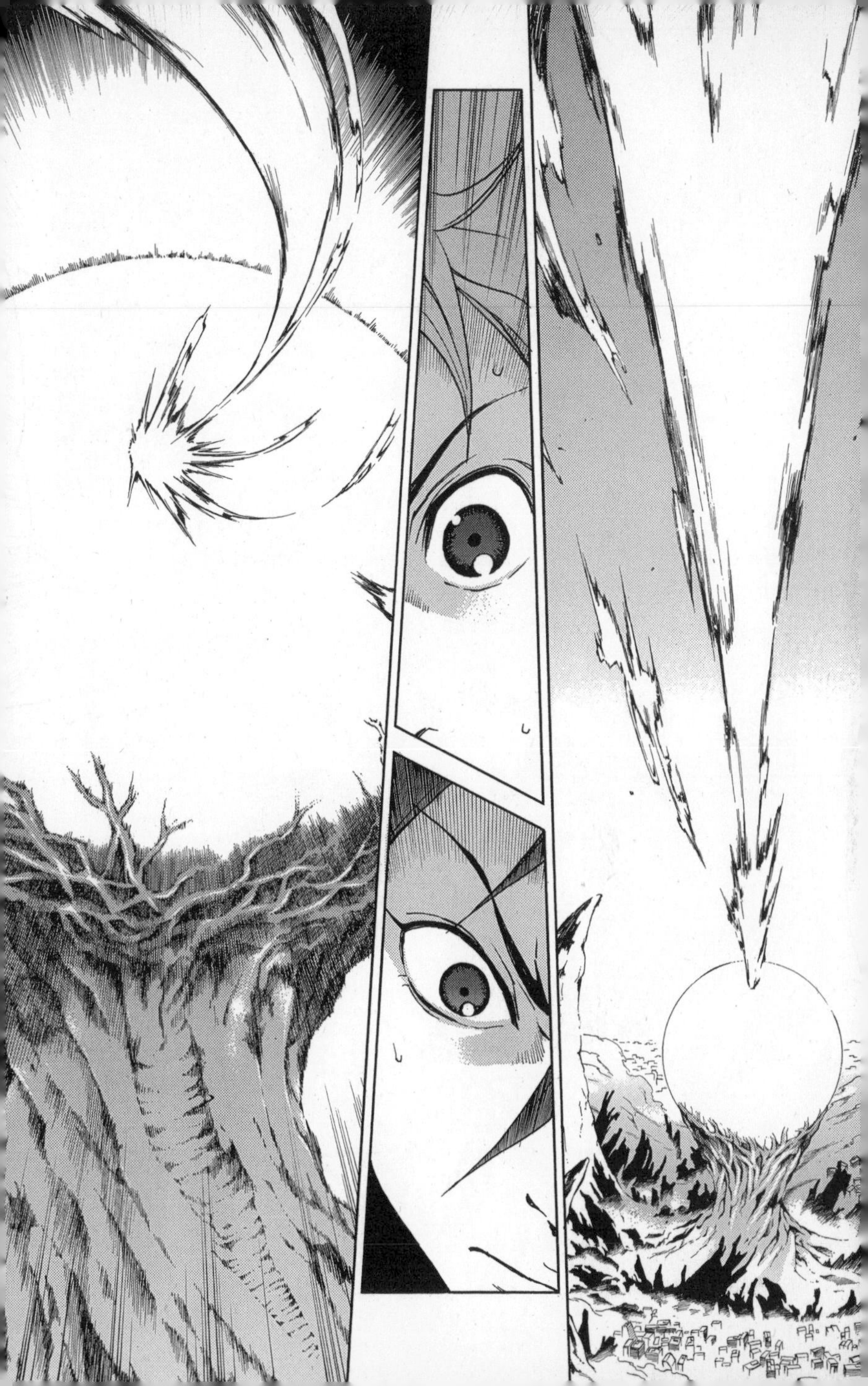

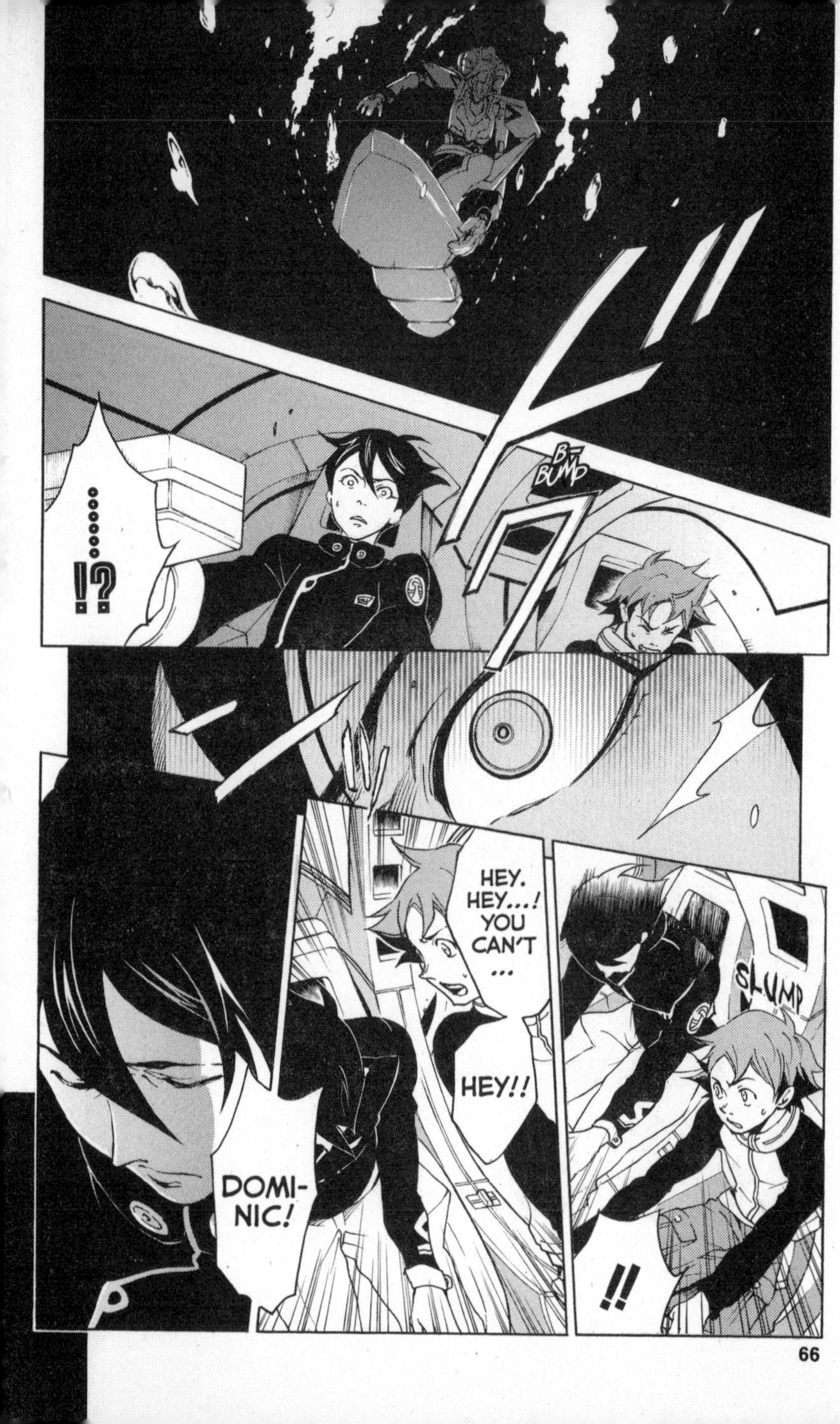
B-BUMP
......!?
SLUMP
!!
HEY. HEY...! YOU CAN'T ...
HEY!!
DOMI-NIC!

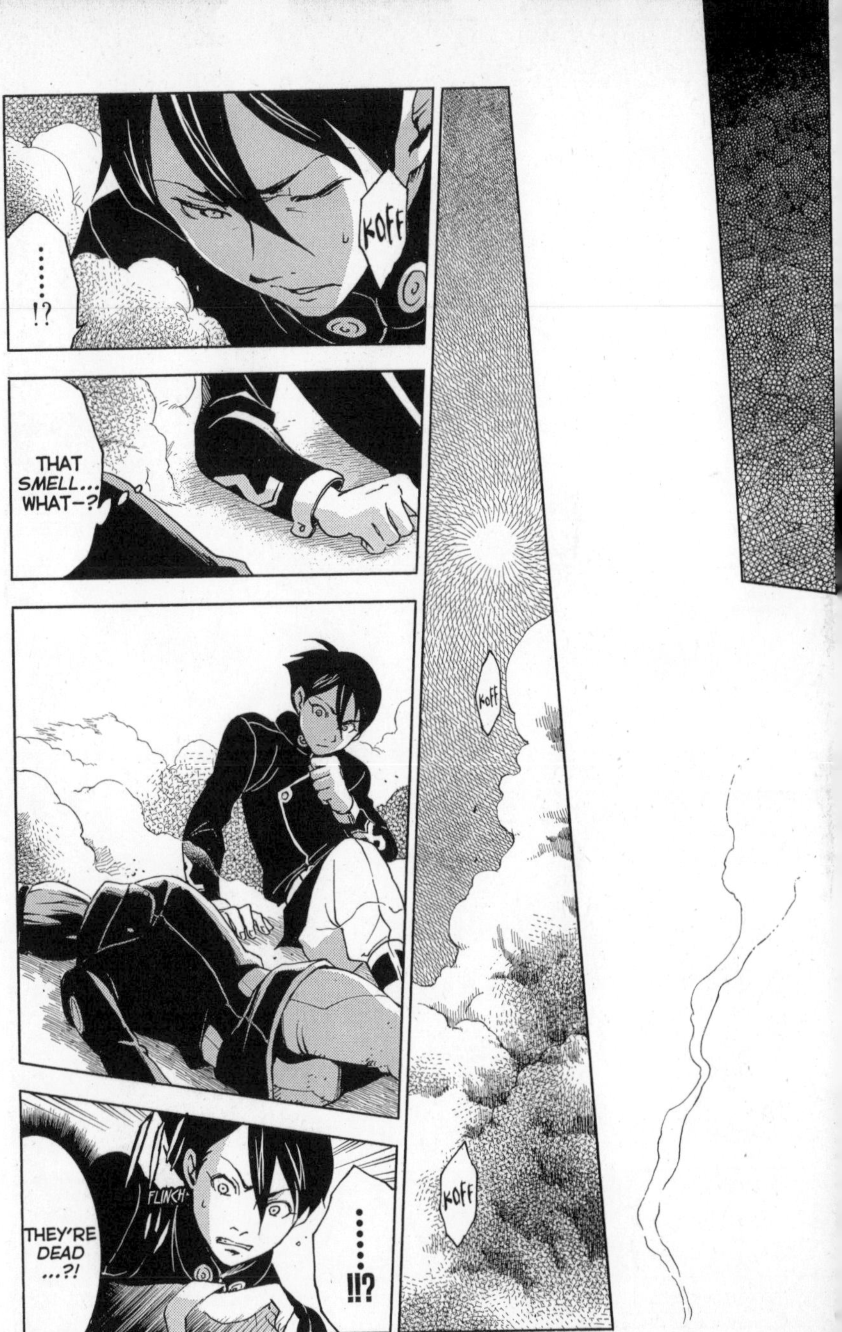
KOFF
KOFF
KOFF
......!?
THAT SMELL... WHAT–?
......!!?
FLINCH
THEY'RE DEAD ...?!

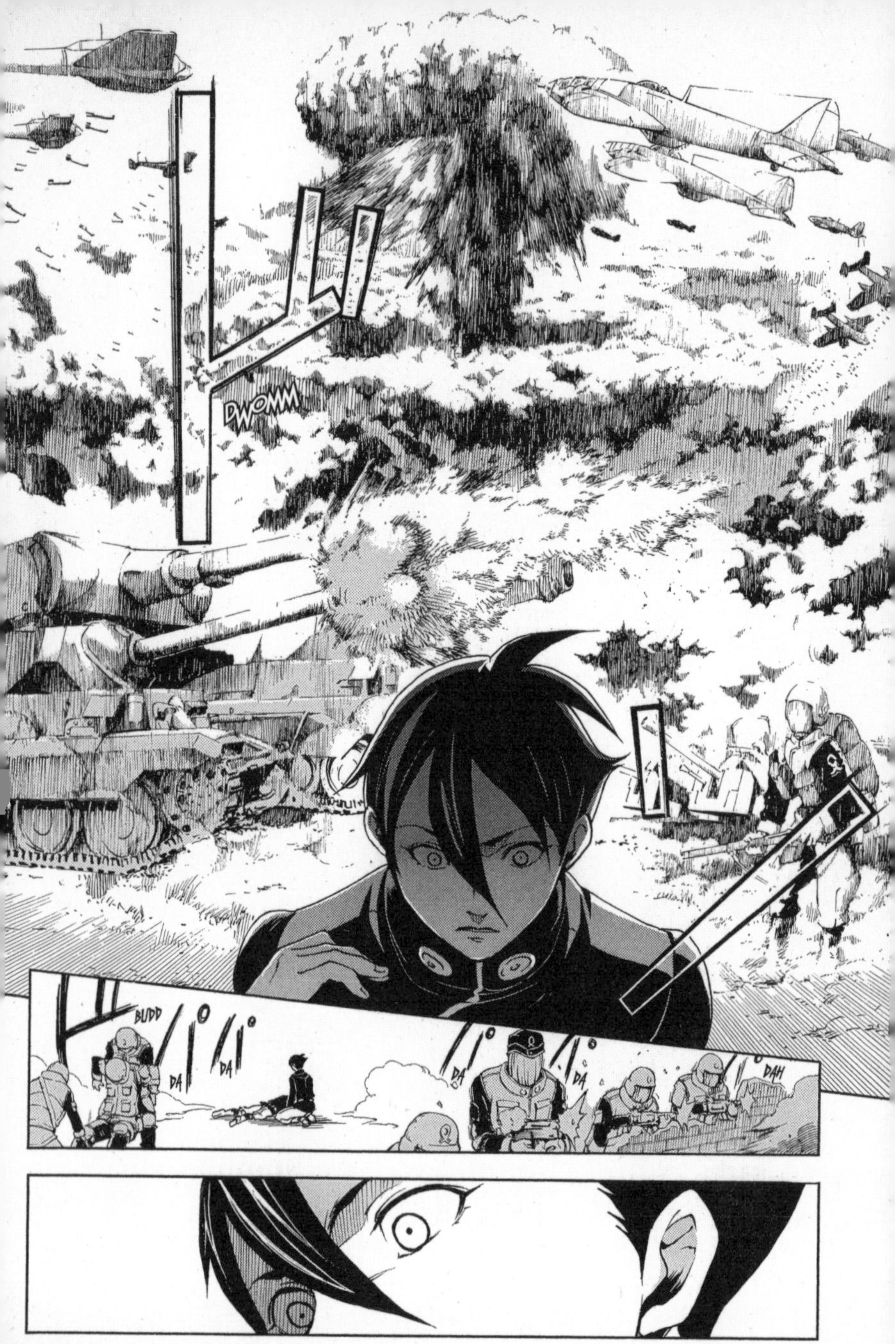
DWOMM
DAH
DA
DA
DA
DA
BUDD

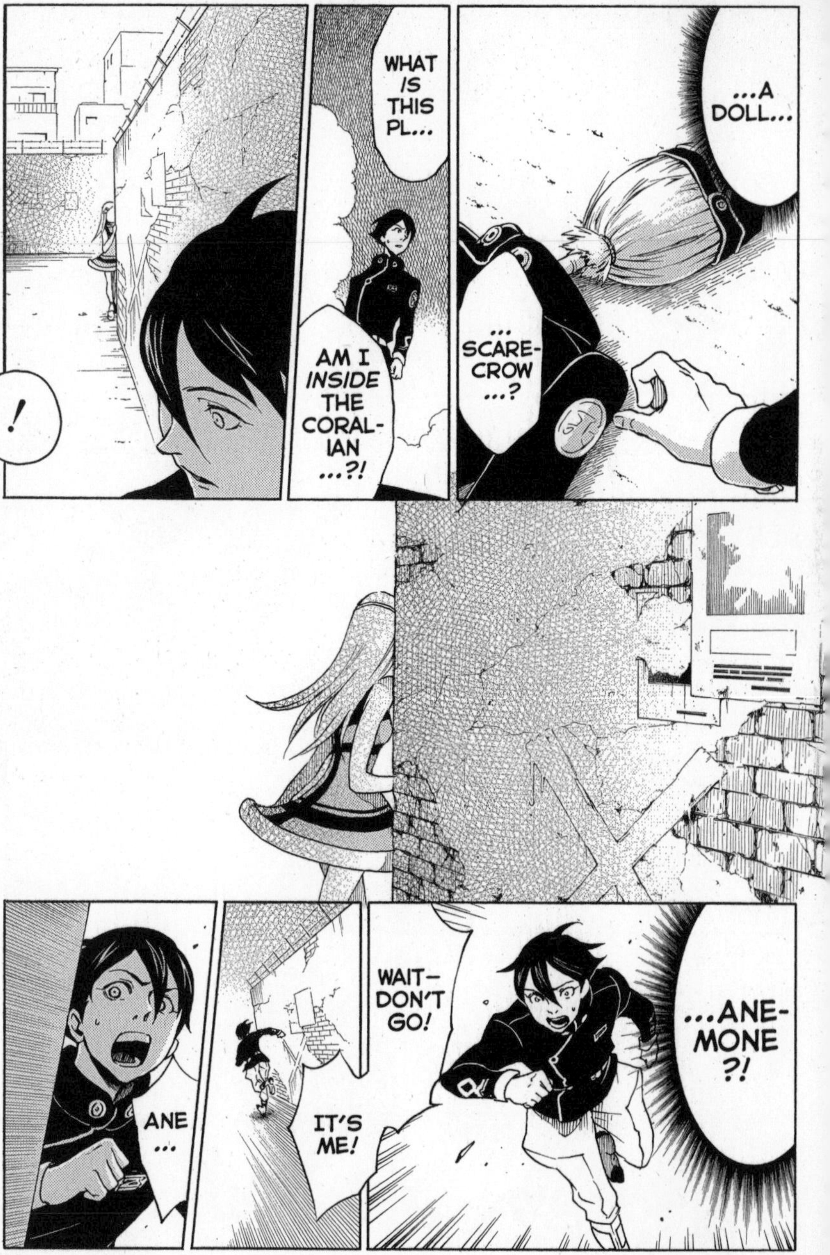

...A DOLL...
...SCARECROW...?
WHAT IS THIS PL...
AM I INSIDE THE CORALIAN...?!
!
...ANEMONE?!
WAIT—DON'T GO!
IT'S ME!
ANE...

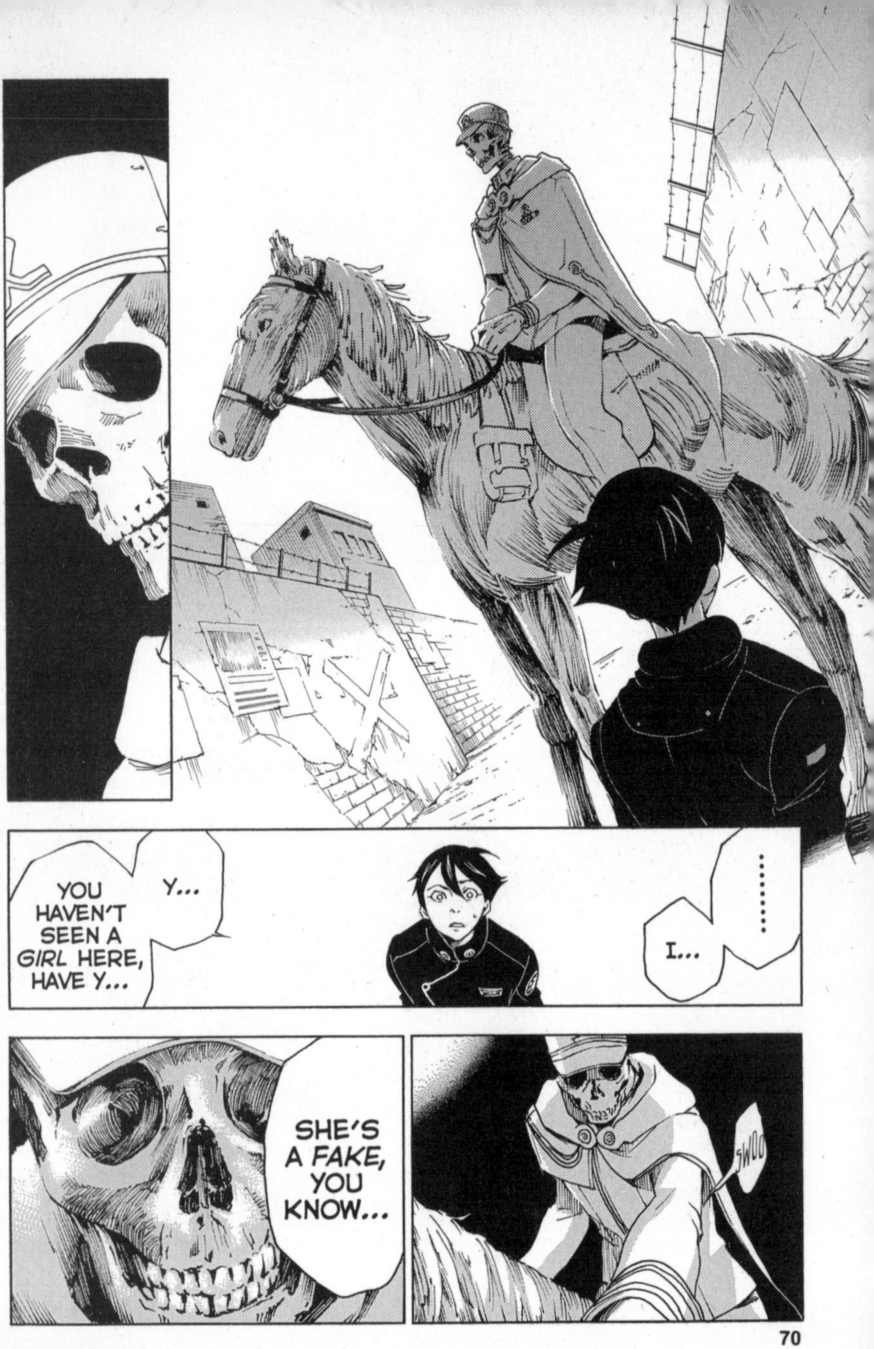
......
I...
Y...
YOU HAVEN'T SEEN A *GIRL* HERE, HAVE Y...
SWOO
SHE'S A *FAKE*, YOU KNOW...

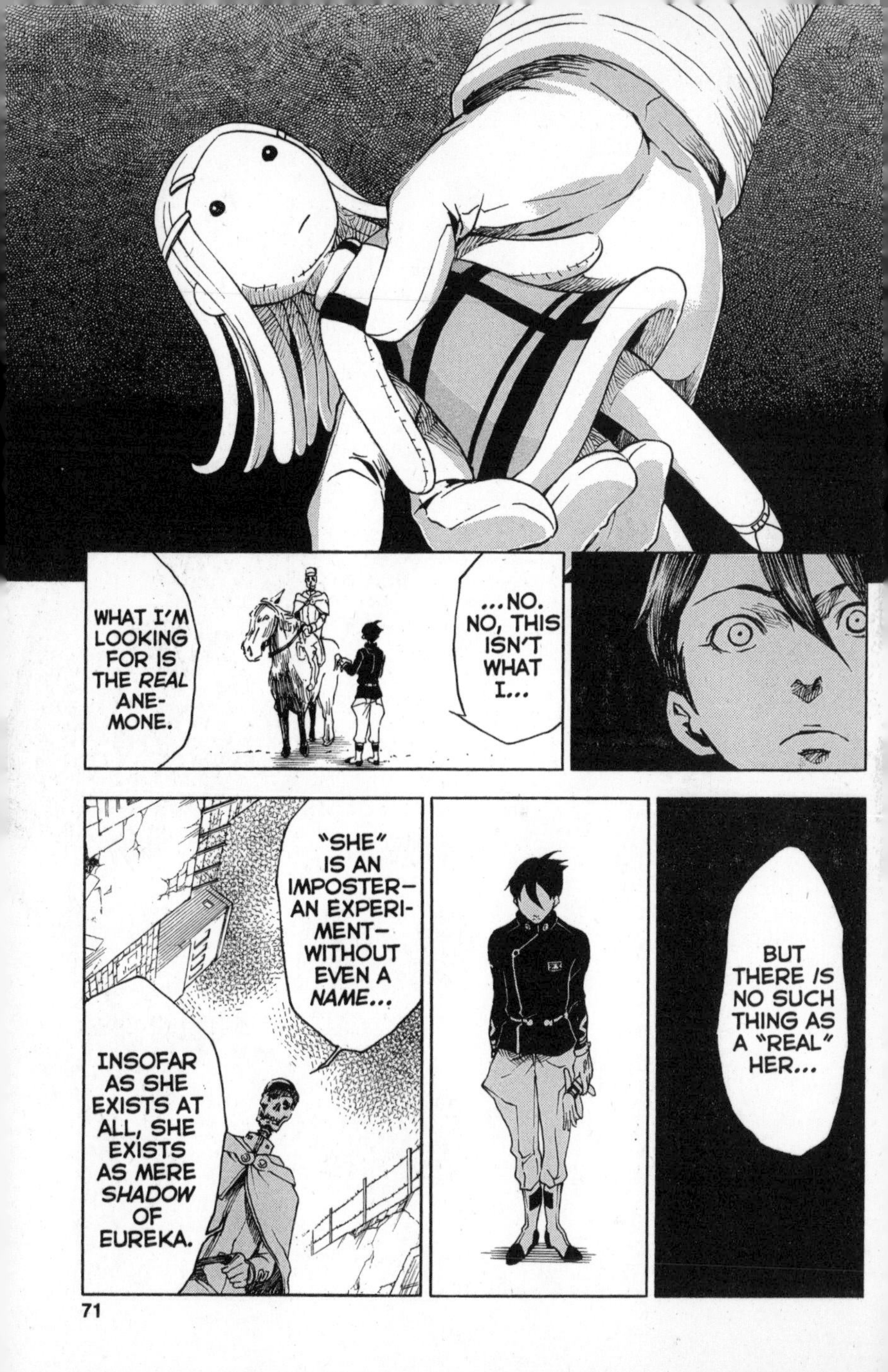
...NO. NO, THIS ISN'T WHAT I...
WHAT I'M LOOKING FOR IS THE *REAL* ANE-MONE.
BUT THERE *IS* NO SUCH THING AS A "REAL" HER...
"SHE" IS AN IMPOSTER—AN EXPERI-MENT—WITHOUT EVEN A *NAME*...
INSOFAR AS SHE EXISTS AT ALL, SHE EXISTS AS MERE *SHADOW* OF EUREKA.

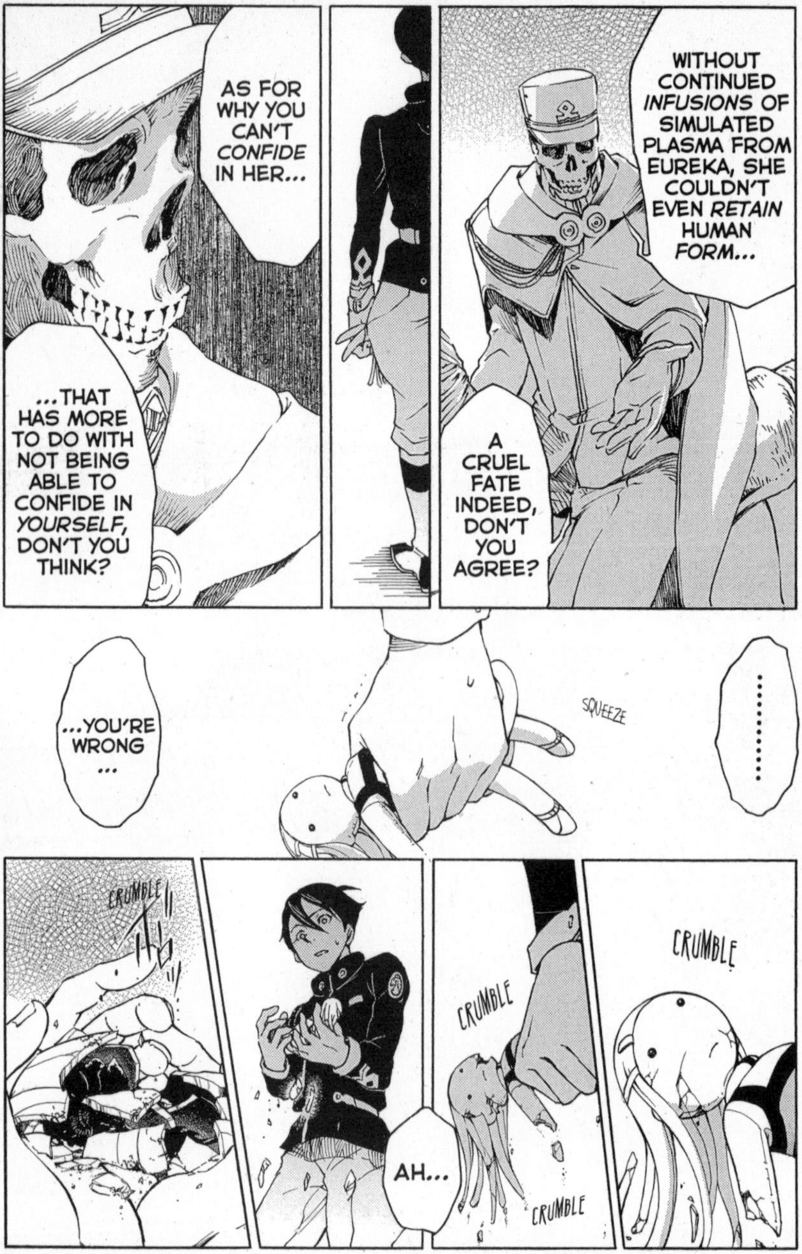
WITHOUT CONTINUED INFUSIONS OF SIMULATED PLASMA FROM EUREKA, SHE COULDN'T EVEN RETAIN HUMAN FORM...
A CRUEL FATE INDEED, DON'T YOU AGREE?
AS FOR WHY YOU CAN'T CONFIDE IN HER...
...THAT HAS MORE TO DO WITH NOT BEING ABLE TO CONFIDE IN YOURSELF, DON'T YOU THINK?
....
SQUEEZE
...YOU'RE WRONG ...
CRUMBLE
CRUMBLE
CRUMBLE
AH...
CRUMBLE

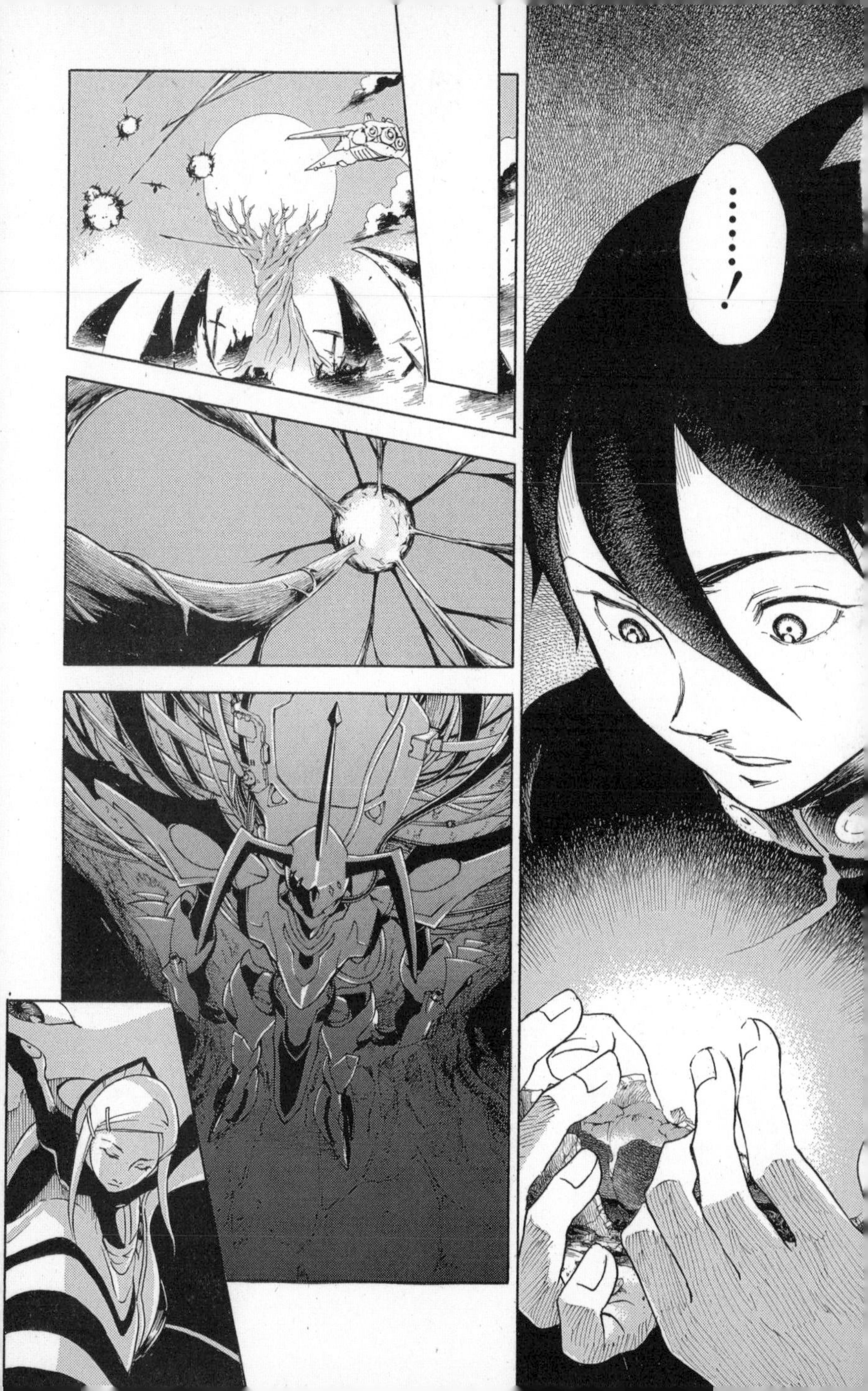
……!

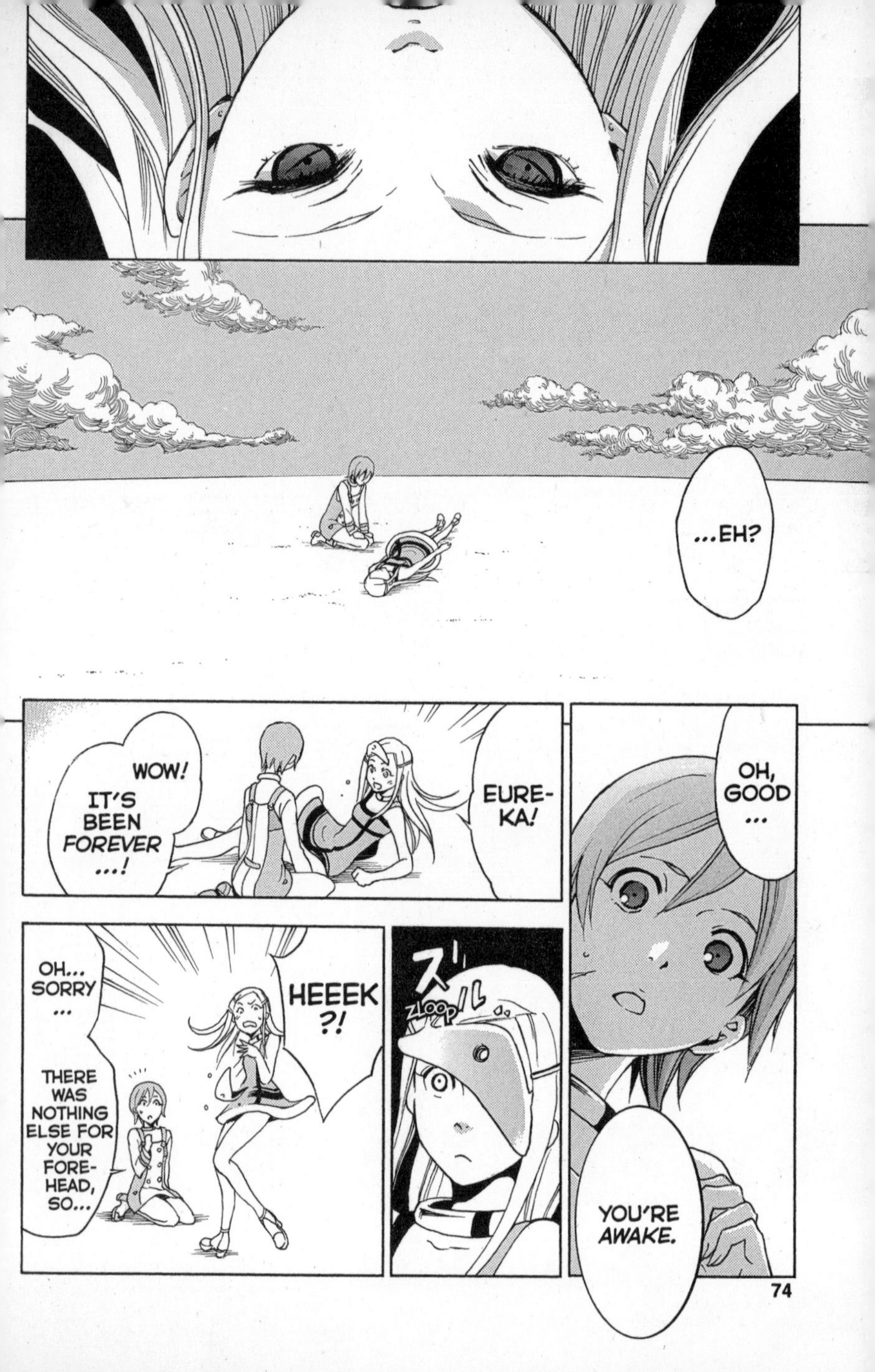
...EH?
OH, GOOD...
YOU'RE AWAKE.
EUREKA!
WOW! IT'S BEEN FOREVER...!
ZLOOP
HEEEK?!
OH... SORRY...
THERE WAS NOTHING ELSE FOR YOUR FOREHEAD, SO...

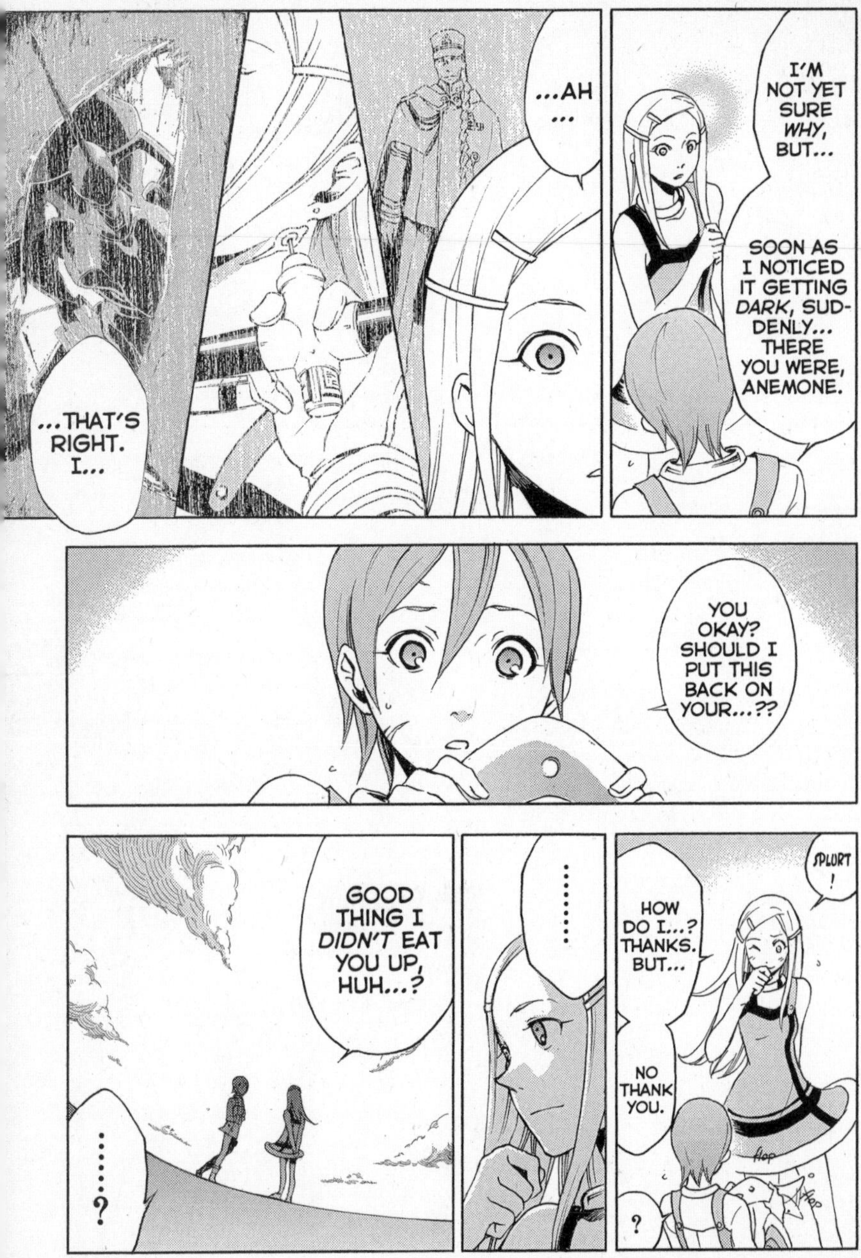
I'M NOT YET SURE *WHY*, BUT...
SOON AS I NOTICED IT GETTING *DARK*, SUDDENLY... THERE YOU WERE, ANEMONE.
...AH ...
...THAT'S RIGHT. I...
YOU OKAY? SHOULD I PUT THIS BACK ON YOUR...??
SPLURT !
HOW DO I...? THANKS. BUT...
NO THANK YOU.
flop
flop
?
....
GOOD THING I *DIDN'T* EAT YOU UP, HUH...?
......?

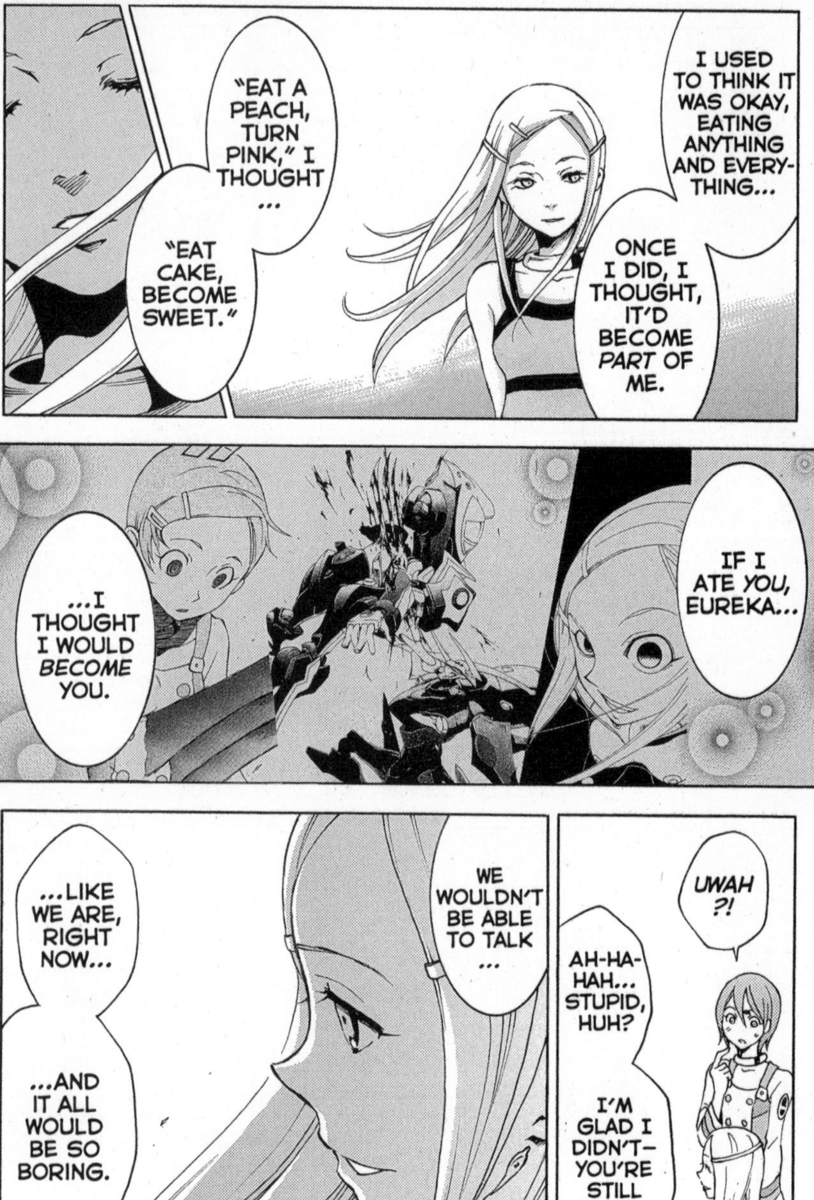
I USED TO THINK IT WAS OKAY, EATING ANYTHING AND EVERY-THING...
ONCE I DID, I THOUGHT, IT'D BECOME *PART* OF ME.
"EAT A PEACH, TURN PINK," I THOUGHT ...
"EAT CAKE, BECOME SWEET."
IF I ATE *YOU*, EUREKA...
...I THOUGHT I WOULD *BECOME* YOU.
UWAH ?!
AH-HA-HAH... STUPID, HUH?
I'M GLAD I DIDN'T– YOU'RE STILL HERE.
WE WOULDN'T BE ABLE TO TALK ...
...LIKE WE ARE, RIGHT NOW...
...AND IT ALL WOULD BE SO BORING.

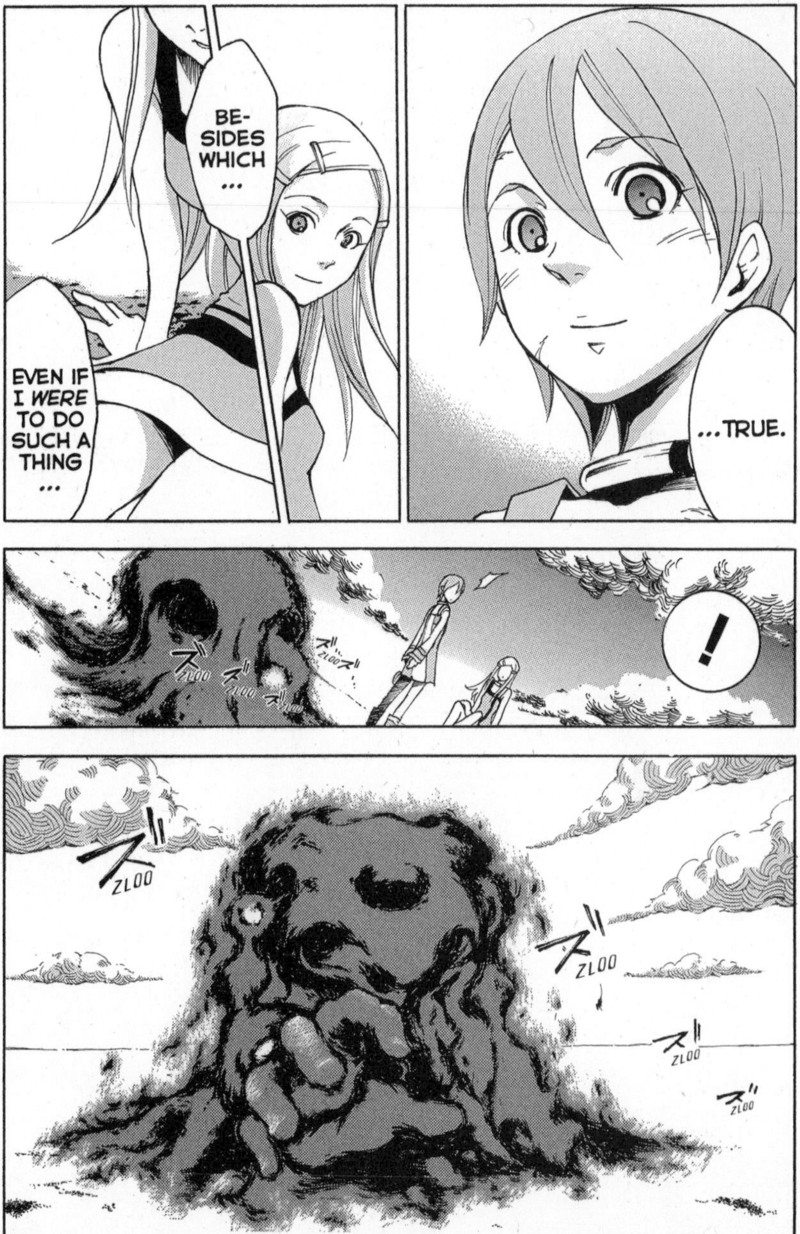
...TRUE.
BE-SIDES WHICH ...
EVEN IF I *WERE* TO DO SUCH A THING ...
!
ZLOO
ZLOO
ZLOO
ZLOO
ZLOO
ZLOO
ZLOO
ZLOO

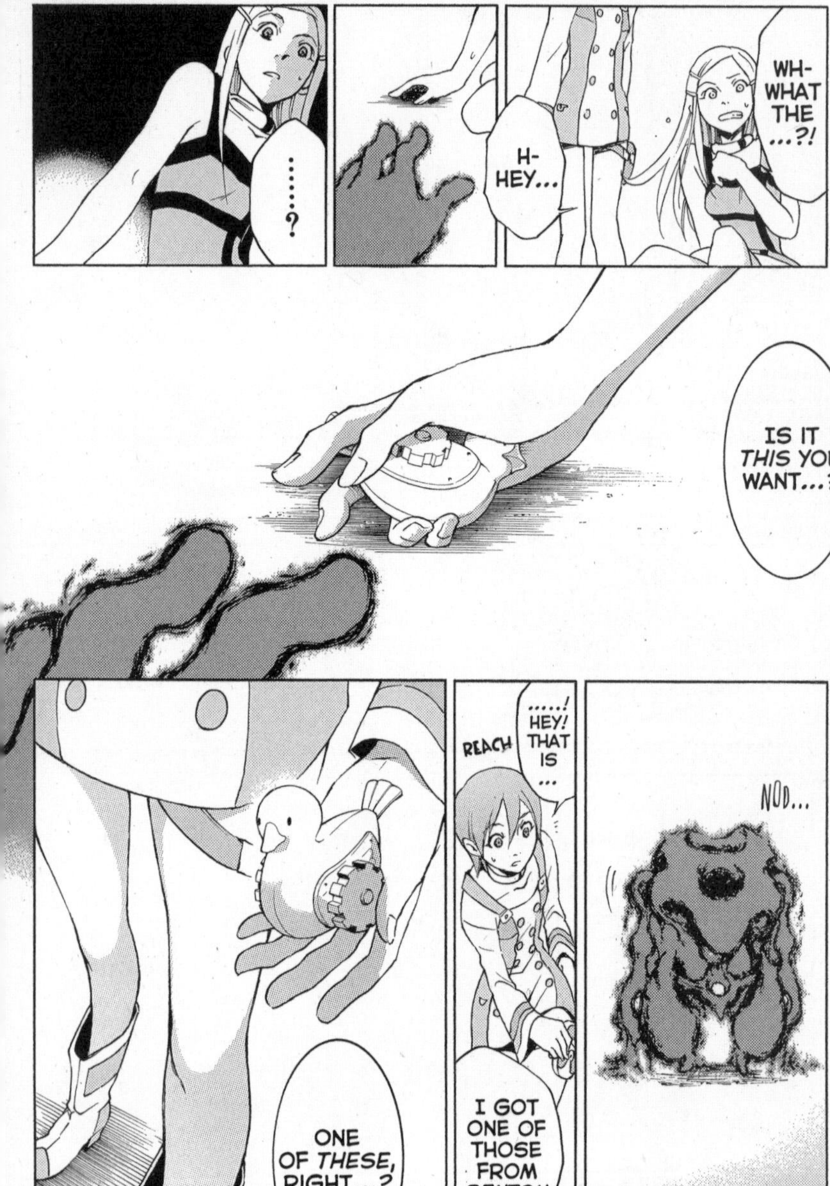
WH-WHAT THE ...?!
H-HEY...
......?
IS IT *THIS* YOU WANT...?
NOD...
......! HEY! THAT IS ...
REACH
I GOT ONE OF THOSE FROM *RENTON* ...
ONE OF *THESE*, RIGHT...?

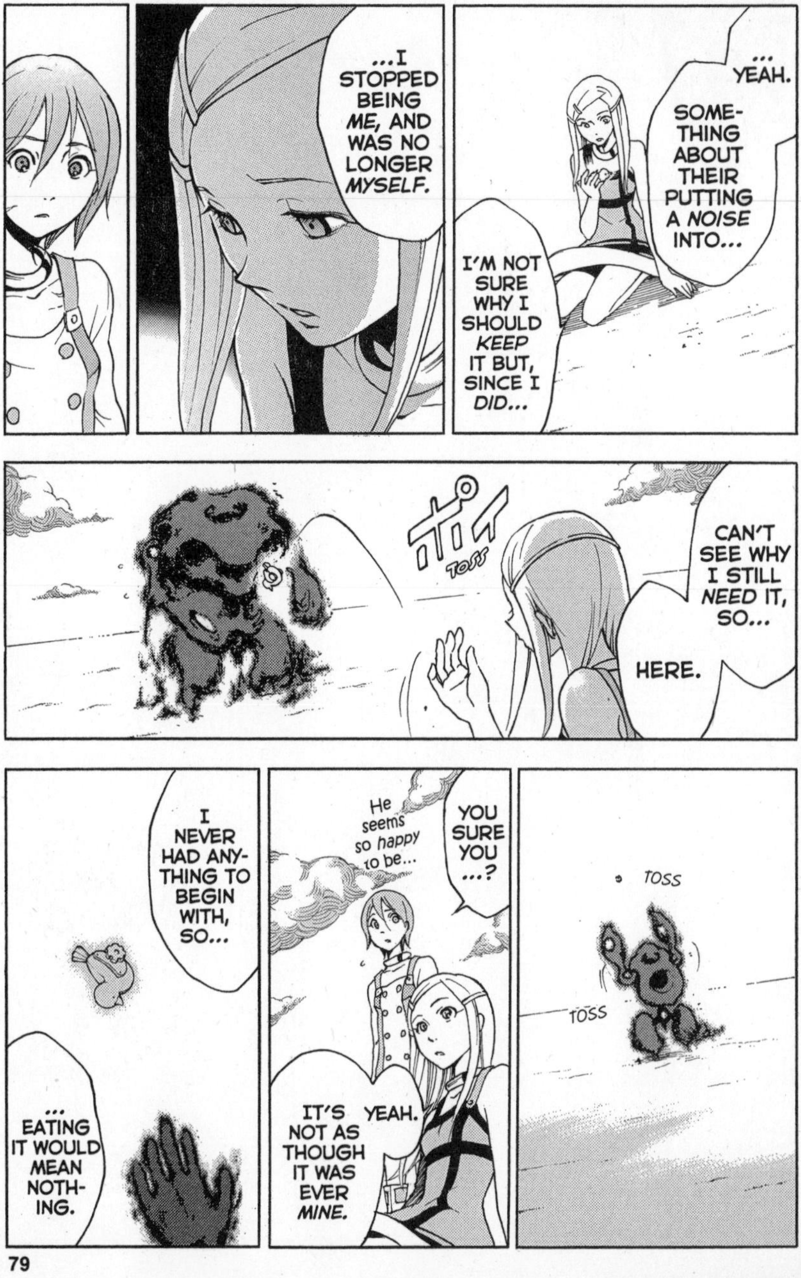
...YEAH.
SOMETHING ABOUT THEIR PUTTING A *NOISE* INTO...
I'M NOT SURE WHY I SHOULD *KEEP* IT BUT, SINCE I *DID*...
...I STOPPED BEING *ME*, AND WAS NO LONGER *MYSELF*.
CAN'T SEE WHY I STILL *NEED* IT, SO...
HERE.
ポイ
TOSS
TOSS
TOSS
YOU SURE YOU ...?
He seems so happy to be...
YEAH.
IT'S NOT AS THOUGH IT WAS EVER *MINE*.
I NEVER HAD ANYTHING TO BEGIN WITH, SO...
...EATING IT WOULD MEAN NOTHING.

KRASH

I'M ALWAYS *EMPTY* ANYWAY.

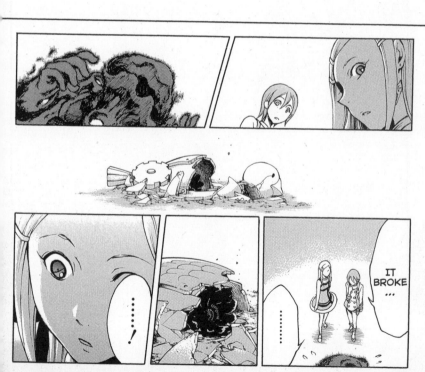

IT BROKE...

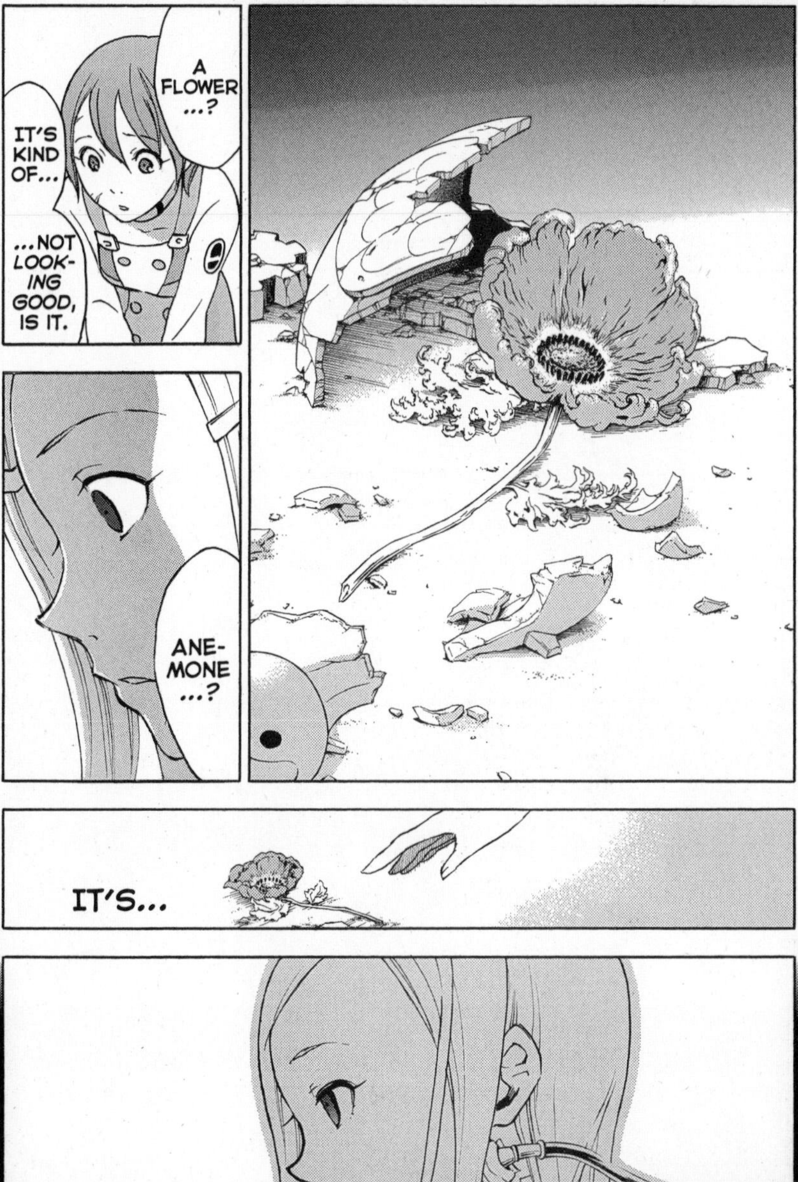
A FLOWER ...?
IT'S KIND OF...
...NOT LOOKING GOOD, IS IT.
ANEMONE ...?
IT'S...

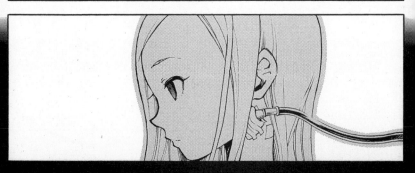

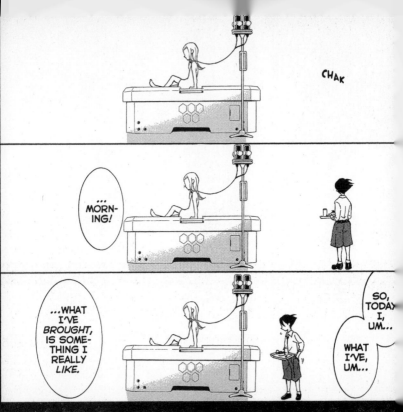

CHAK

...MORN-ING!

...WHAT I'VE BROUGHT, IS SOMETHING I REALLY LIKE.

SO, TODAY I, UM...

WHAT I'VE, UM...

IT BROKE UP THE DAILY ROUTINE

I KNOW YOU CAN'T GO OUTSIDE, SO, I THOUGHT MAYBE YOU HADN'T SEEN...

THE THINGS BROUGHT BY THIS ONE WHO CARED FOR ME

No.

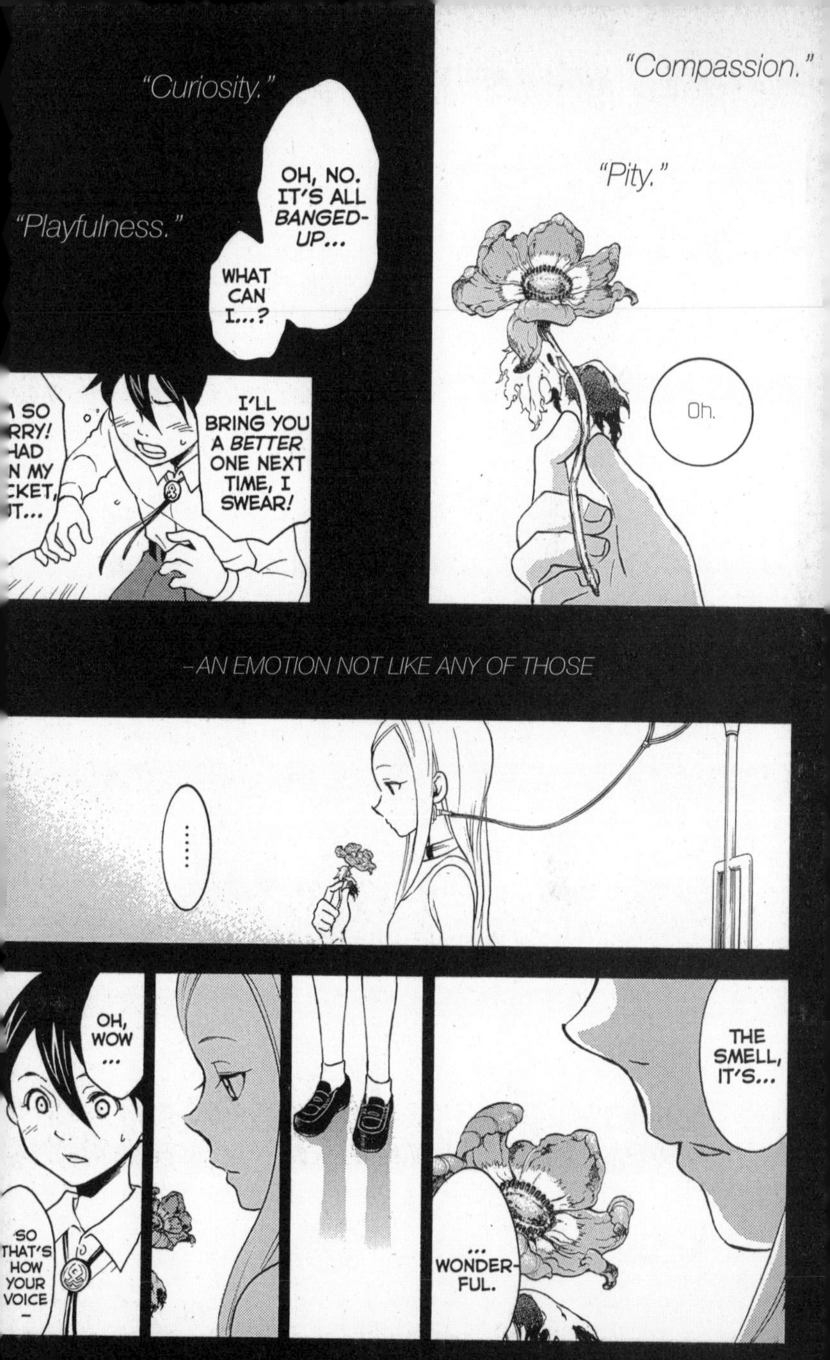
"Compassion."
"Pity."
Oh.
"Curiosity."
OH, NO. IT'S ALL BANGED-UP...
WHAT CAN I...?
"Playfulness."
I'LL BRING YOU A BETTER ONE NEXT TIME, I SWEAR!
–AN EMOTION NOT LIKE ANY OF THOSE
......
THE SMELL, IT'S...
...WONDERFUL.
OH, WOW...
SO THAT'S HOW YOUR VOICE–

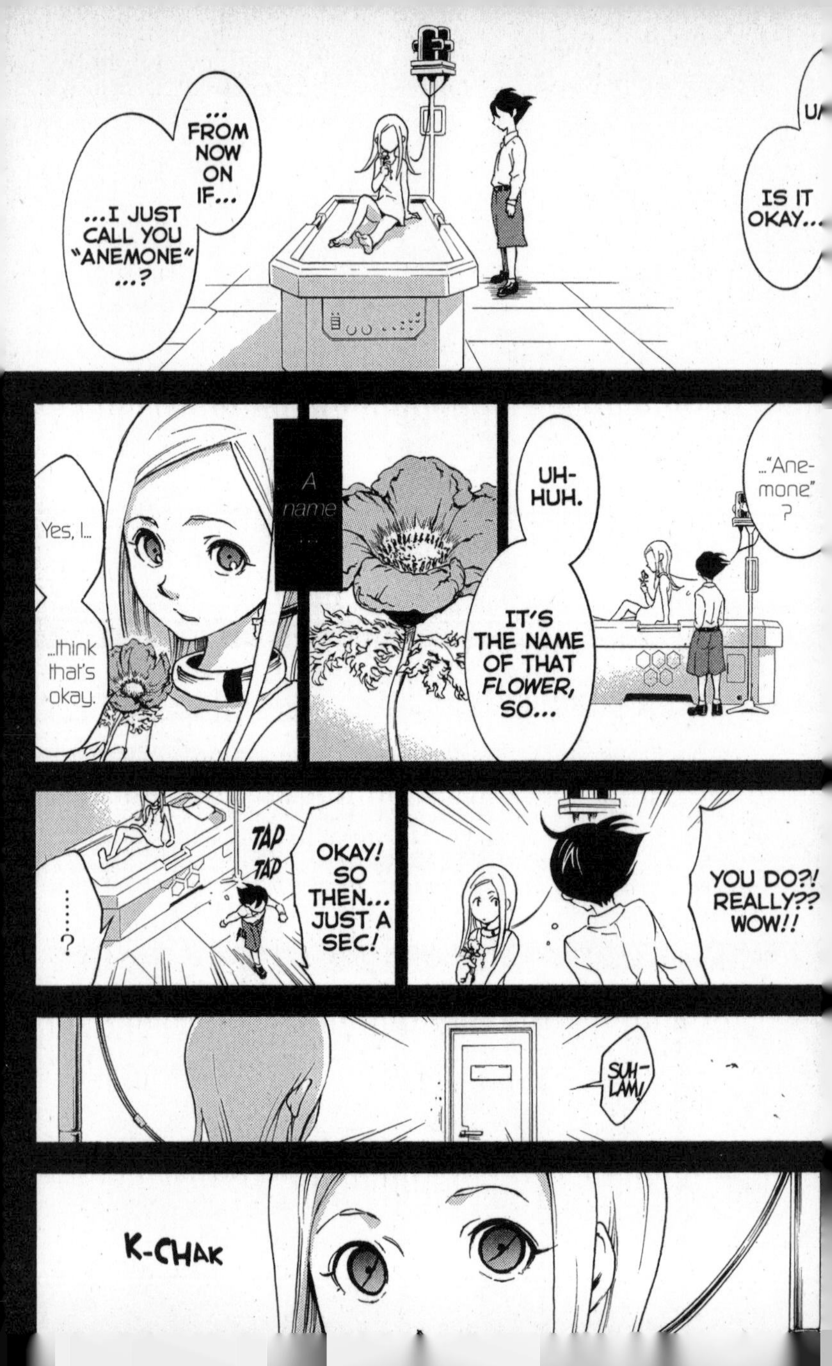
IS IT OKAY...
...FROM NOW ON IF...
...I JUST CALL YOU "ANEMONE" ...?
..."Ane-mone" ?
UH-HUH.
IT'S THE NAME OF THAT *FLOWER*, SO...
A name ...
Yes, I...
...think that's okay.
YOU DO?! REALLY?? WOW!!
OKAY! SO THEN... JUST A SEC!
TAP TAP
......?
SUH-LAM!
K-CHAK

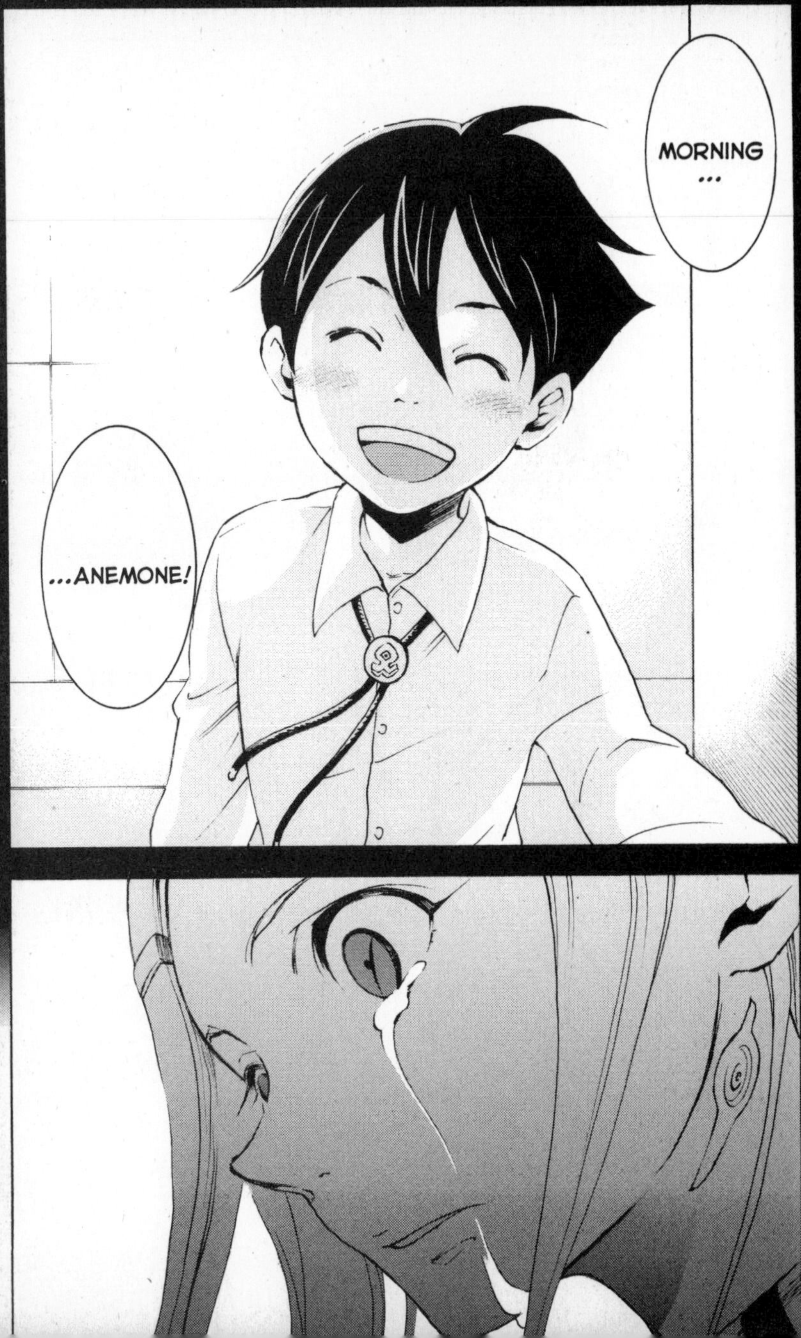
MORNING
...
...ANEMONE!

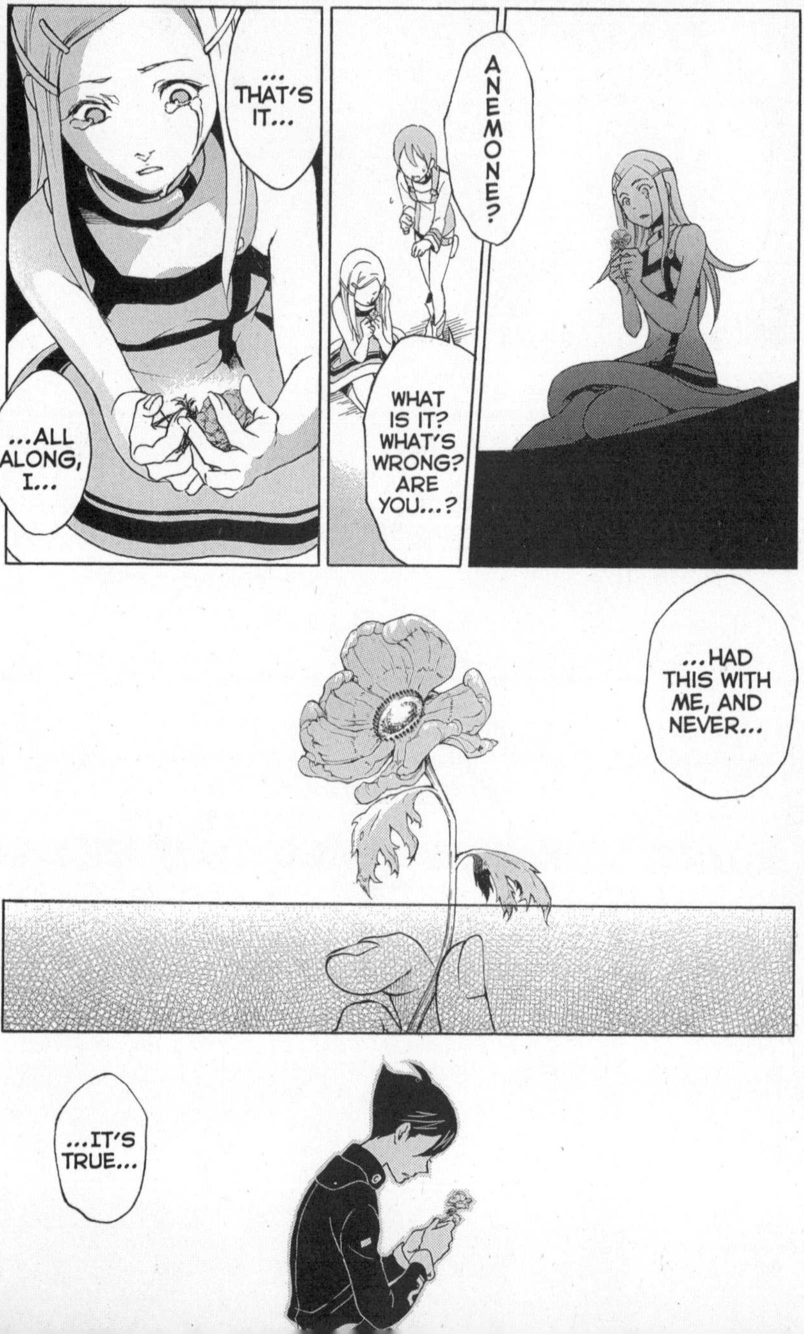
ANEMONE?
WHAT IS IT? WHAT'S WRONG? ARE YOU...?
...THAT'S IT...
...ALL ALONG, I...
...HAD THIS WITH ME, AND NEVER...
...IT'S TRUE...

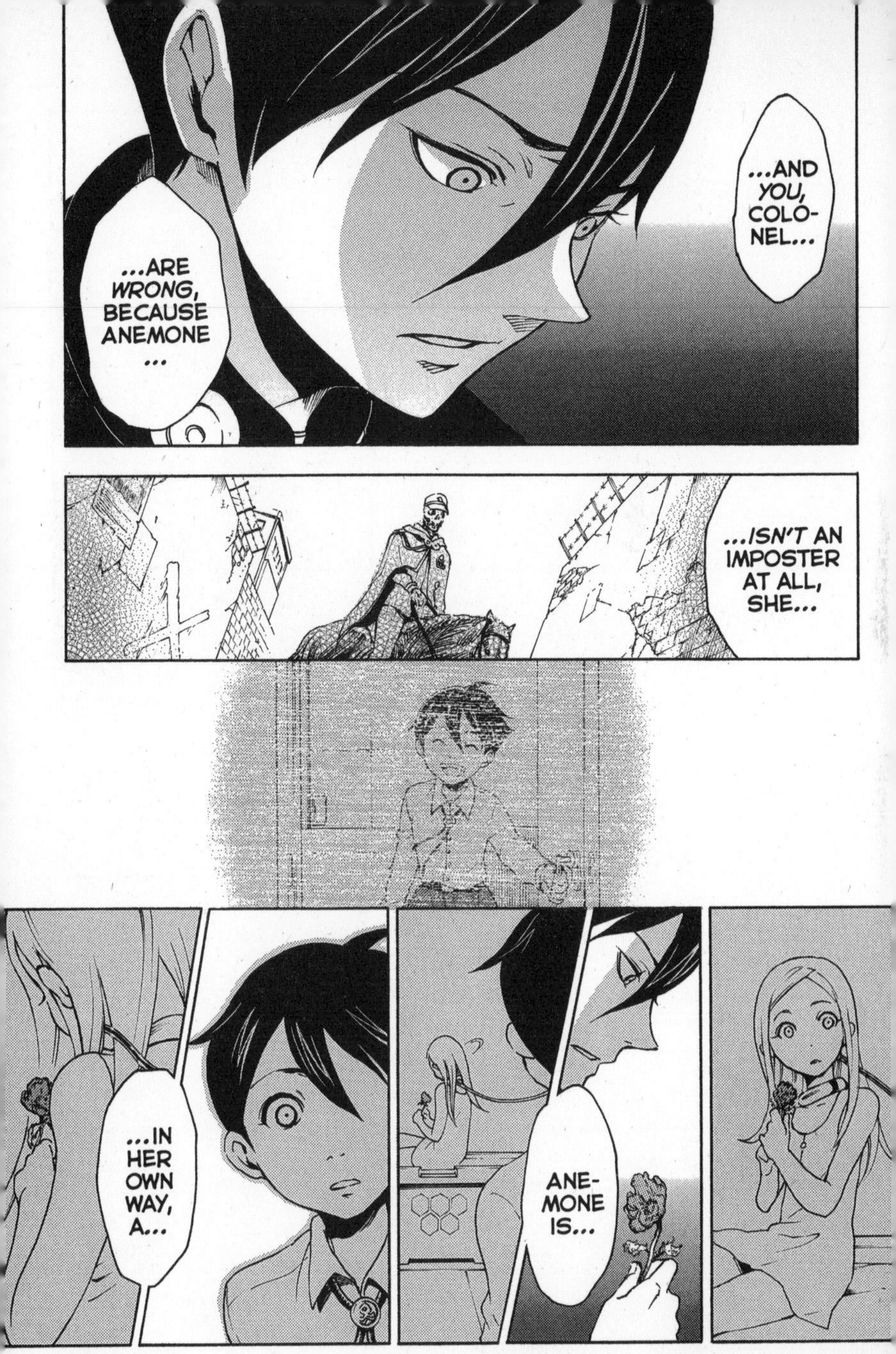
...AND YOU, COLO-NEL...
...ARE *WRONG*, BECAUSE ANEMONE ...
...*ISN'T* AN IMPOSTER AT ALL, SHE...
ANE-MONE IS...
...IN HER OWN WAY, A...

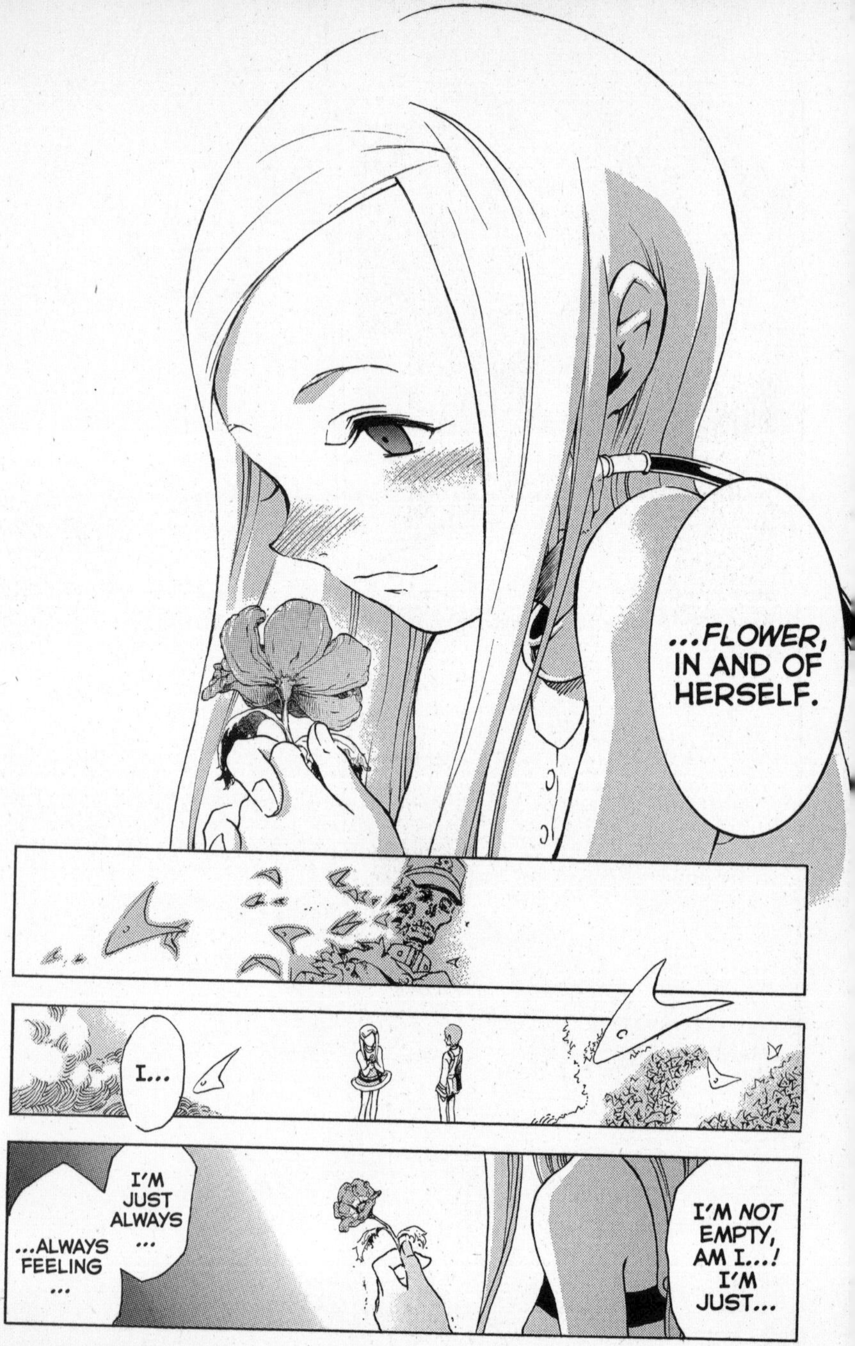
...FLOWER, IN AND OF HERSELF.
I...
I'M NOT EMPTY, AM I...! I'M JUST...
I'M JUST ALWAYS ...
...ALWAYS FEELING ...

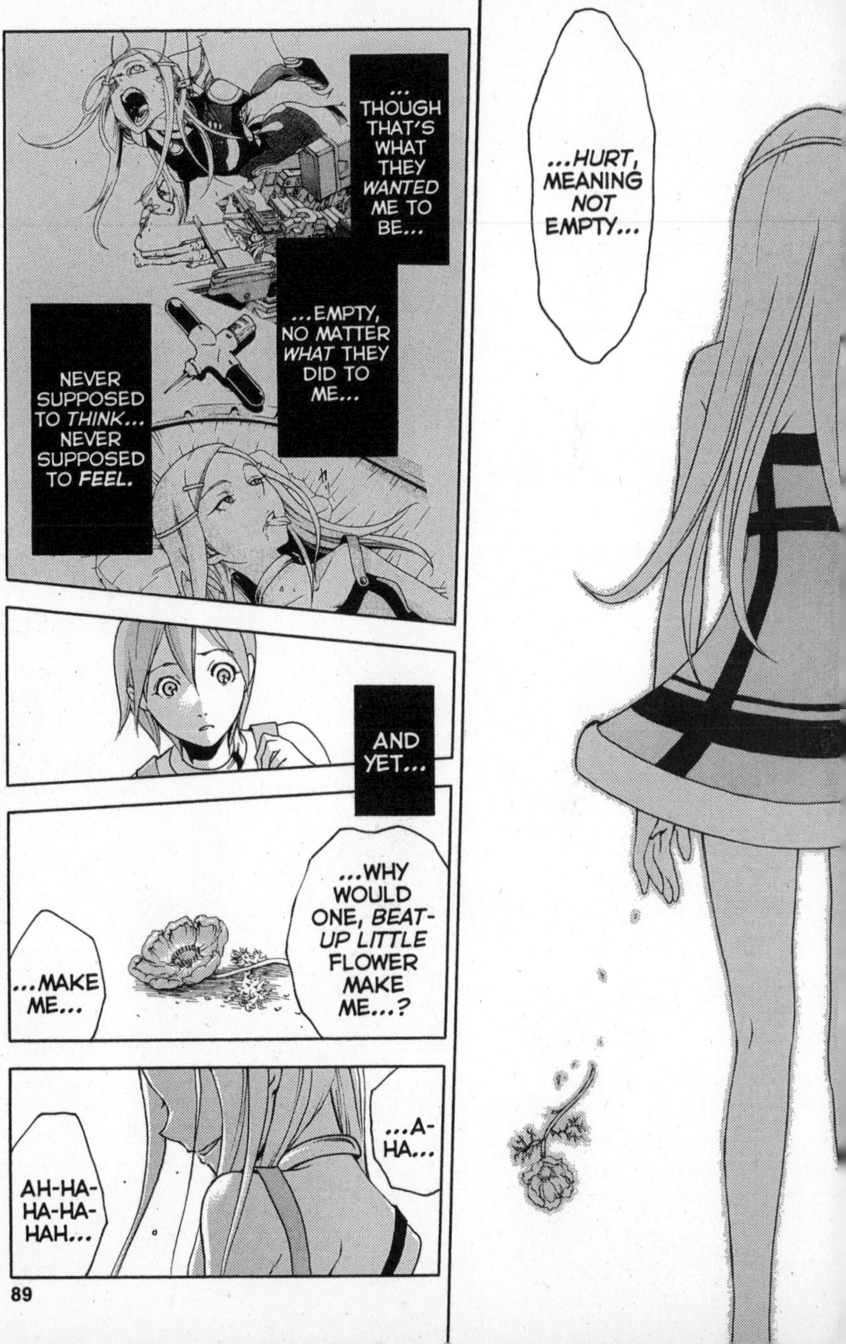
...THOUGH THAT'S WHAT THEY *WANTED* ME TO BE...
...EMPTY, NO MATTER *WHAT* THEY DID TO ME...
NEVER SUPPOSED TO *THINK*... NEVER SUPPOSED TO *FEEL*.
AND YET...
...WHY WOULD ONE, *BEAT-UP LITTLE* FLOWER MAKE ME...?
...MAKE ME...
...A-HA...
AH-HA-HA-HA-HAH...
...*HURT*, MEANING *NOT* EMPTY...

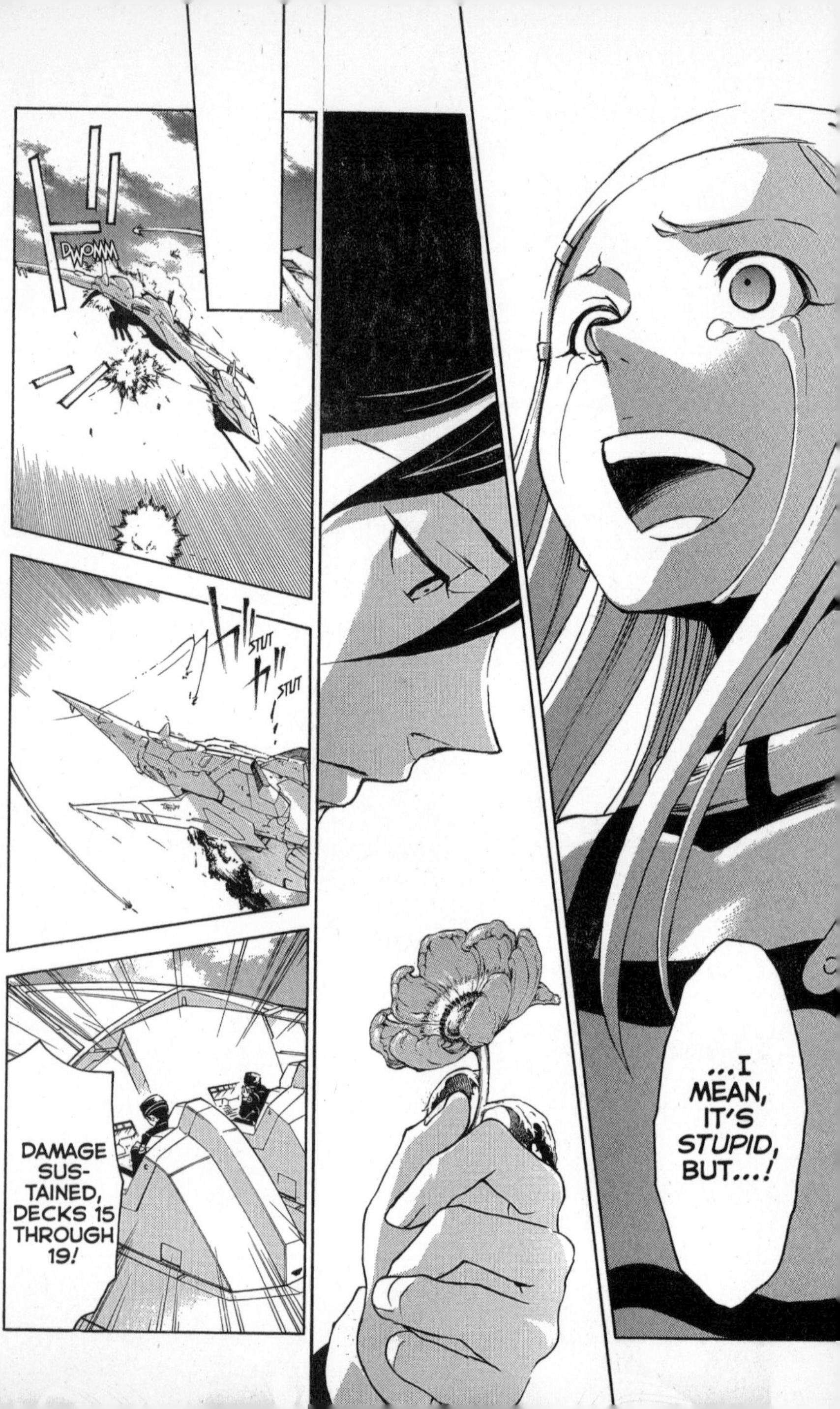
...I MEAN, IT'S STUPID, BUT...!
DWOMM
STUT
STUT
DAMAGE SUS-TAINED, DECKS 15 THROUGH 19!

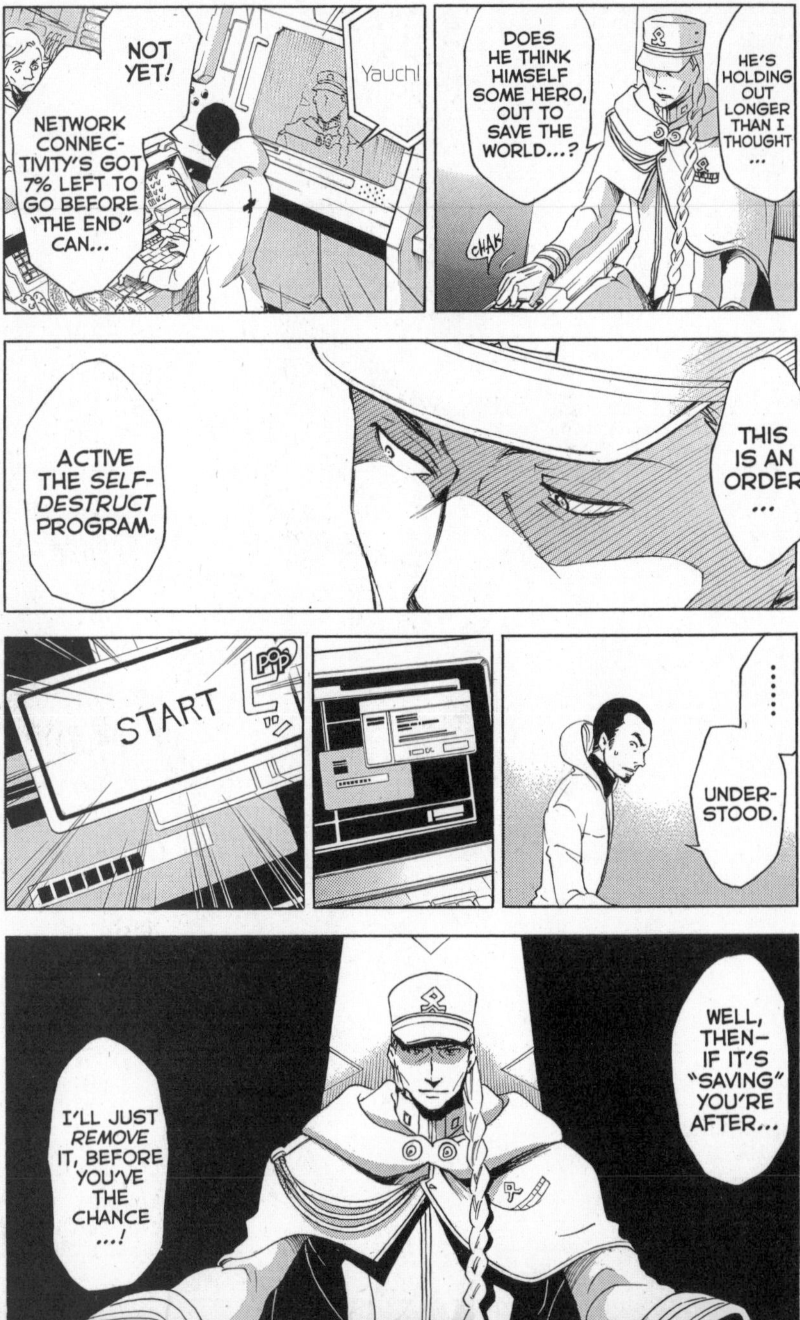
HE'S HOLDING OUT LONGER THAN I THOUGHT...
DOES HE THINK HIMSELF SOME HERO, OUT TO SAVE THE WORLD...?
CHAK
Yauch!
NOT YET!
NETWORK CONNEC-TIVITY'S GOT 7% LEFT TO GO BEFORE "THE END" CAN...
THIS IS AN ORDER...
ACTIVE THE *SELF-DESTRUCT* PROGRAM.
......
UNDER-STOOD.
POP
START
WELL, THEN— IF IT'S "SAVING" YOU'RE AFTER...
I'LL JUST *REMOVE* IT, BEFORE YOU'VE THE CHANCE...!

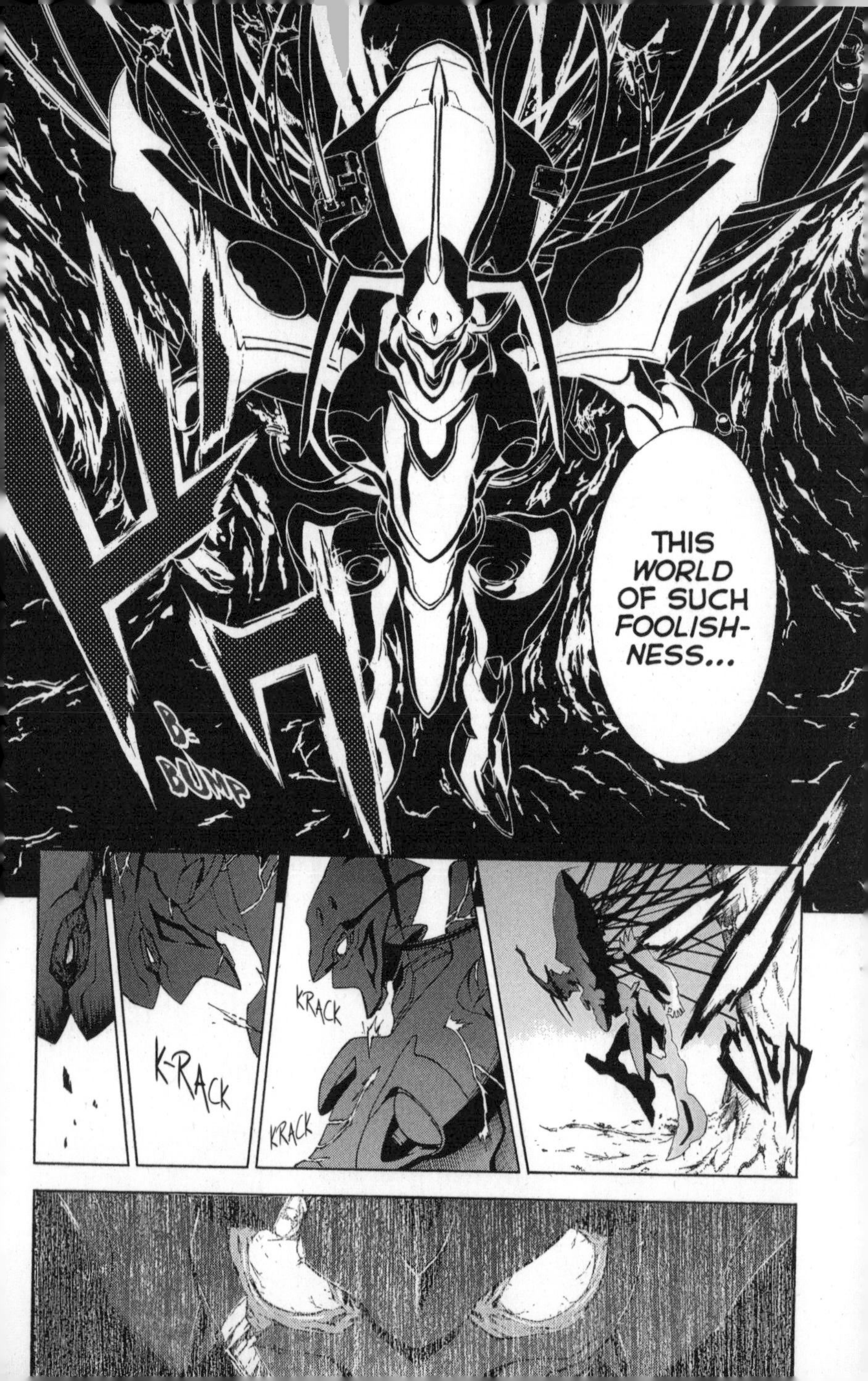
THIS WORLD OF SUCH FOOLISHNESS...
B-BUMP
KRACK
KRACK
K-RACK

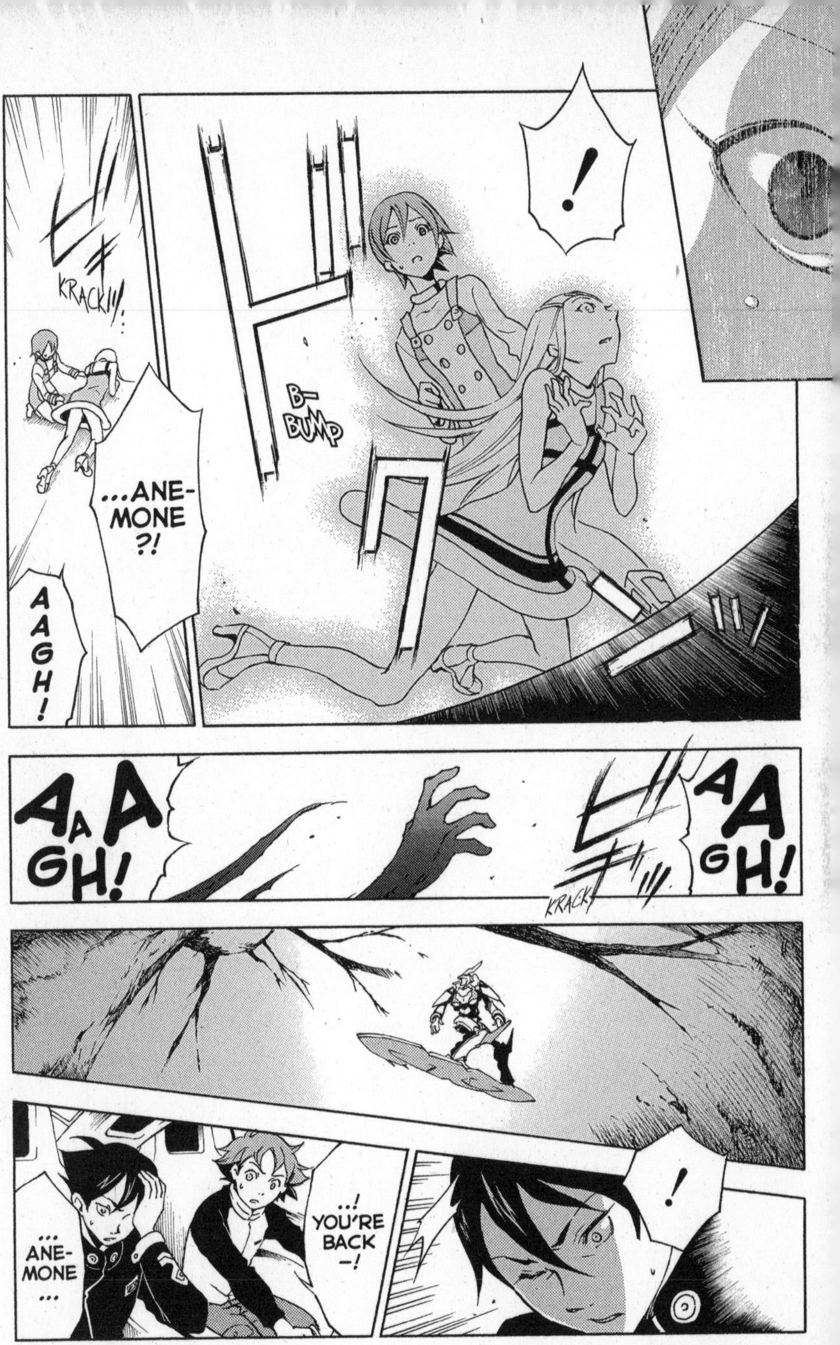
!
B-BUMP
KRACK!!
...ANE-MONE?!
AAGH!
AAGH!
KRACK
AAAGH!
!
...! YOU'RE BACK—!
...ANE-MONE...

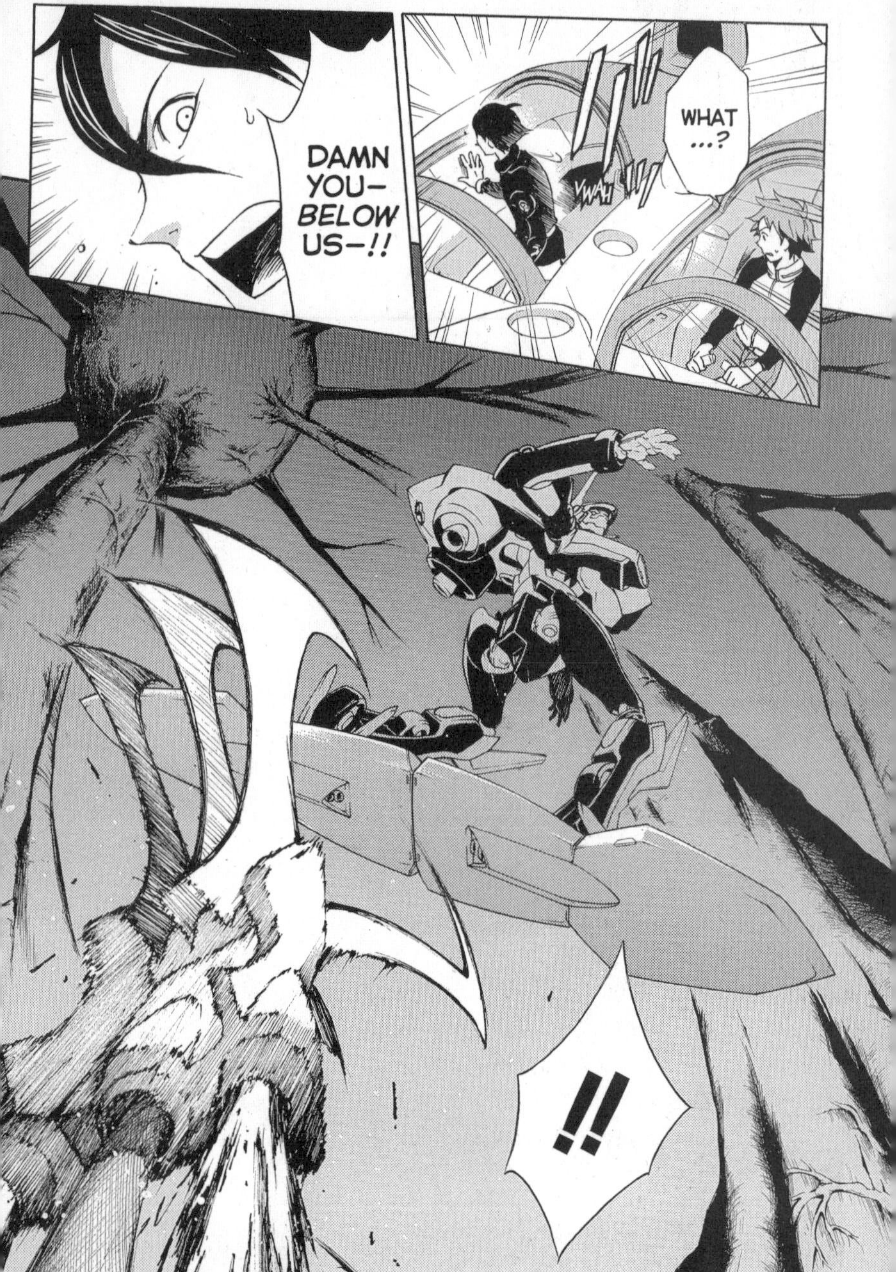
WHAT ...?
VWAH
DAMN YOU— BELOW US—!!
!!

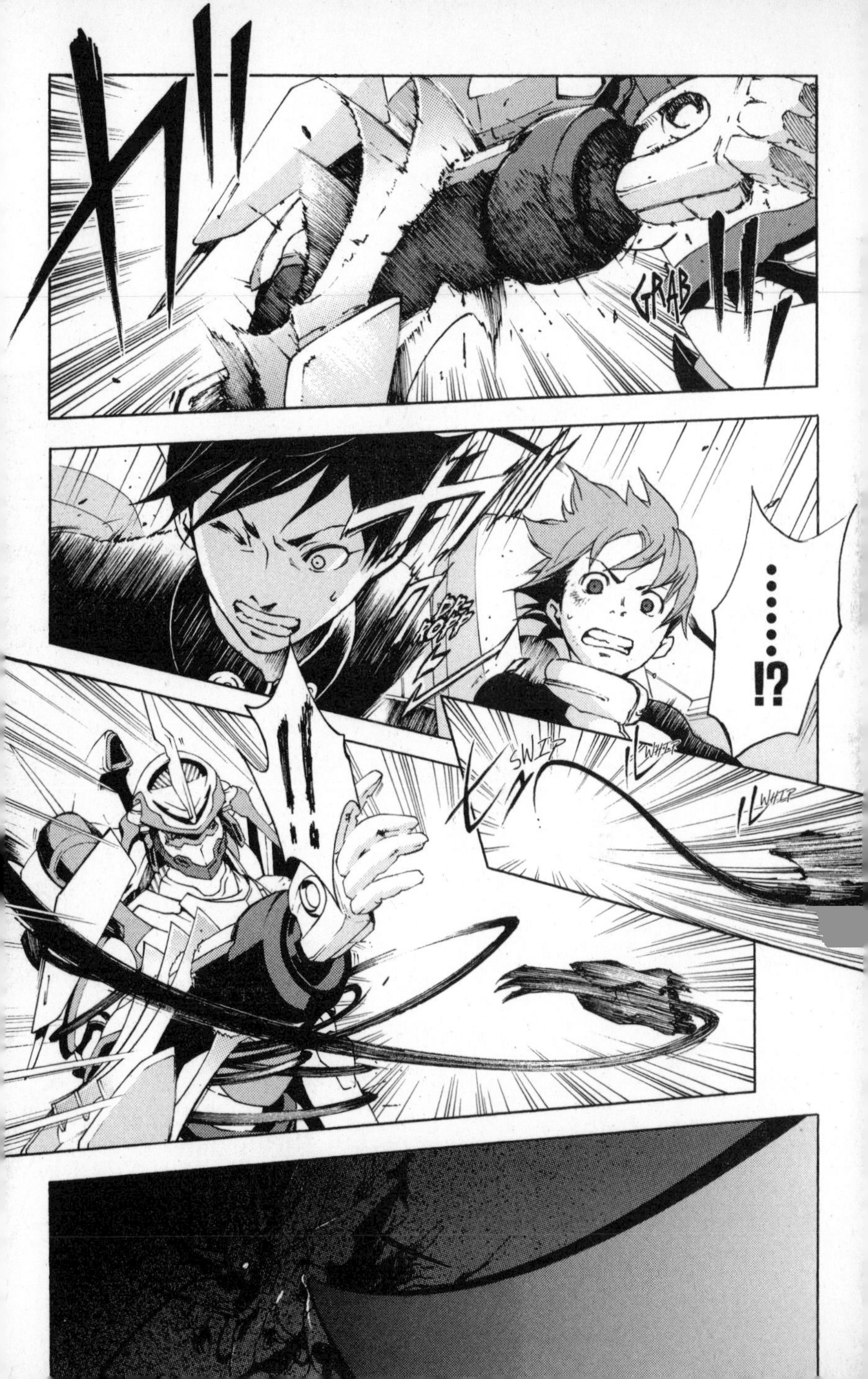
GRAB
DROPP
......!?
!!
WHIP
WHIP
SWIP

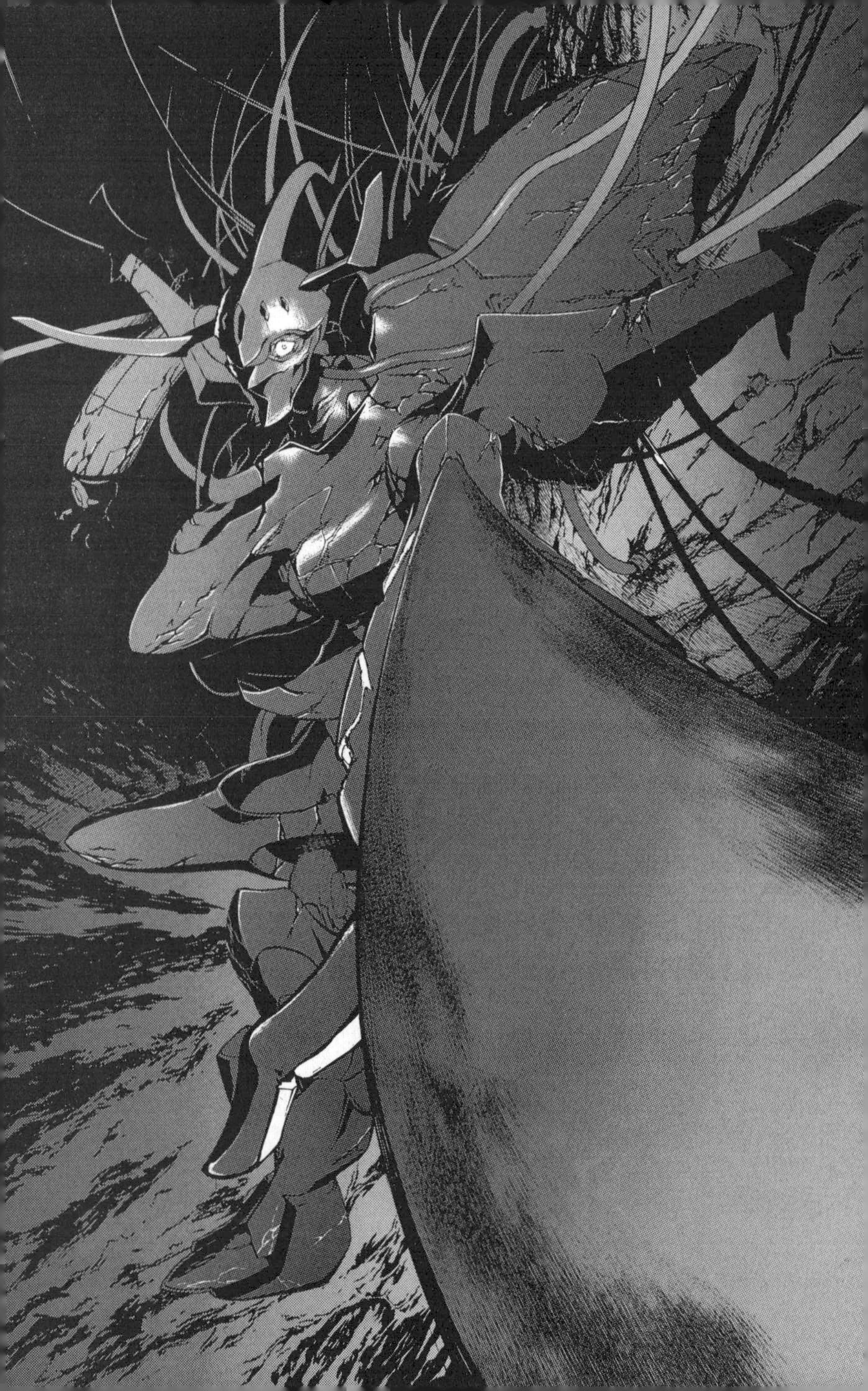

Psalms of
Planet
Eureka seveN

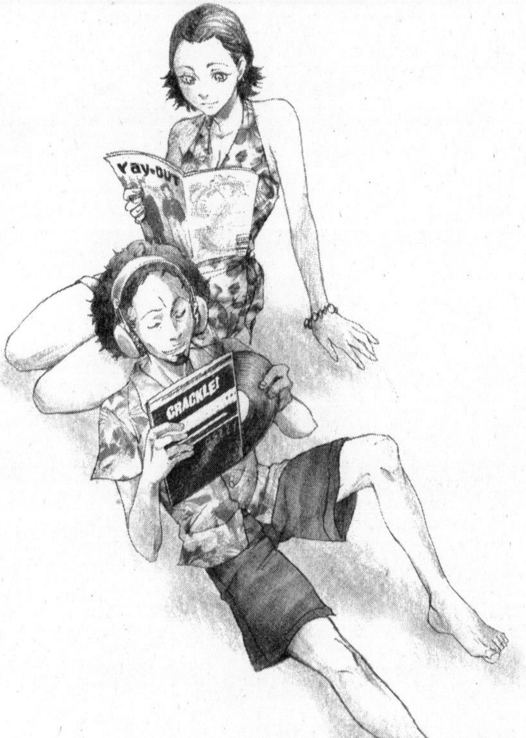
Yay-OUT
CRACKLE!

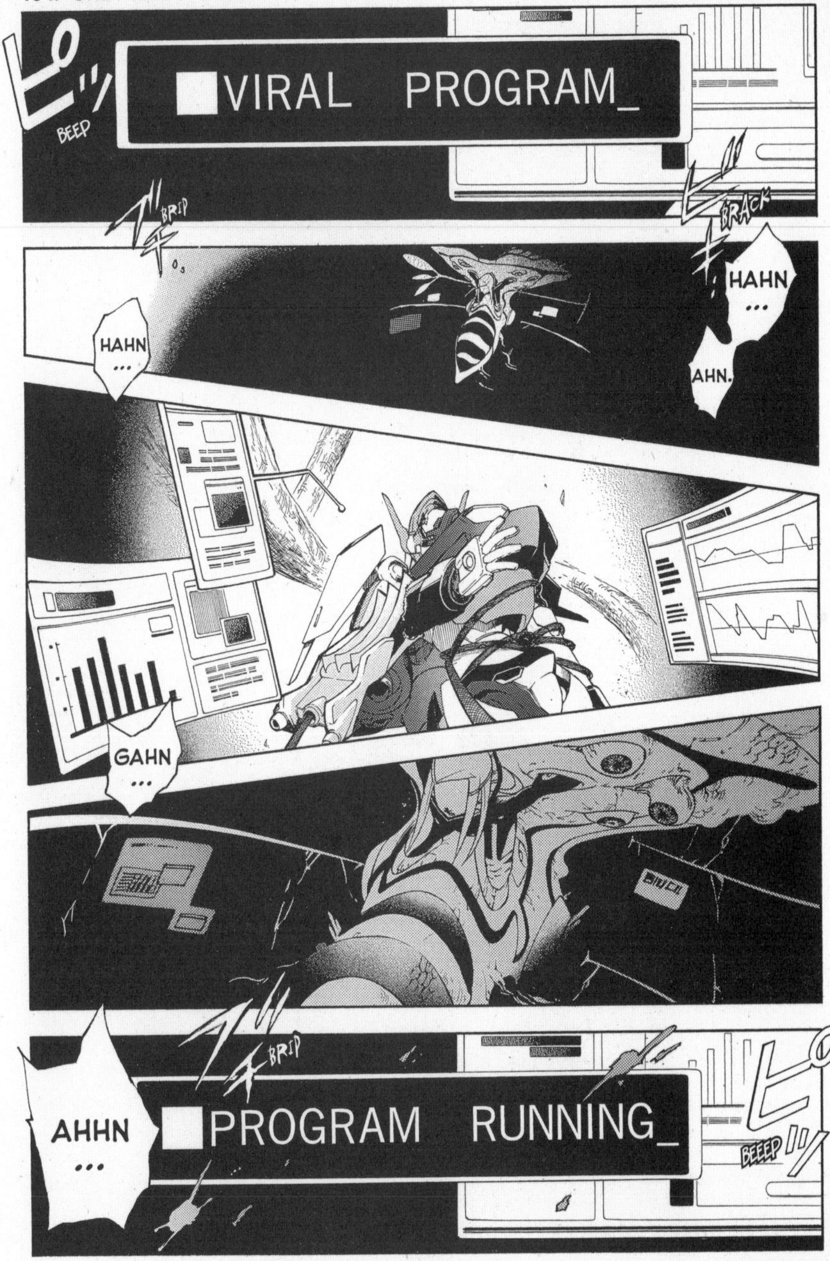
ピッ
BEEP
■VIRAL PROGRAM_
BRACK
HAHN...
AHN.
BRIP
HAHN...
GAHN...
BEEEP
■PROGRAM RUNNING_
BRIP
AHHN...

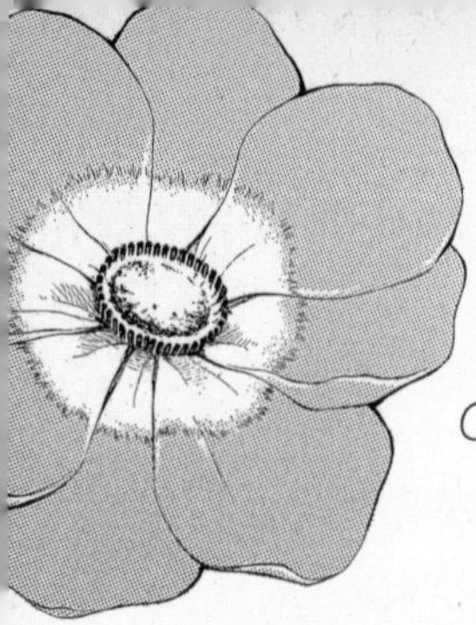

I could while away the hours
Conferrin' with the flowers, consultin' with the rain

I would be not just a nuffin'
My head all full of stuffin', my heart all full of pain

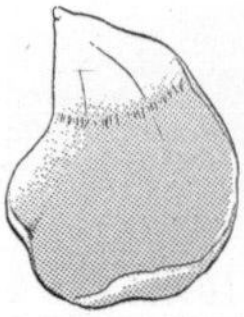

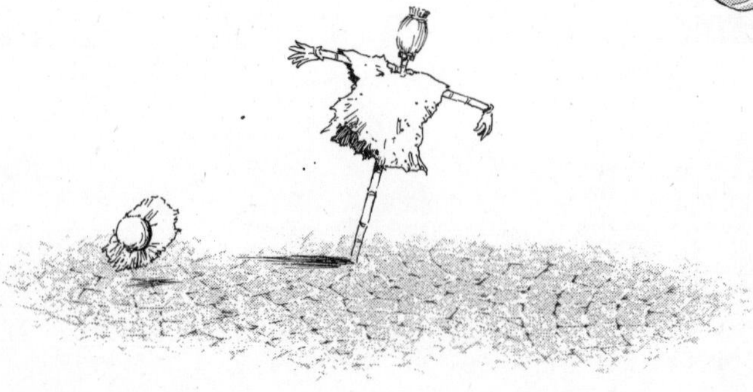

I would dance and be merry
Life would be a ding-a-derry
If I only had a brain

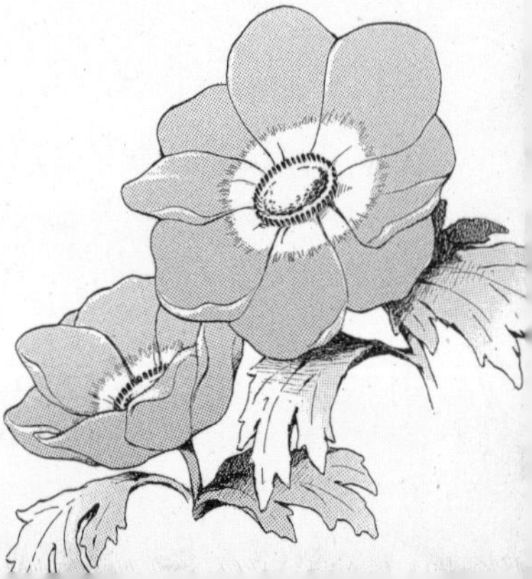

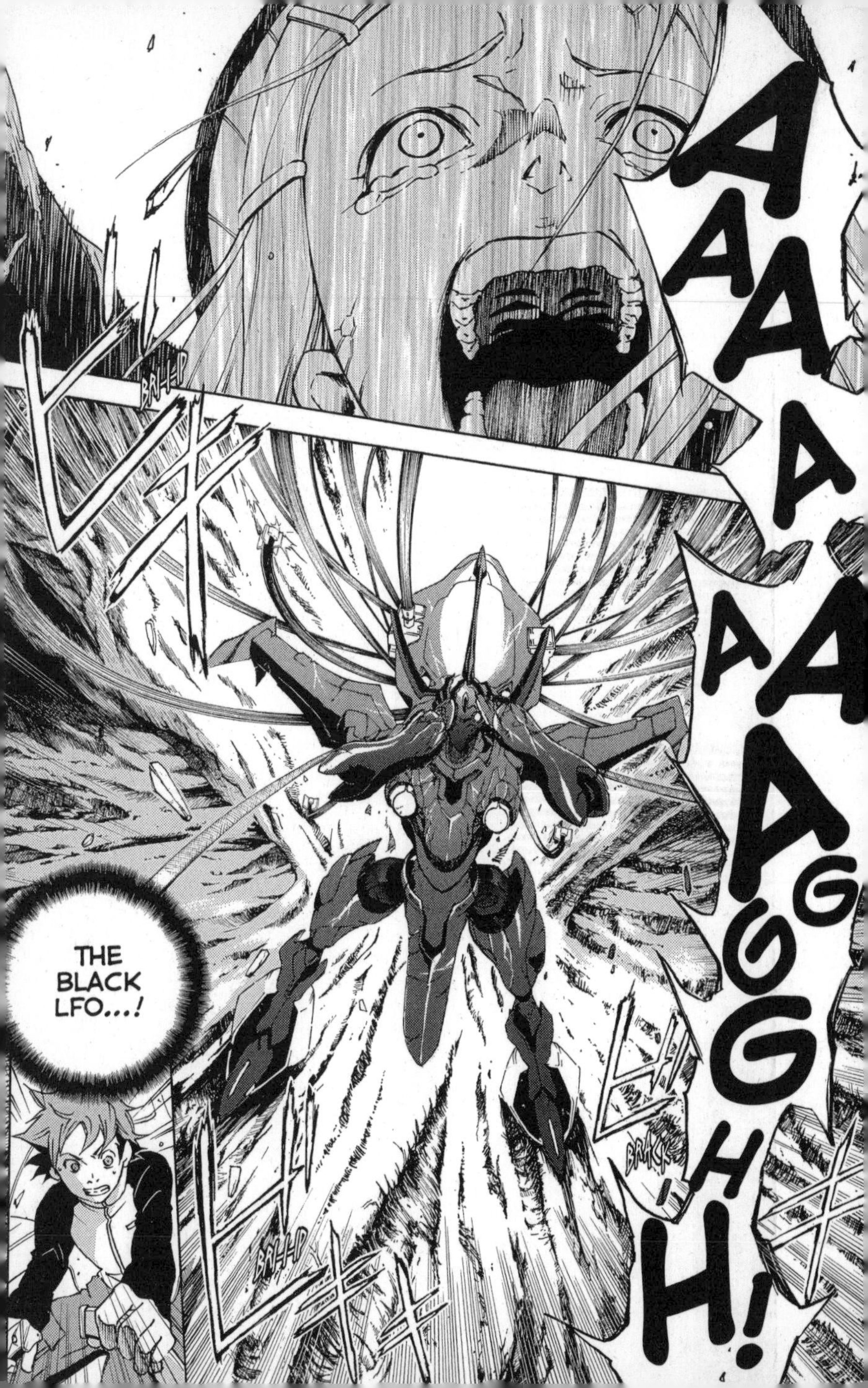
AAAAAAAGGGHH!
BRI-I-P
BRACK
BRI-I-P
THE BLACK LFO...!

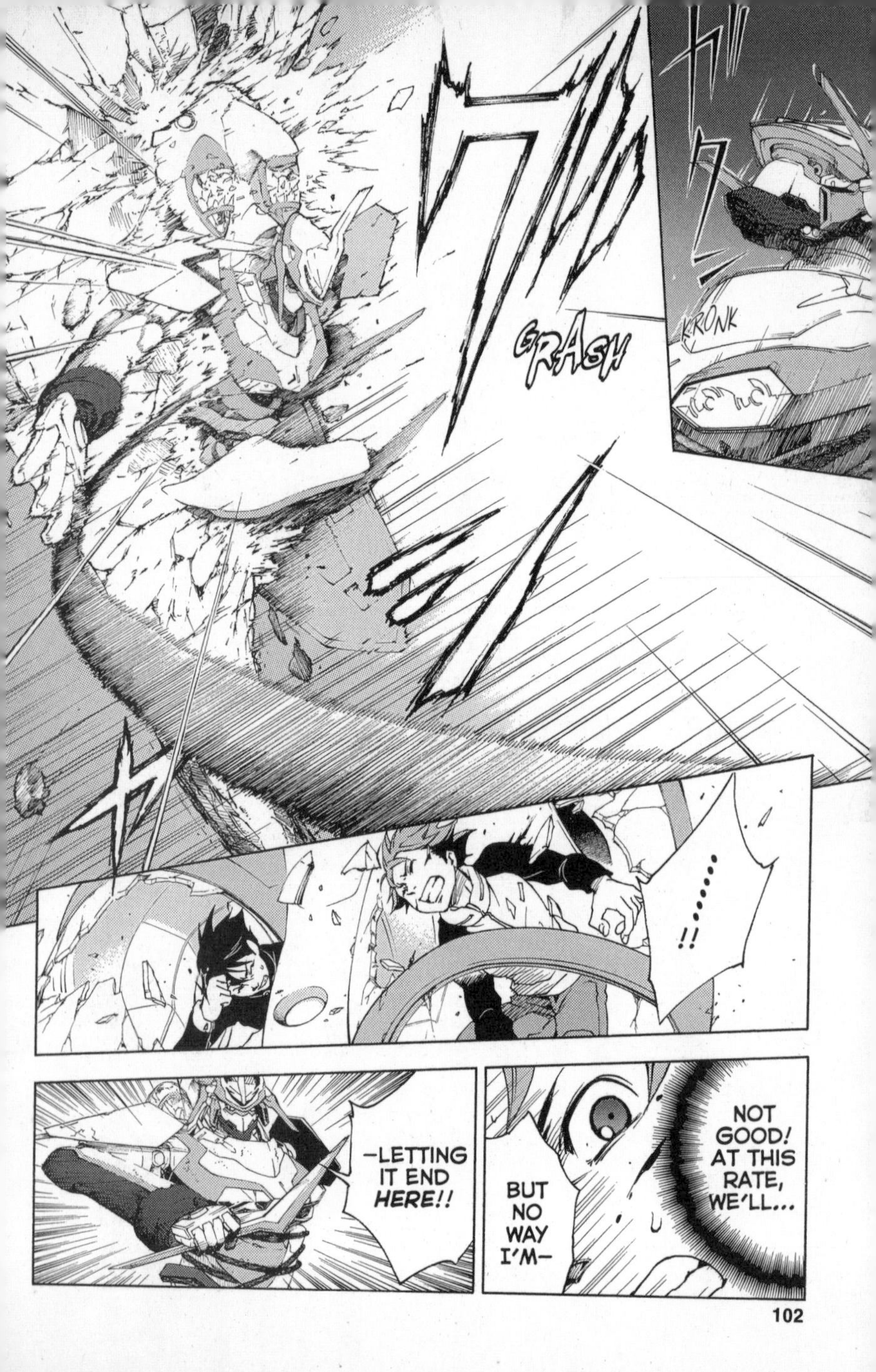
KRONK
CRASH
!!
......
NOT GOOD! AT THIS RATE, WE'LL...
BUT NO WAY I'M—
—LETTING IT END HERE!!

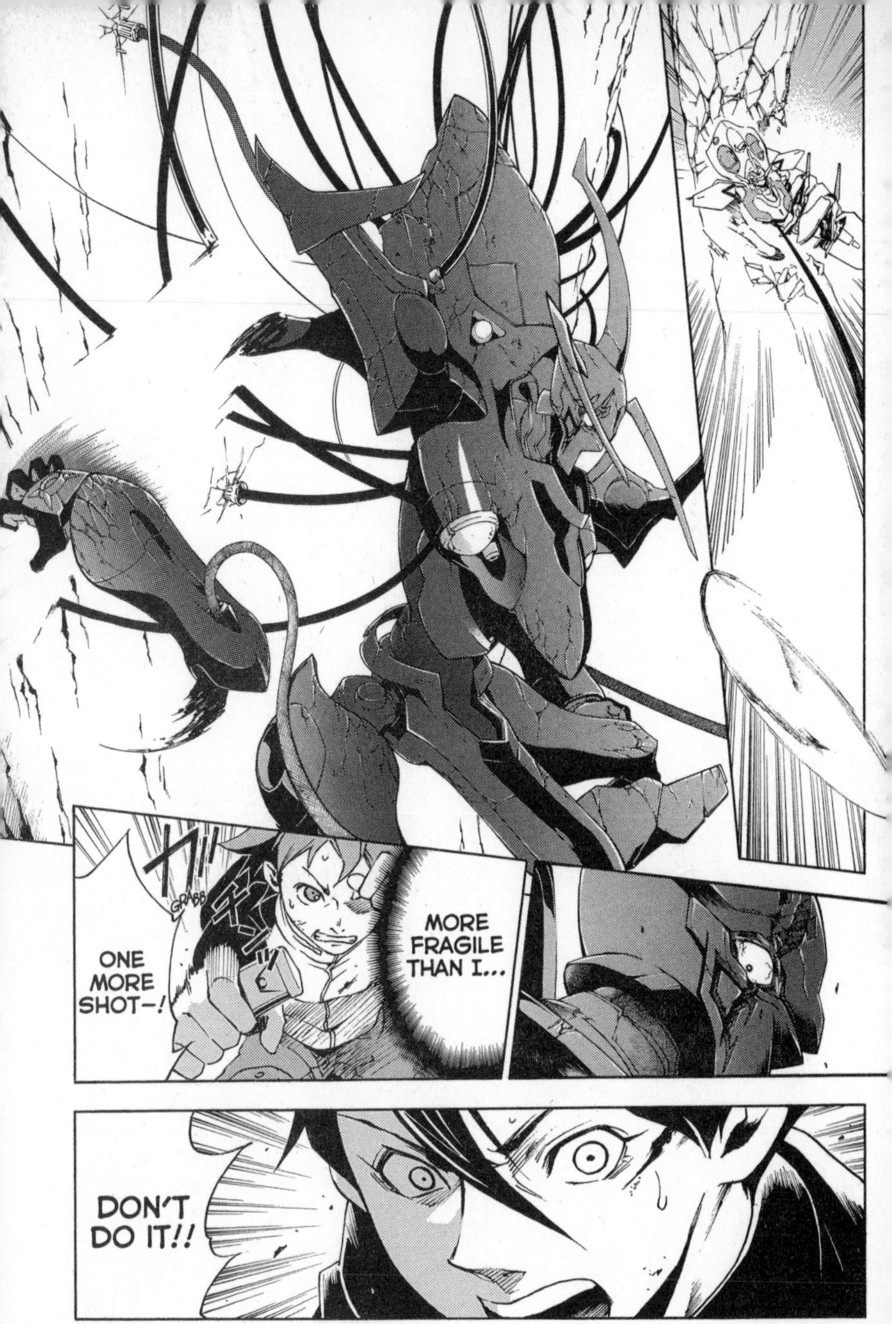
MORE FRAGILE THAN I...
GRABB
ONE MORE SHOT-!
DON'T DO IT!!

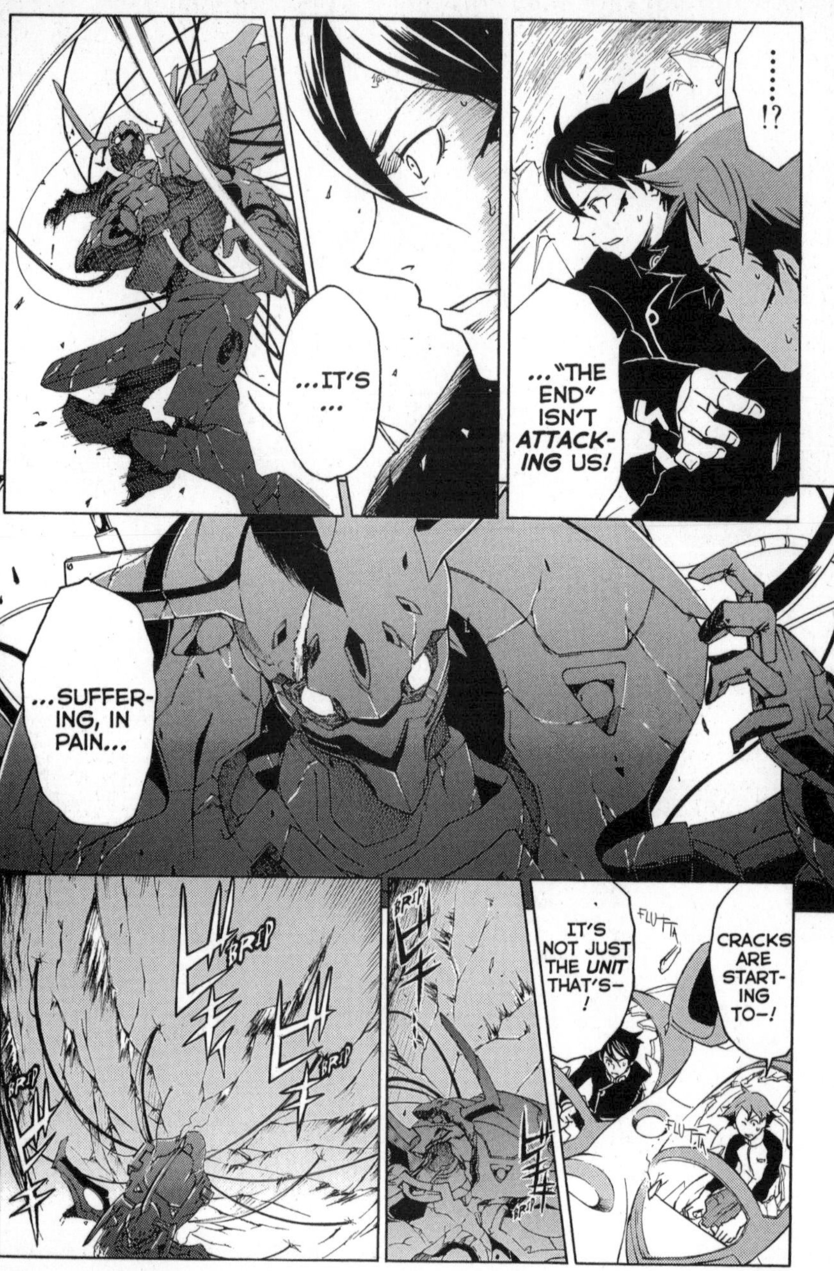
......!?
..."THE END" ISN'T *ATTACKING* US!
...IT'S ...
...SUFFERING, IN PAIN...
CRACKS ARE STARTING TO—!
FLUTTA
IT'S NOT JUST THE *UNIT* THAT'S—!
FLUTTA
BRIP
BRIP
BRIP
BRIP
BRIP

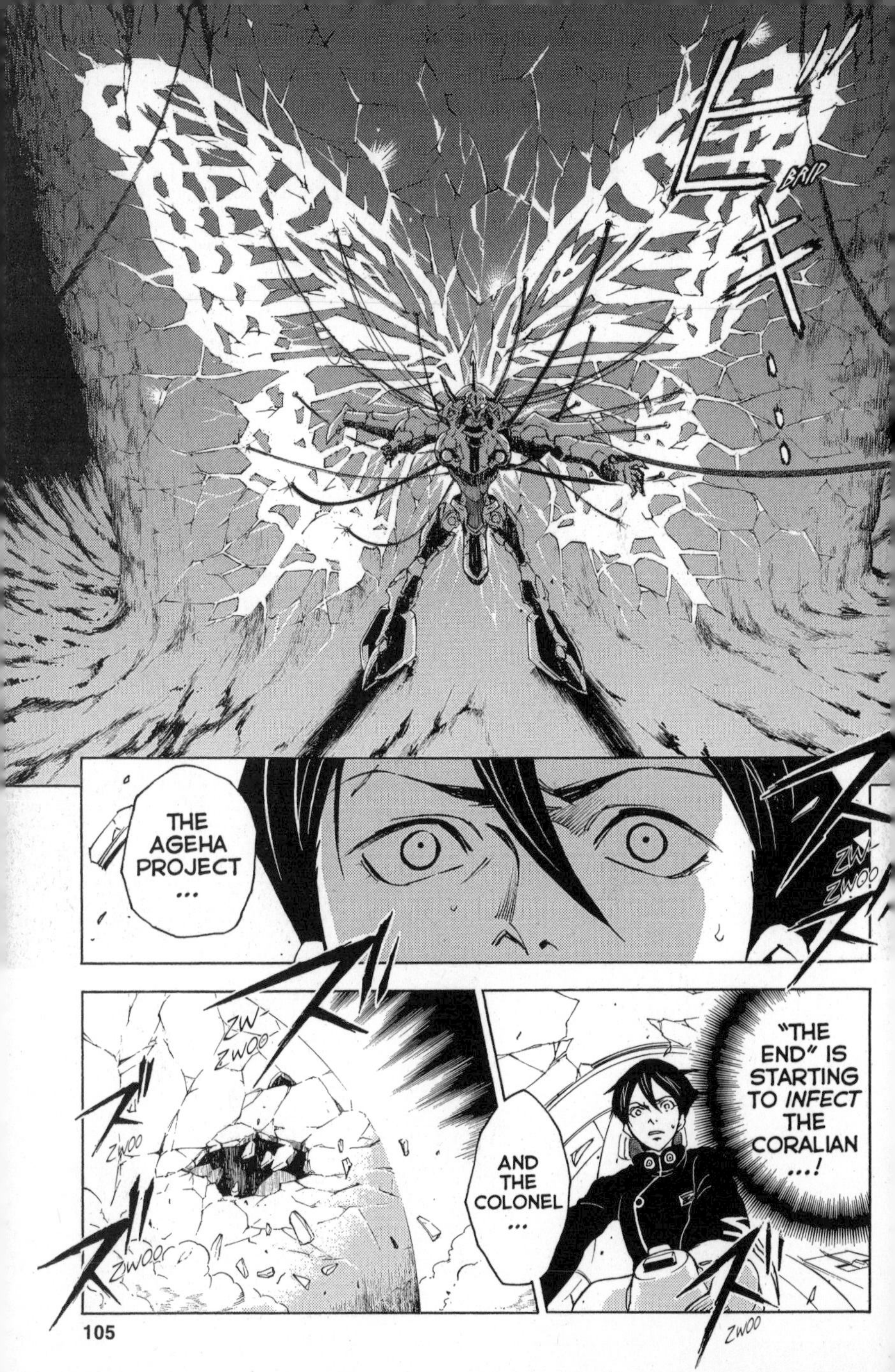
BRIP
ZW-ZWOO
THE AGEHA PROJECT ...
"THE END" IS STARTING TO *INFECT* THE CORALIAN ...!
AND THE COLONEL ...
ZWOO
ZW-ZWOO
ZWOO
ZWOO

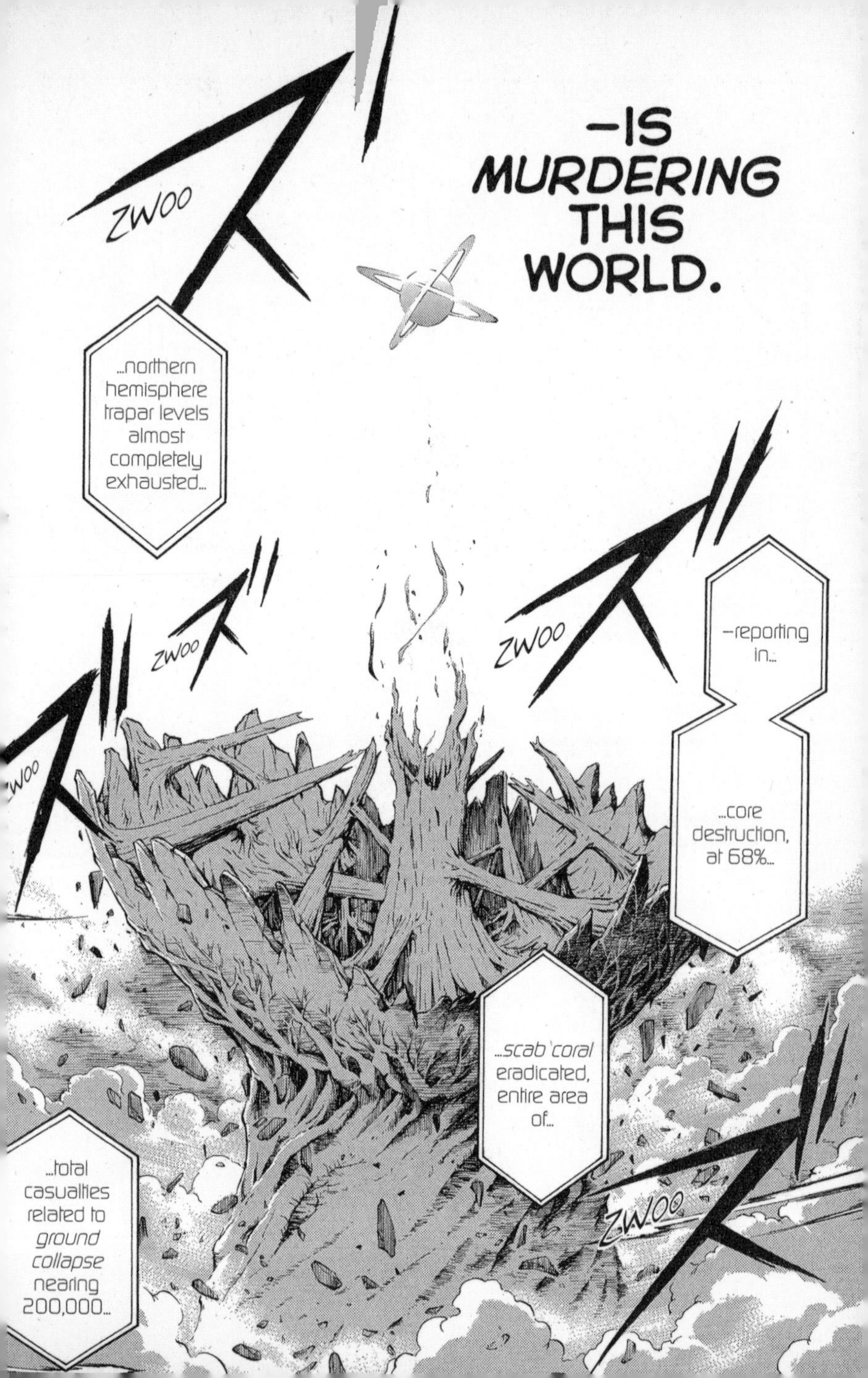
—IS MURDERING THIS WORLD.
ZWOO
...northern hemisphere trapar levels almost completely exhausted...
ZWOO
—reporting in...
...core destruction, at 68%...
ZWOO
ZWOO
...scab 'coral eradicated, entire area of...
ZWOO
...total casualties related to ground collapse nearing 200,000...

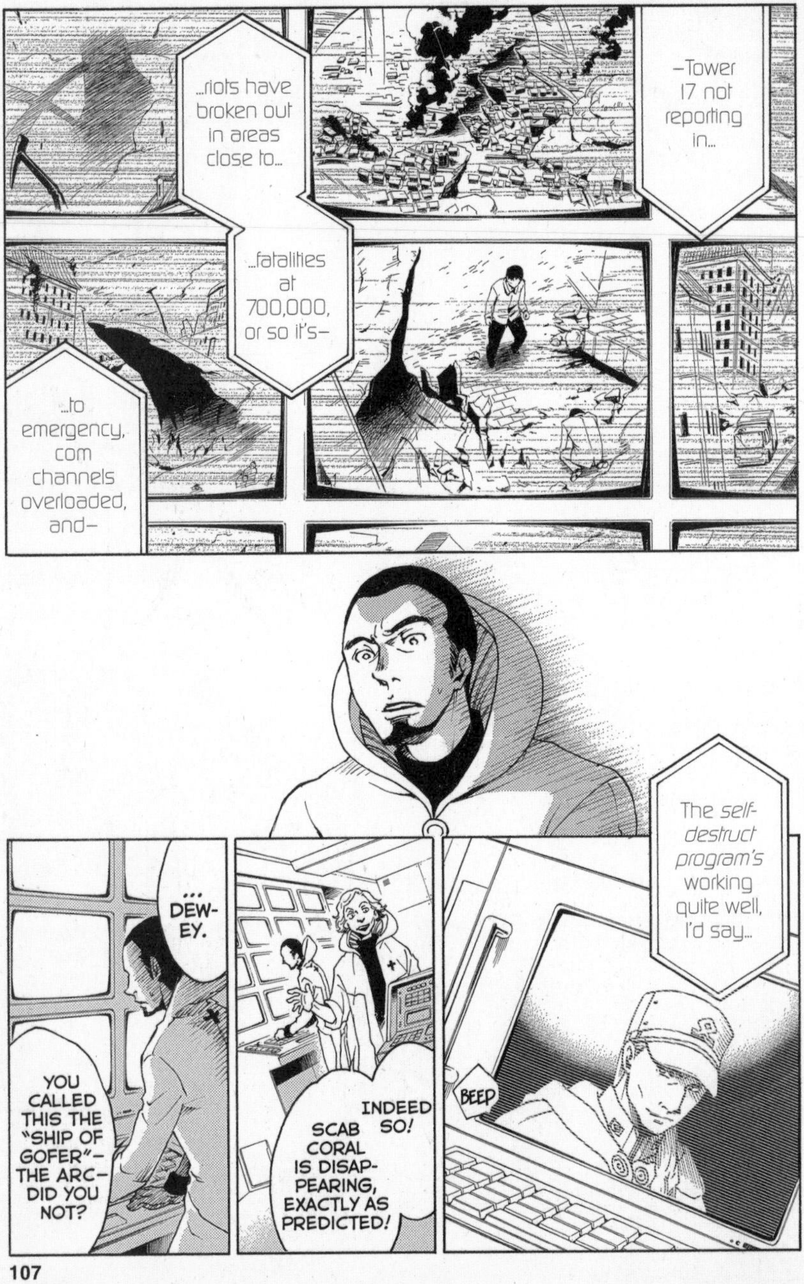

—Tower 17 not reporting in...
...riots have broken out in areas close to...
...fatalities at 700,000, or so it's—
...to emergency, com channels overloaded, and—
The *self-destruct program's* working quite well, I'd say...
BEEP
INDEED SO!
SCAB CORAL IS DISAPPEARING, EXACTLY AS PREDICTED!
... DEWEY.
YOU CALLED THIS THE "SHIP OF GOFER"—THE ARC—DID YOU NOT?

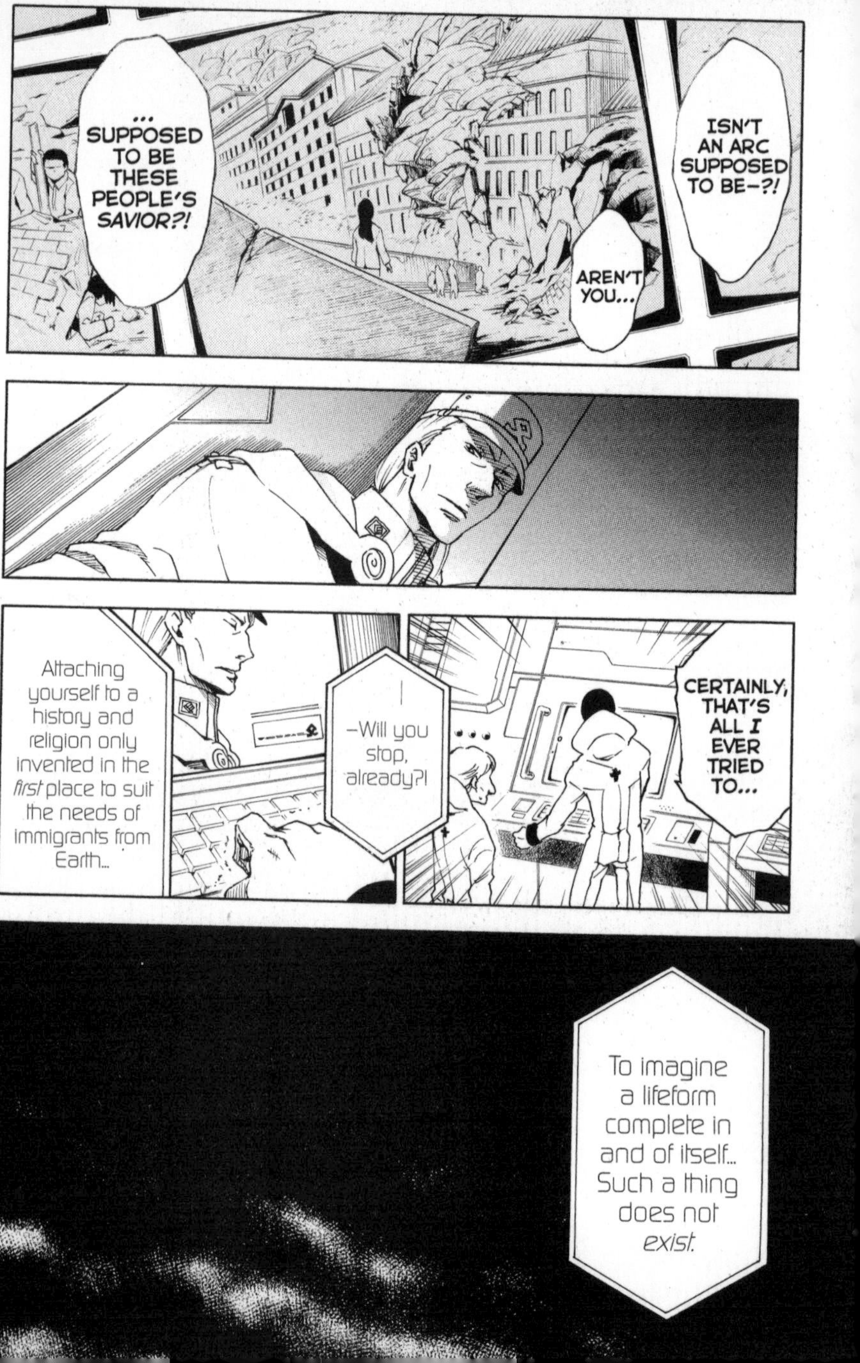
ISN'T AN ARC SUPPOSED TO BE–?!
AREN'T YOU...
...SUPPOSED TO BE THESE PEOPLE'S *SAVIOR?!*
CERTAINLY, THAT'S ALL *I* EVER TRIED TO...
–Will you stop, already?!
Attaching yourself to a history and religion only invented in the *first* place to suit the needs of immigrants from Earth...
To imagine a lifeform complete in and of itself... Such a thing does not *exist.*

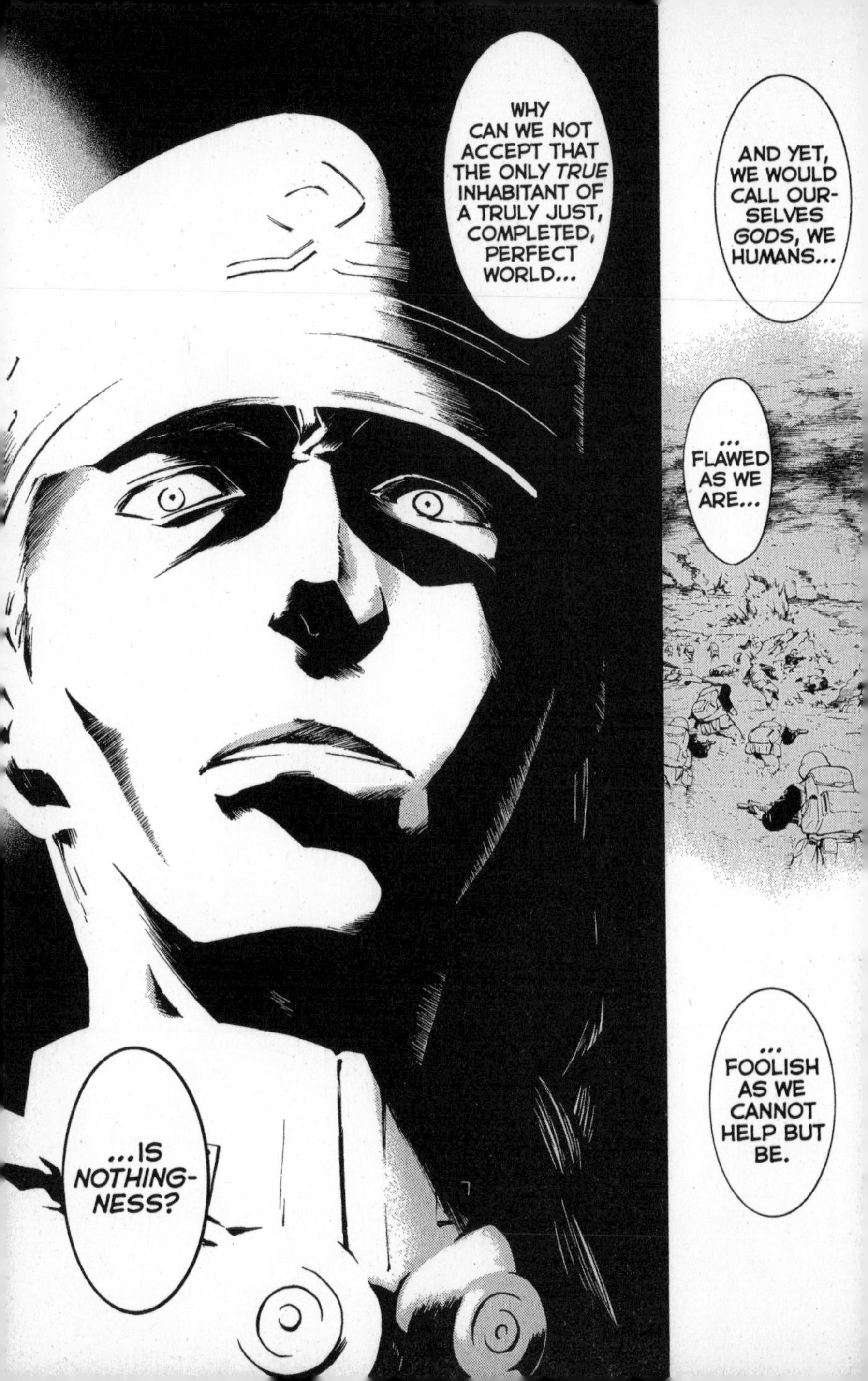
AND YET, WE WOULD CALL OUR-SELVES *GODS*, WE HUMANS...
...FLAWED AS WE ARE...
...FOOLISH AS WE CANNOT HELP BUT BE.
WHY CAN WE NOT ACCEPT THAT THE ONLY *TRUE* INHABITANT OF A TRULY JUST, COMPLETED, PERFECT WORLD...
...IS NOTHING-NESS?

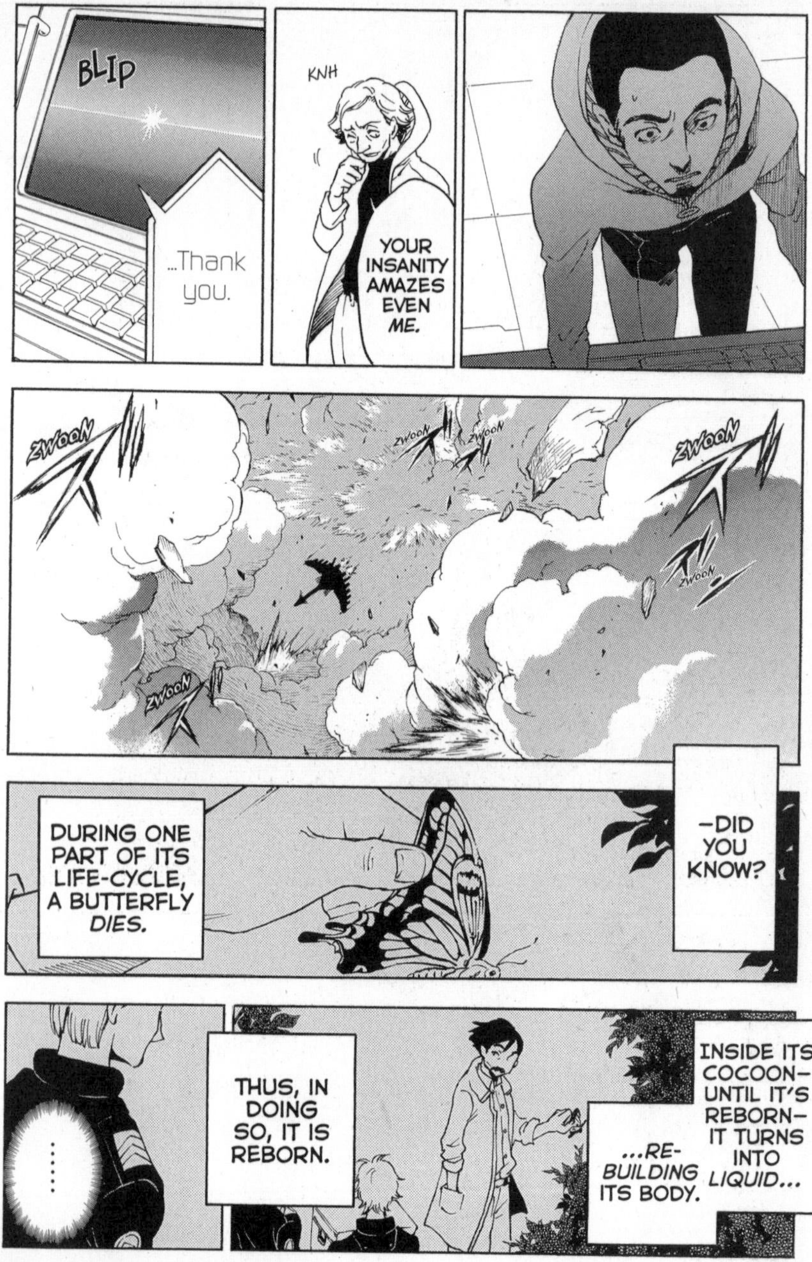
KNH
YOUR INSANITY AMAZES EVEN *ME.*
BLIP
...Thank you.
ZWOON
ZWOON
ZWOON
ZWOON
ZWOON
ZWOON
–DID YOU KNOW?
DURING ONE PART OF ITS LIFE-CYCLE, A BUTTERFLY *DIES.*
INSIDE ITS COCOON— UNTIL IT'S REBORN— IT TURNS INTO *LIQUID...*
...RE-BUILDING ITS BODY.
THUS, IN DOING SO, IT IS REBORN.
......

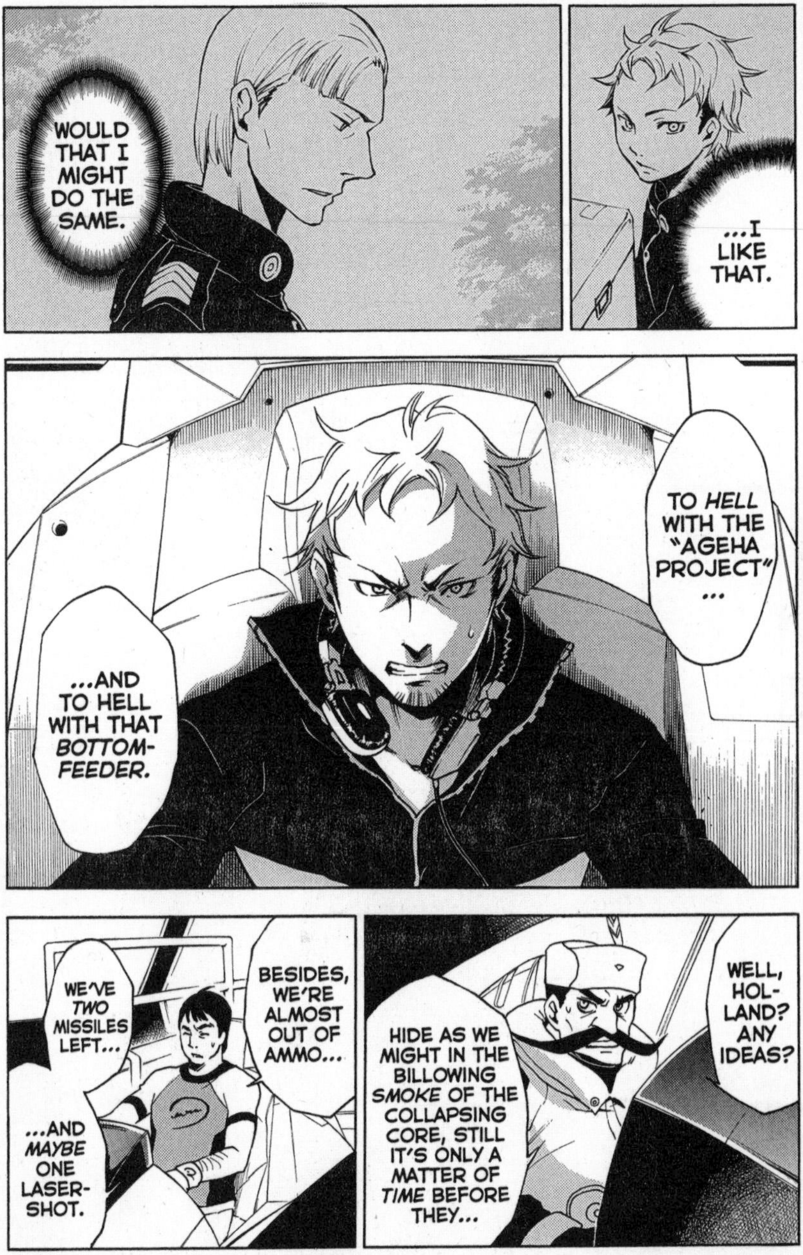
...I LIKE THAT.
WOULD THAT I MIGHT DO THE SAME.
TO *HELL* WITH THE "AGEHA PROJECT"...
...AND TO HELL WITH THAT *BOTTOM-FEEDER.*
WELL, HOL-LAND? ANY IDEAS?
HIDE AS WE MIGHT IN THE BILLOWING *SMOKE* OF THE COLLAPSING CORE, STILL IT'S ONLY A MATTER OF *TIME* BEFORE THEY...
BESIDES, WE'RE ALMOST OUT OF AMMO...
WE'VE *TWO* MISSILES LEFT...
...AND *MAYBE* ONE LASER-SHOT.

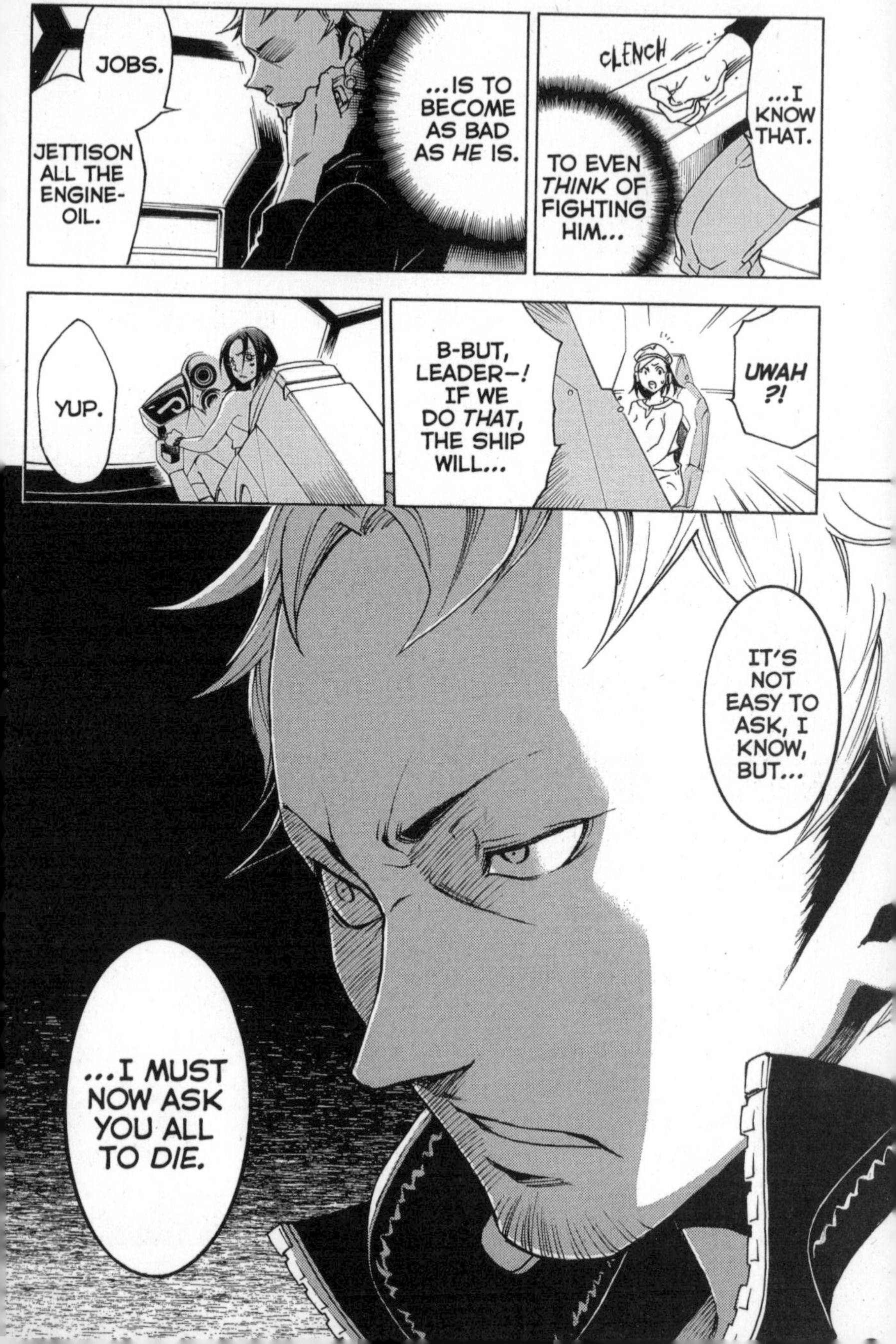
CLENCH
...I KNOW THAT.
TO EVEN THINK OF FIGHTING HIM...
...IS TO BECOME AS BAD AS HE IS.
JOBS.
JETTISON ALL THE ENGINE-OIL.
UWAH ?!
B-BUT, LEADER—! IF WE DO THAT, THE SHIP WILL...
YUP.
IT'S NOT EASY TO ASK, I KNOW, BUT...
...I MUST NOW ASK YOU ALL TO DIE.

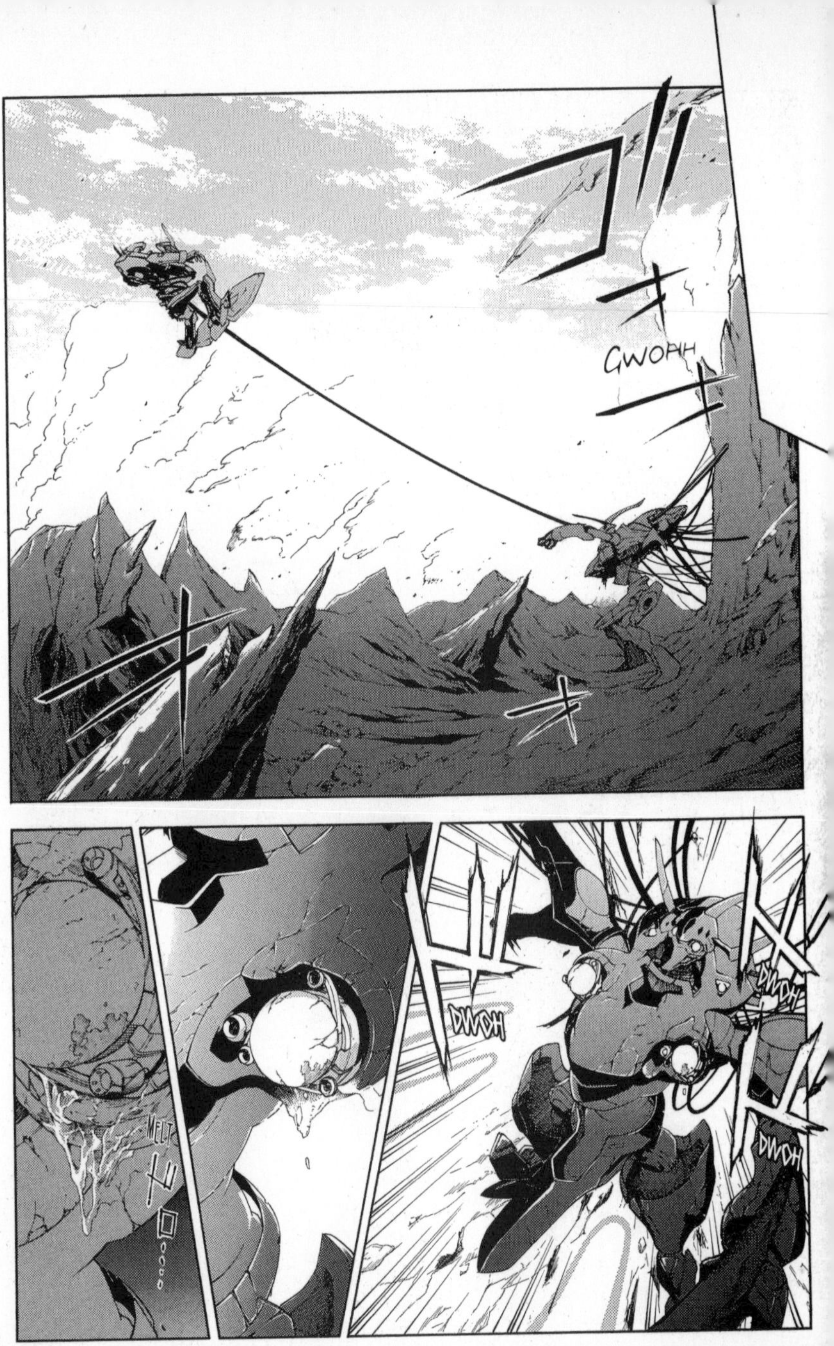
GWOHH
DWOH
DWOH
DWOH
MELT

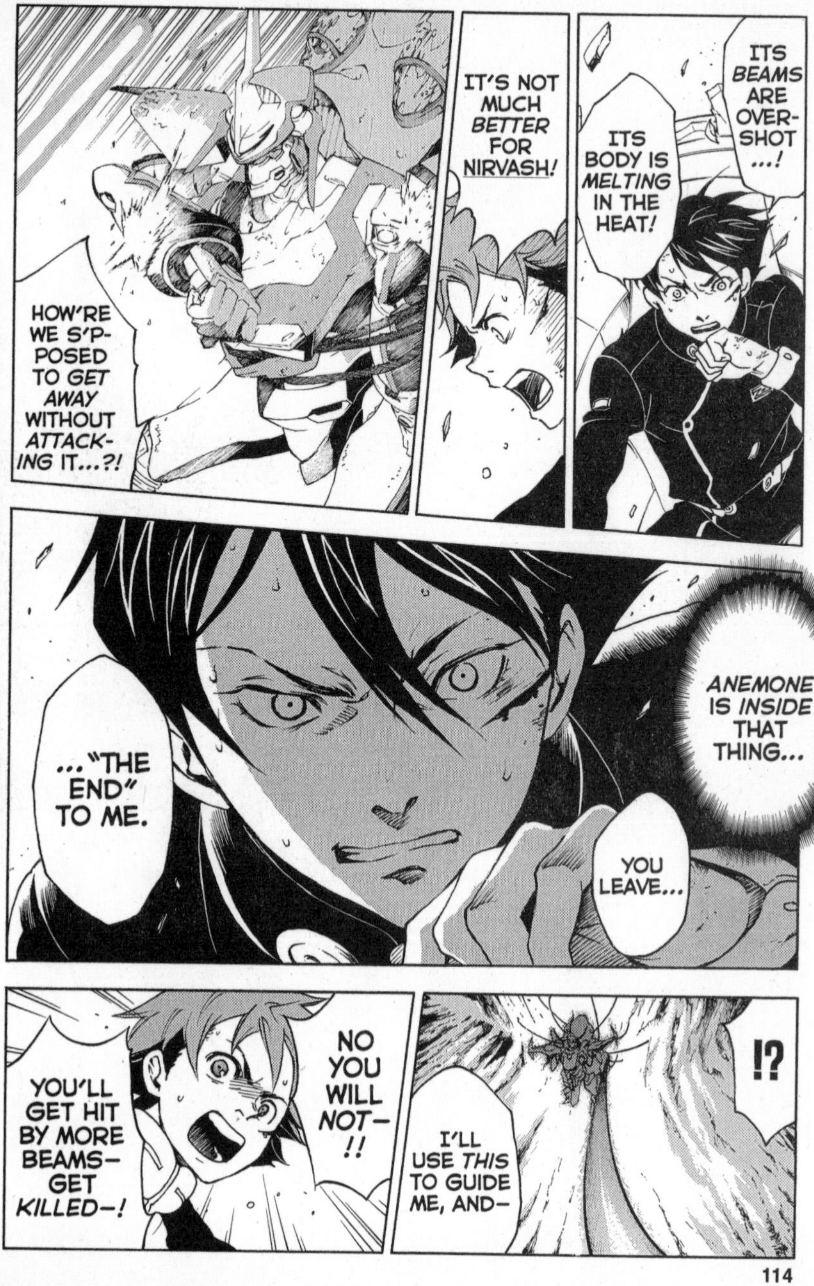
ITS BEAMS ARE OVER-SHOT ...!
ITS BODY IS MELTING IN THE HEAT!
IT'S NOT MUCH BETTER FOR NIRVASH!
HOW'RE WE S'P-POSED TO GET AWAY WITHOUT ATTACK-ING IT...?!
ANEMONE IS INSIDE THAT THING...
YOU LEAVE...
..."THE END" TO ME.
!?
I'LL USE THIS TO GUIDE ME, AND-
NO YOU WILL NOT- !!
YOU'LL GET HIT BY MORE BEAMS- GET KILLED-!

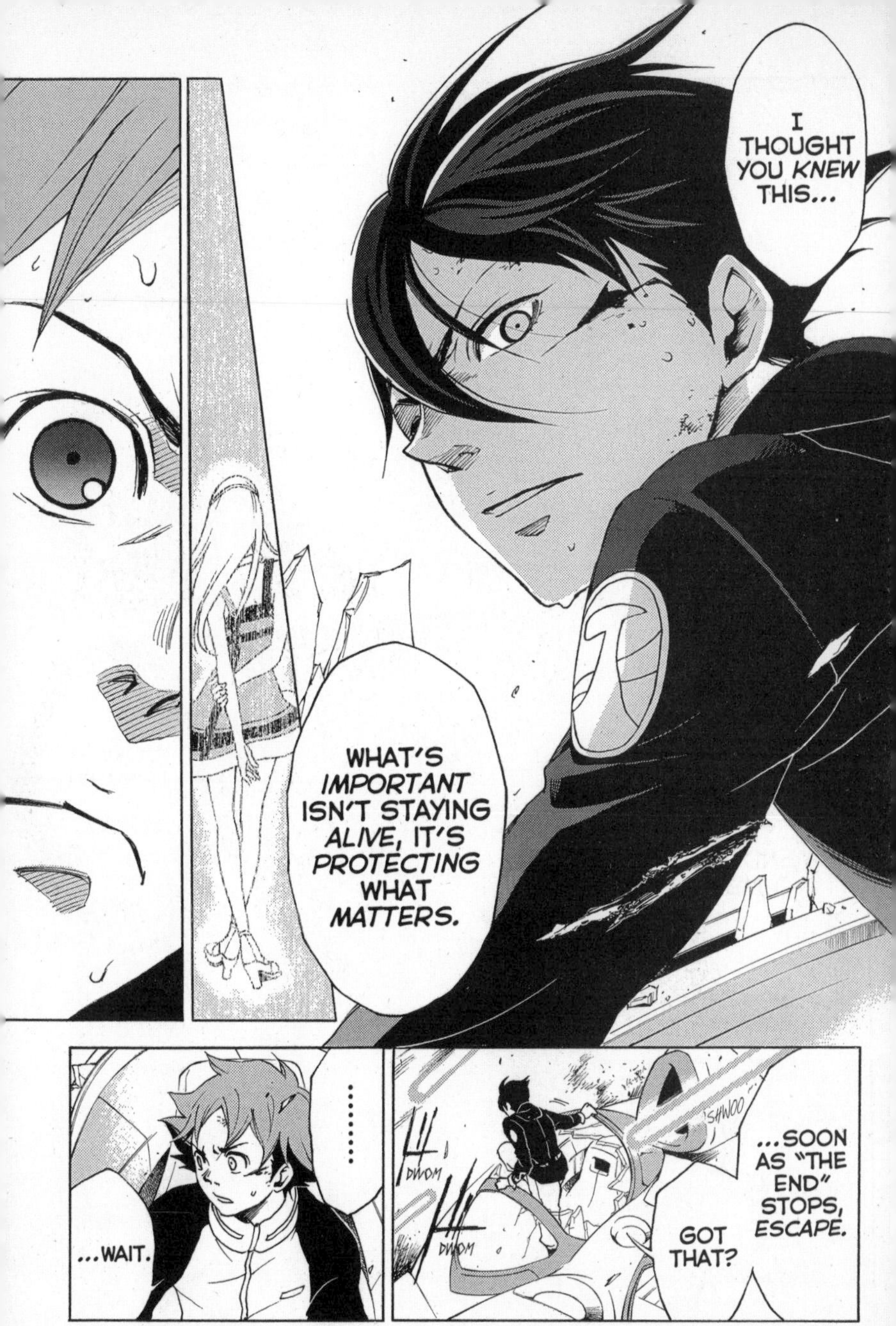
I THOUGHT YOU *KNEW* THIS...
WHAT'S *IMPORTANT* ISN'T STAYING *ALIVE*, IT'S *PROTECTING* WHAT *MATTERS*.
SHWOO
DWOM
DWOM
...SOON AS "THE END" STOPS, *ESCAPE*.
GOT THAT?
......
...WAIT.

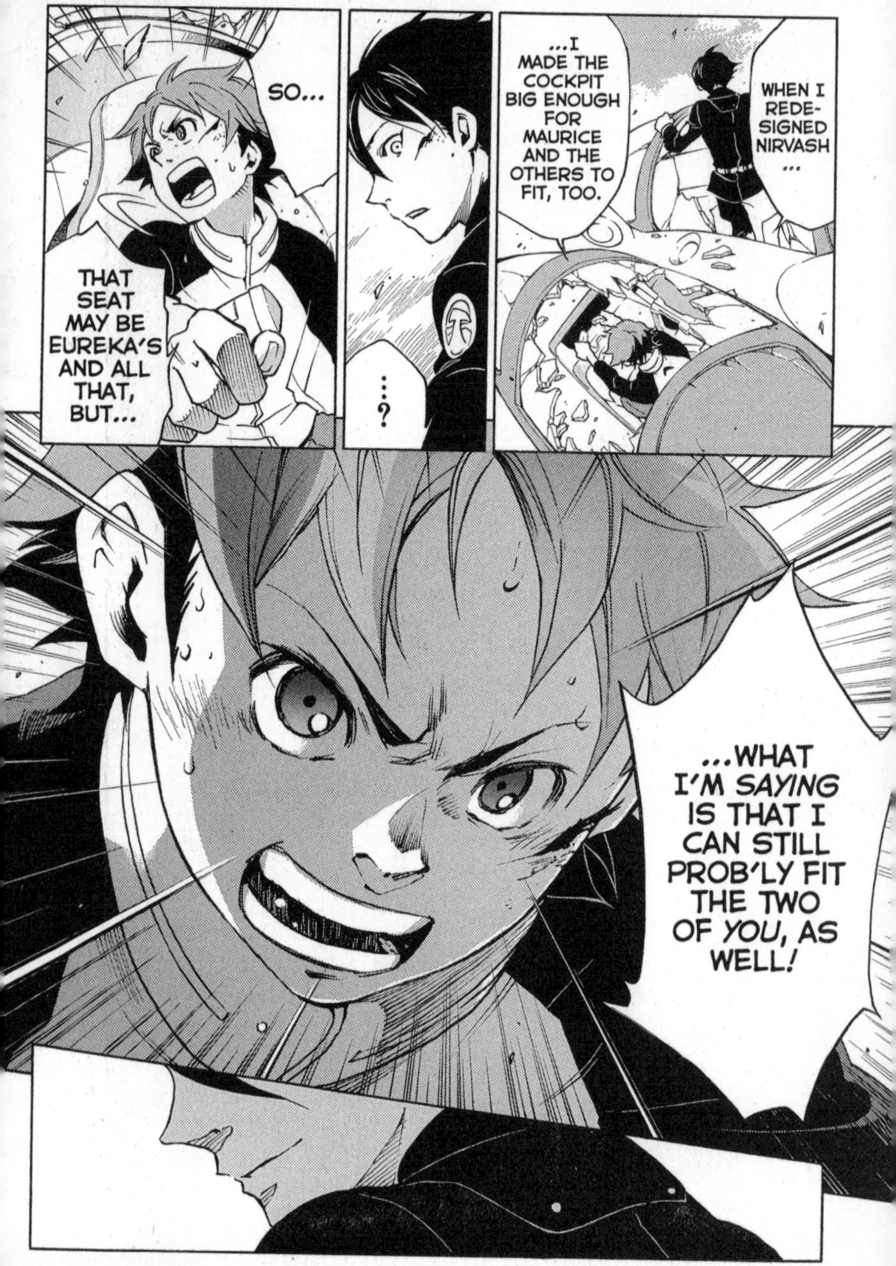
WHEN I REDE-SIGNED NIRVASH ...
...I MADE THE COCKPIT BIG ENOUGH FOR MAURICE AND THE OTHERS TO FIT, TOO.
...?
SO...
THAT SEAT MAY BE EUREKA'S AND ALL THAT, BUT...
...WHAT I'M *SAYING* IS THAT I CAN STILL PROB'LY FIT THE TWO OF *YOU*, AS WELL!

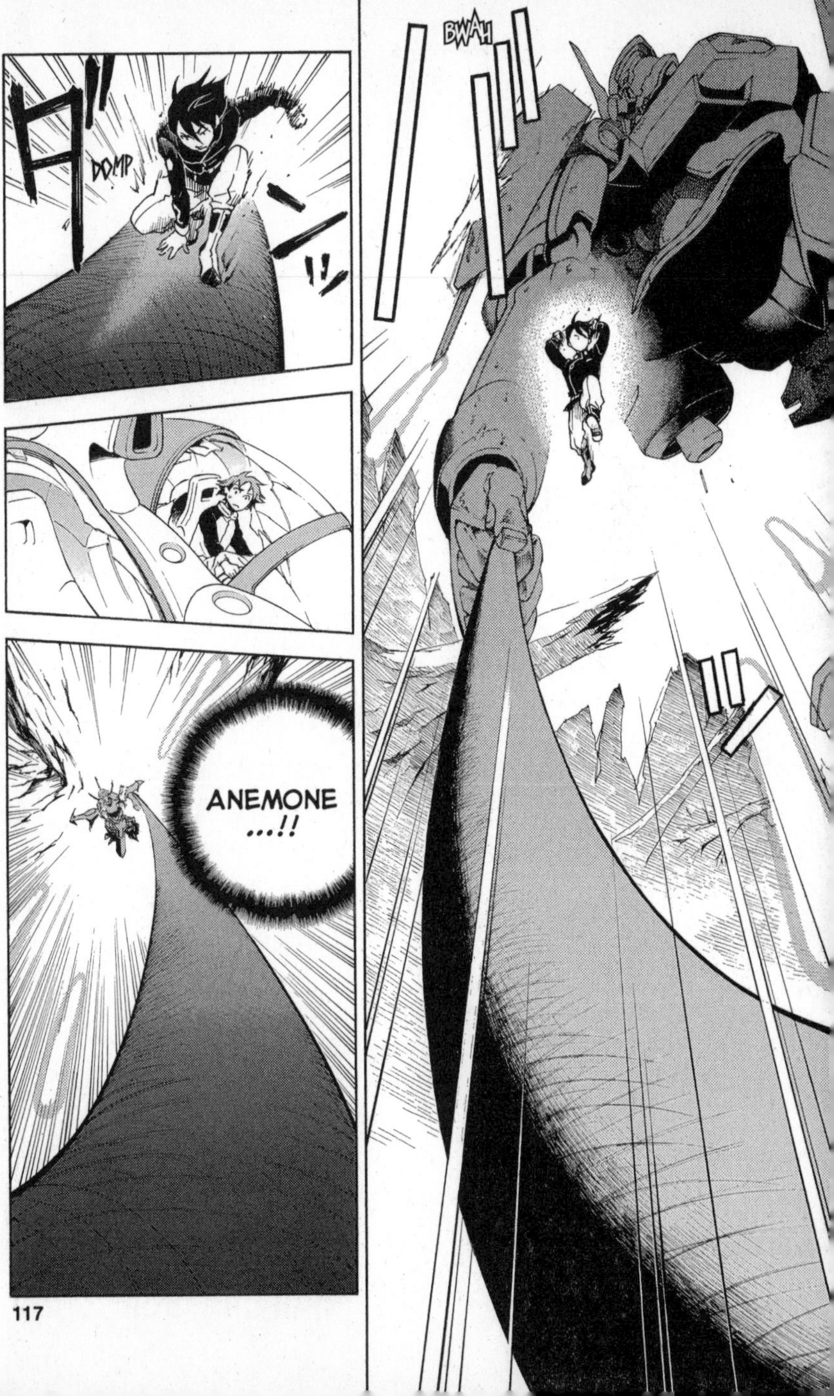
BWAH
DOMP
ANEMONE ...!!

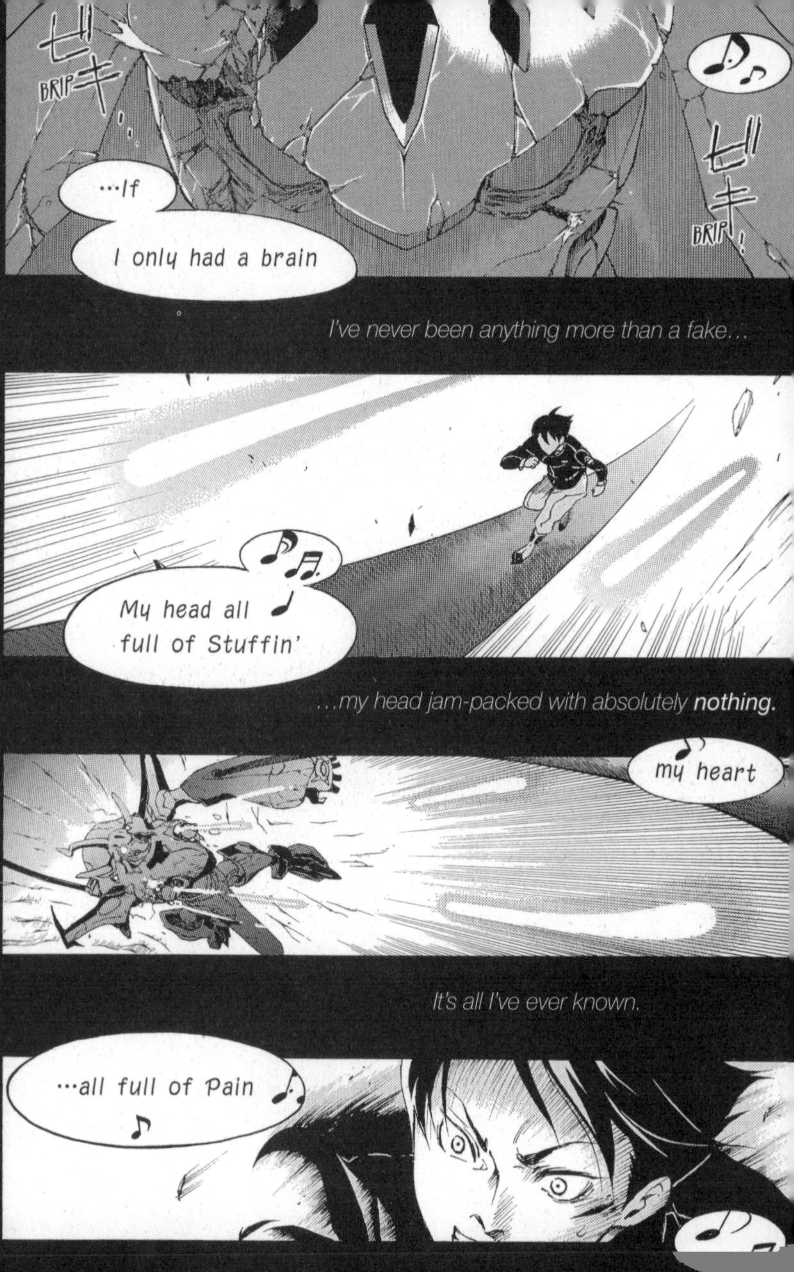
ビキ BRIP!
ビキ BRIP
...If
I only had a brain
I've never been anything more than a fake...
My head all full of Stuffin'
...my head jam-packed with absolutely **nothing.**
my heart
It's all I've ever known.
...all full of Pain

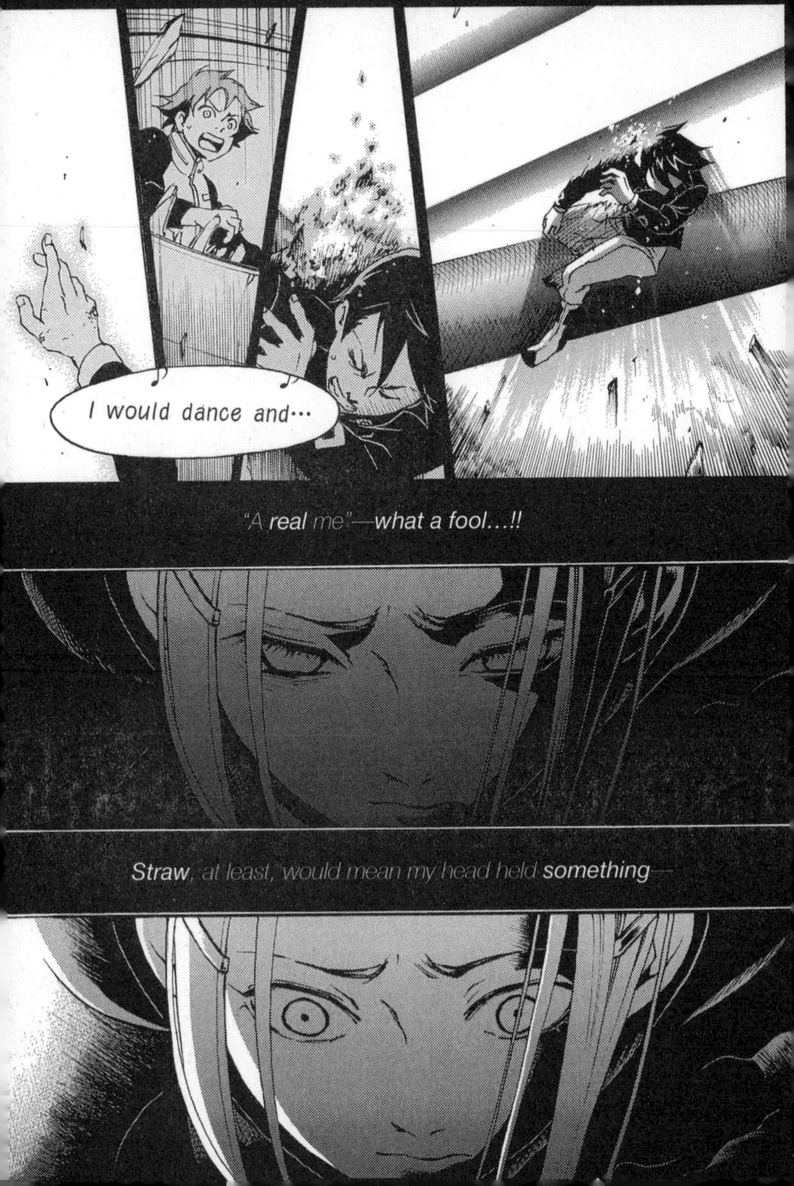
I would dance and…
"A real me"—what a fool…!!
Straw, at least, would mean my head held something—

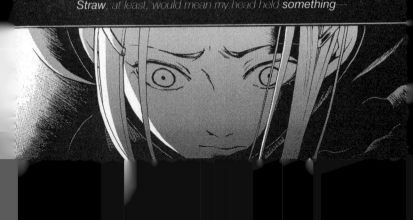

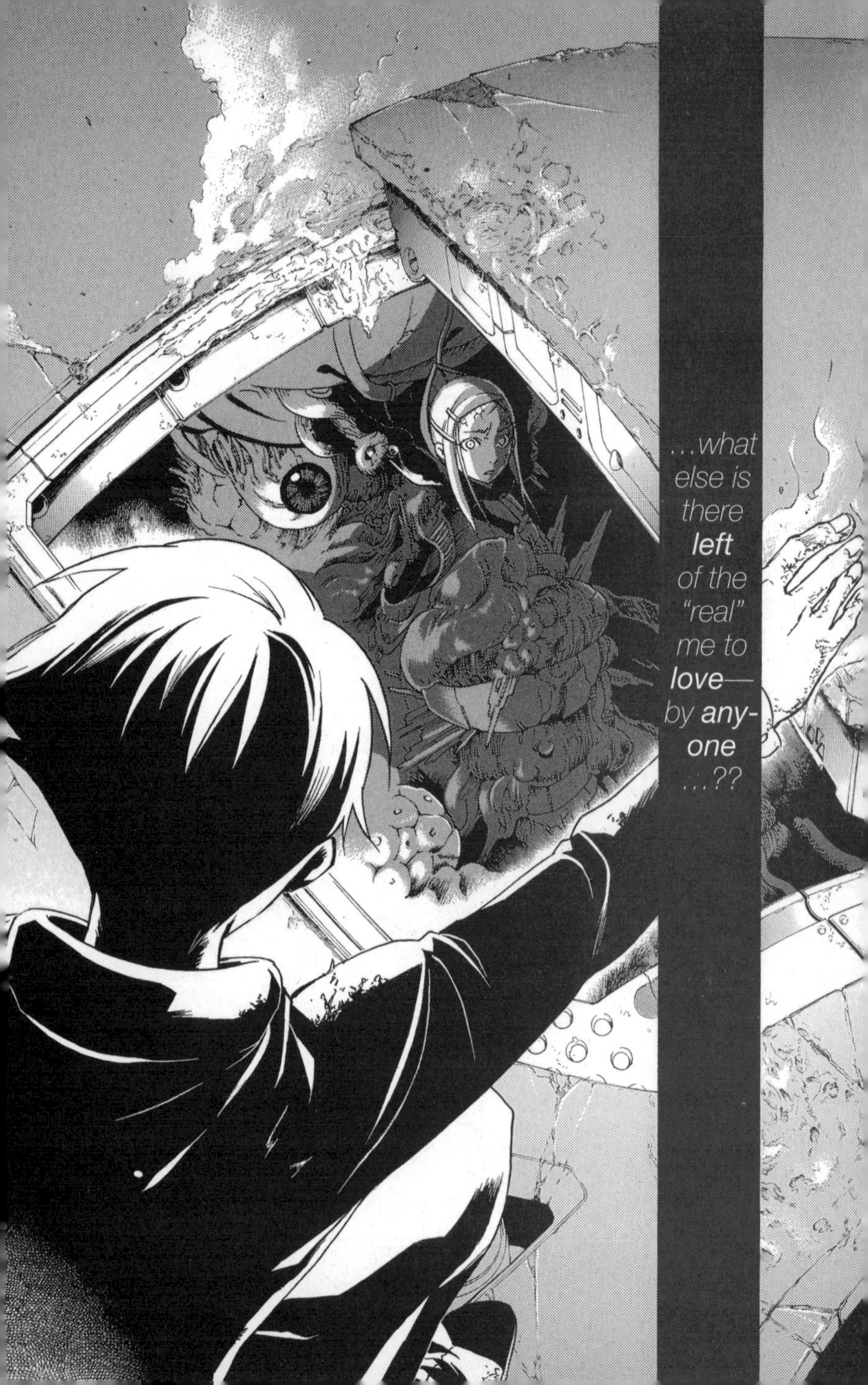

...what else is there **left** of the "real" me to **love**— by **any-one** ...??

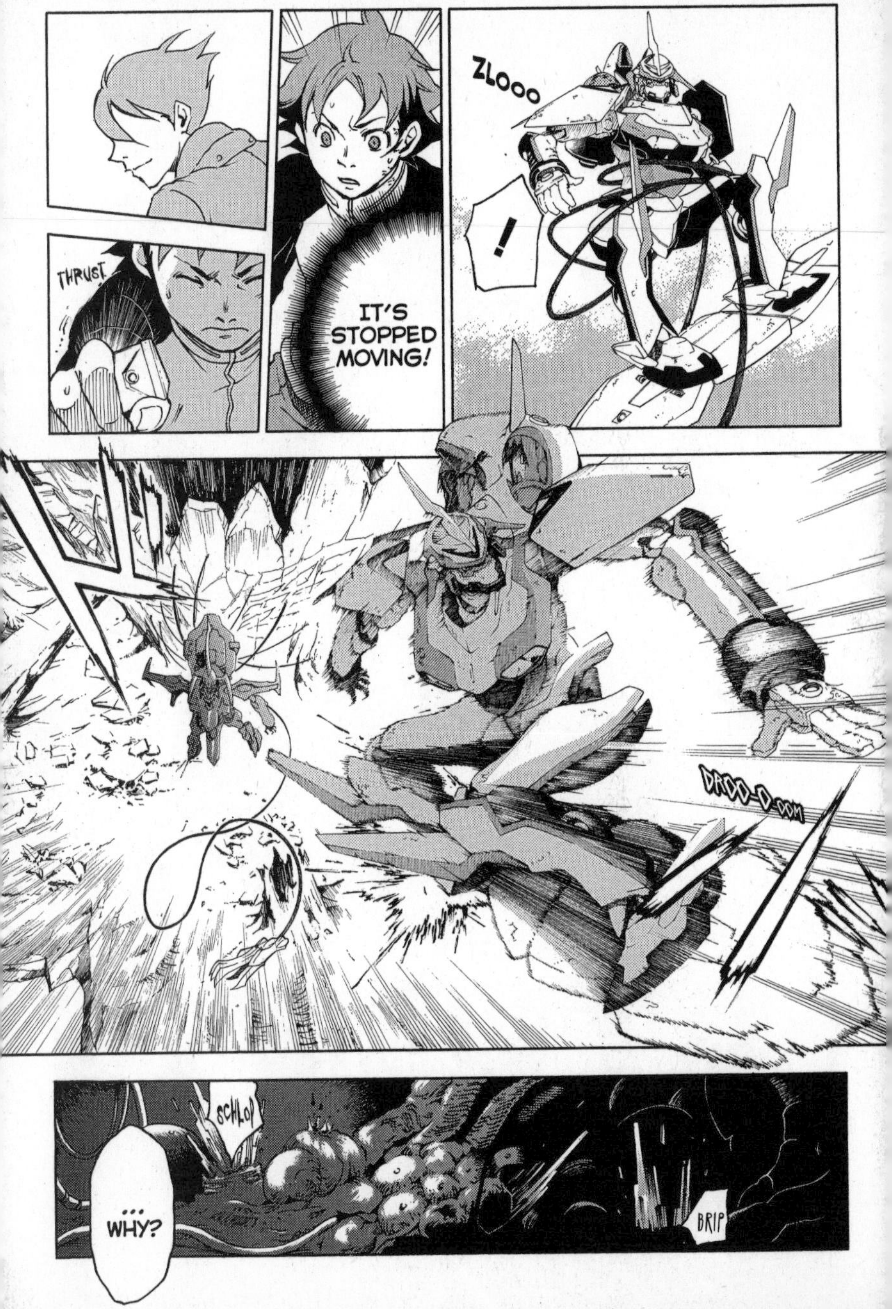
ZLOOO
!
IT'S STOPPED MOVING!
THRUST
DRDO-O-OOM
BRIP
SCHLOP
...WHY?

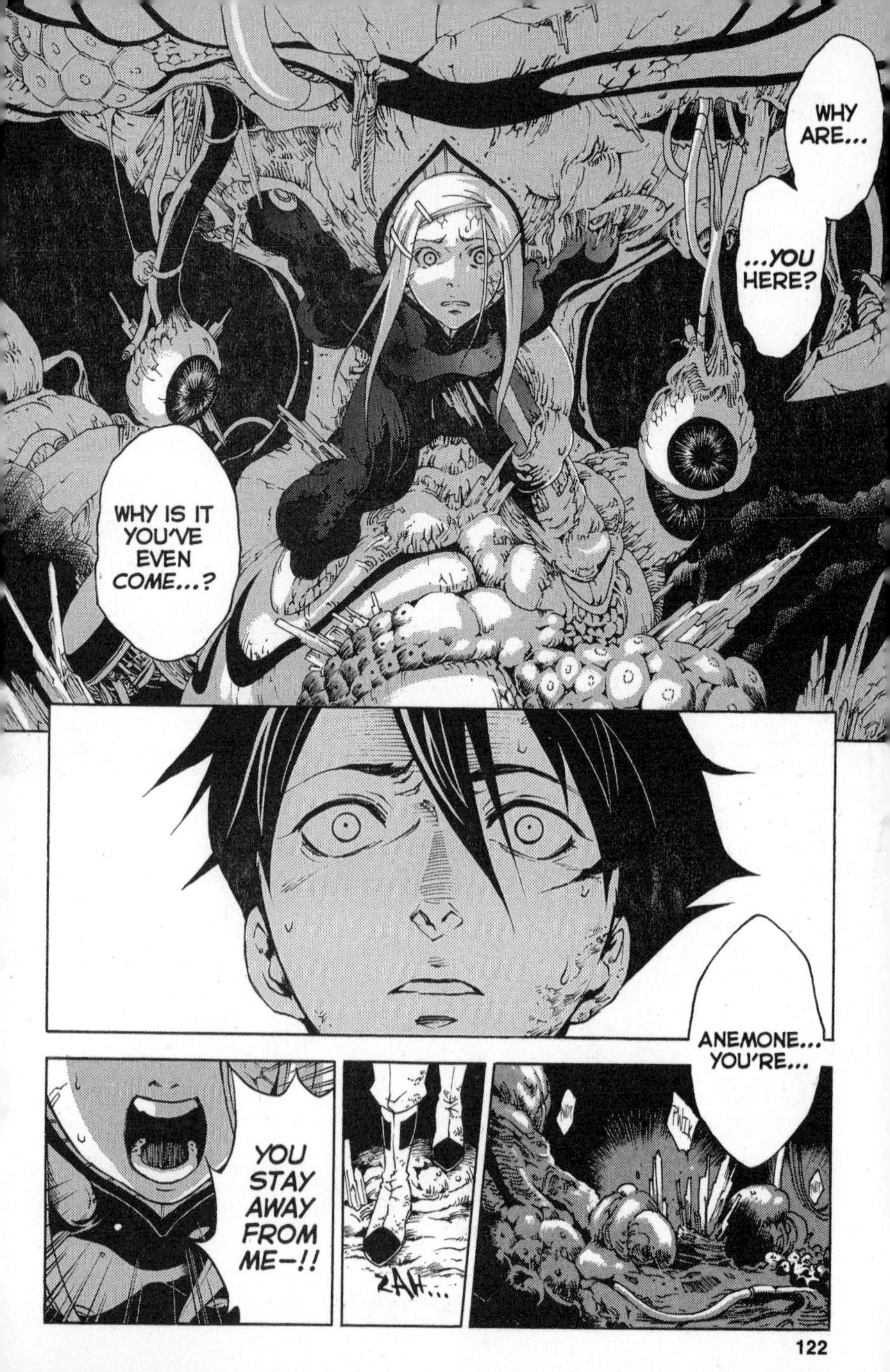
WHY ARE...
...YOU HERE?
WHY IS IT YOU'VE EVEN COME...?
ANEMONE... YOU'RE...
PWIK
ZAH...
YOU STAY AWAY FROM ME—!!

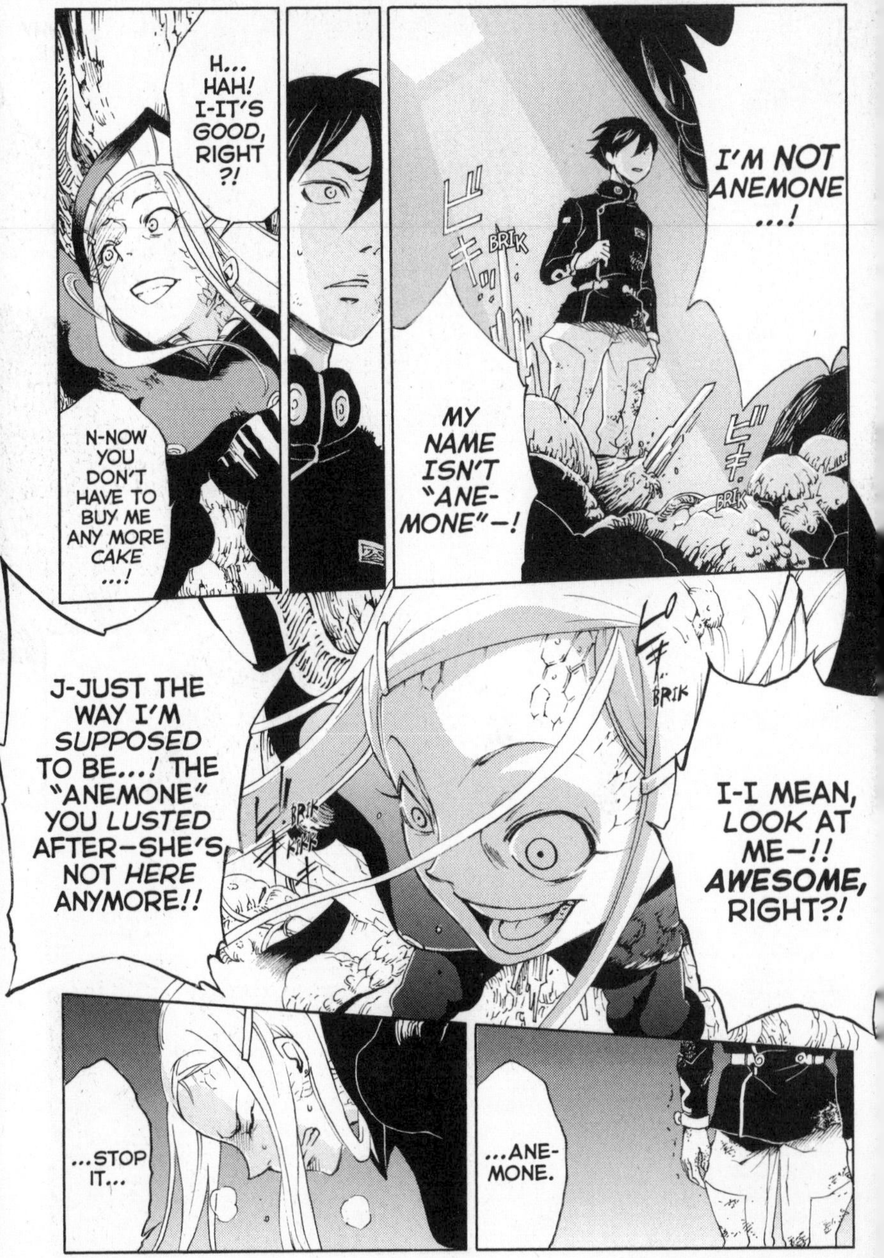
I'M NOT ANEMONE ...!
BRIK
MY NAME ISN'T "ANE-MONE"-!
BRIK
H... HAH! I-IT'S GOOD, RIGHT?!
N-NOW YOU DON'T HAVE TO BUY ME ANY MORE CAKE ...!
BRIK
I-I MEAN, LOOK AT ME-!! AWESOME, RIGHT?!
BRIK KRIK
J-JUST THE WAY I'M SUPPOSED TO BE...! THE "ANEMONE" YOU LUSTED AFTER-SHE'S NOT HERE ANYMORE!!
...ANE-MONE.
...STOP IT...

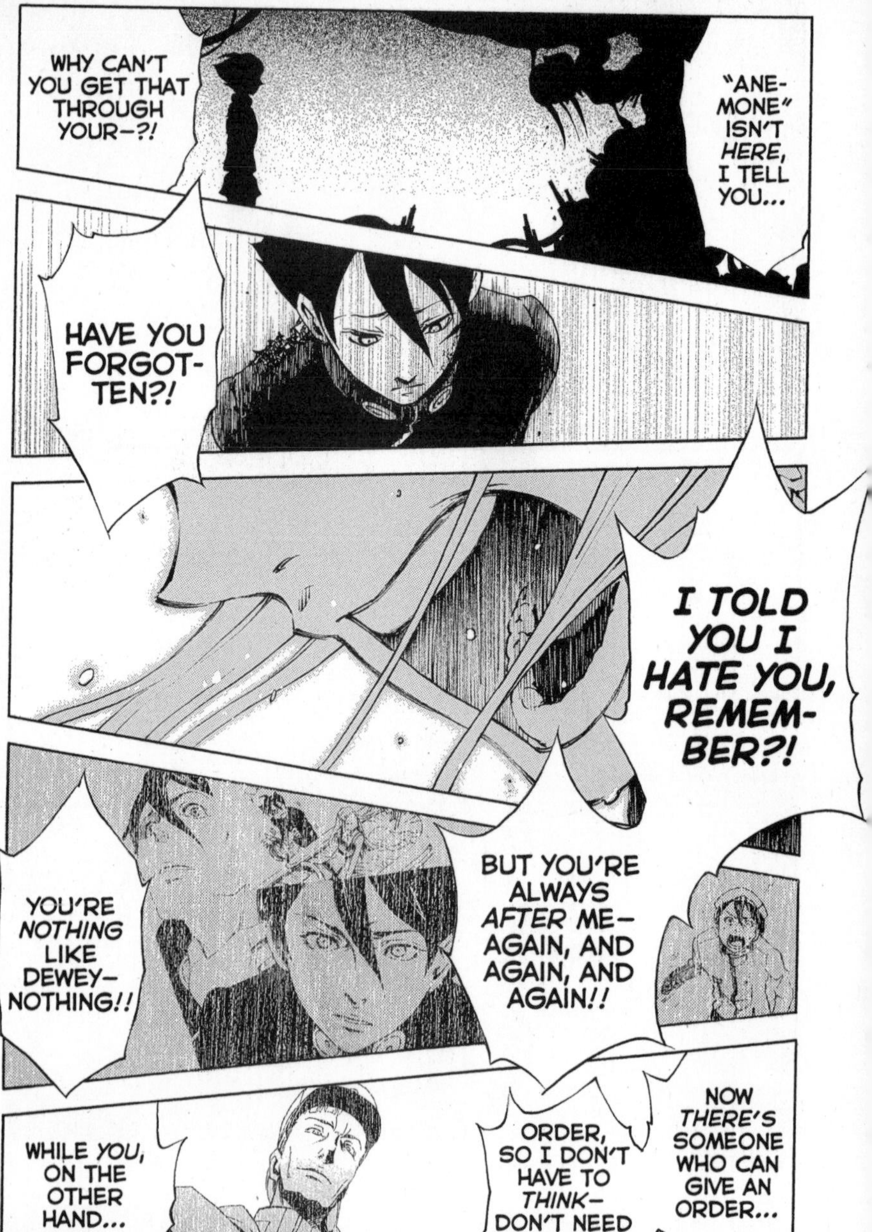
"ANEMONE" ISN'T HERE, I TELL YOU...
WHY CAN'T YOU GET THAT THROUGH YOUR—?!
HAVE YOU FORGOTTEN?!
I TOLD YOU I HATE YOU, REMEMBER?!
BUT YOU'RE ALWAYS AFTER ME—AGAIN, AND AGAIN, AND AGAIN!!
YOU'RE NOTHING LIKE DEWEY—NOTHING!!
NOW THERE'S SOMEONE WHO CAN GIVE AN ORDER...
ORDER, SO I DON'T HAVE TO THINK—DON'T NEED A BRAIN!
WHILE YOU, ON THE OTHER HAND...

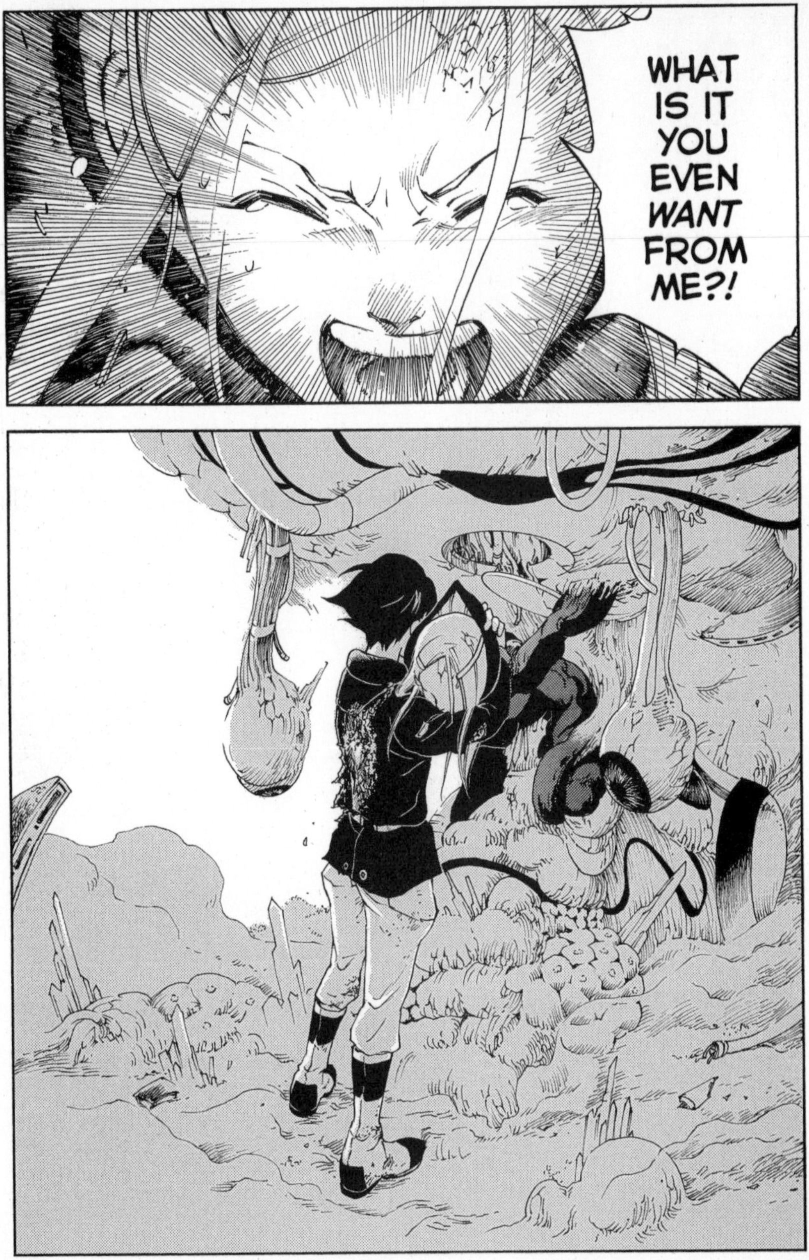
WHAT IS IT YOU EVEN *WANT* FROM ME?!

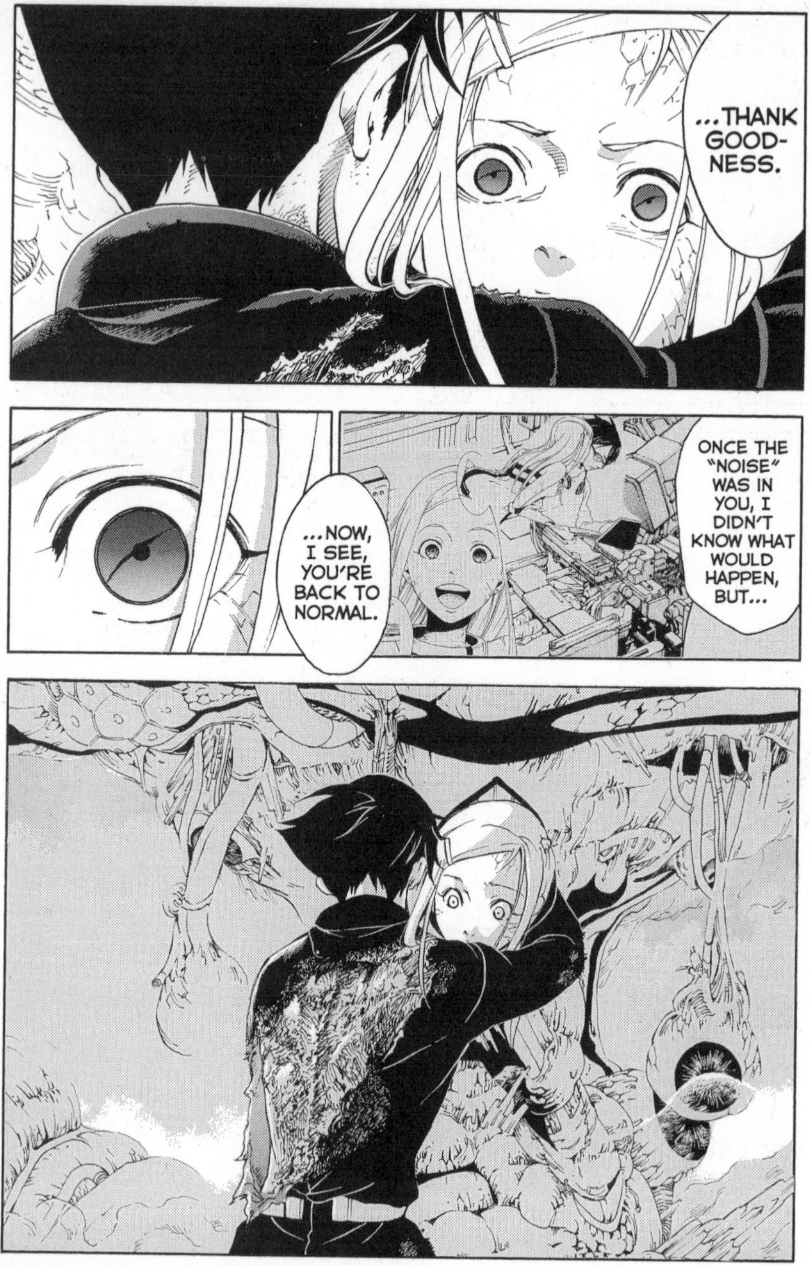
...THANK GOODNESS.
ONCE THE "NOISE" WAS IN YOU, I DIDN'T KNOW WHAT WOULD HAPPEN, BUT...
...NOW, I SEE, YOU'RE BACK TO NORMAL.

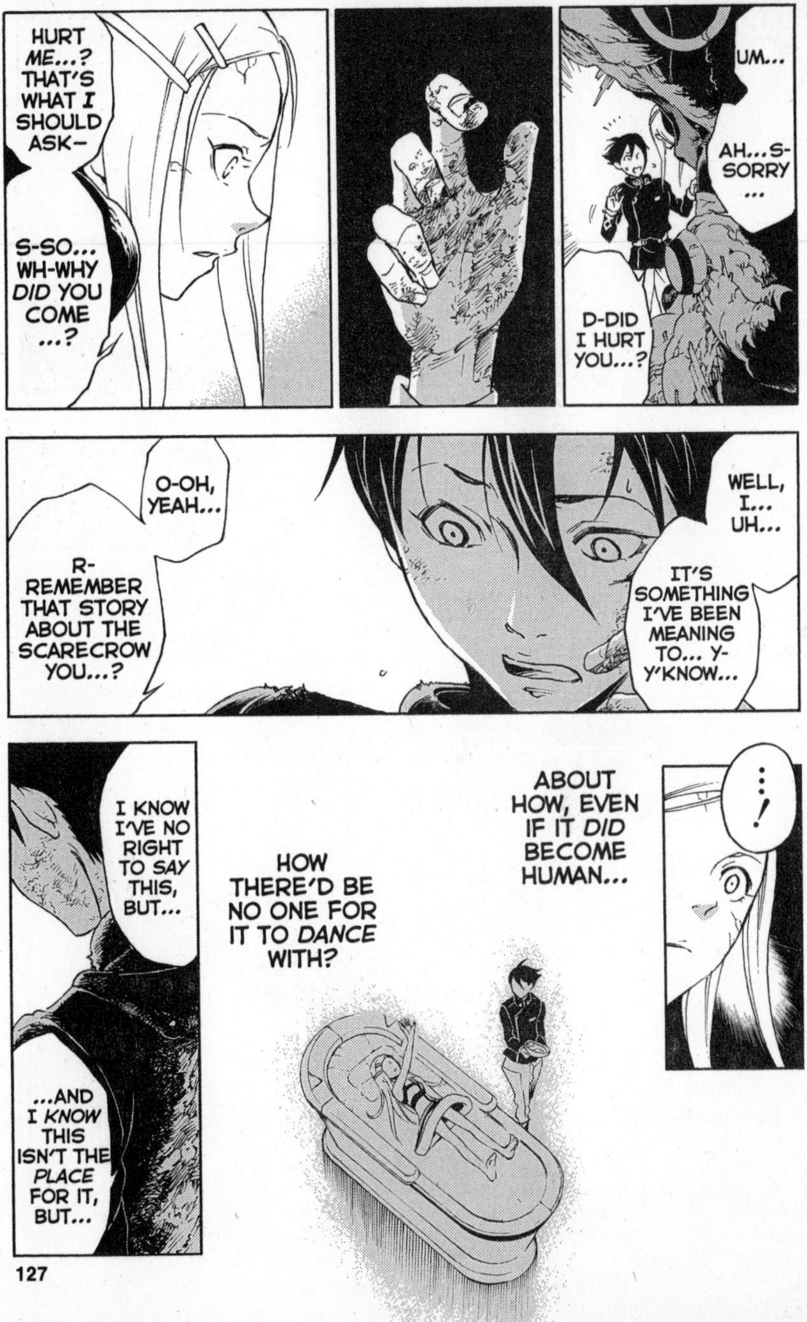
UM...
AH... S-SORRY ...
D-DID I HURT YOU...?
HURT *ME*...? THAT'S WHAT *I* SHOULD ASK—
S-SO... WH-WHY *DID* YOU COME ...?
WELL, I... UH...
IT'S SOMETHING I'VE BEEN MEANING TO... Y-Y'KNOW...
O-OH, YEAH...
R-REMEMBER THAT STORY ABOUT THE SCARECROW YOU...?
...!
ABOUT HOW, EVEN IF IT *DID* BECOME HUMAN...
HOW THERE'D BE NO ONE FOR IT TO *DANCE* WITH?
I KNOW I'VE NO RIGHT TO *SAY* THIS, BUT...
...AND I *KNOW* THIS ISN'T THE *PLACE* FOR IT, BUT...

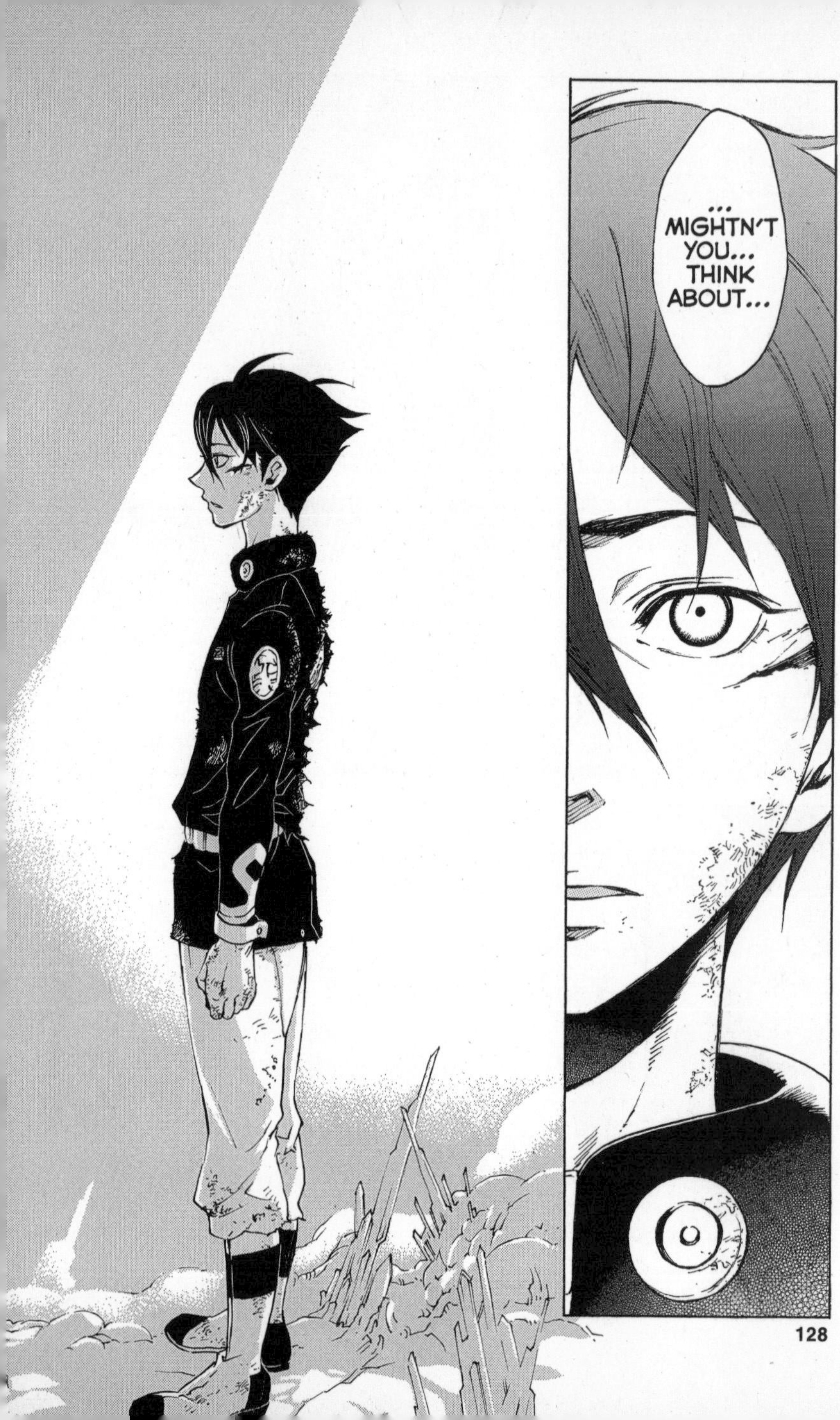
...
MIGHTN'T YOU... THINK ABOUT...

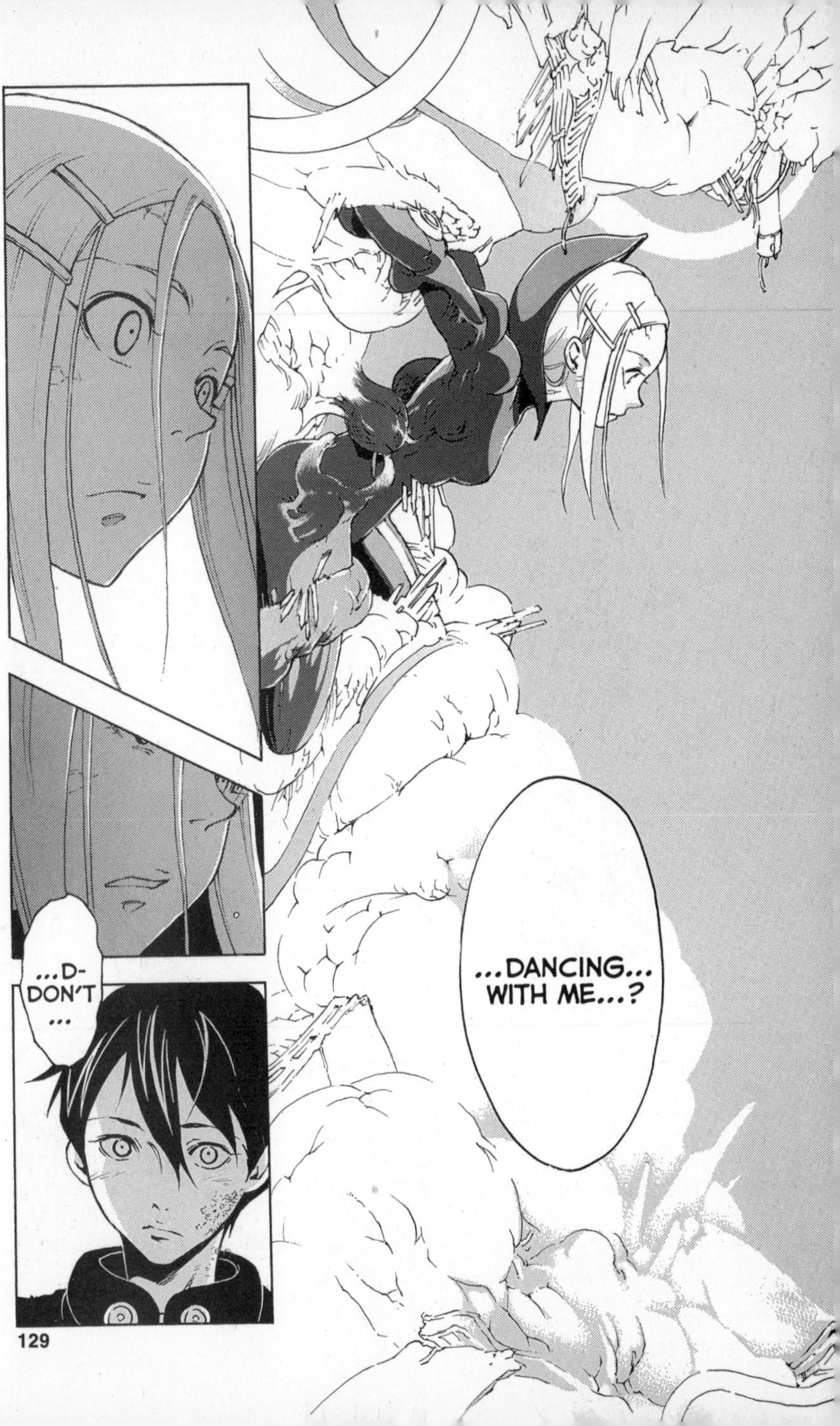
...DANCING... WITH ME...?
...D- DON'T ...

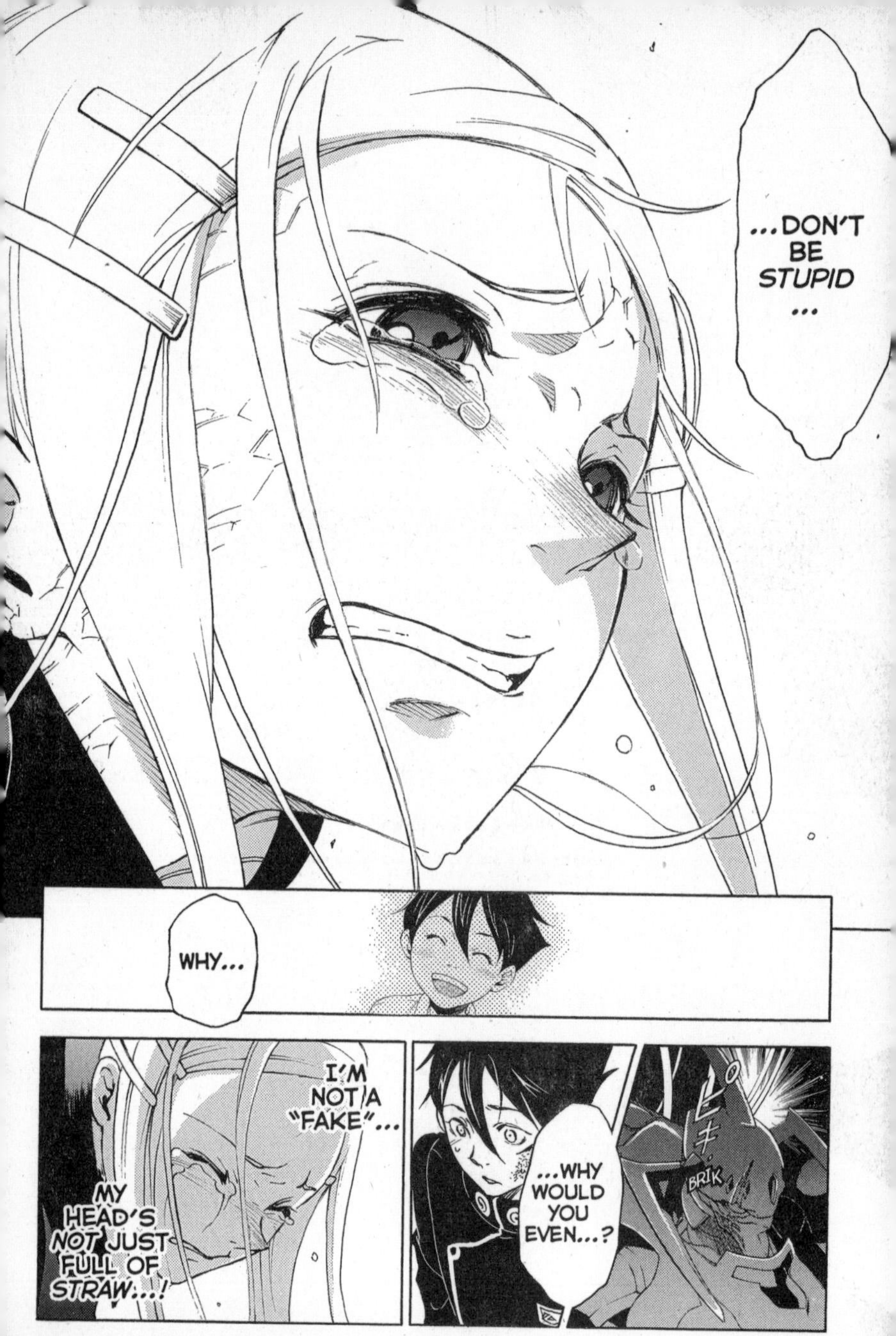
...DON'T BE STUPID...
WHY...
...WHY WOULD YOU EVEN...?
BRIK
I'M NOT A "FAKE"...
MY HEAD'S NOT JUST FULL OF STRAW...!

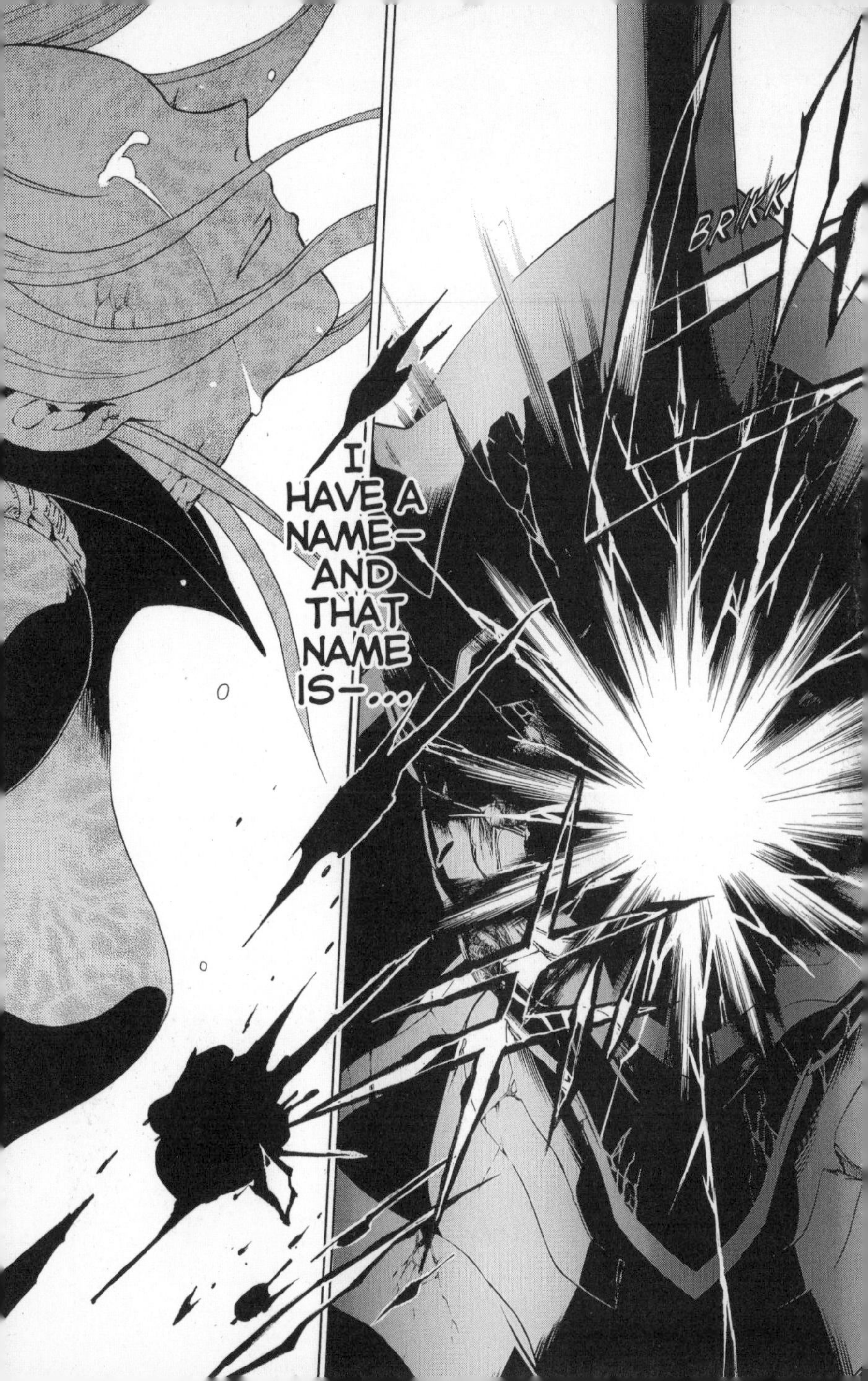
BRIKK
I HAVE A NAME— AND THAT NAME IS—...

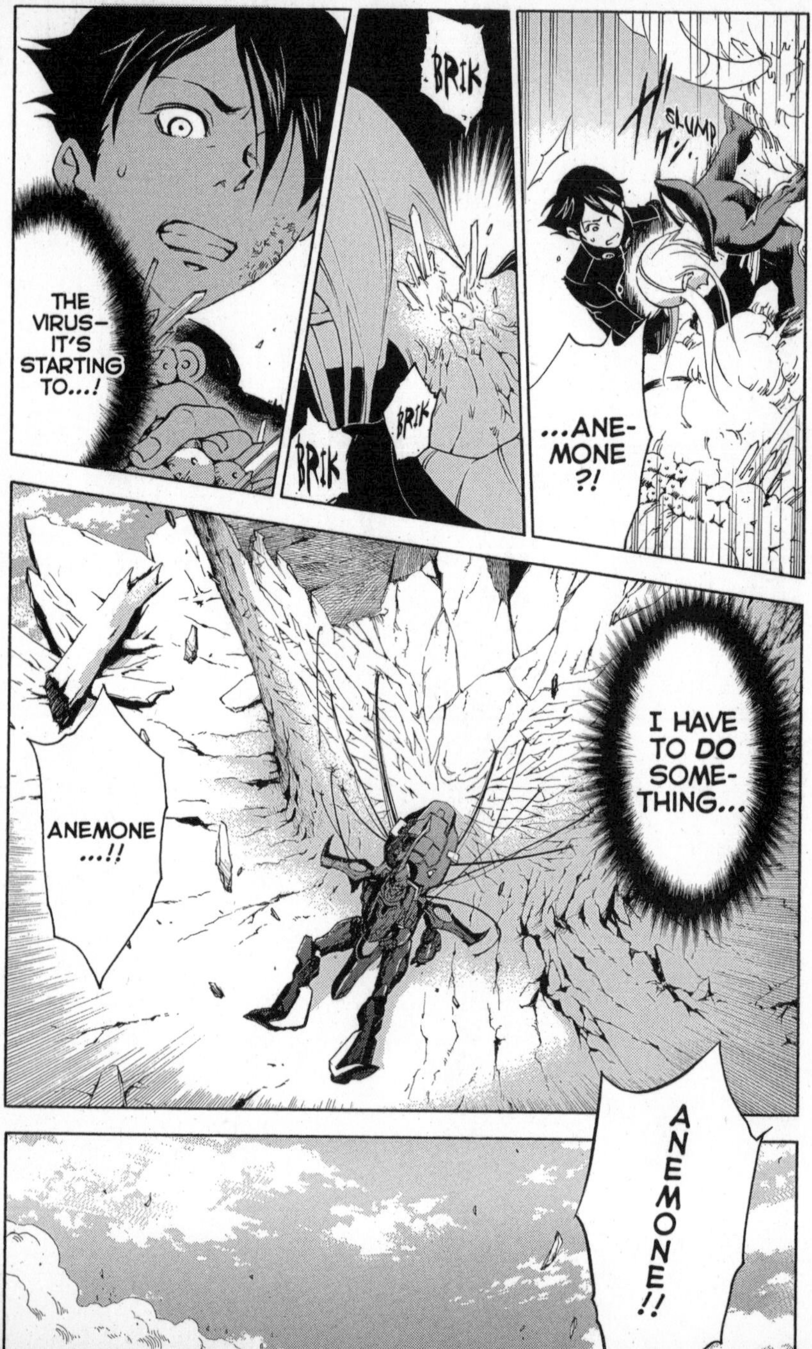
SLUMP
...ANEMONE?!
BRIK
BRIK
BRIK
THE VIRUS—IT'S STARTING TO...!
I HAVE TO *DO* SOMETHING...
ANEMONE...!!
ANEMONE!!

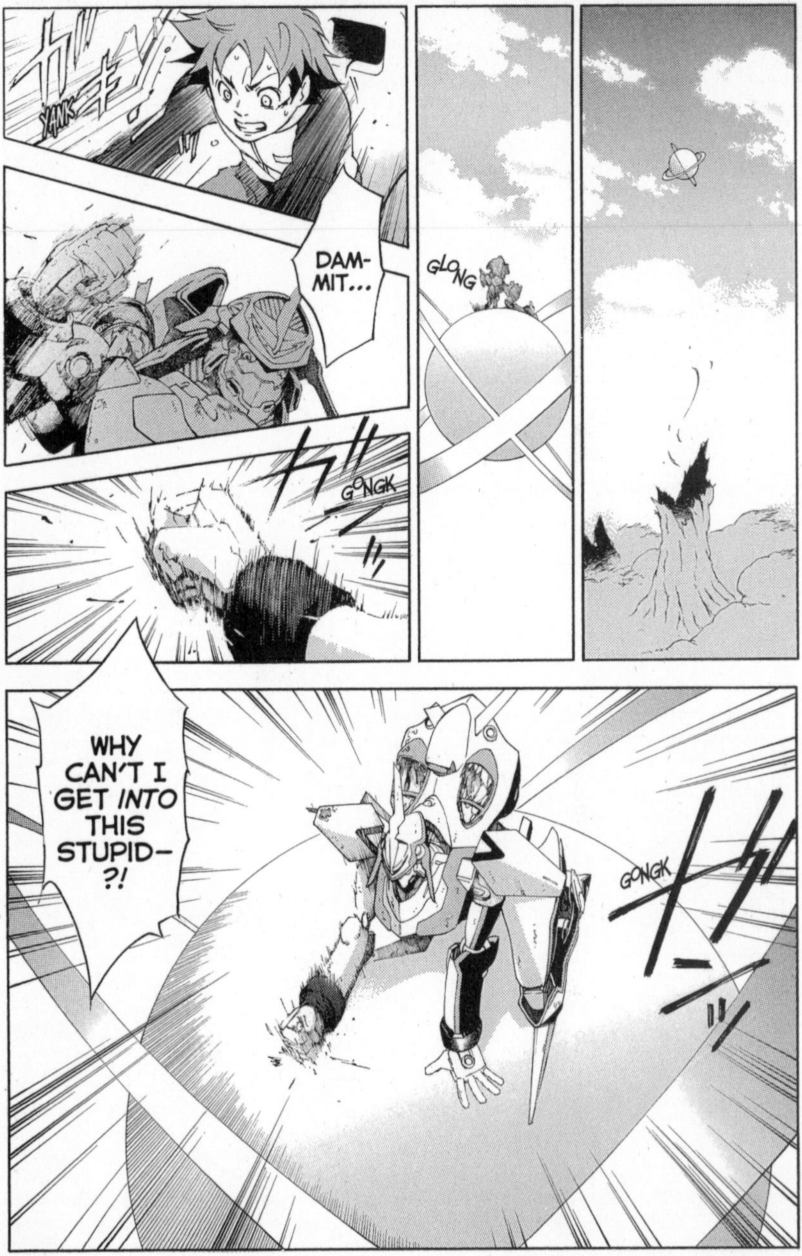
GLONG
YANK
DAM-MIT...
GONGK
WHY CAN'T I GET *INTO* THIS STUPID—?!
GONGK

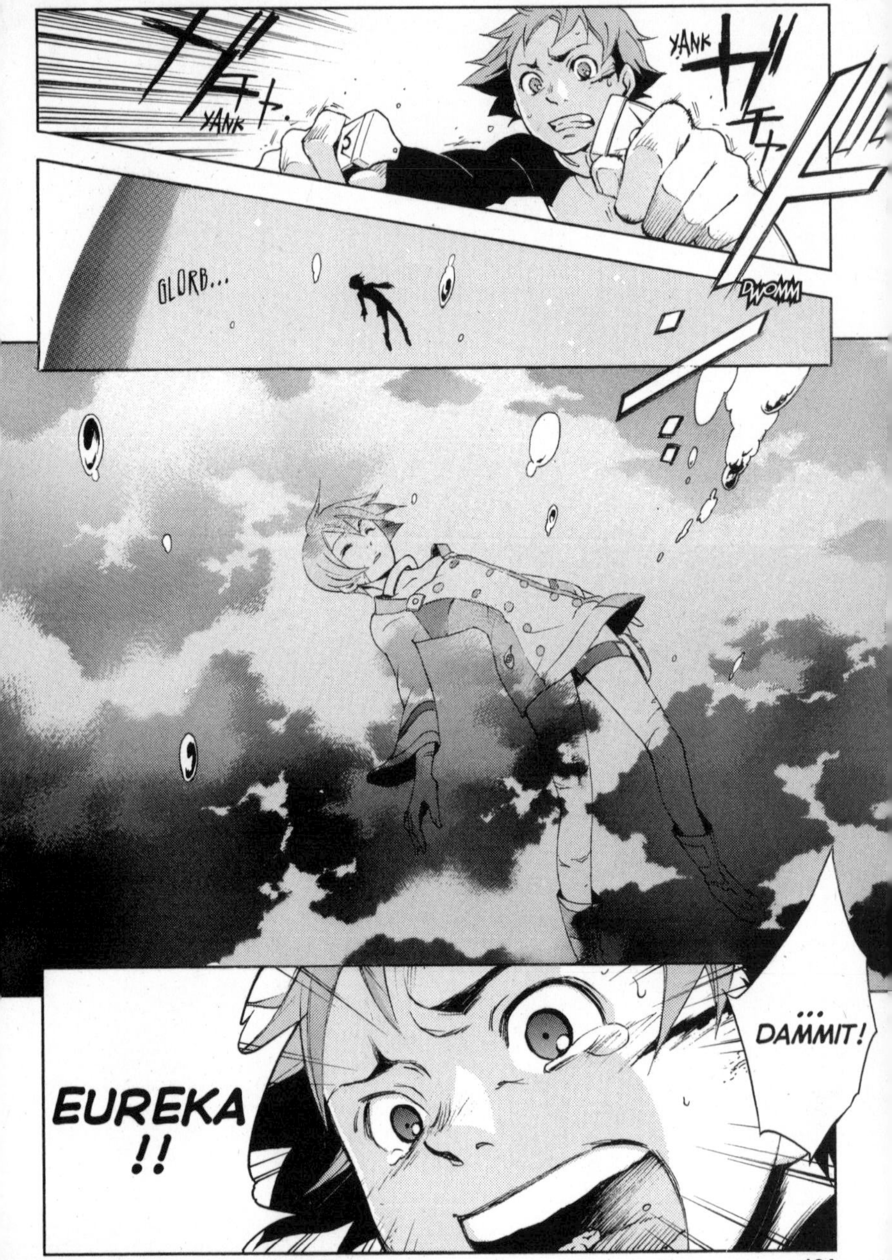
YANK
YANK
DWOMM
GLORB...
...DAMMIT!
EUREKA !!

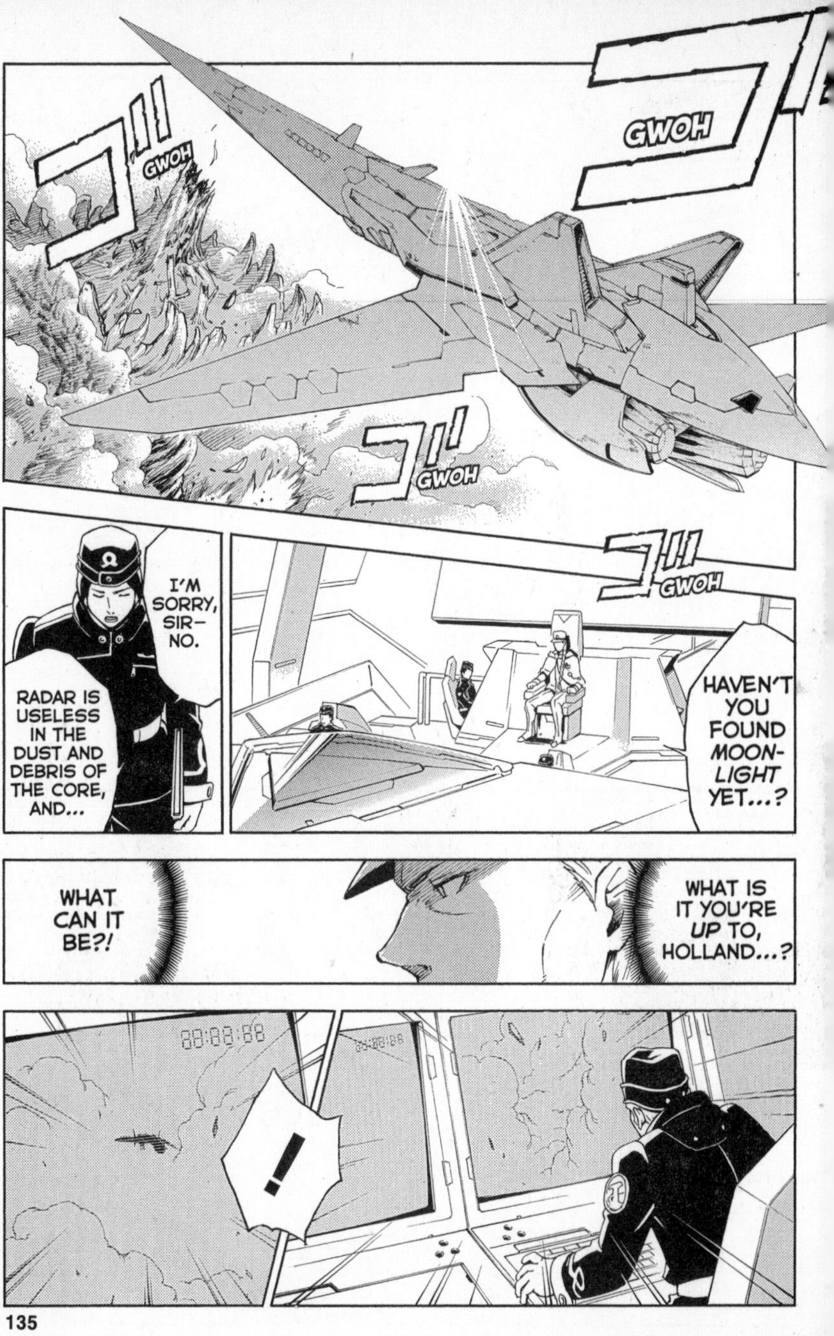
GWOH
GWOH
GWOH
GWOH
HAVEN'T YOU FOUND *MOON-LIGHT* YET...?
I'M SORRY, SIR— NO.
RADAR IS USELESS IN THE DUST AND DEBRIS OF THE CORE, AND...
WHAT IS IT YOU'RE *UP TO*, HOLLAND...?
WHAT CAN IT BE?!
!

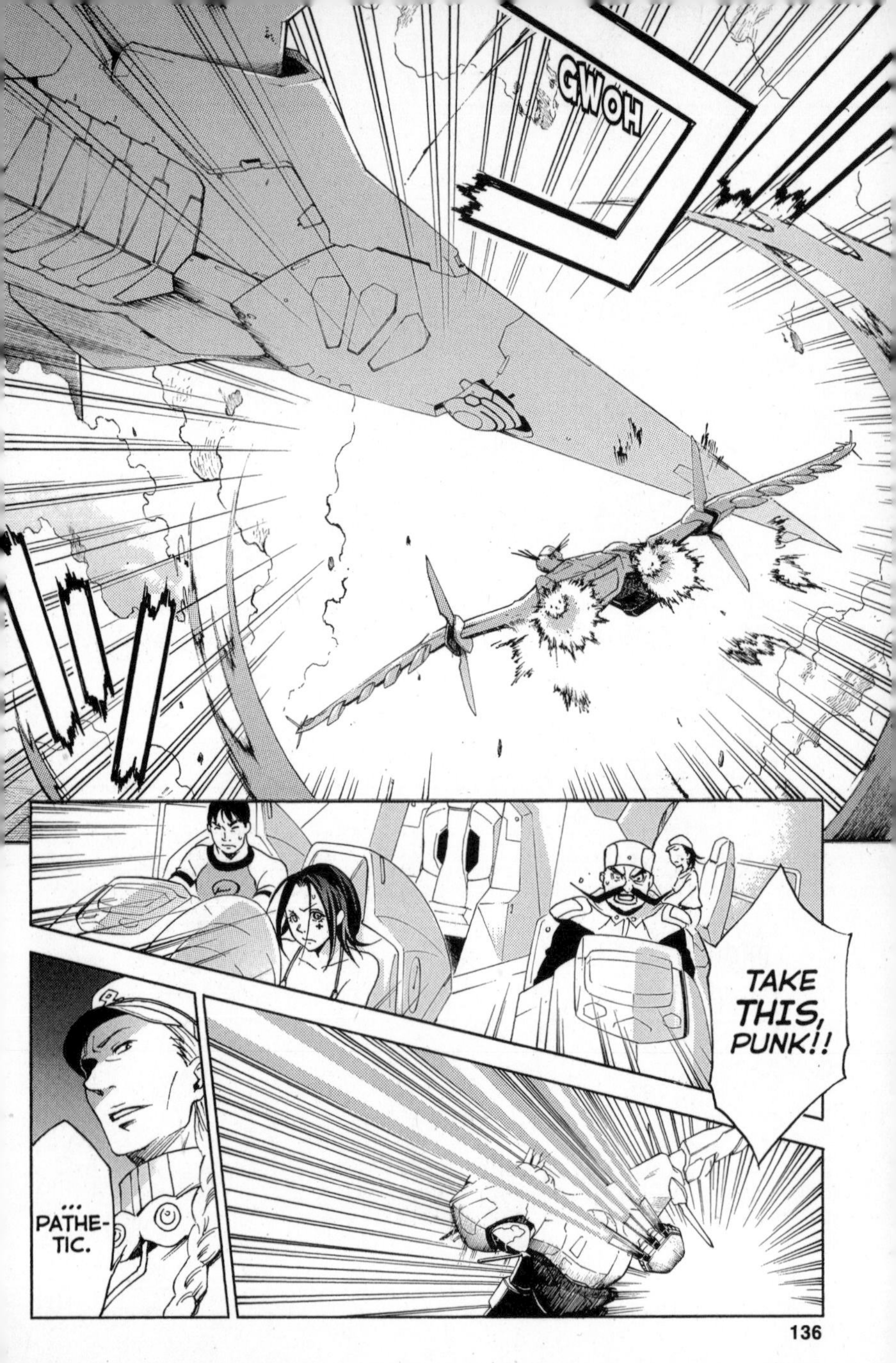
GWOH
TAKE THIS, PUNK!!
...PATHE-TIC.

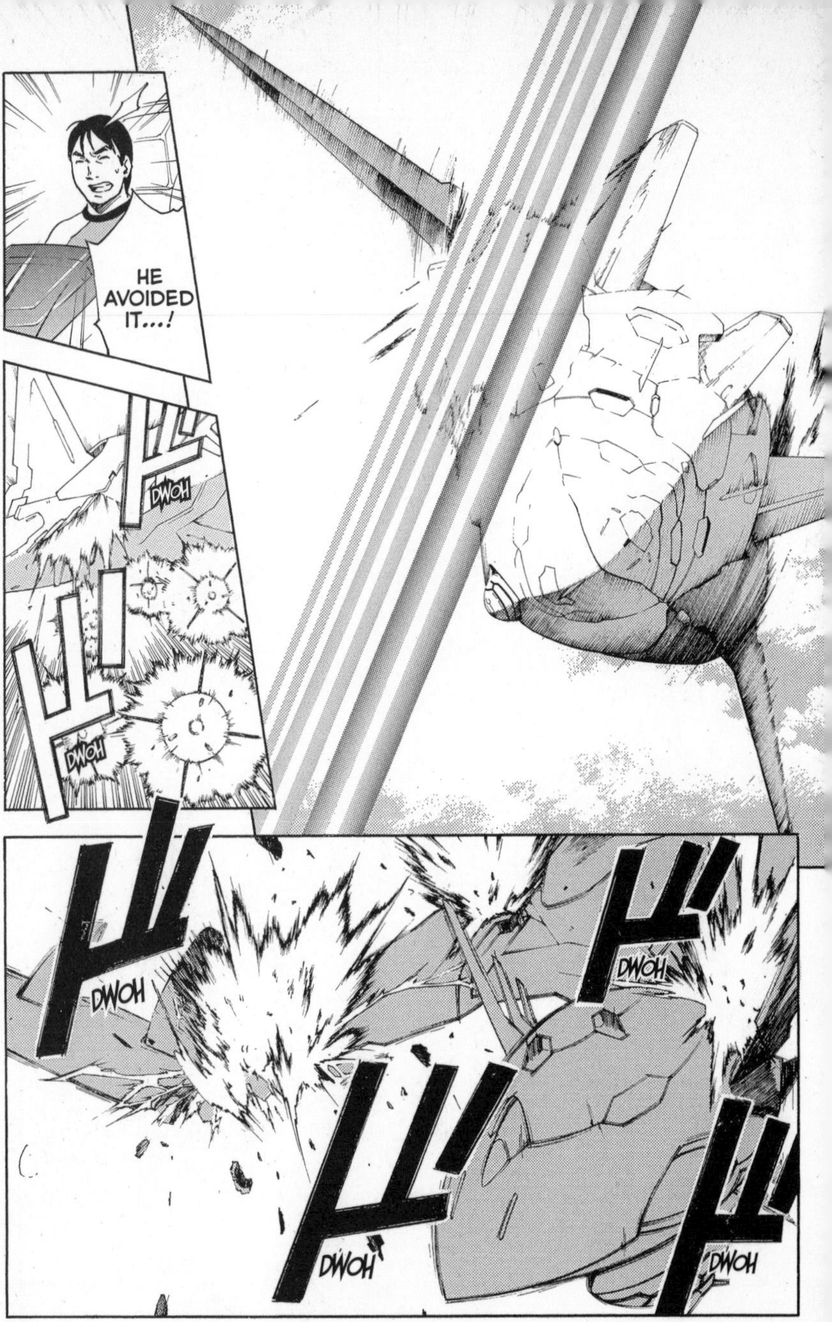
HE AVOIDED IT...!
DWOH
DWOH
DWOH
DWOH
DWOH
DWOH

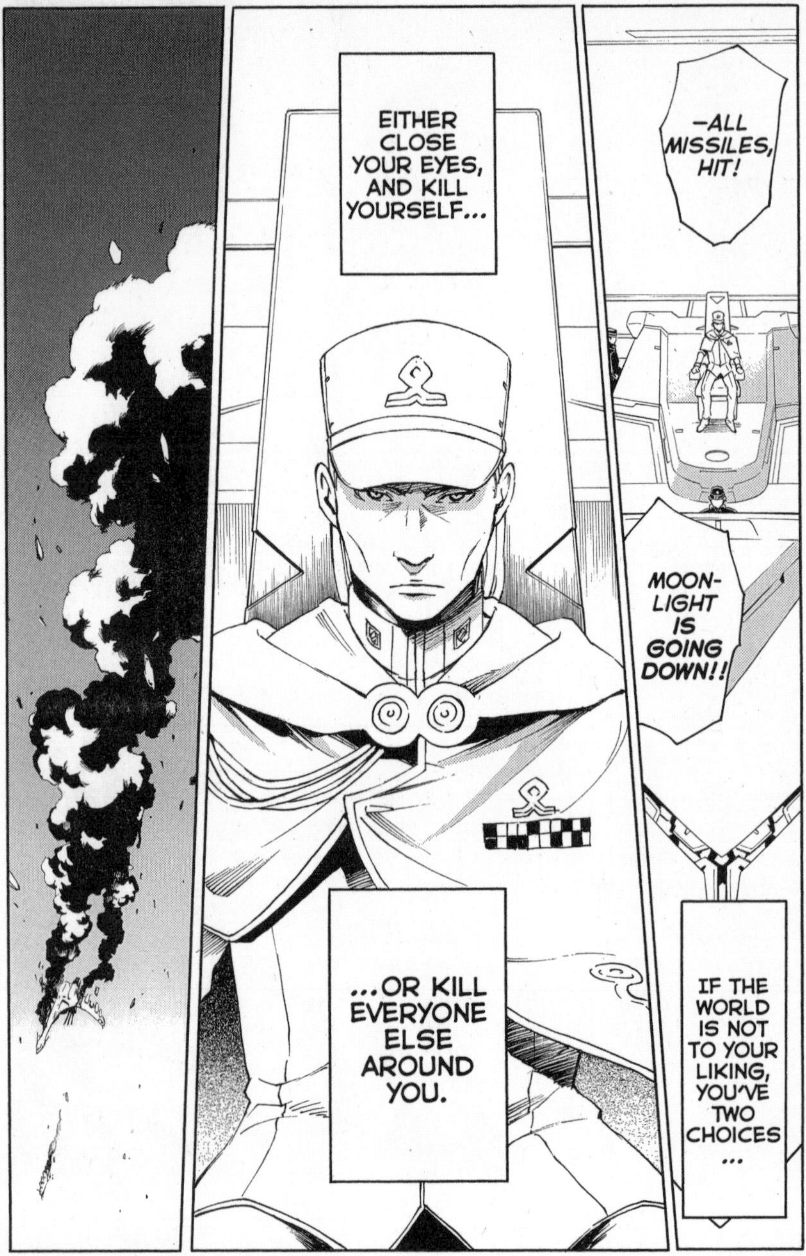
—ALL MISSILES, HIT!
MOON-LIGHT IS GOING DOWN!!
IF THE WORLD IS NOT TO YOUR LIKING, YOU'VE TWO CHOICES ...
EITHER CLOSE YOUR EYES, AND KILL YOURSELF...
...OR KILL EVERYONE ELSE AROUND YOU.

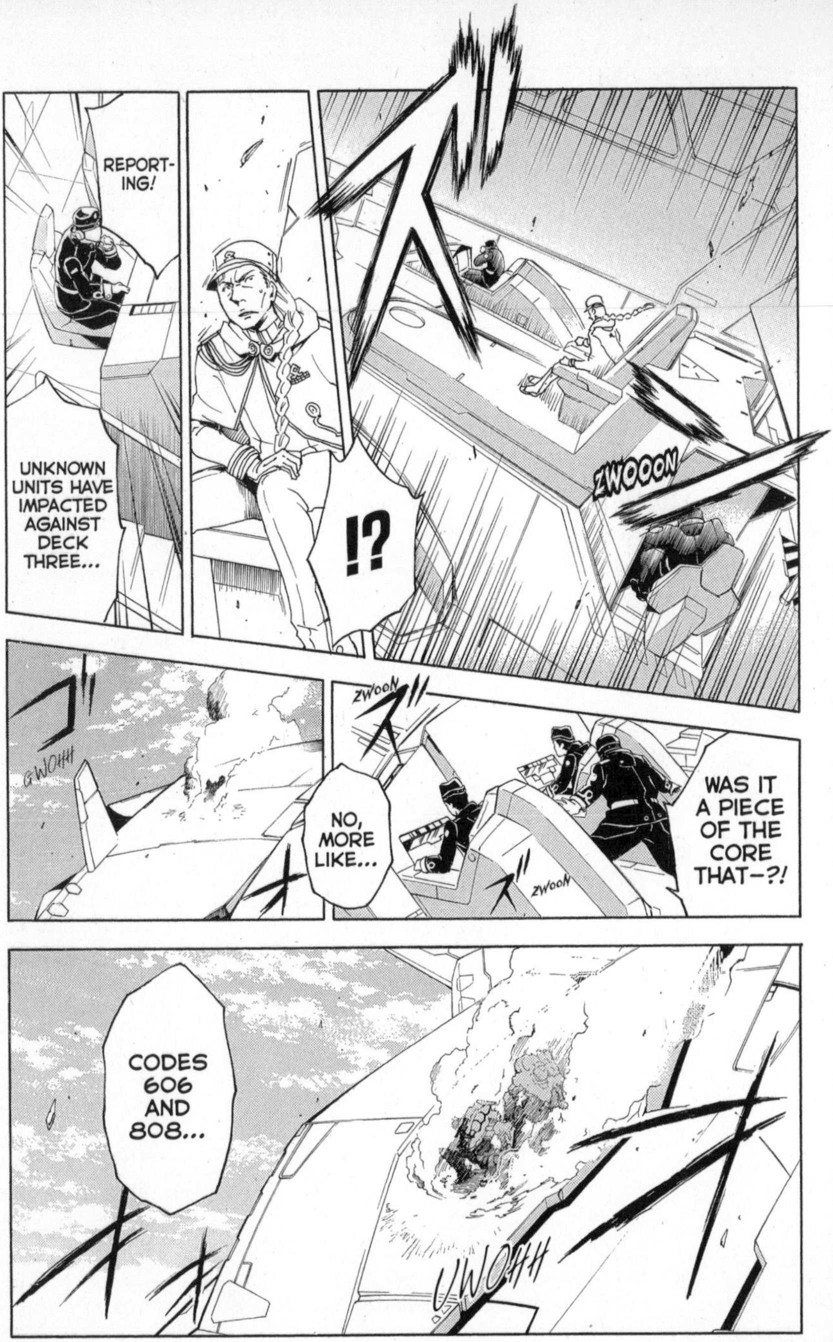

ZWOOON
!?
REPORTING!
UNKNOWN UNITS HAVE IMPACTED AGAINST DECK THREE...
ZWOON
WAS IT A PIECE OF THE CORE THAT—?!
NO, MORE LIKE...
ZWOON
GWOHH
CODES 606 AND 808...
UWOHH

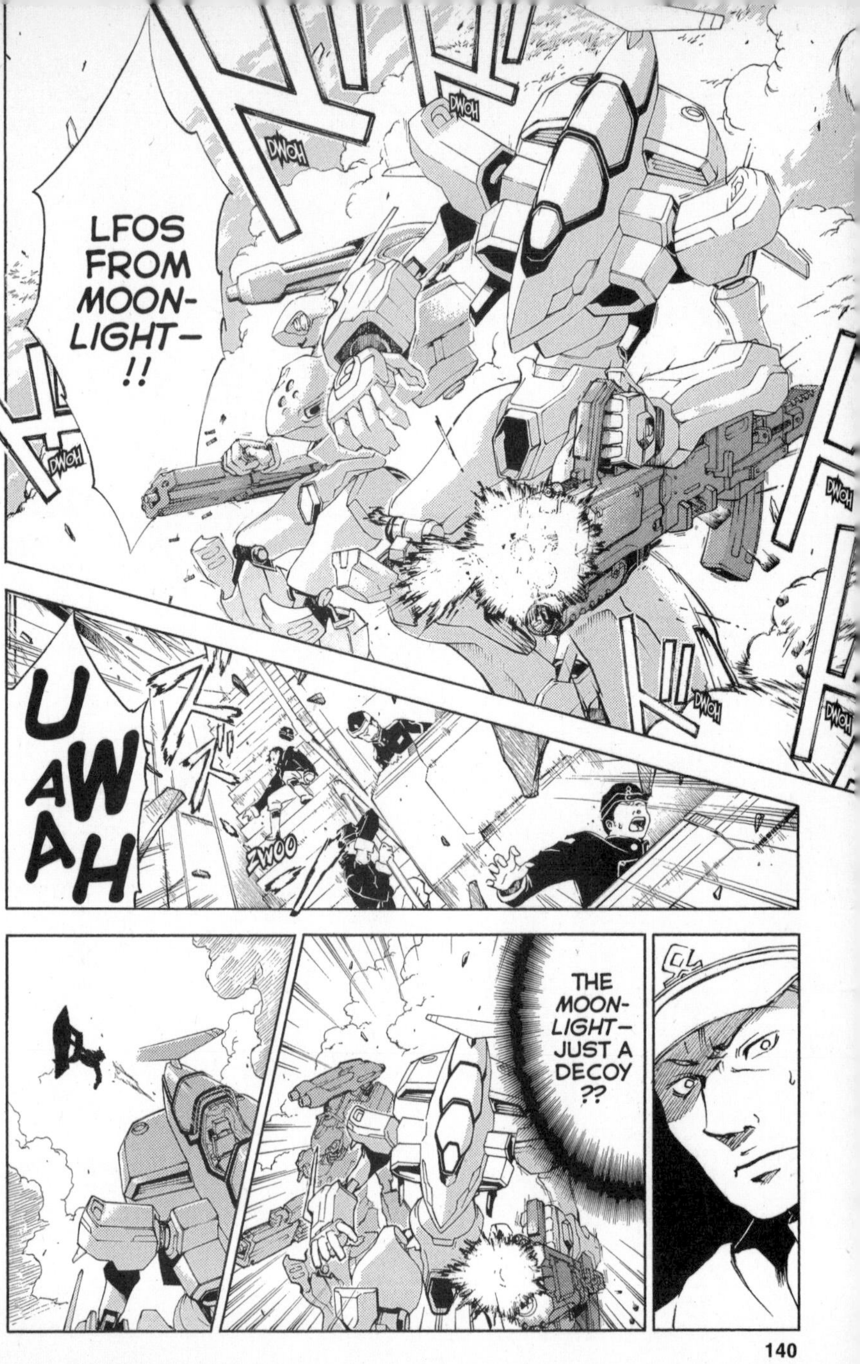
DWOH
DWOH
LFOS FROM MOON-LIGHT—!!
DWOH
DWOH
DWOH
DWOH
UAWAH
ZWOO
THE MOON-LIGHT—JUST A DECOY??

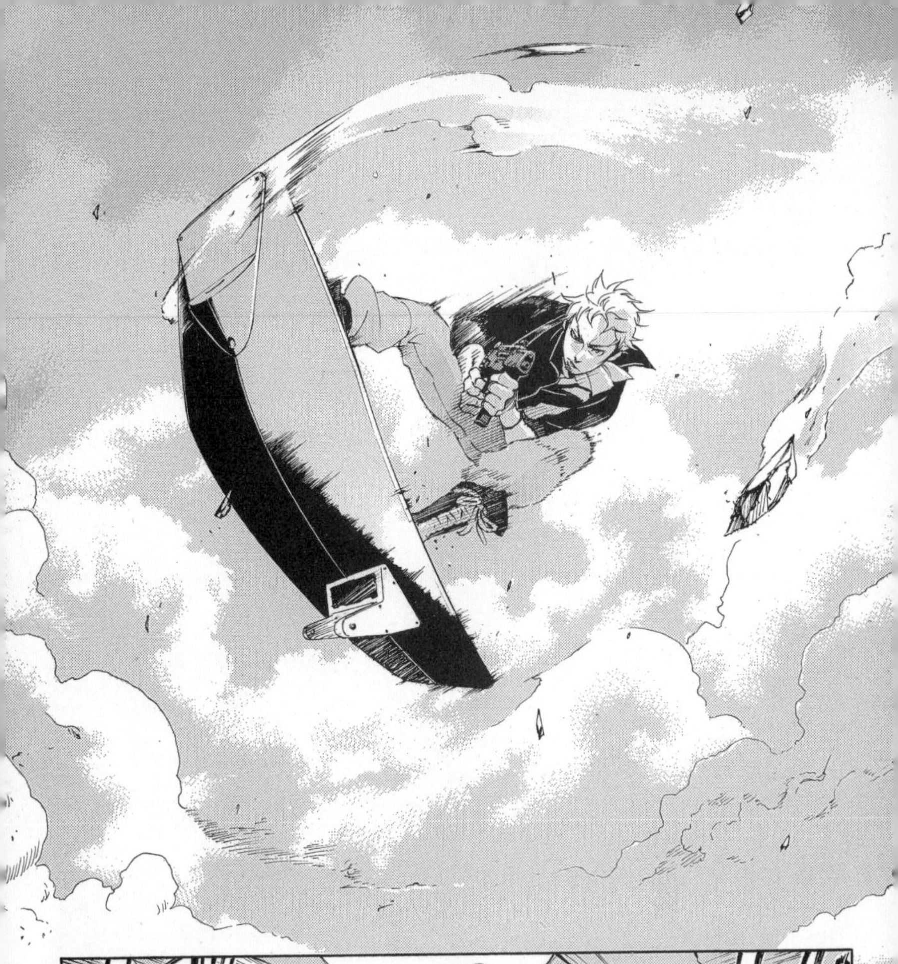

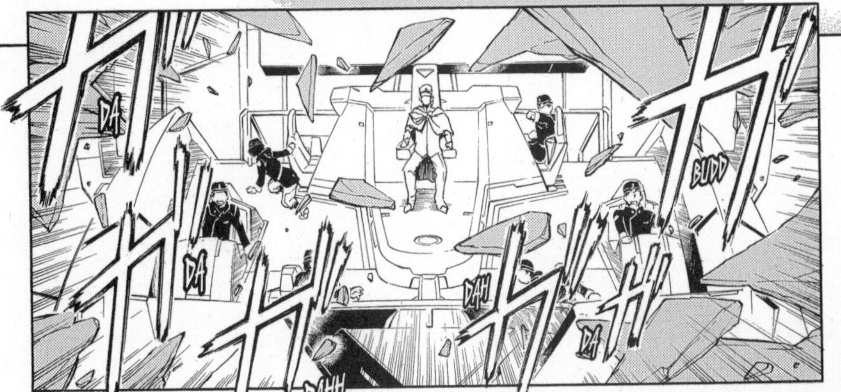
BUDD
DA
DAH
DAHH
DA
DA

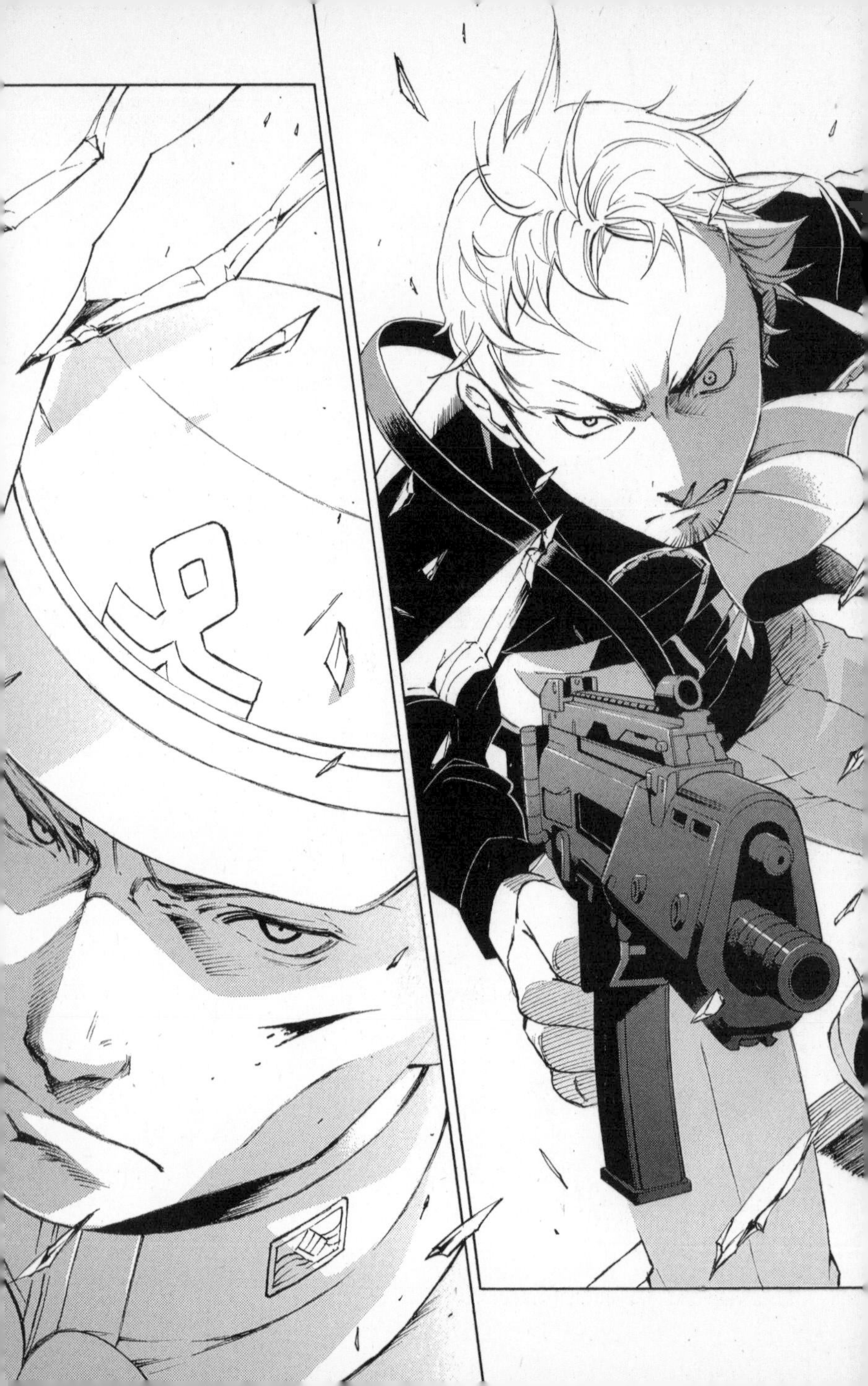

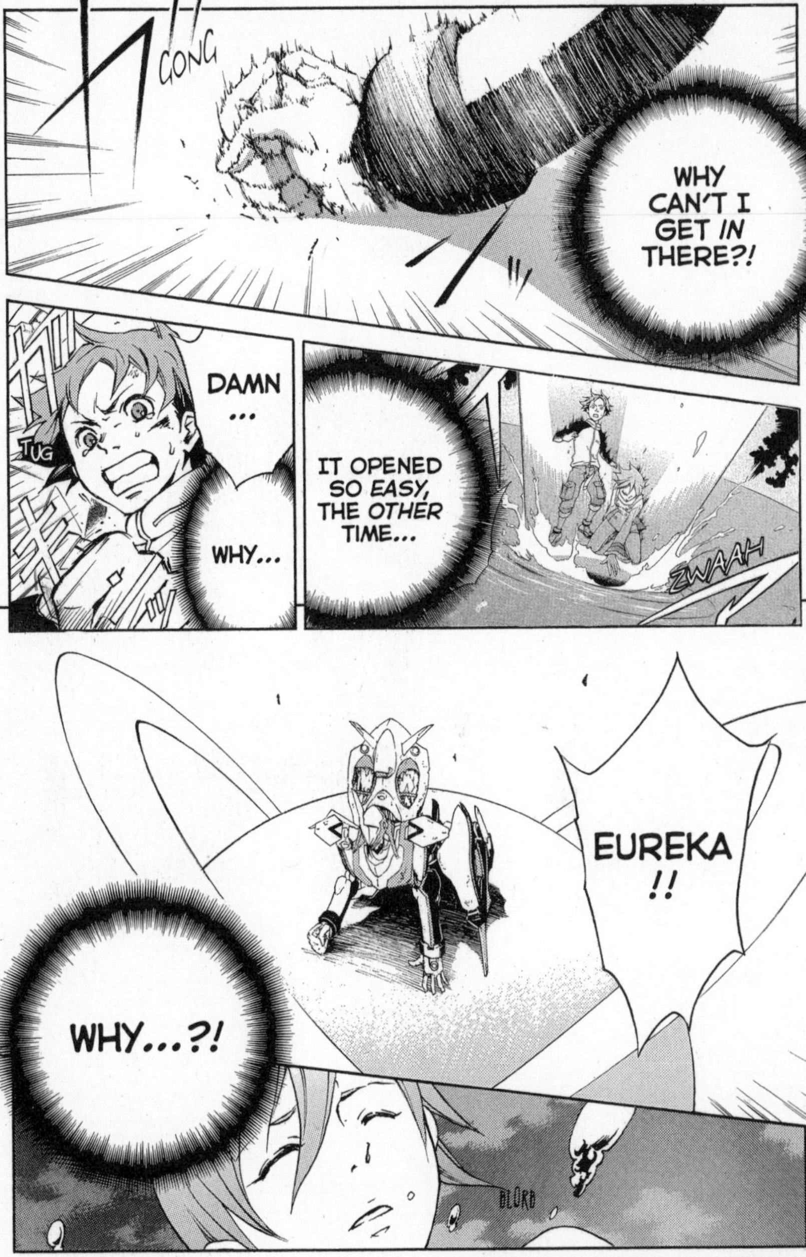
GONG
WHY CAN'T I GET *IN* THERE?!
IT OPENED SO *EASY*, THE *OTHER* TIME...
ZWAAH
DAMN...
WHY...
TUG
EUREKA!!
WHY...?!

19 What can you see from your place

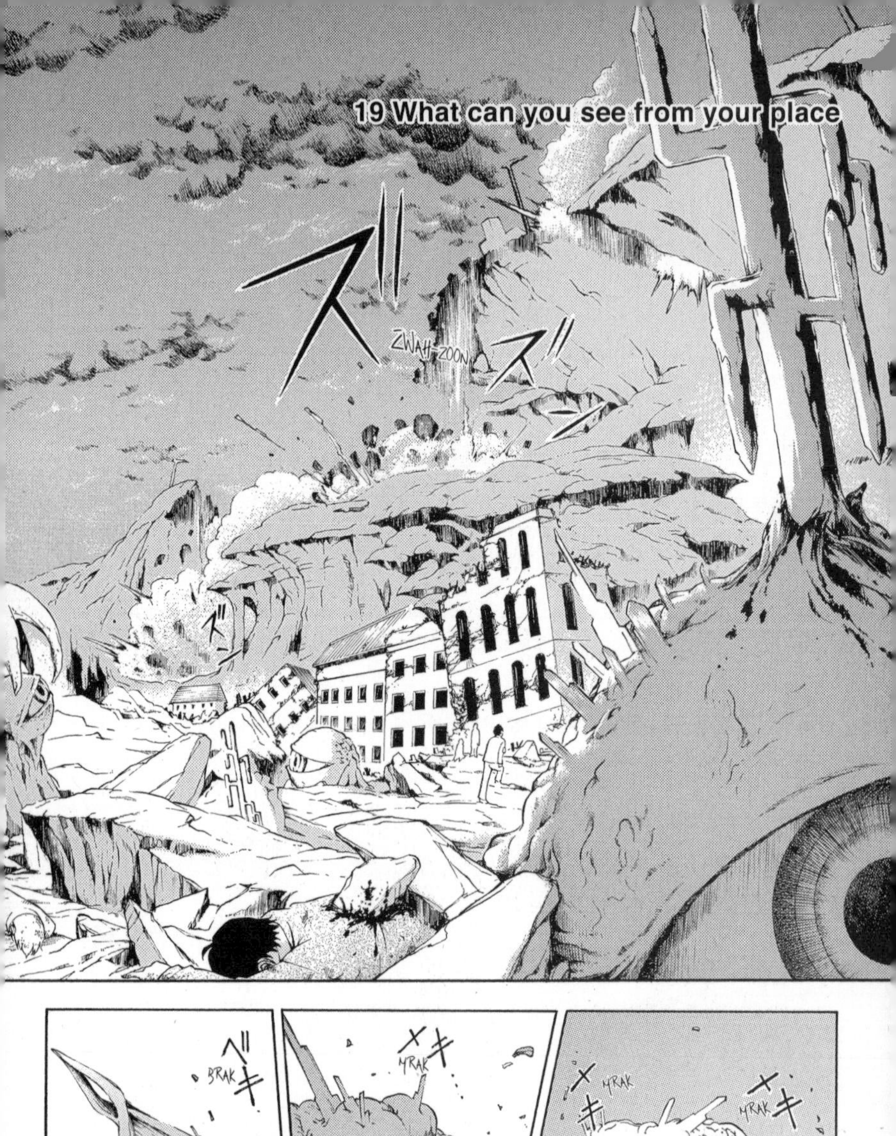
ZWAH-ZOON
MYRAK
MYRAK
MYRAK
BRAK
BRAK

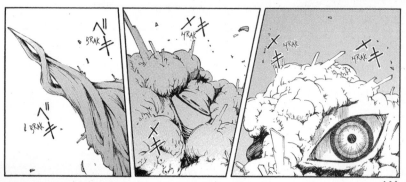

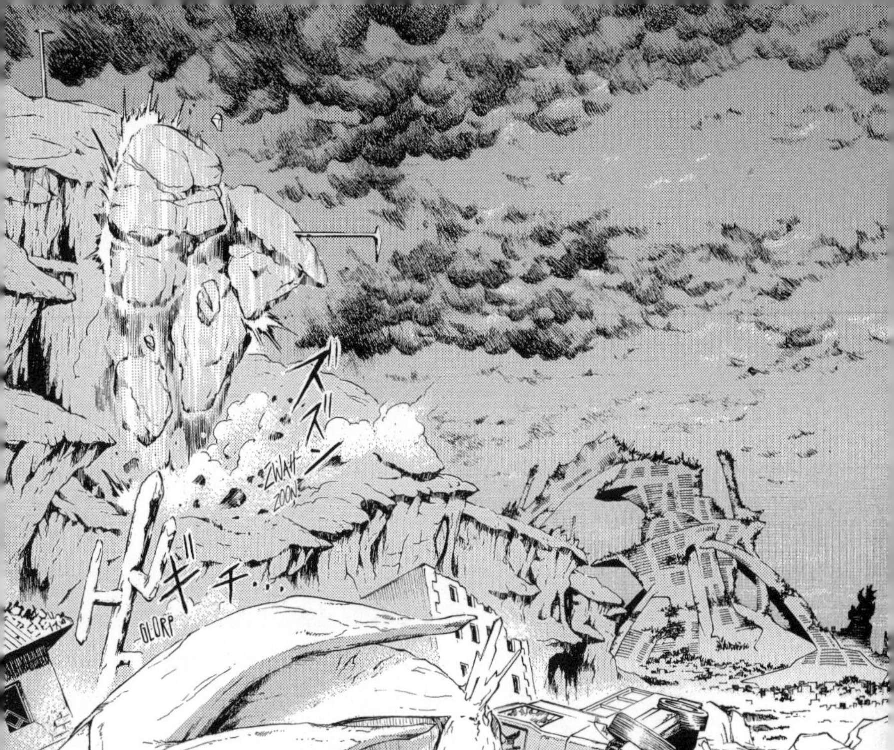
ズズーン
ZWAAH
ZOON
ドギチ...
GLORP

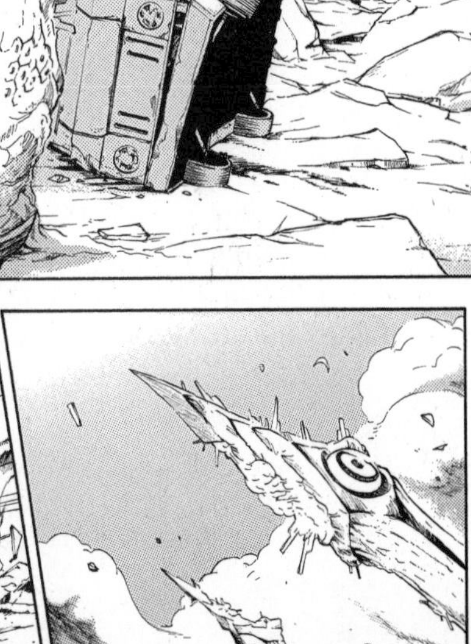

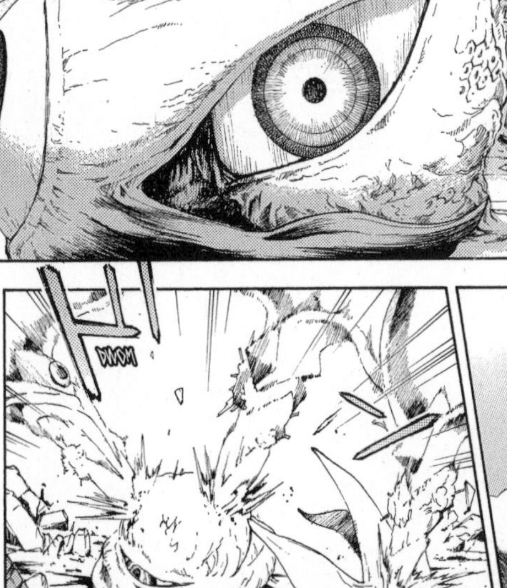

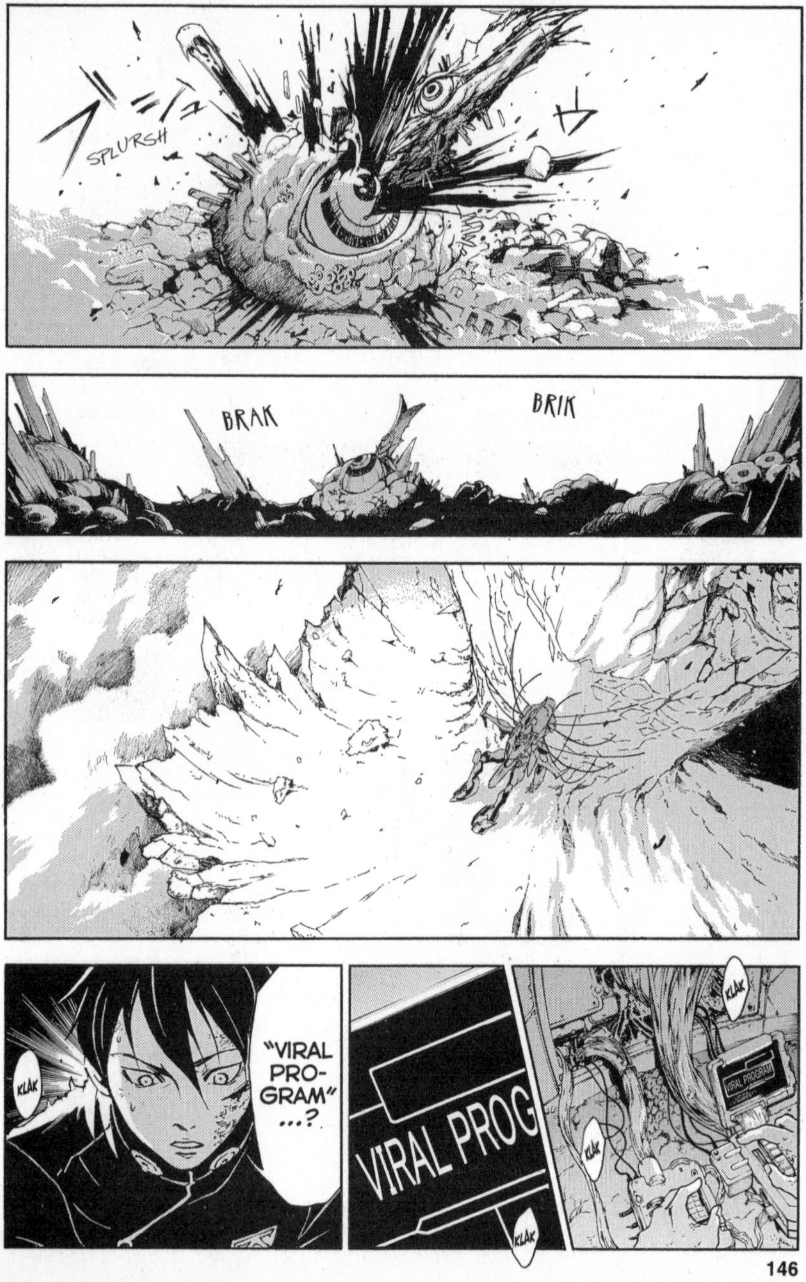
SPLURSH
BRIK
BRAK
KLAK
VIRAL PROG
VIRAL_PROGRAM
KLAK
KLAK
KLAK
"VIRAL PRO-GRAM" ...?

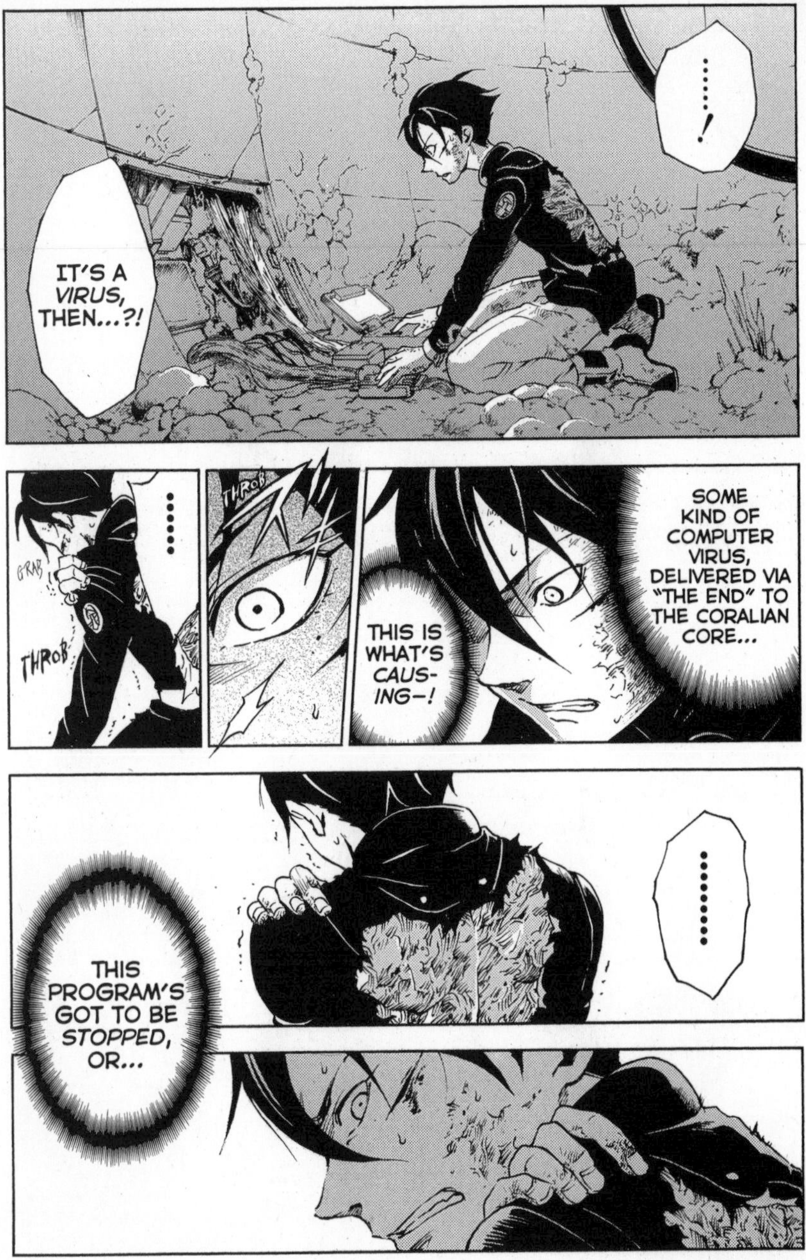
......!
IT'S A VIRUS, THEN...?!
SOME KIND OF COMPUTER VIRUS, DELIVERED VIA "THE END" TO THE CORALIAN CORE...
THIS IS WHAT'S CAUS-ING–!
THROB
......
GRAB
THROB
....
THIS PROGRAM'S GOT TO BE STOPPED, OR...

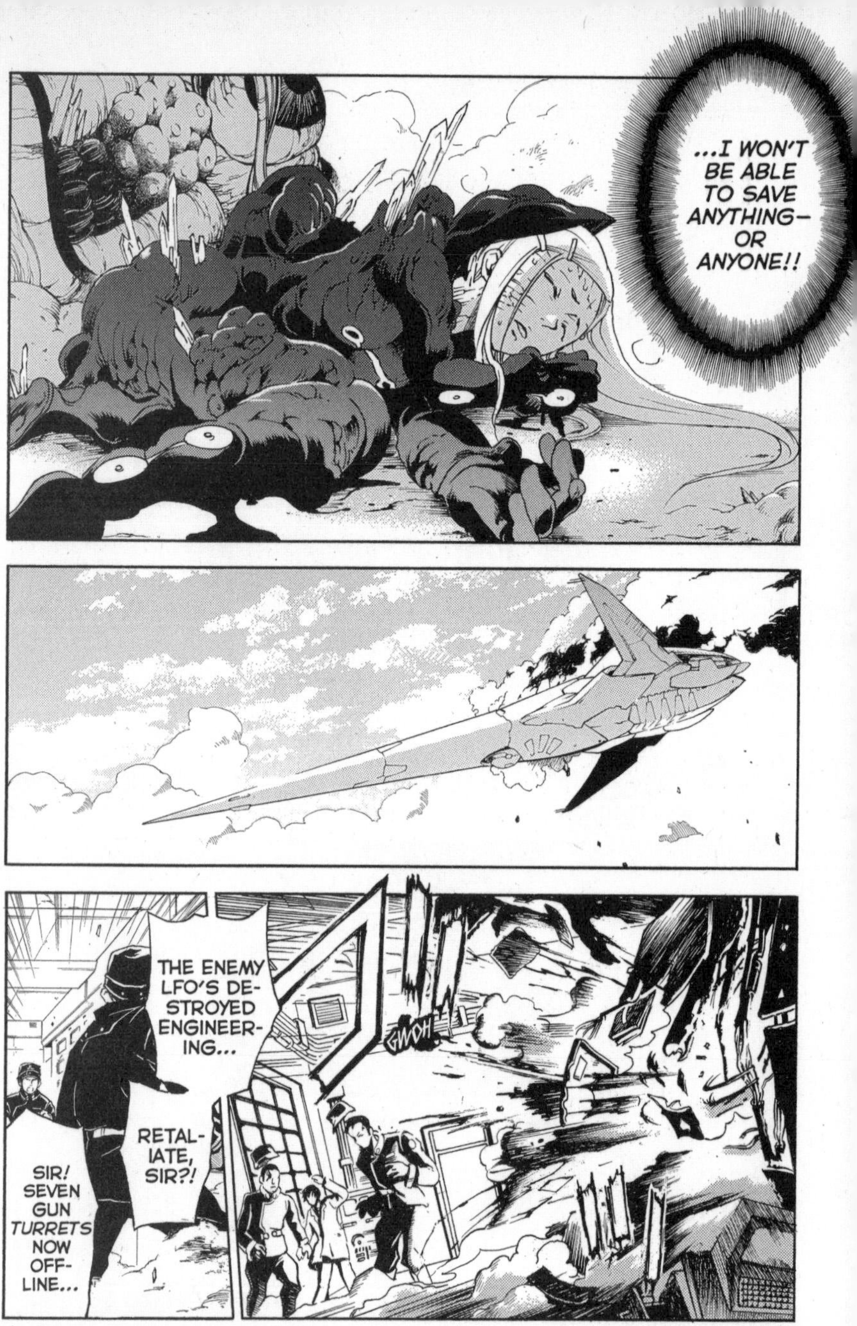
...I WON'T BE ABLE TO SAVE ANYTHING— OR ANYONE!!
THE ENEMY LFO'S DESTROYED ENGINEERING...
GWOH
RETALIATE, SIR?!
SIR! SEVEN GUN *TURRETS* NOW OFFLINE...

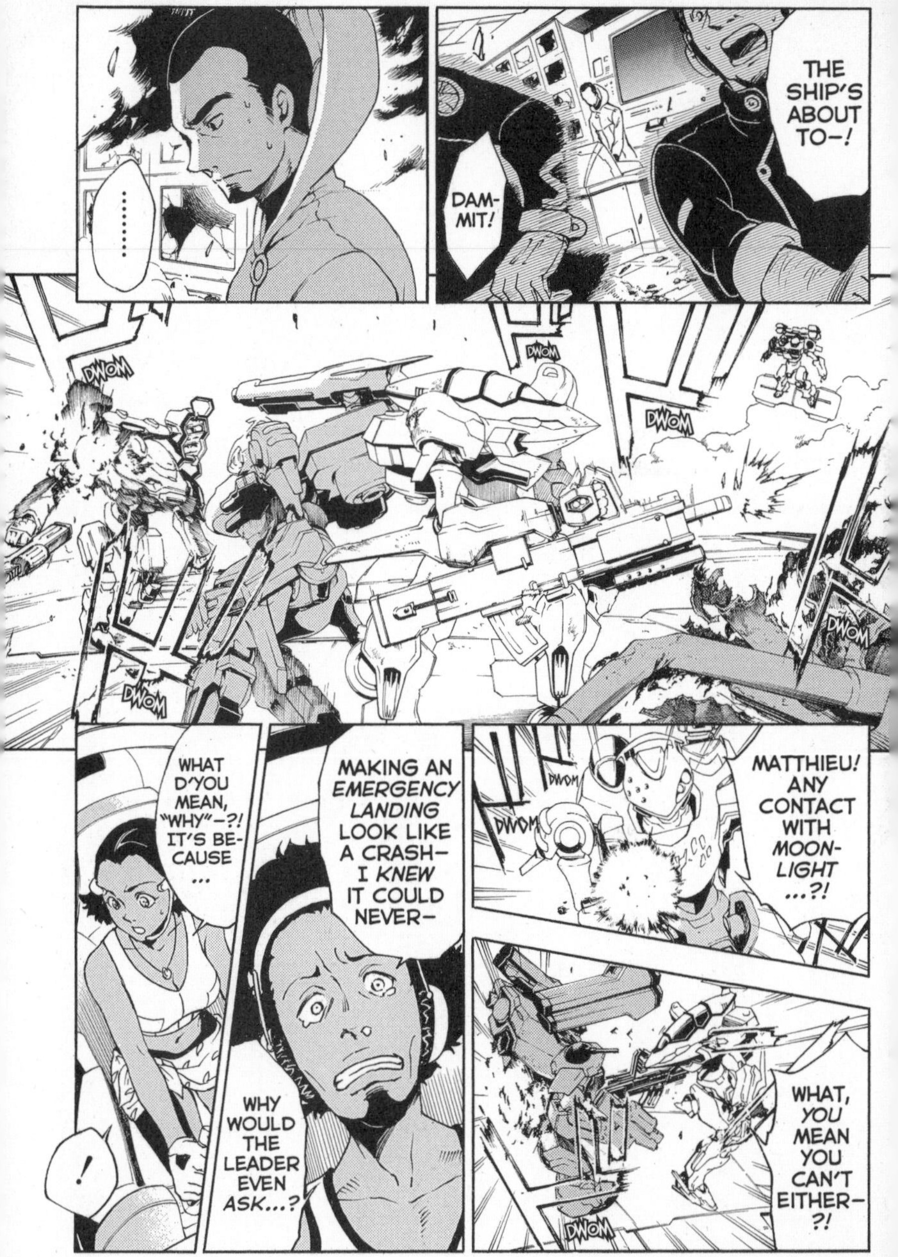
THE SHIP'S ABOUT TO-!
DAM-MIT!
......
DWOM
DWOM
DWOM
DWOM
DWOM
MATTHIEU! ANY CONTACT WITH MOON-LIGHT ...?!
DWOM
DWOM
WHAT, YOU MEAN YOU CAN'T EITHER-?!
DWOM
MAKING AN EMERGENCY LANDING LOOK LIKE A CRASH- I KNEW IT COULD NEVER-
WHY WOULD THE LEADER EVEN ASK...?
WHAT D'YOU MEAN, "WHY"-?! IT'S BE-CAUSE ...
!

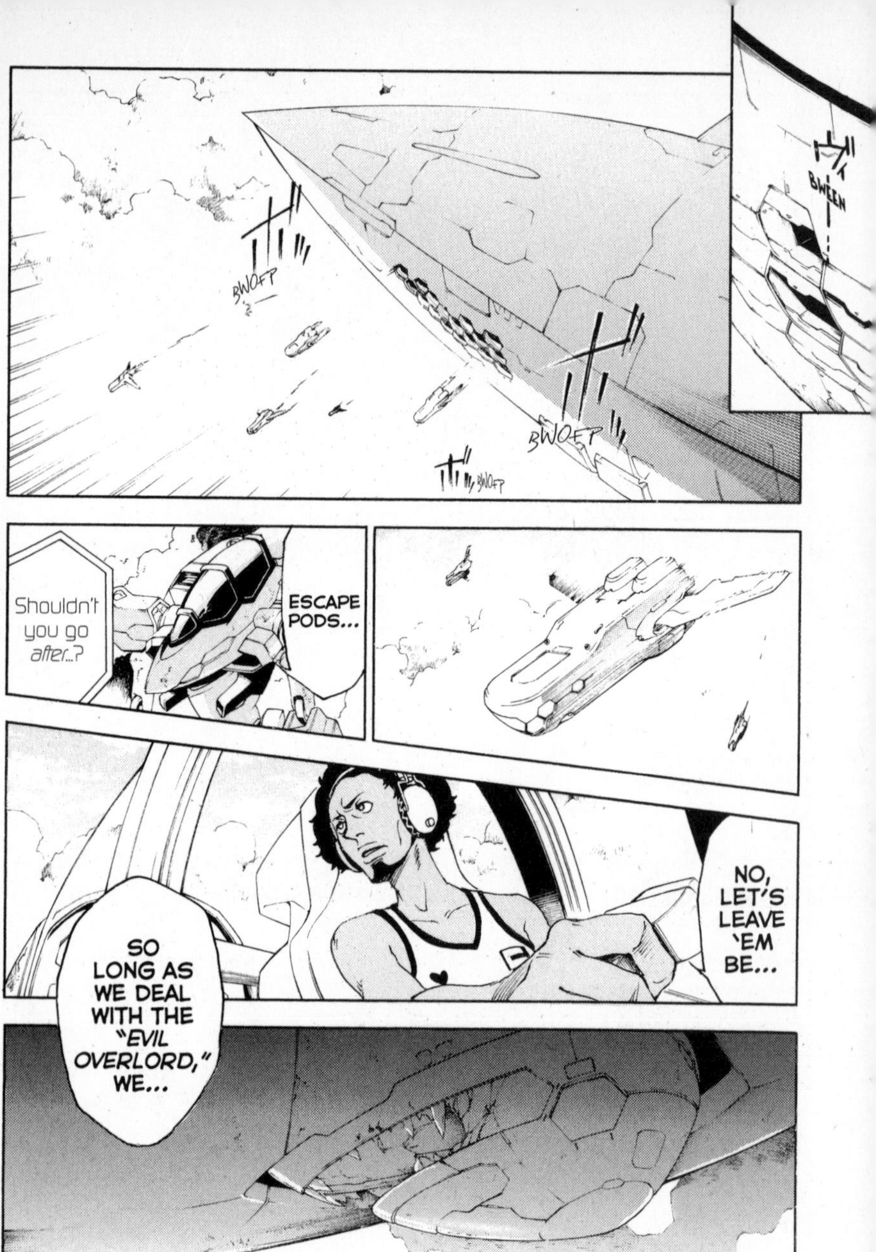
BWEEN
BWOFP
BWOFP
BWOFP
ESCAPE PODS...
Shouldn't you go *after*...?
NO, LET'S LEAVE 'EM BE...
SO LONG AS WE DEAL WITH THE "*EVIL OVERLORD*," WE...

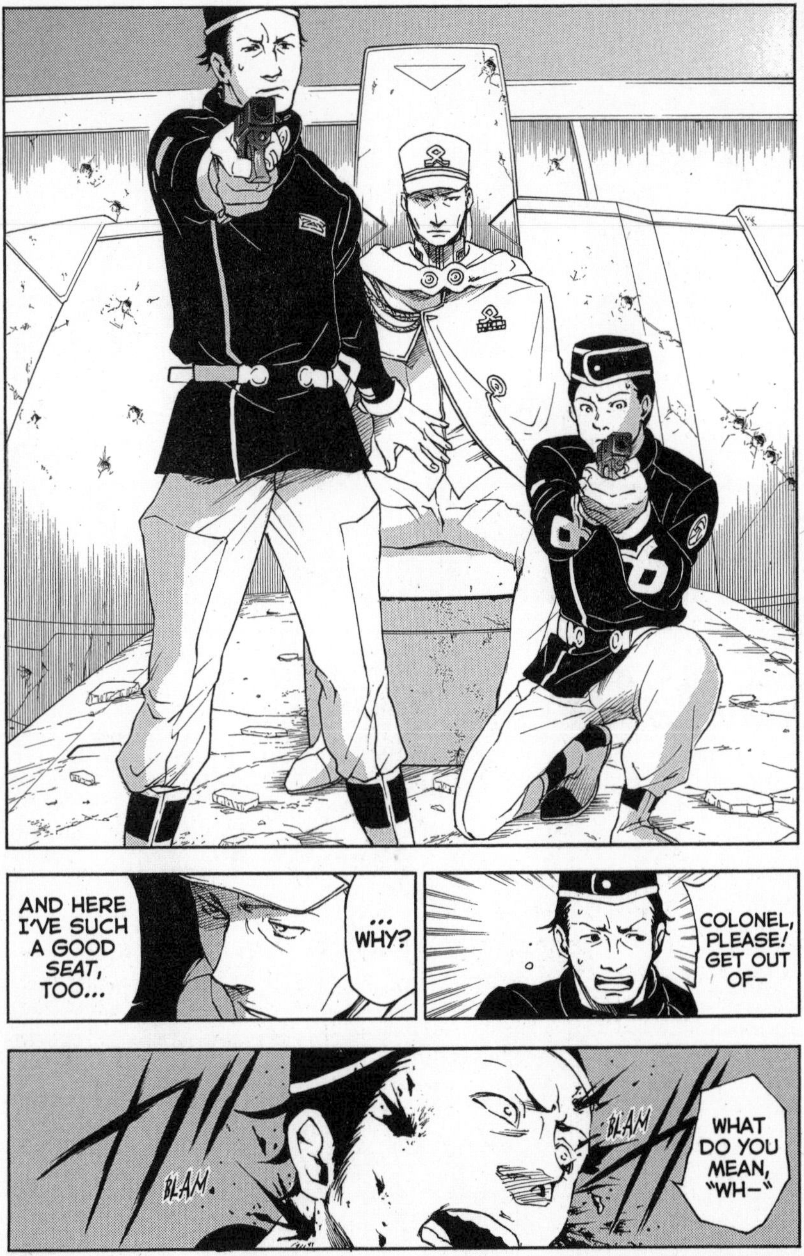
COLONEL, PLEASE! GET OUT OF–
... WHY?
AND HERE I'VE SUCH A GOOD *SEAT*, TOO...
WHAT DO YOU MEAN, "WH–"
BLAM
BLAM

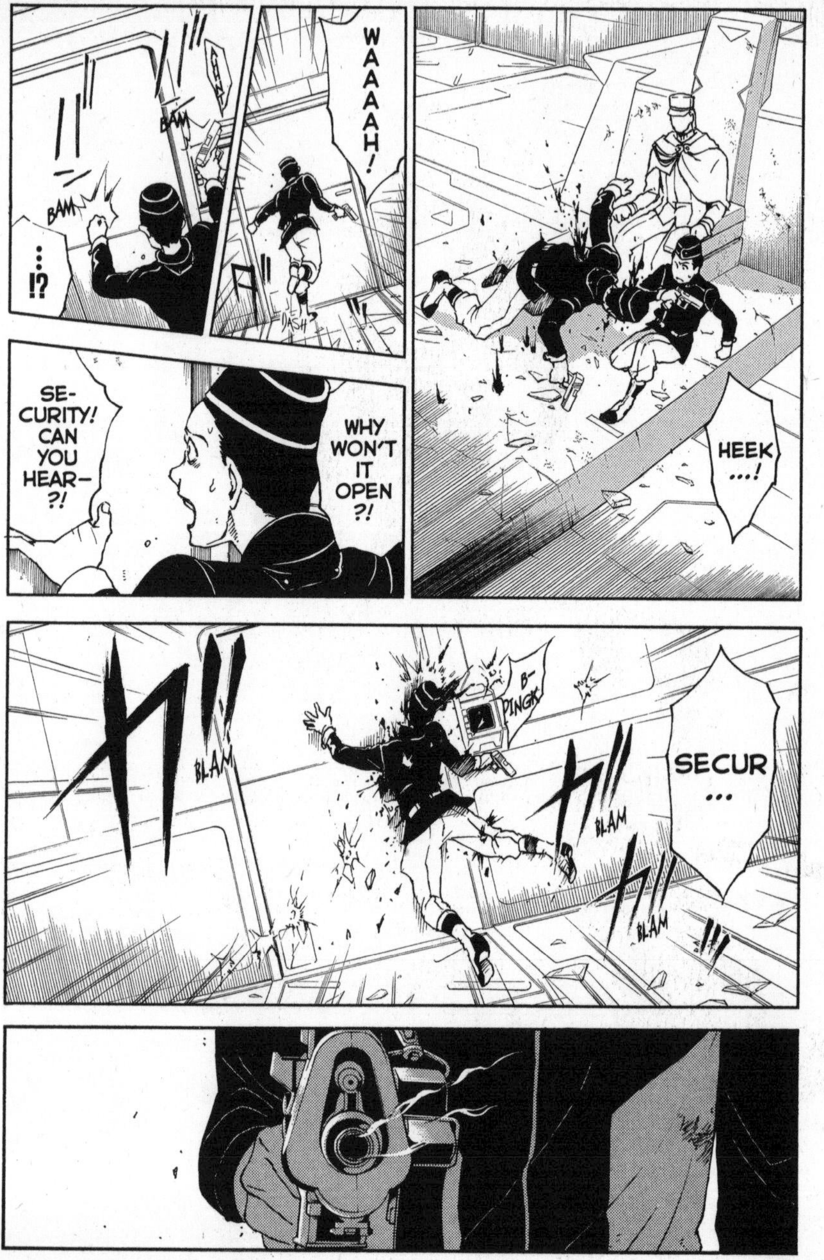
HEEK ...!
WAAAAAH!
DASH
BAM
BAM
...!?
WHY WON'T IT OPEN ?!
SE-CURITY! CAN YOU HEAR– ?!
SECUR ...
B-PINGK
BLAM
BLAM
BLAM

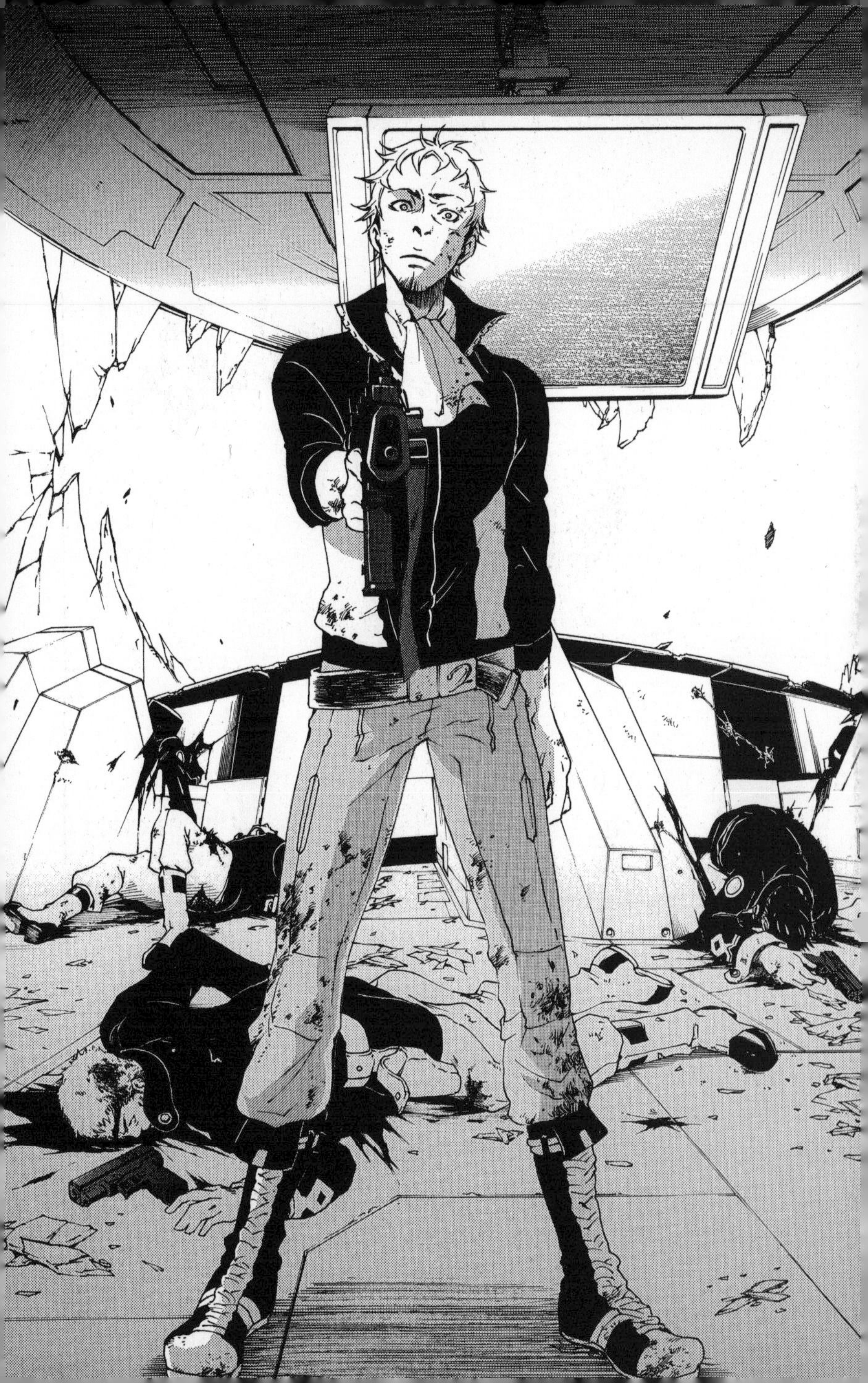

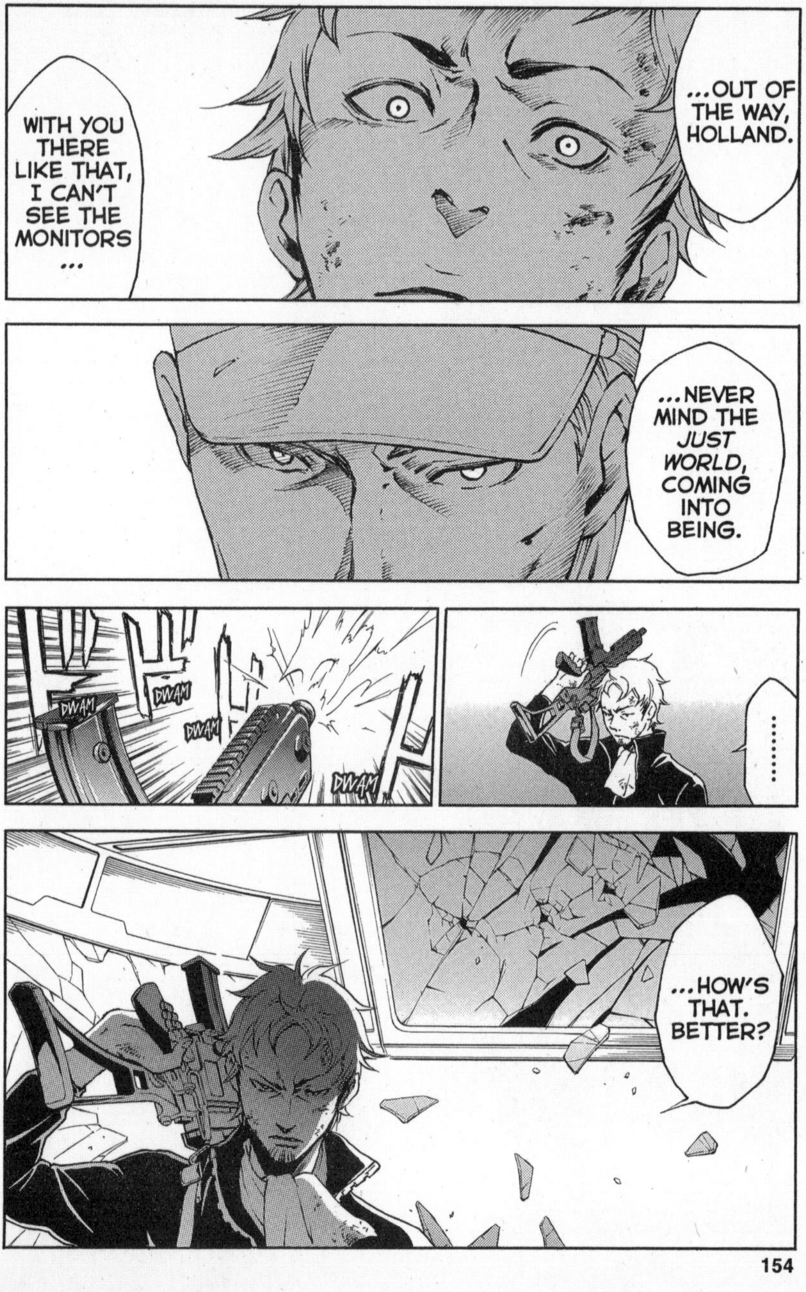
...OUT OF THE WAY, HOLLAND.
WITH YOU THERE LIKE THAT, I CAN'T SEE THE MONITORS ...
...NEVER MIND THE *JUST WORLD*, COMING INTO BEING.
....
DWAM
DWAM
DWAM
DWAM
...HOW'S THAT. BETTER?

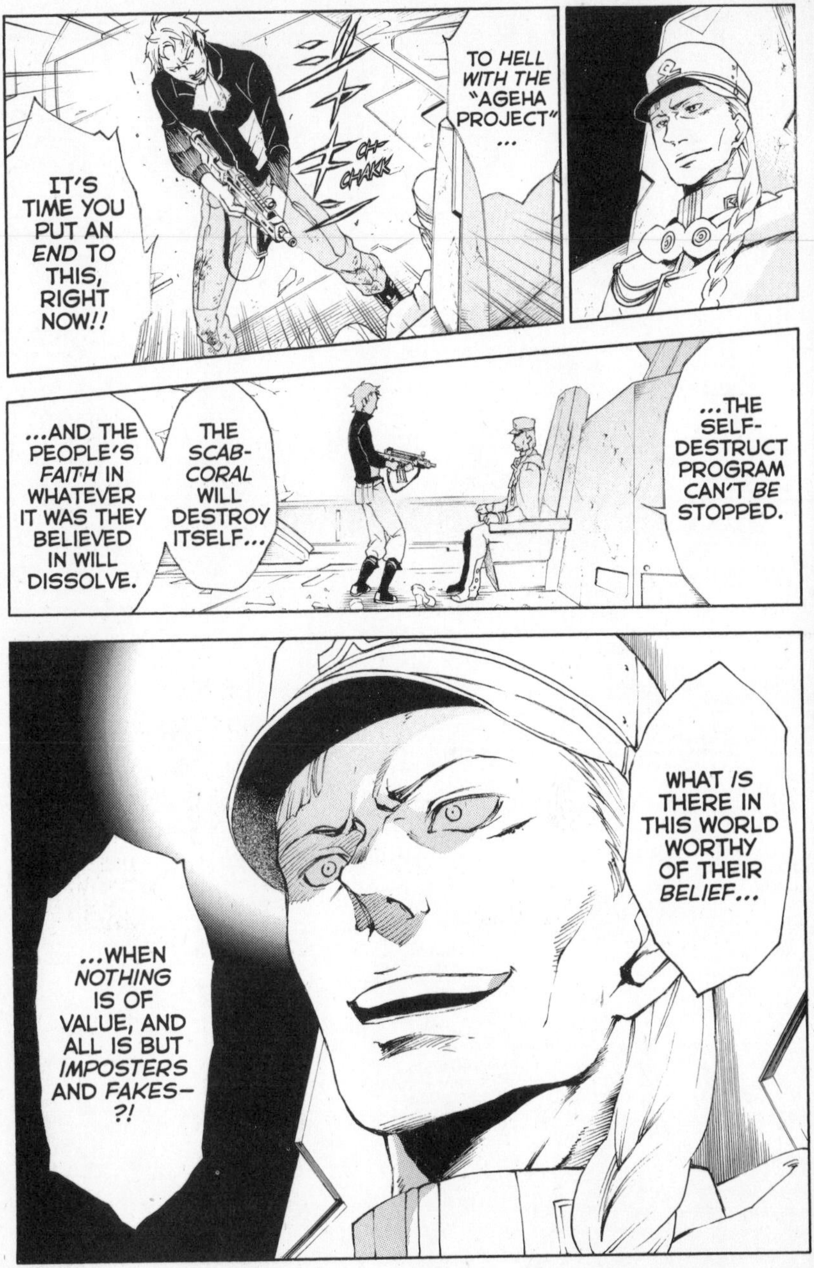
TO HELL WITH THE "AGEHA PROJECT"...
CH-CHAKK
IT'S TIME YOU PUT AN END TO THIS, RIGHT NOW!!
...THE SELF-DESTRUCT PROGRAM CAN'T BE STOPPED.
THE SCAB-CORAL WILL DESTROY ITSELF...
...AND THE PEOPLE'S FAITH IN WHATEVER IT WAS THEY BELIEVED IN WILL DISSOLVE.
WHAT IS THERE IN THIS WORLD WORTHY OF THEIR BELIEF...
...WHEN NOTHING IS OF VALUE, AND ALL IS BUT IMPOSTERS AND FAKES—?!

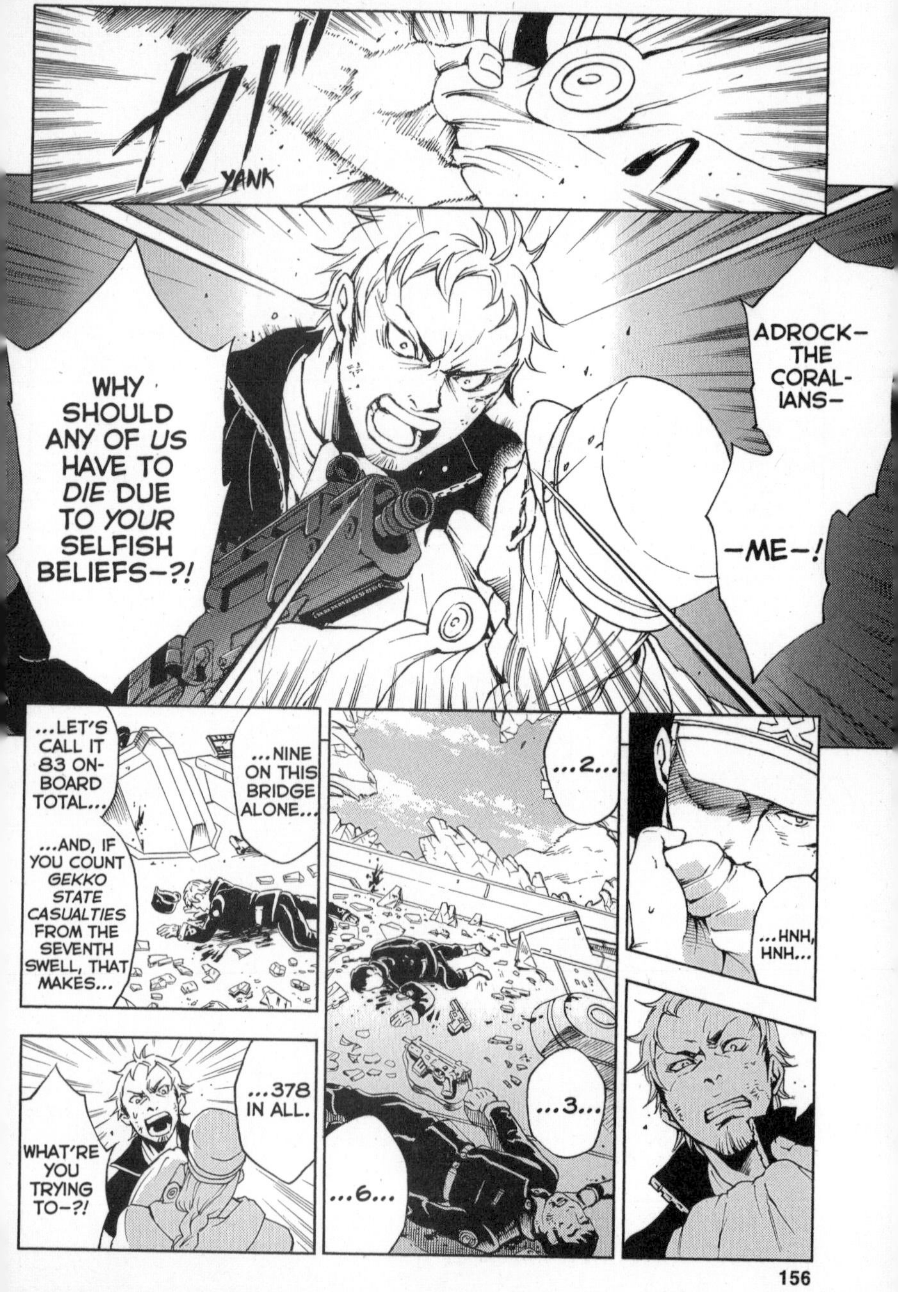
YANK
ADROCK— THE CORAL- IANS—
—ME—!
WHY SHOULD ANY OF *US* HAVE TO *DIE* DUE TO *YOUR* SELFISH BELIEFS—?!
...HNH, HNH...
...2...
...3...
...6...
...NINE ON THIS BRIDGE ALONE...
...LET'S CALL IT 83 ON-BOARD TOTAL...
...AND, IF YOU COUNT *GEKKO STATE CASUALTIES* FROM THE SEVENTH SWELL, THAT MAKES...
...378 IN ALL.
WHAT'RE YOU TRYING TO—?!

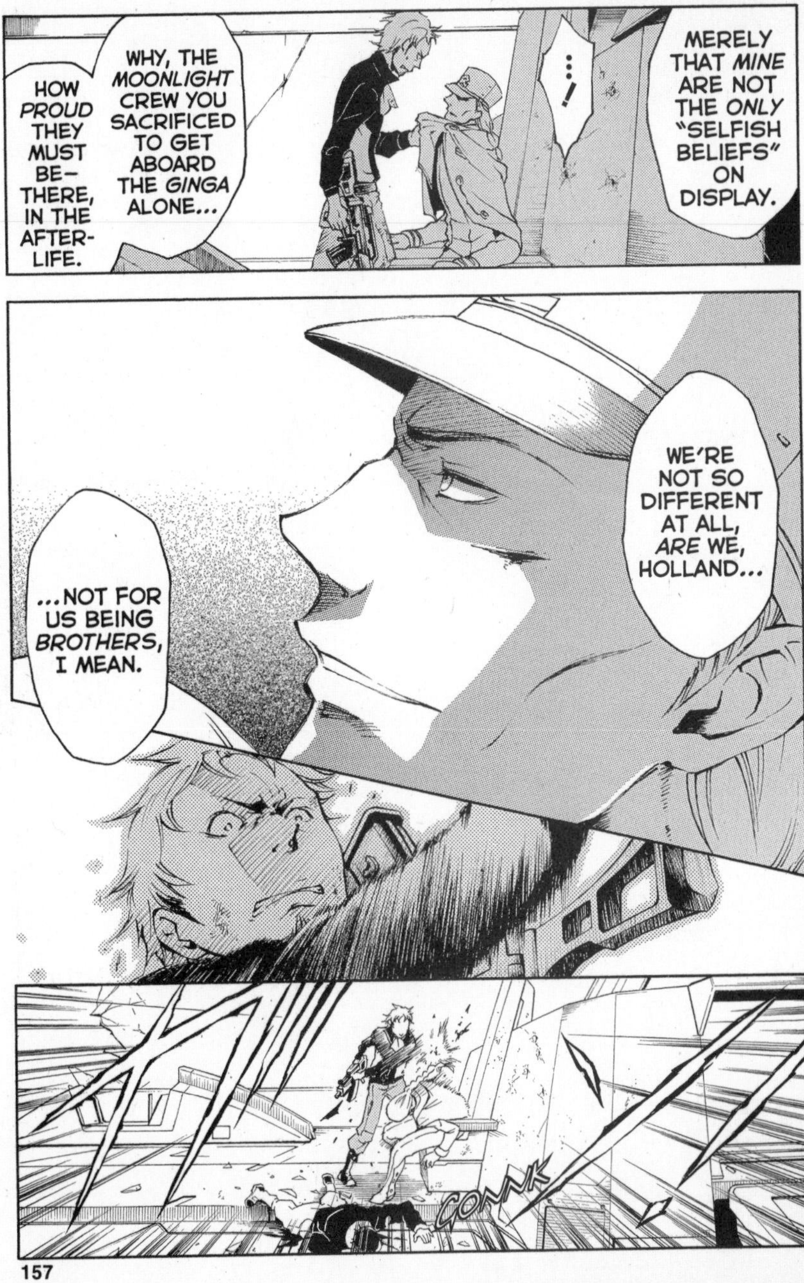
MERELY THAT *MINE* ARE NOT THE *ONLY* "SELFISH BELIEFS" ON DISPLAY.
...!
WHY, THE *MOONLIGHT* CREW YOU SACRIFICED TO GET ABOARD THE *GINGA* ALONE...
HOW *PROUD* THEY MUST BE—THERE, IN THE AFTER-LIFE.
WE'RE NOT SO DIFFERENT AT ALL, *ARE* WE, HOLLAND...
...NOT FOR US BEING *BROTHERS*, I MEAN.
GONNK

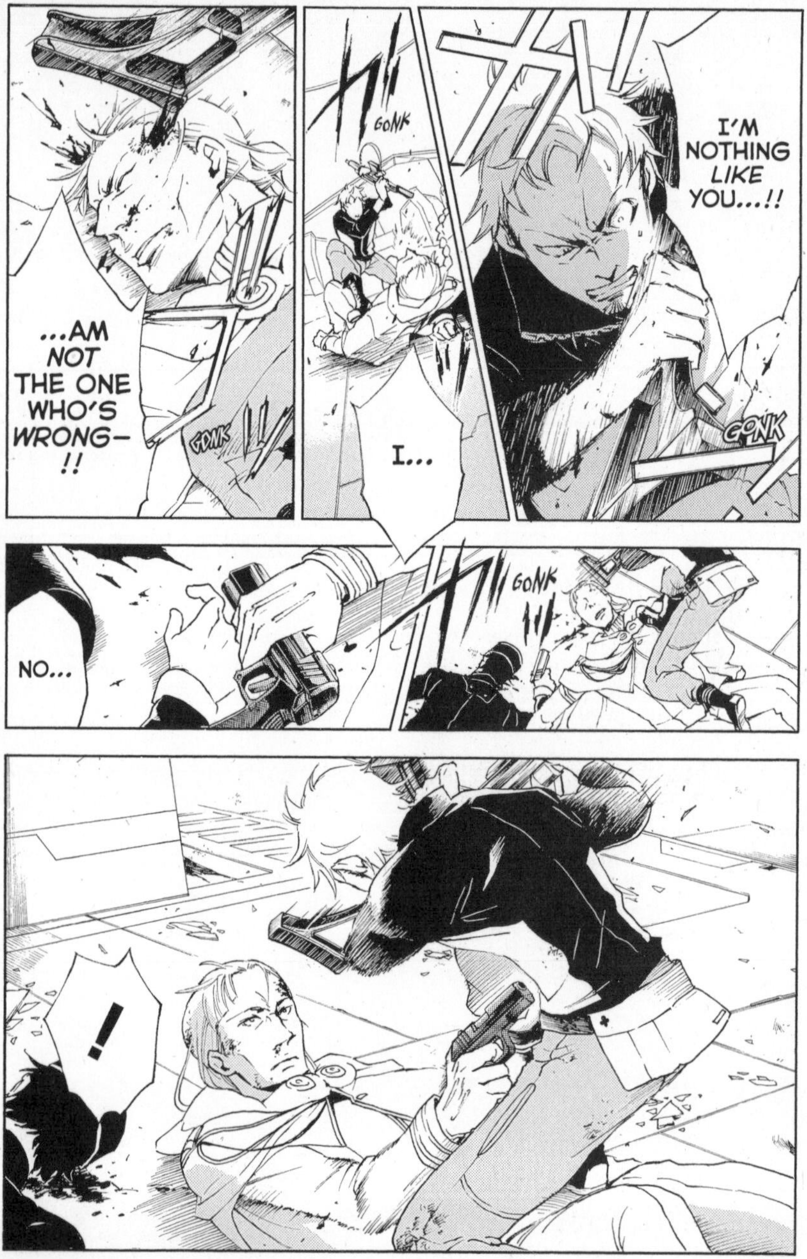
I'M NOTHING LIKE YOU...!!
GONK
GONK
I...
...AM NOT THE ONE WHO'S WRONG—!!
GONK
GONK
NO...
!

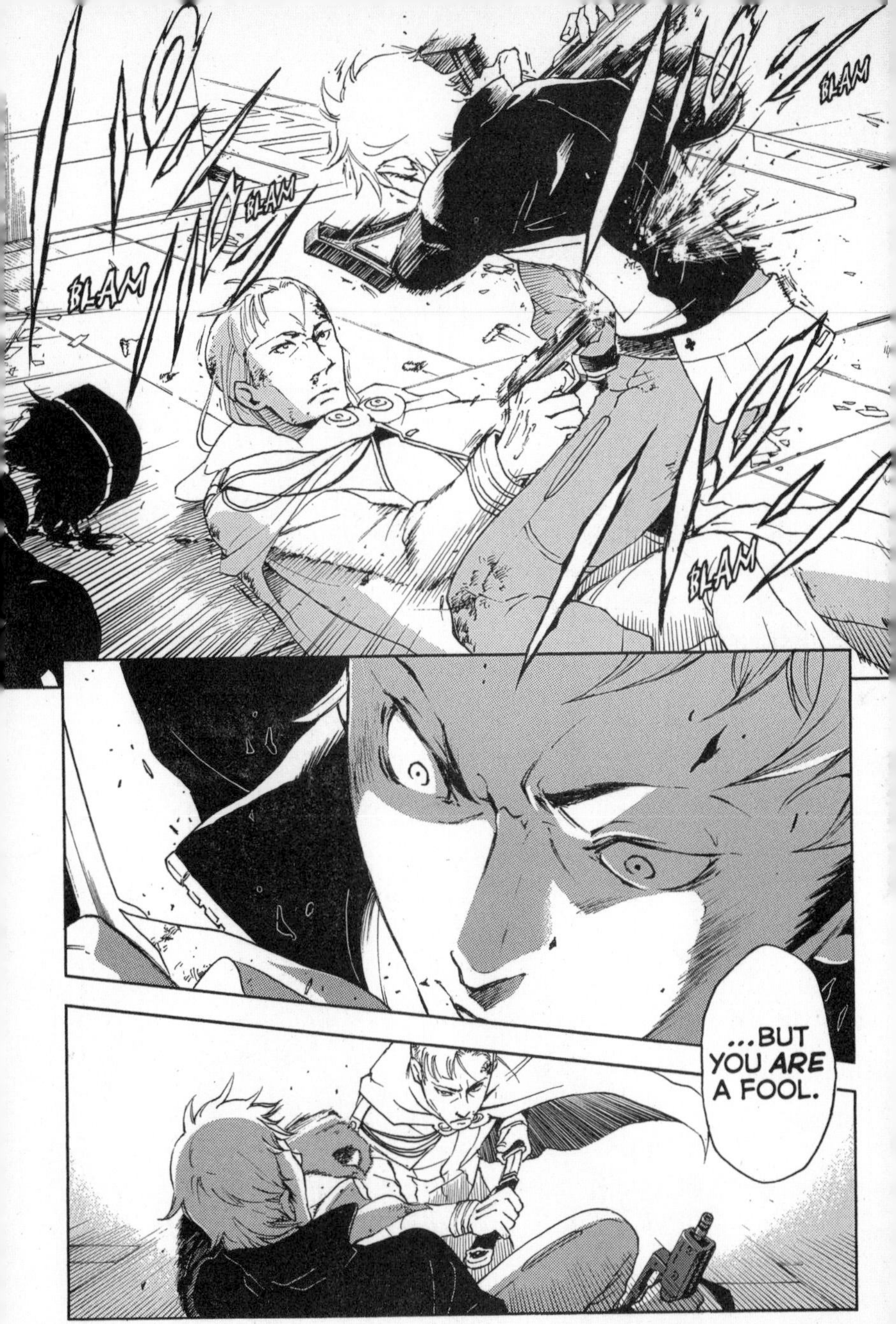
BLAM
BLAM
BLAM
BLAM
...BUT YOU ARE A FOOL.

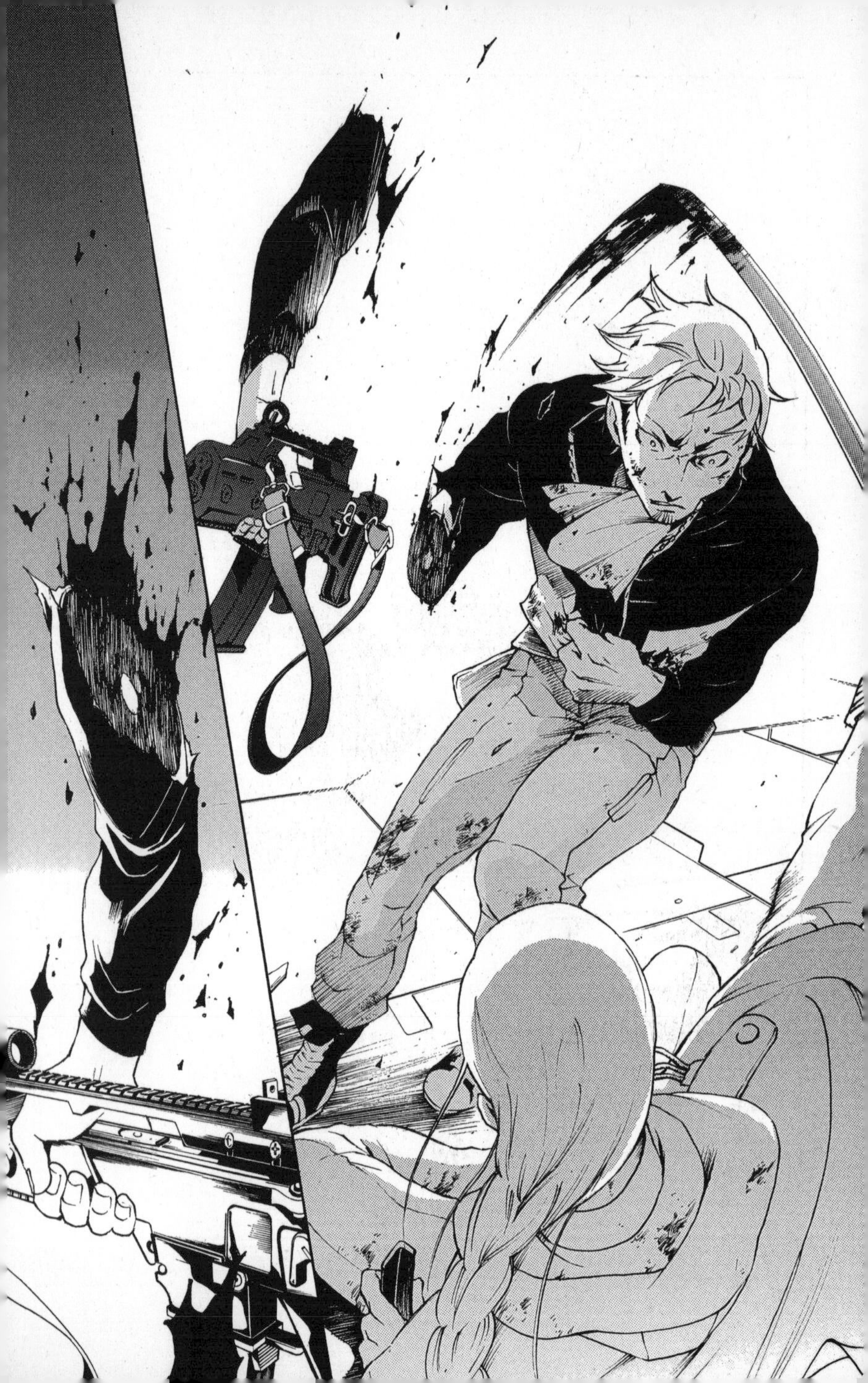

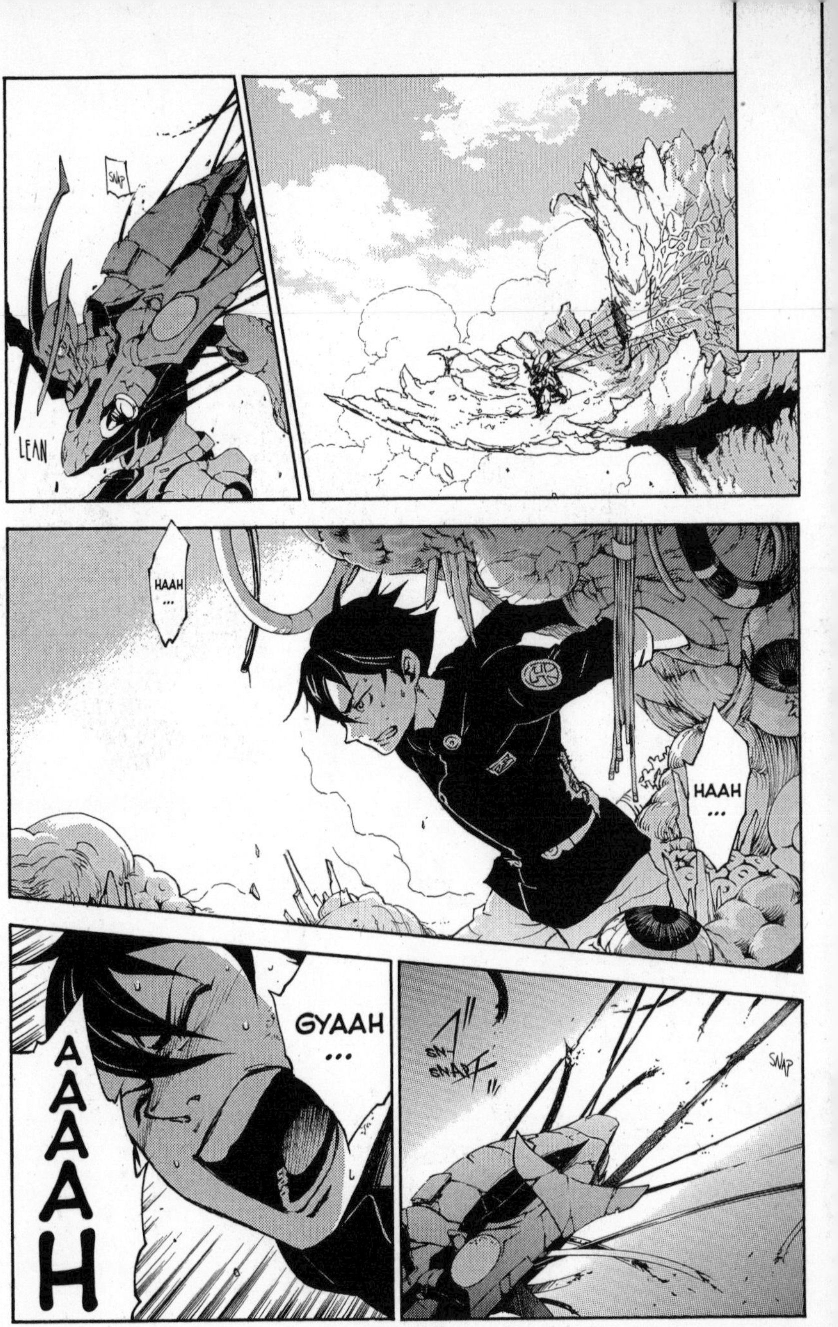

SNAP
LEAN
HAAH ...
HAAH ...
SNAP
SH- SNAP!!
GYAAH ...
AAAAH

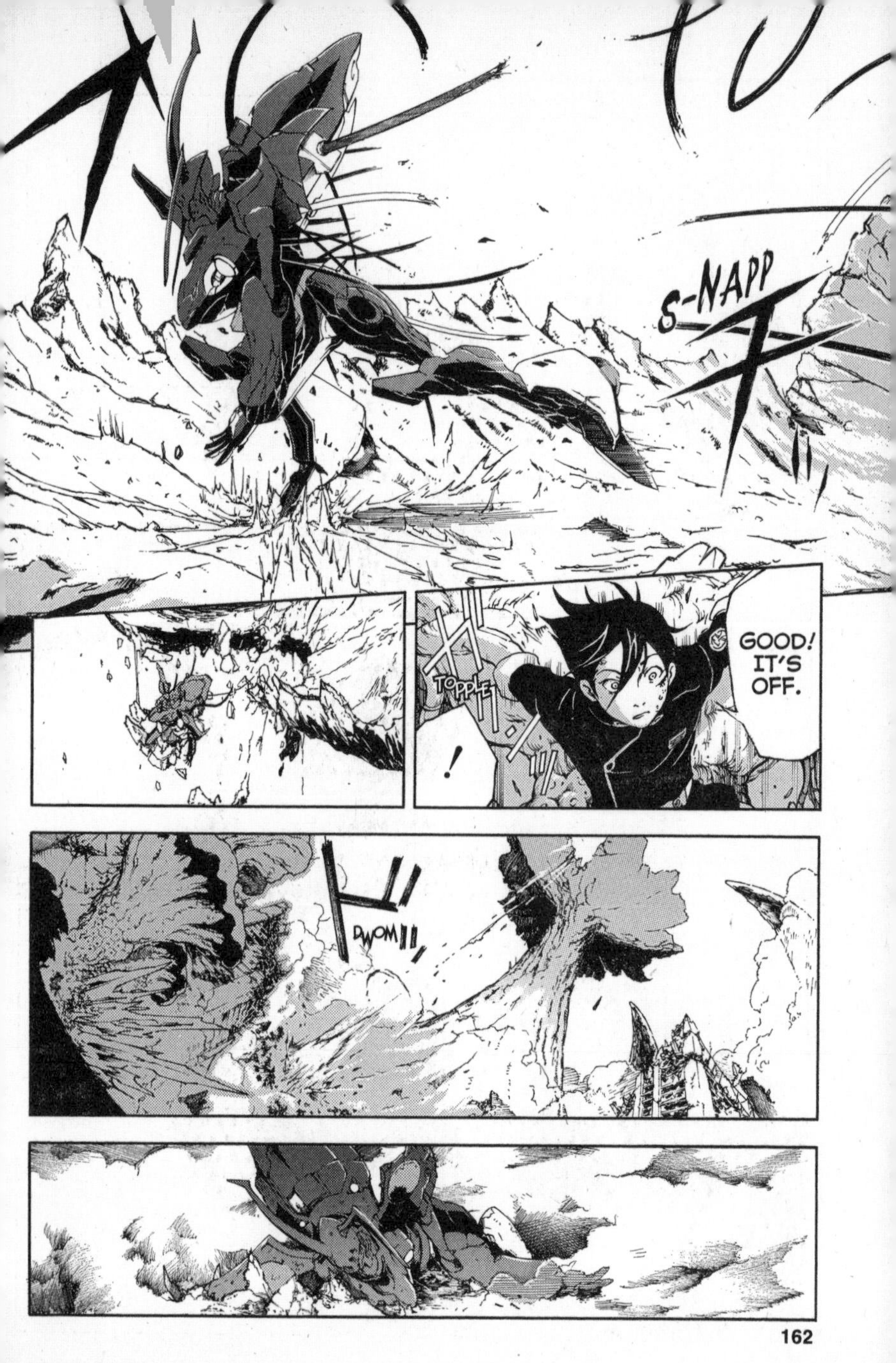
S-NAPP
TOPPLE
!
GOOD! IT'S OFF.
DWOM

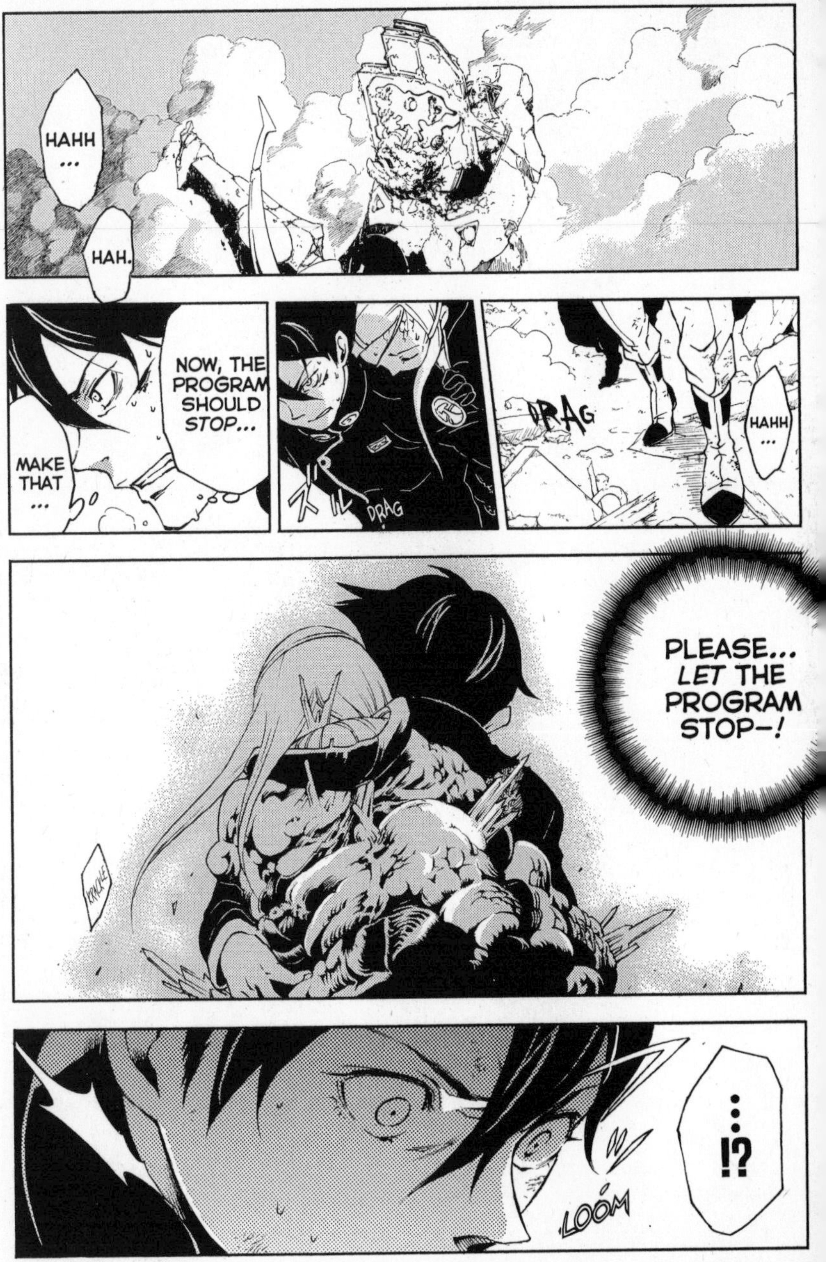
HAHH...
HAH.
HAHH...
DRAG
DRAG
NOW, THE PROGRAM SHOULD STOP...
MAKE THAT...
PLEASE... LET THE PROGRAM STOP–!
KRACKLE
...!?
LOOM

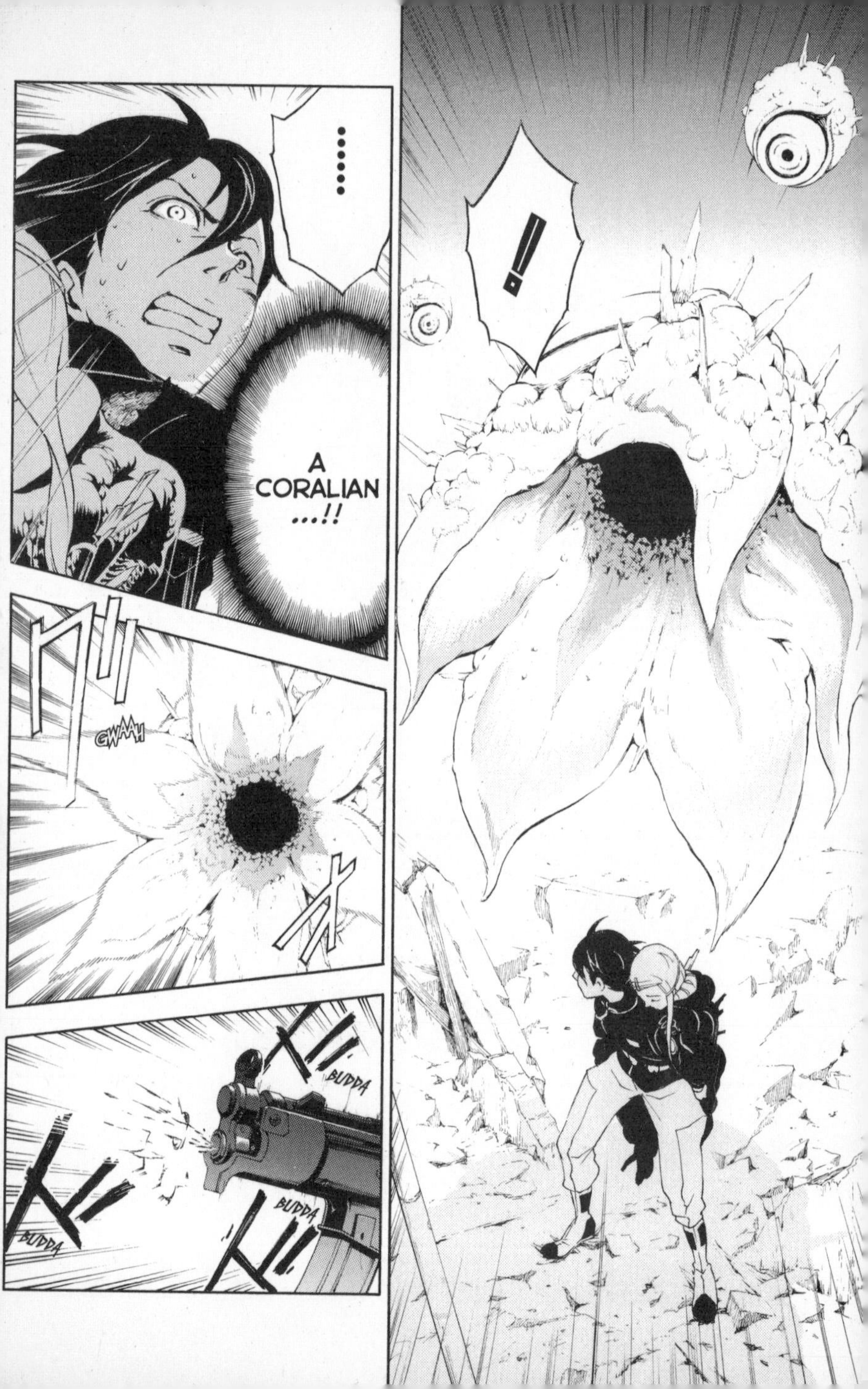
!
......
A CORALIAN ...!!
GWAAH
BUDDA
BUDDA
BUDDA

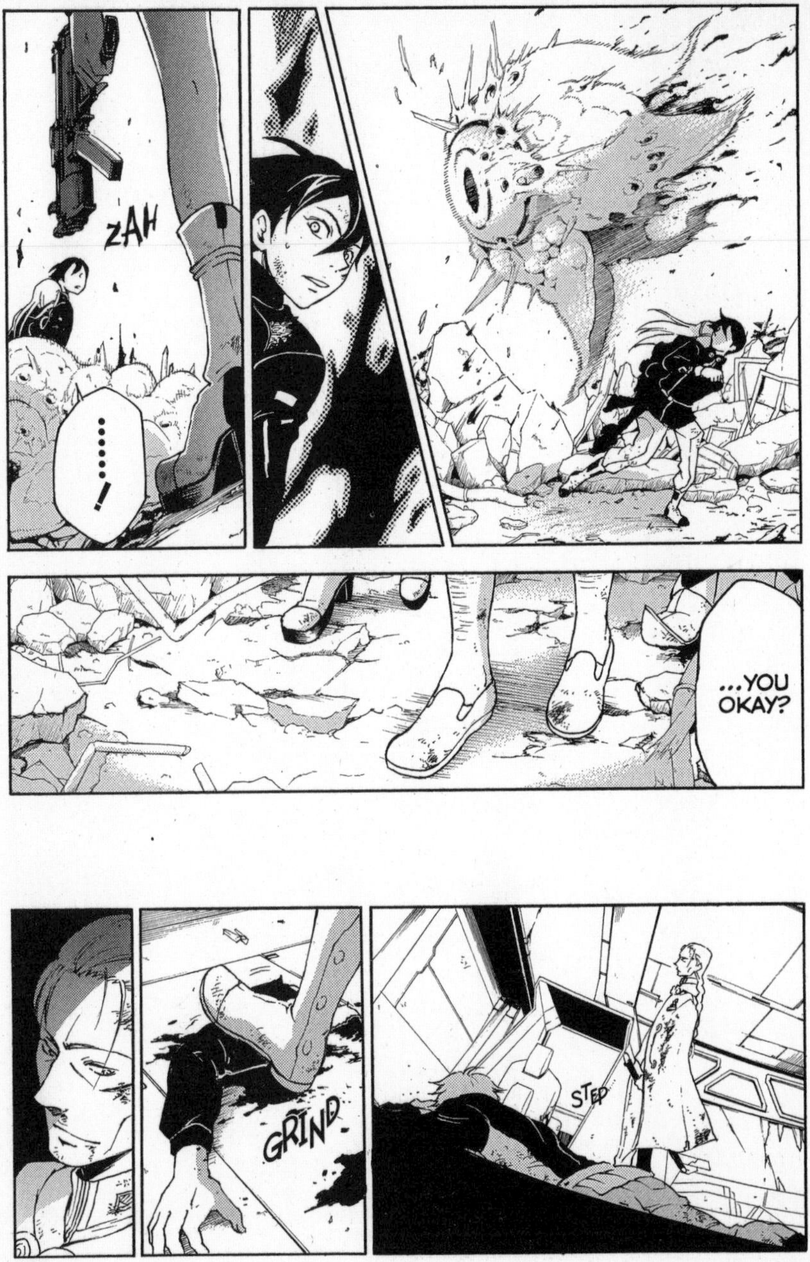
ZAH
......!
...YOU OKAY?
STEP
GRIND

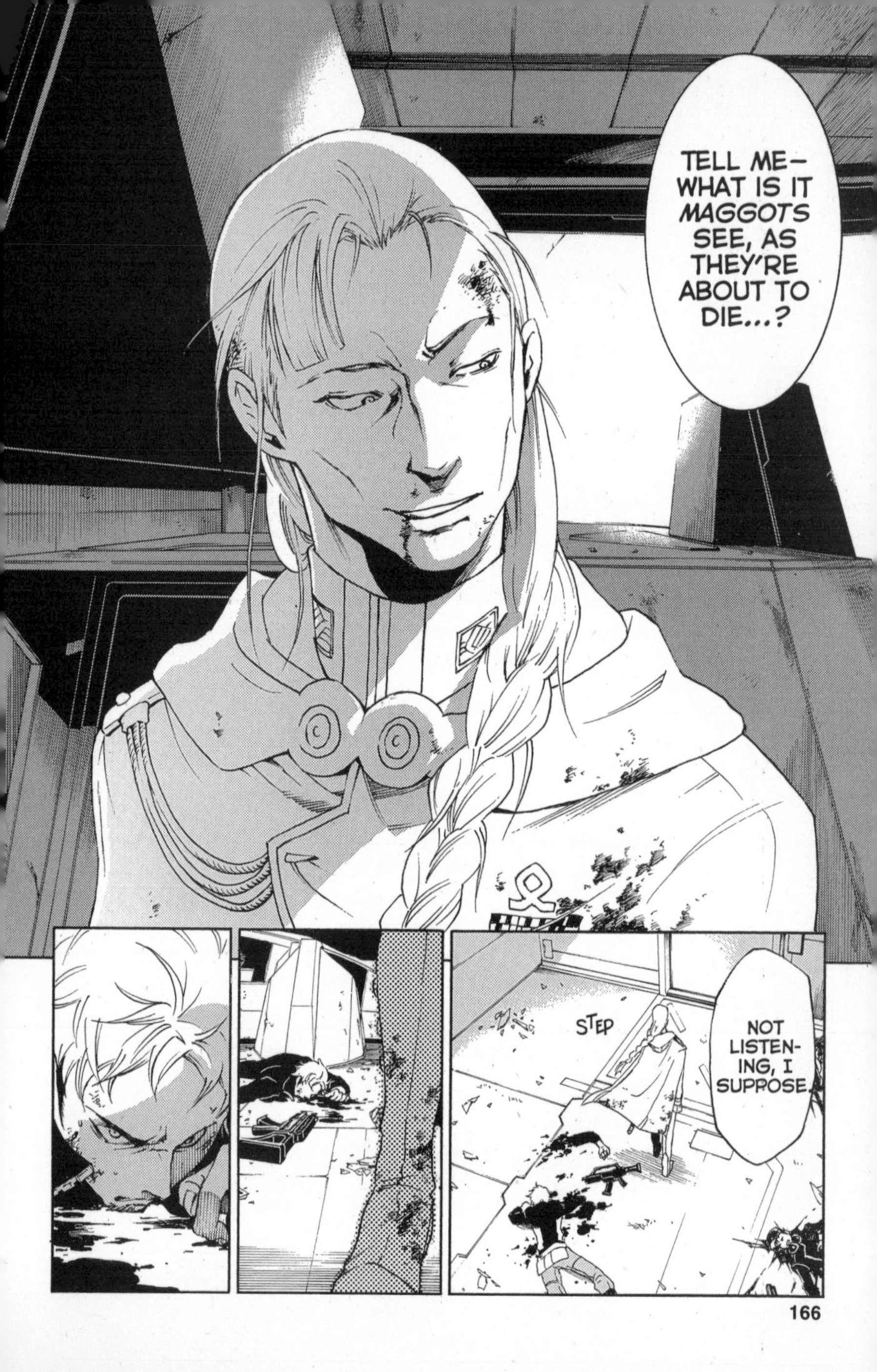
TELL ME—WHAT IS IT *MAGGOTS* SEE, AS THEY'RE ABOUT TO DIE...?
NOT LISTEN-ING, I SUPPOSE.
STEP

...IT'S BEEN LOCKED.

MIGHT'VE BEEN *YAUCH*, I SUPPO—

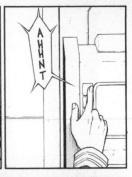

AHHNT

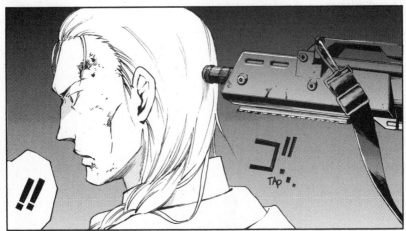

!!

コ!!
TAP

NO CAVALRY YET, HUH?

WHY AREN'T I SUR-PRISED.

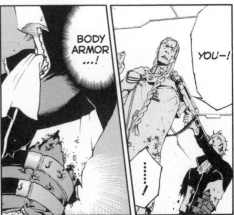

BODY ARMOR....!

YOU—!

......!

167

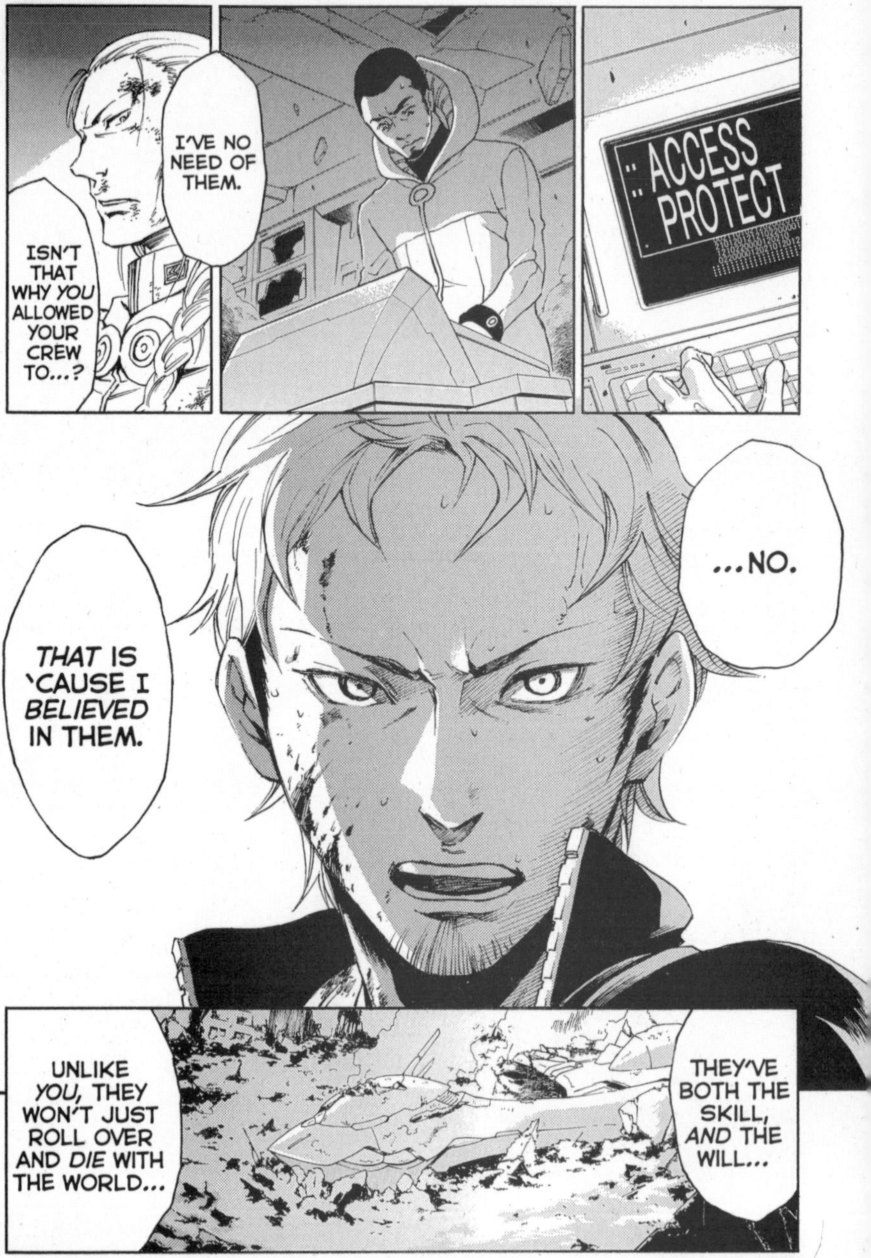
ACCESS PROTECT
I'VE NO NEED OF THEM.
ISN'T THAT WHY *YOU* ALLOWED YOUR CREW TO...?
...NO.
THAT IS 'CAUSE I *BELIEVED* IN THEM.
THEY'VE BOTH THE SKILL, *AND* THE WILL...
UNLIKE *YOU*, THEY WON'T JUST ROLL OVER AND *DIE* WITH THE WORLD...

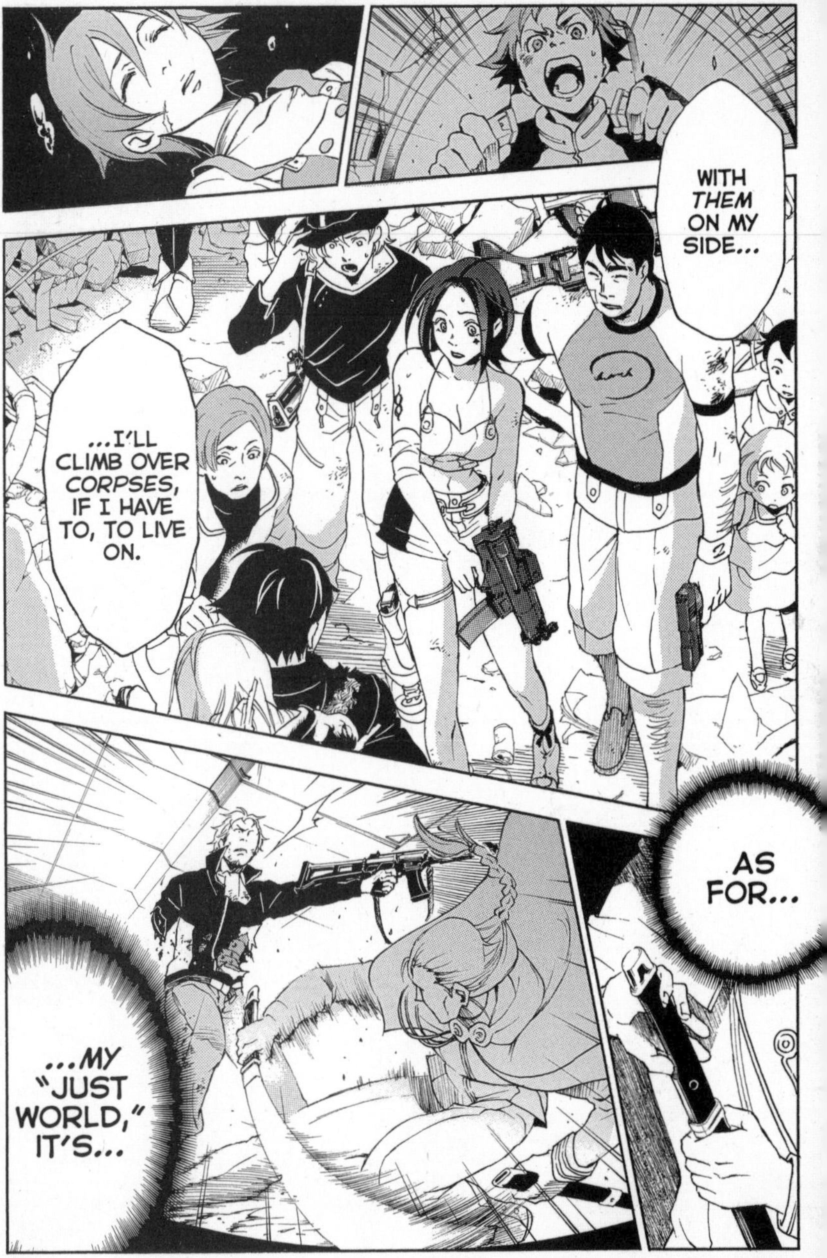
WITH THEM ON MY SIDE...
...I'LL CLIMB OVER CORPSES, IF I HAVE TO, TO LIVE ON.
AS FOR...
...MY "JUST WORLD," IT'S...

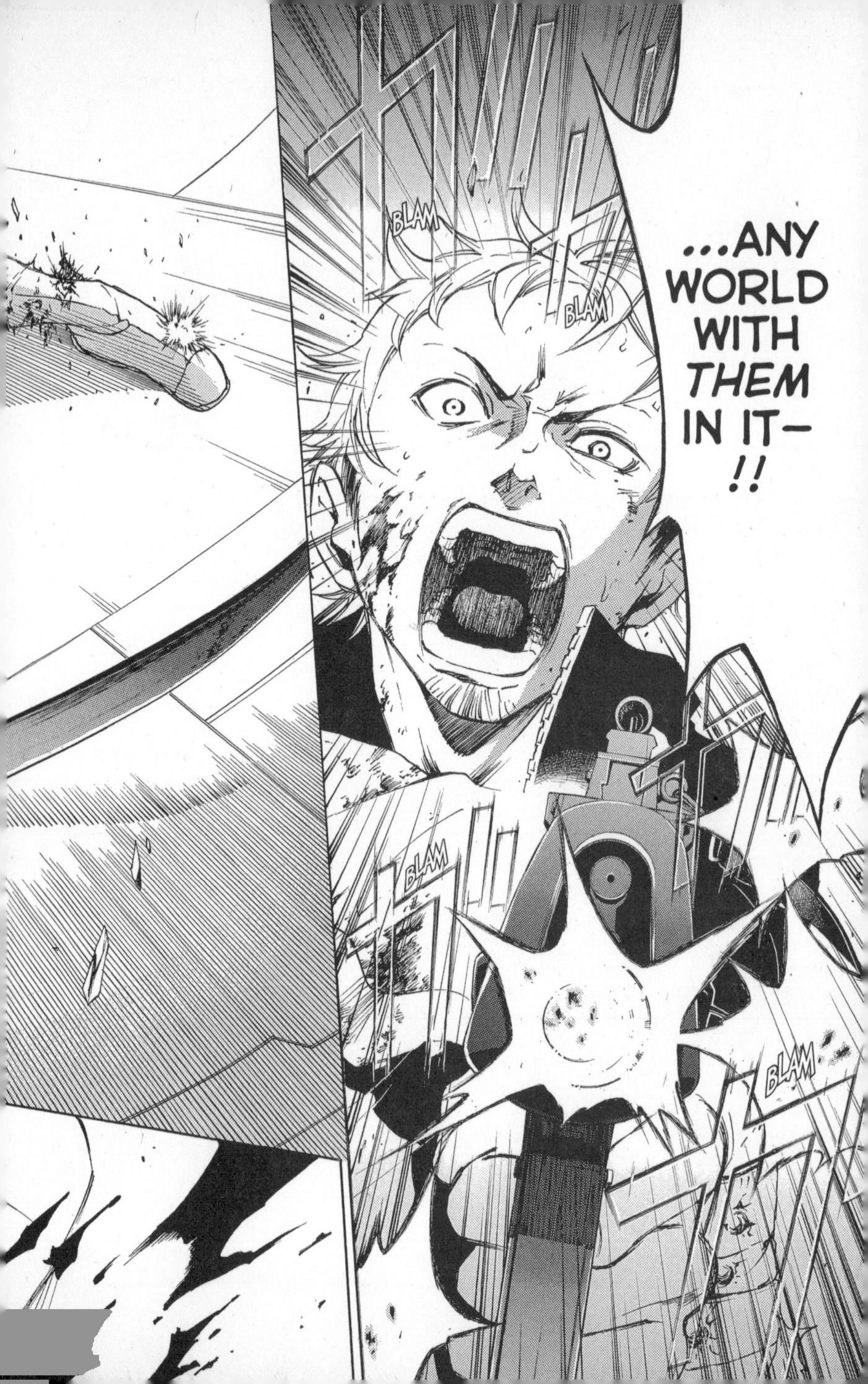
...ANY WORLD WITH *THEM* IN IT—!!
BLAM
BLAM
BLAM
BLAM

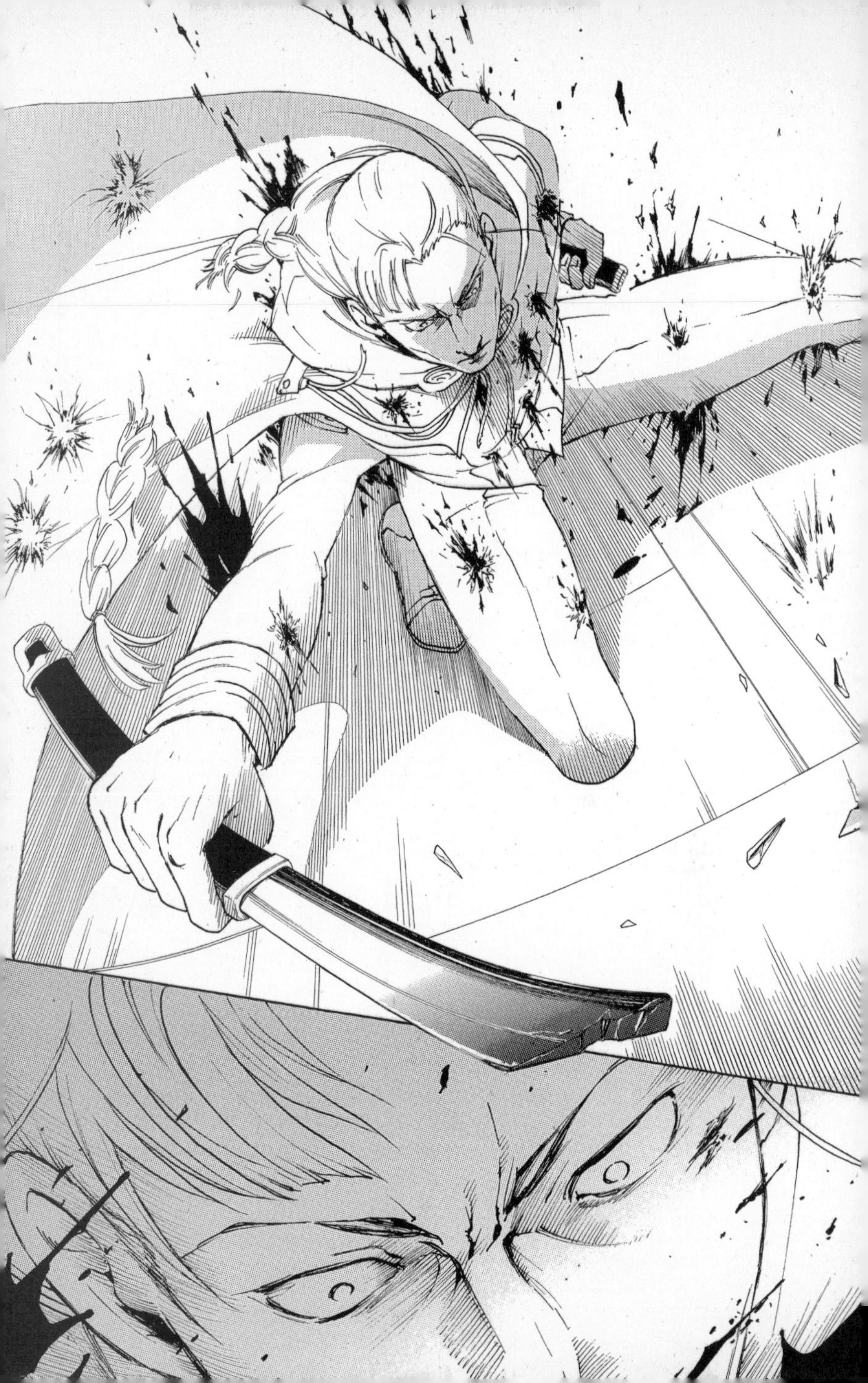

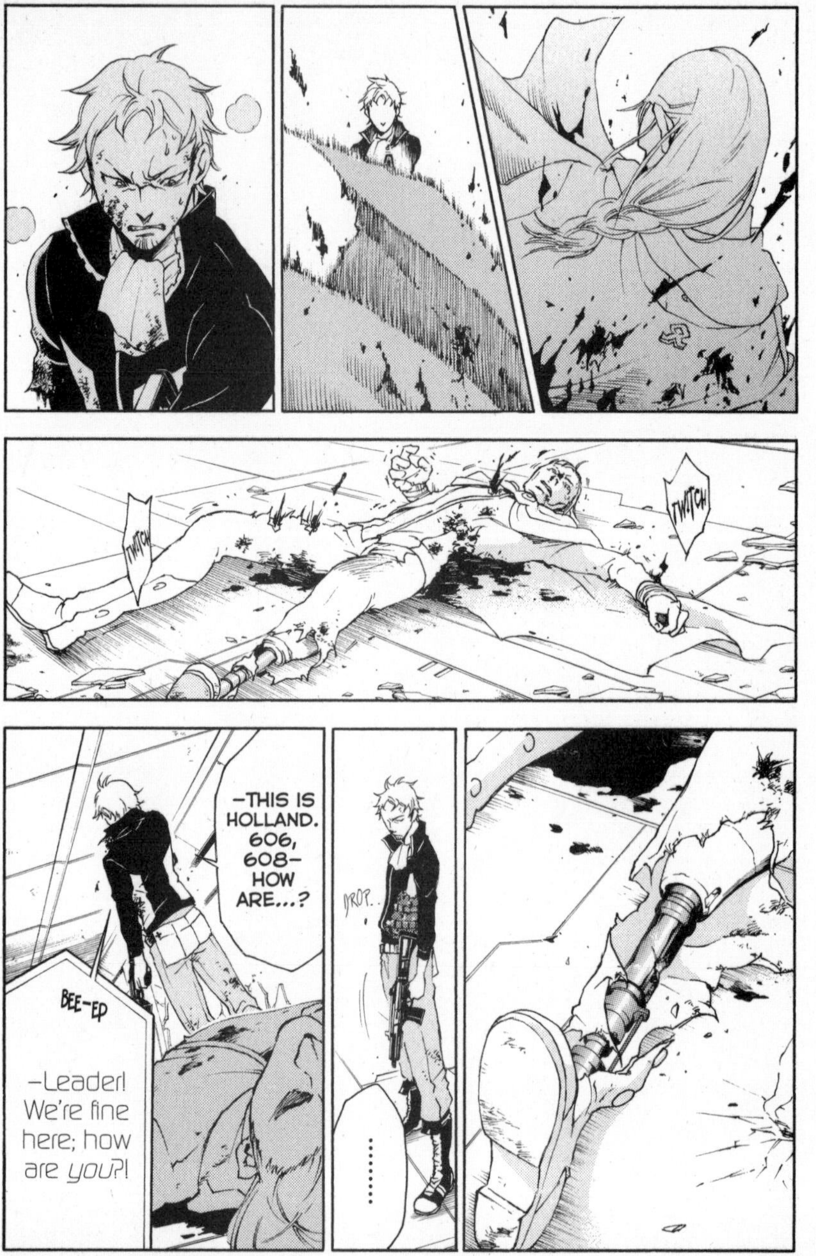
TWITCH
TWITCH
DROP...
......
—THIS IS HOLLAND. 606, 608— HOW ARE...?
BEE—EP
—Leader! We're fine here; how are *you*?!

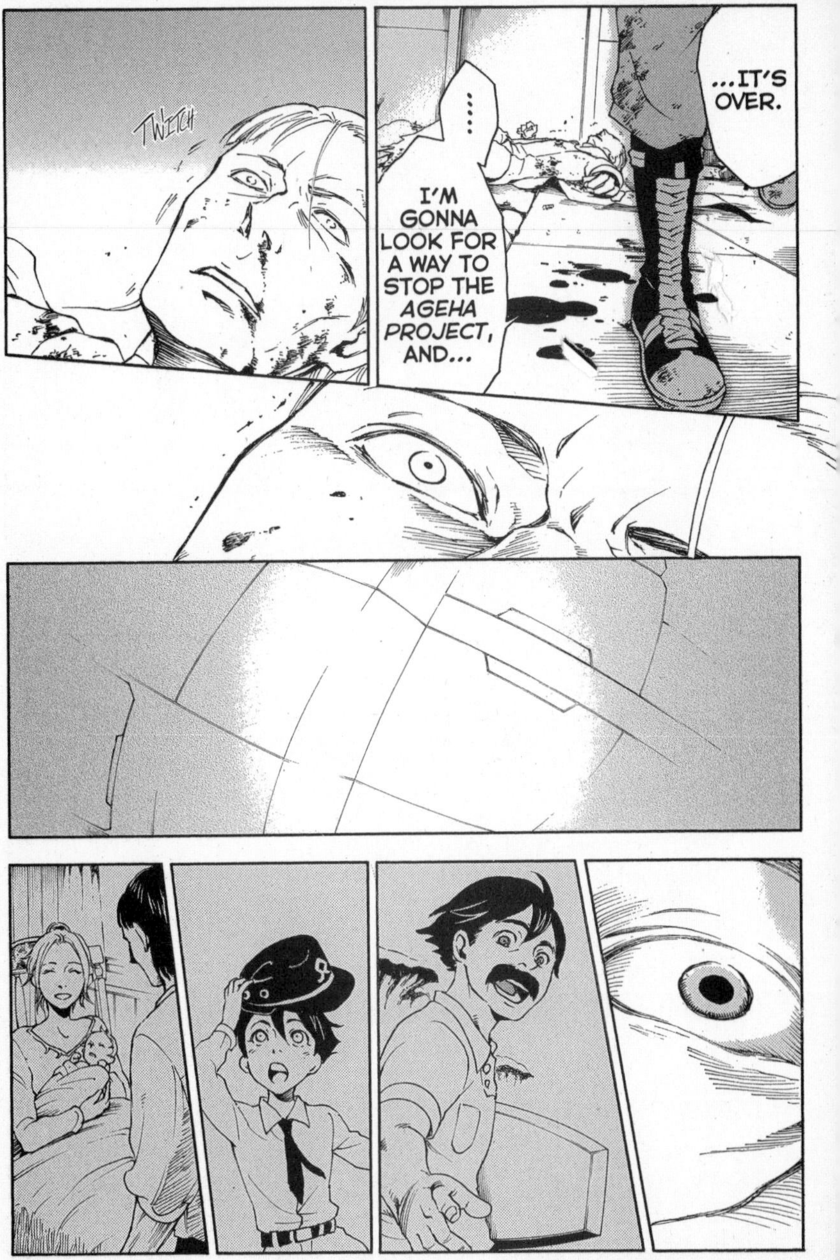
...IT'S OVER.
.....
I'M GONNA LOOK FOR A WAY TO STOP THE *AGEHA PROJECT*, AND...
TWITCH

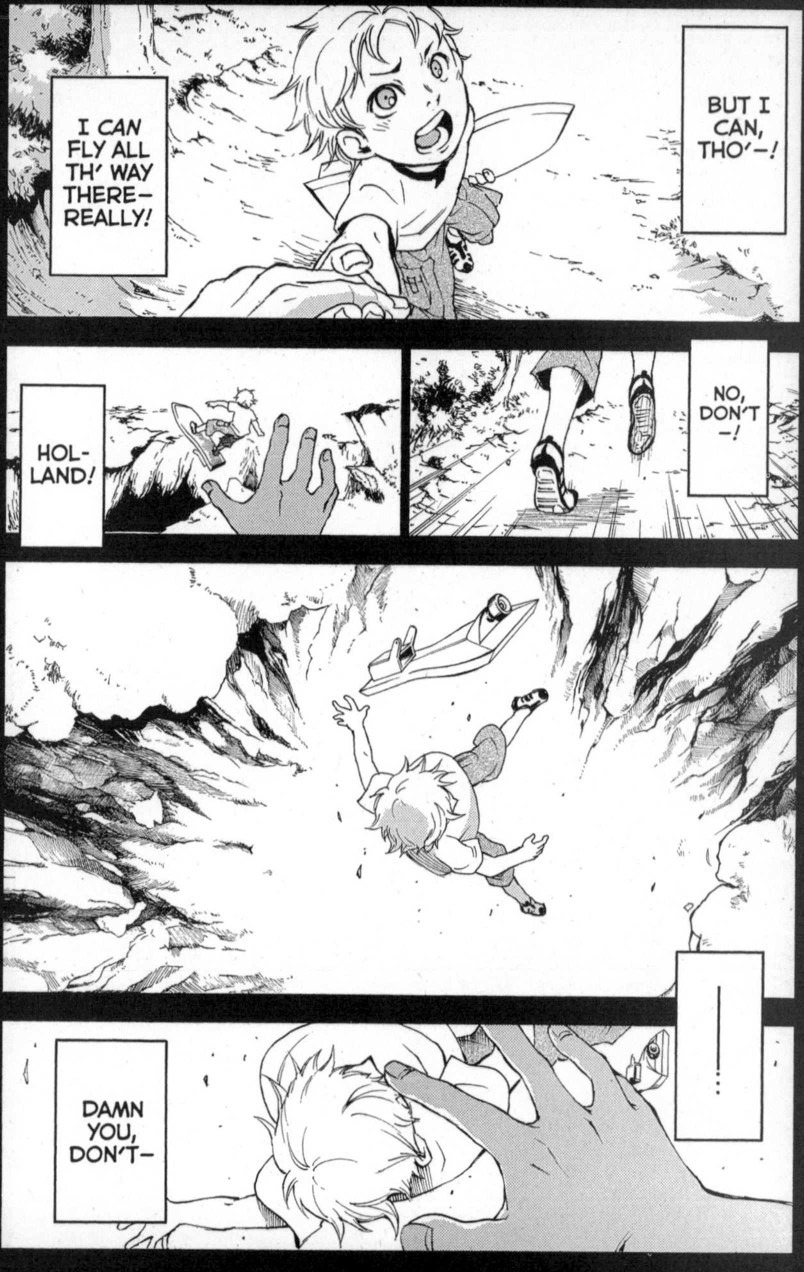
BUT I CAN, THO'–!
I CAN FLY ALL TH' WAY THERE–REALLY!
NO, DON'T–!
HOL-LAND!
–......
DAMN YOU, DON'T–

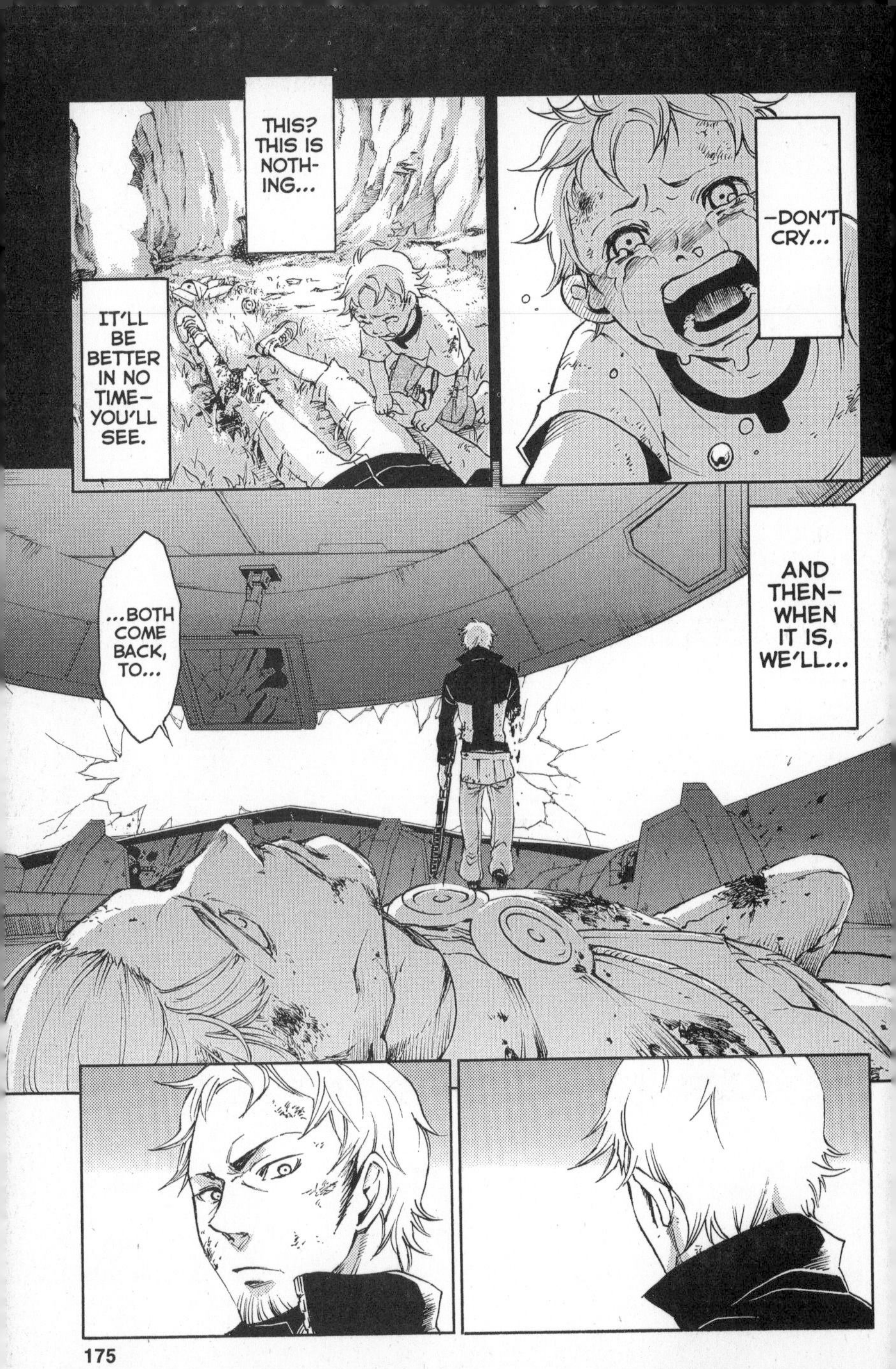
—DON'T CRY...
THIS? THIS IS NOTHING...
IT'LL BE BETTER IN NO TIME—YOU'LL SEE.
AND THEN—WHEN IT IS, WE'LL...
...BOTH COME BACK, TO...

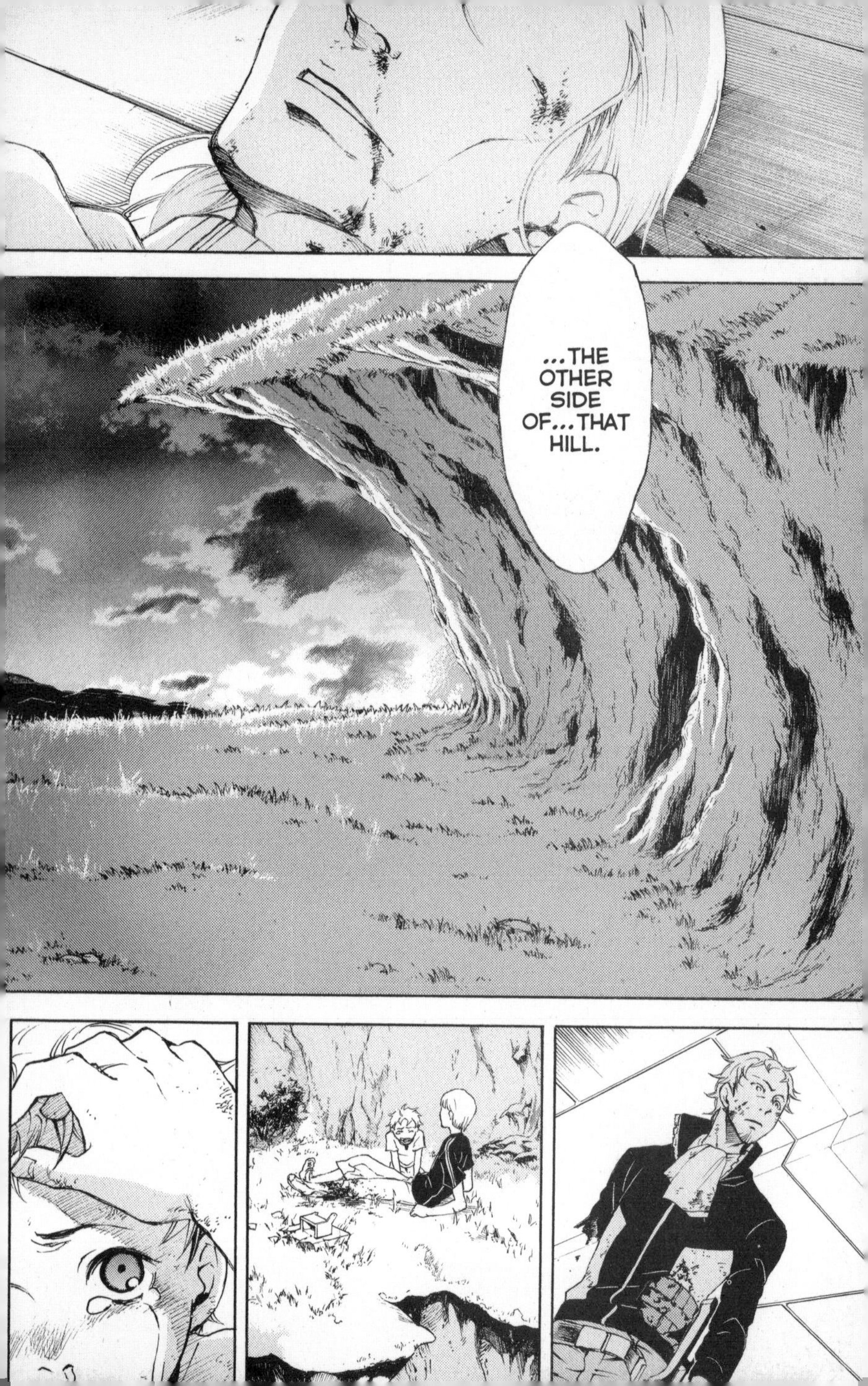
...THE OTHER SIDE OF...THAT HILL.

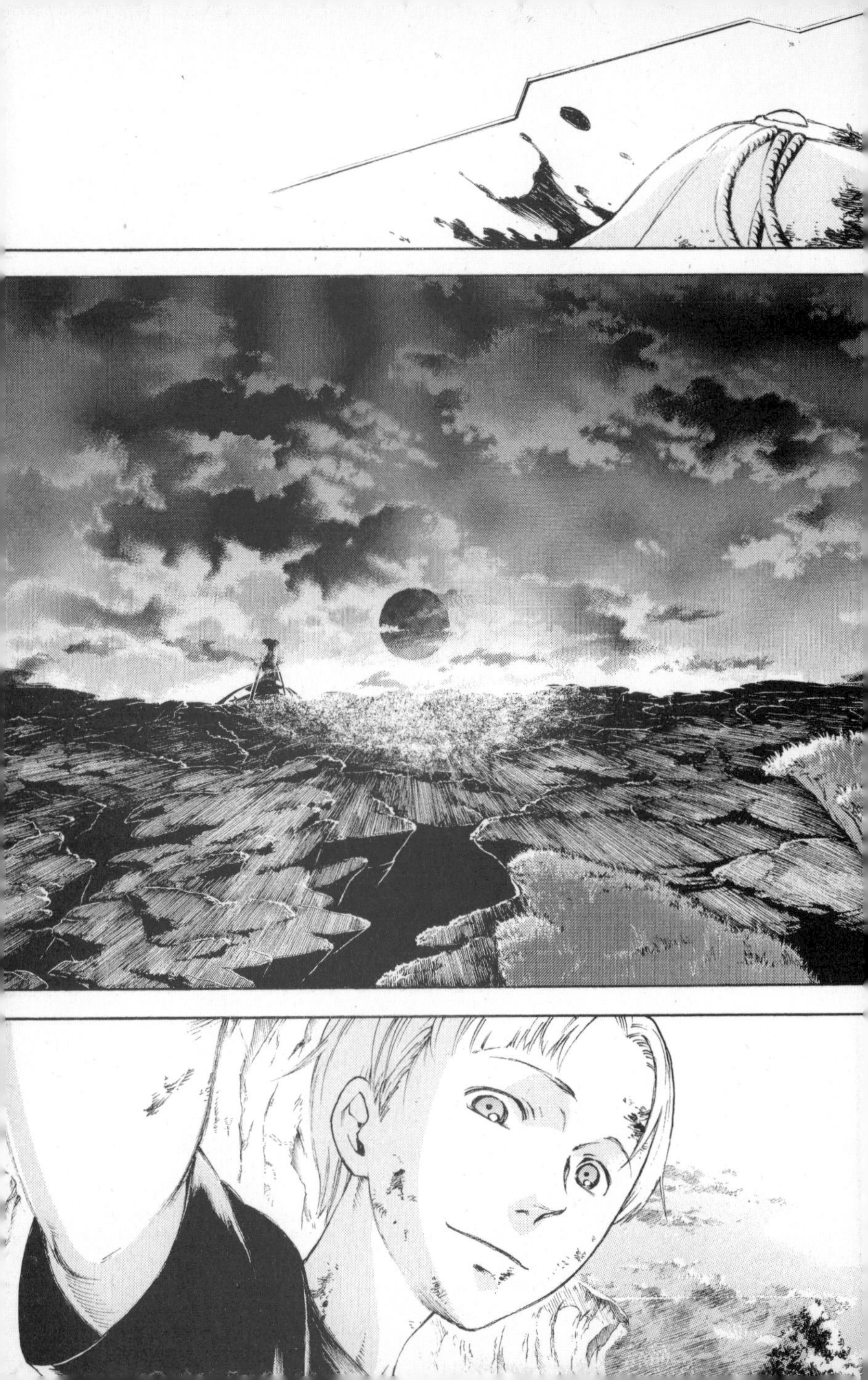

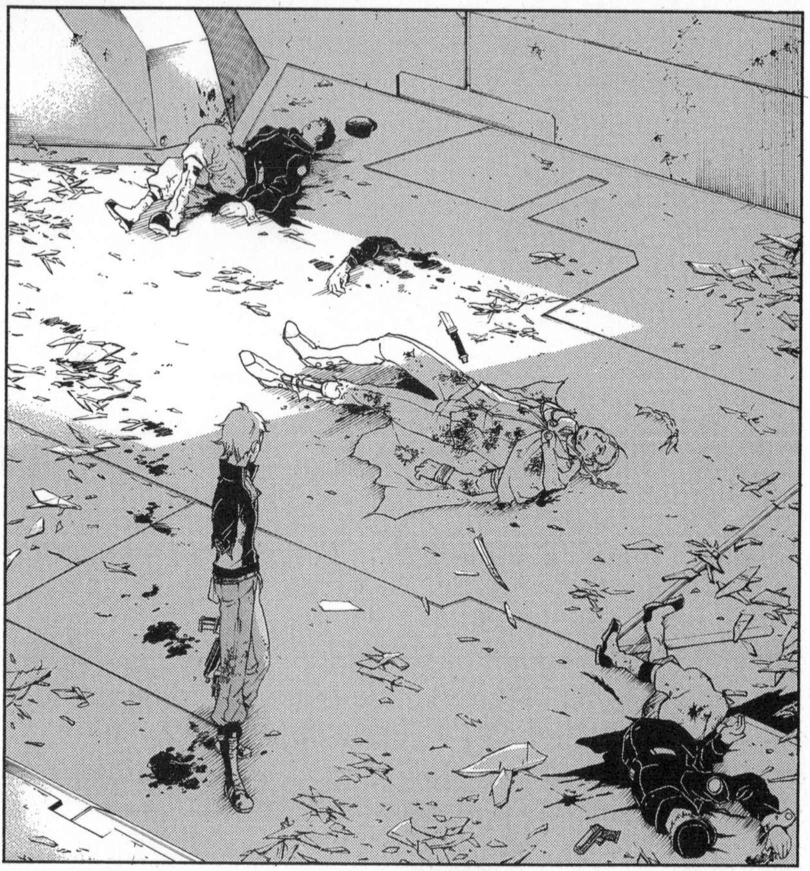

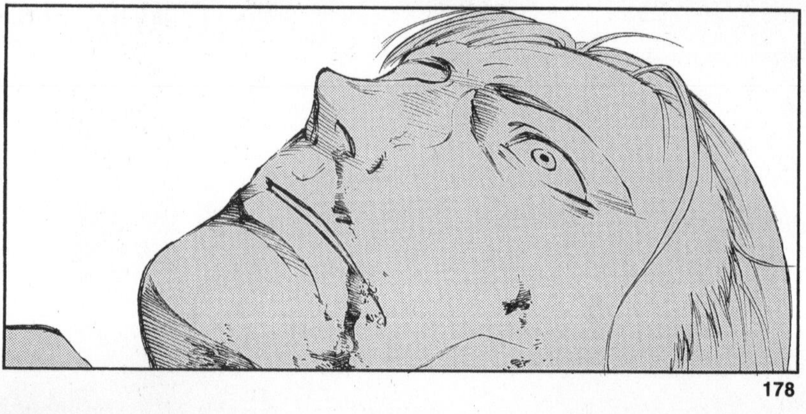

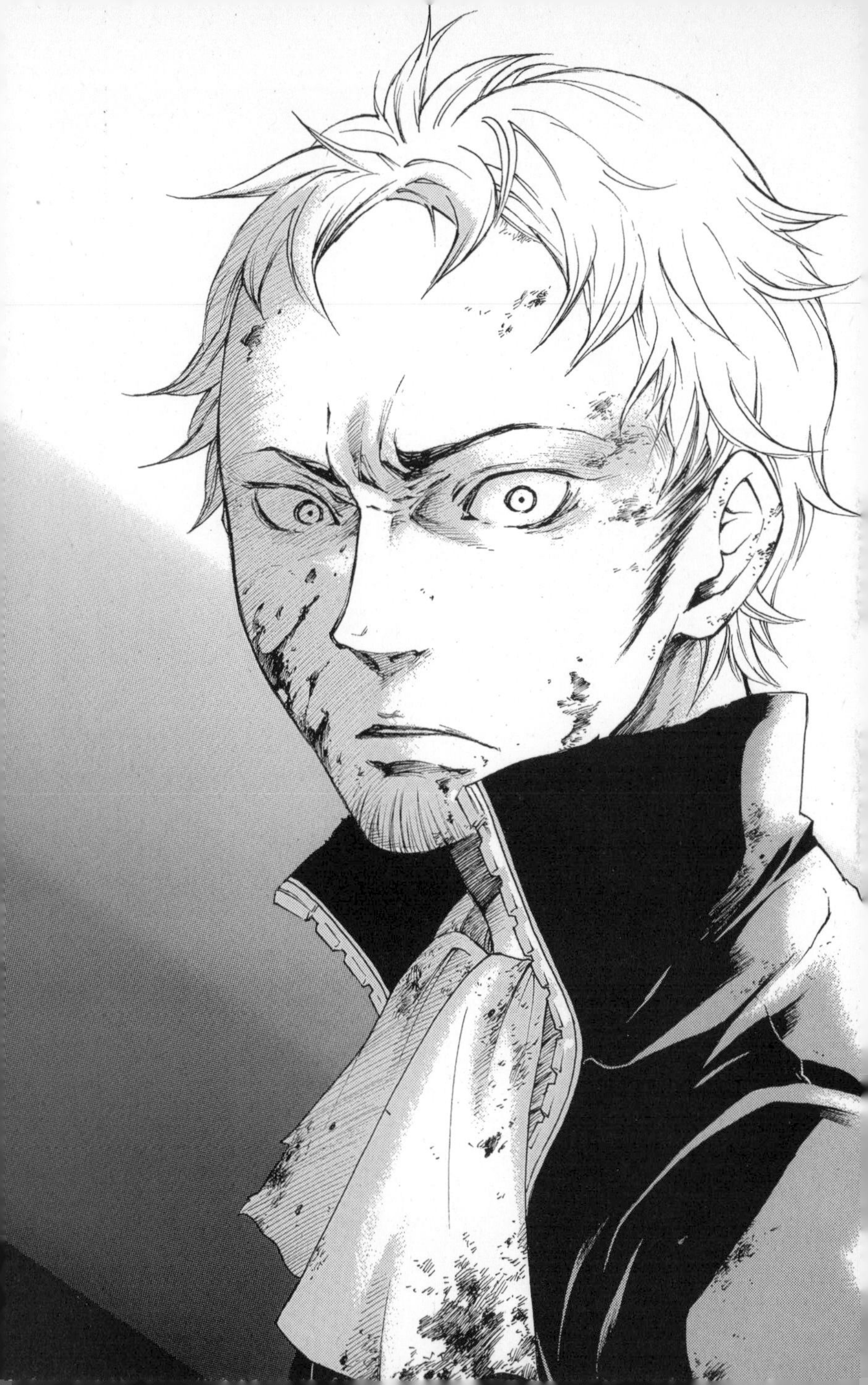

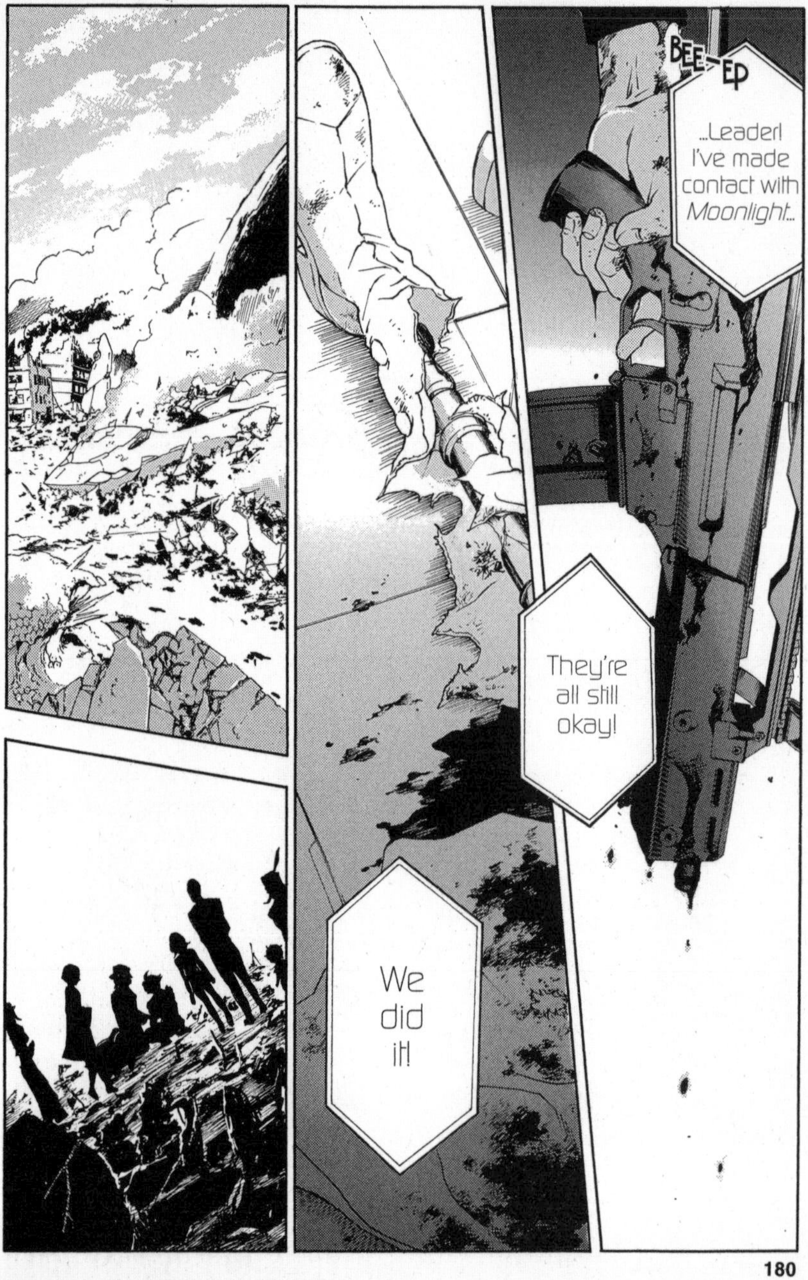
BEE-EP
...Leader! I've made contact with *Moonlight*...
They're all still okay!
We did it!

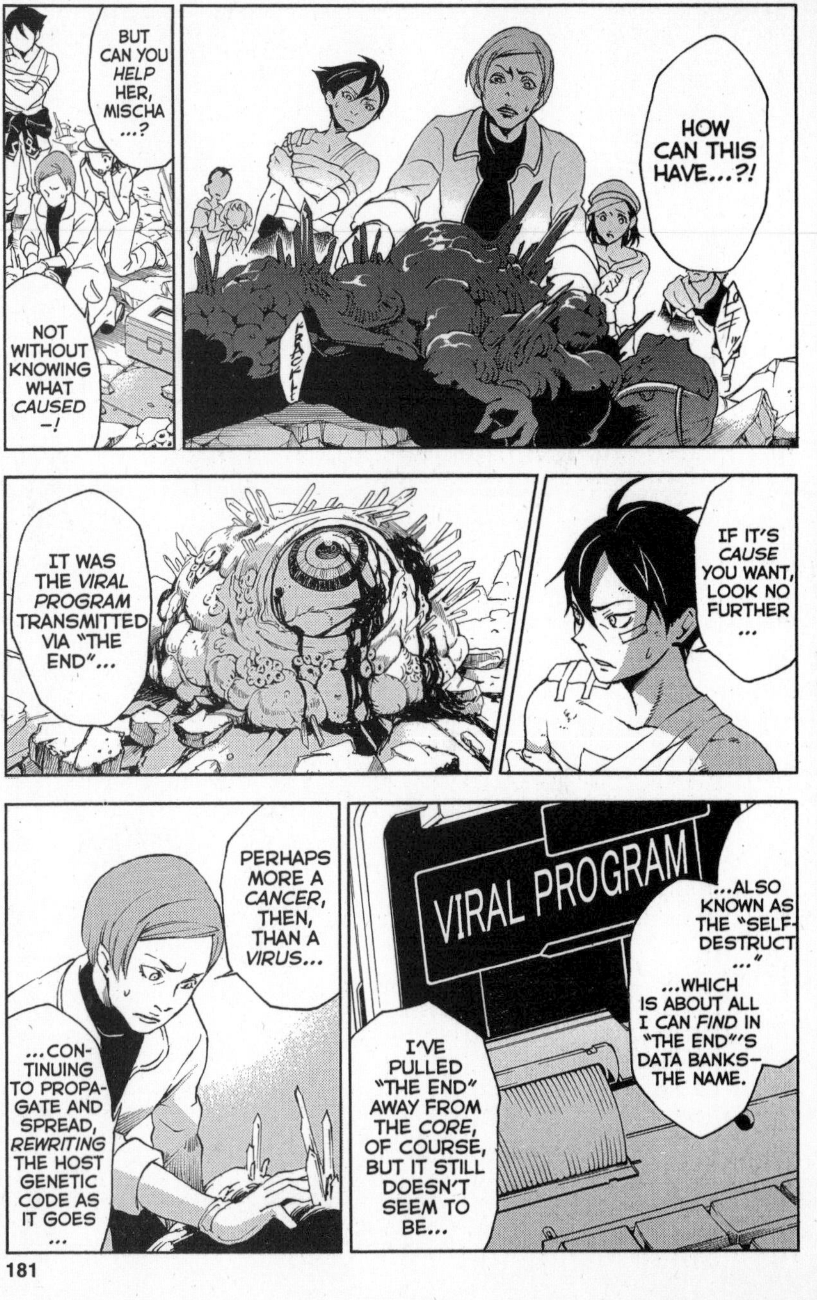
HOW CAN THIS HAVE...?!
KRACKLE
BUT CAN YOU *HELP* HER, MISCHA...?
NOT WITHOUT KNOWING WHAT *CAUSED*—!
IF IT'S *CAUSE* YOU WANT, LOOK NO FURTHER...
IT WAS THE *VIRAL PROGRAM* TRANSMITTED VIA "THE END"...
VIRAL PROGRAM
...ALSO KNOWN AS THE "SELF-DESTRUCT..."
...WHICH IS ABOUT ALL I CAN *FIND* IN "THE END"'S DATA BANKS—THE NAME.
I'VE PULLED "THE END" AWAY FROM THE *CORE*, OF COURSE, BUT IT STILL DOESN'T SEEM TO BE...
PERHAPS MORE A *CANCER*, THEN, THAN A *VIRUS*...
...CONTINUING TO PROPAGATE AND SPREAD, *REWRITING* THE HOST GENETIC CODE AS IT GOES...

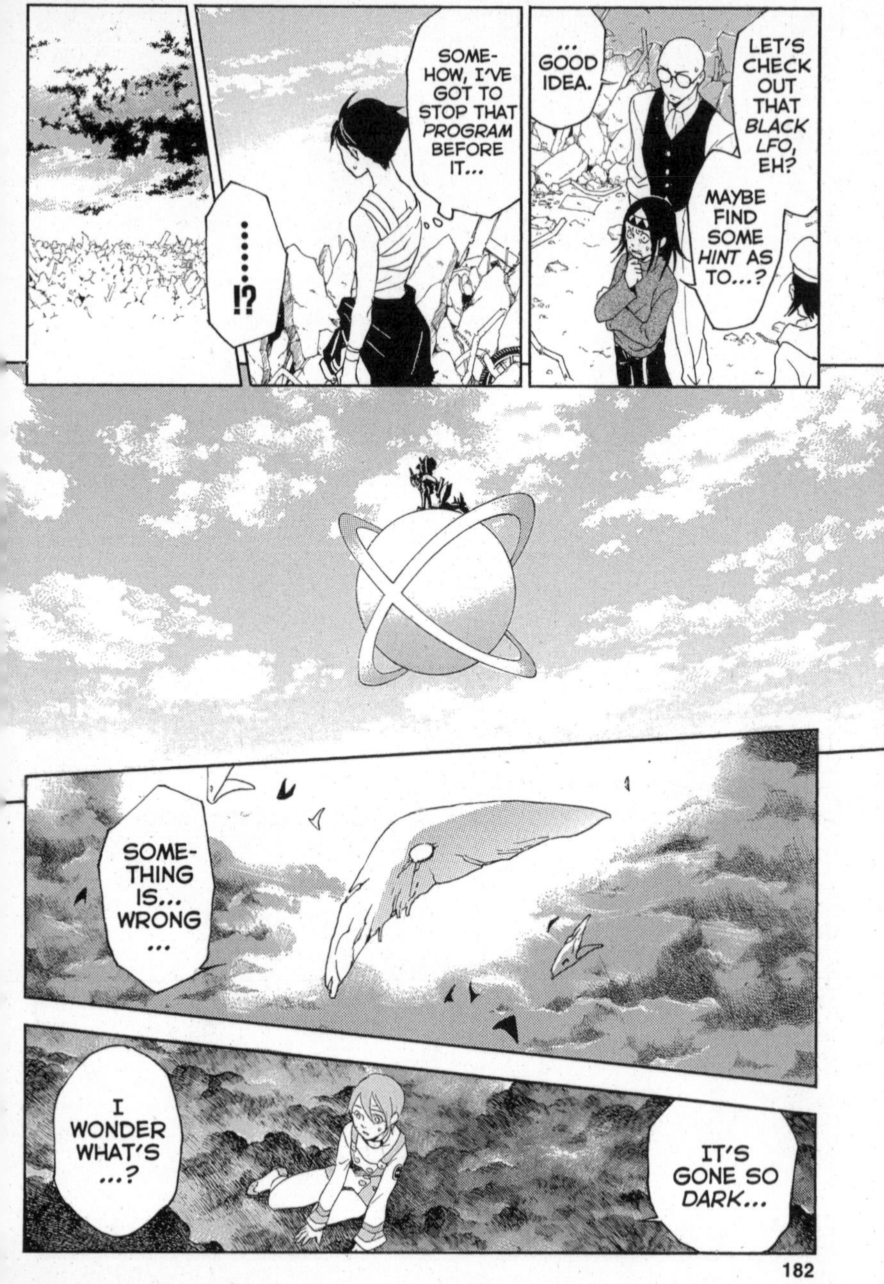
LET'S CHECK OUT THAT *BLACK LFO*, EH?
MAYBE FIND SOME *HINT* AS TO...?
...GOOD IDEA.
SOME-HOW, I'VE GOT TO STOP THAT *PROGRAM* BEFORE IT...
......!?
SOME-THING IS... WRONG...
IT'S GONE SO *DARK*...
I WONDER WHAT'S ...?

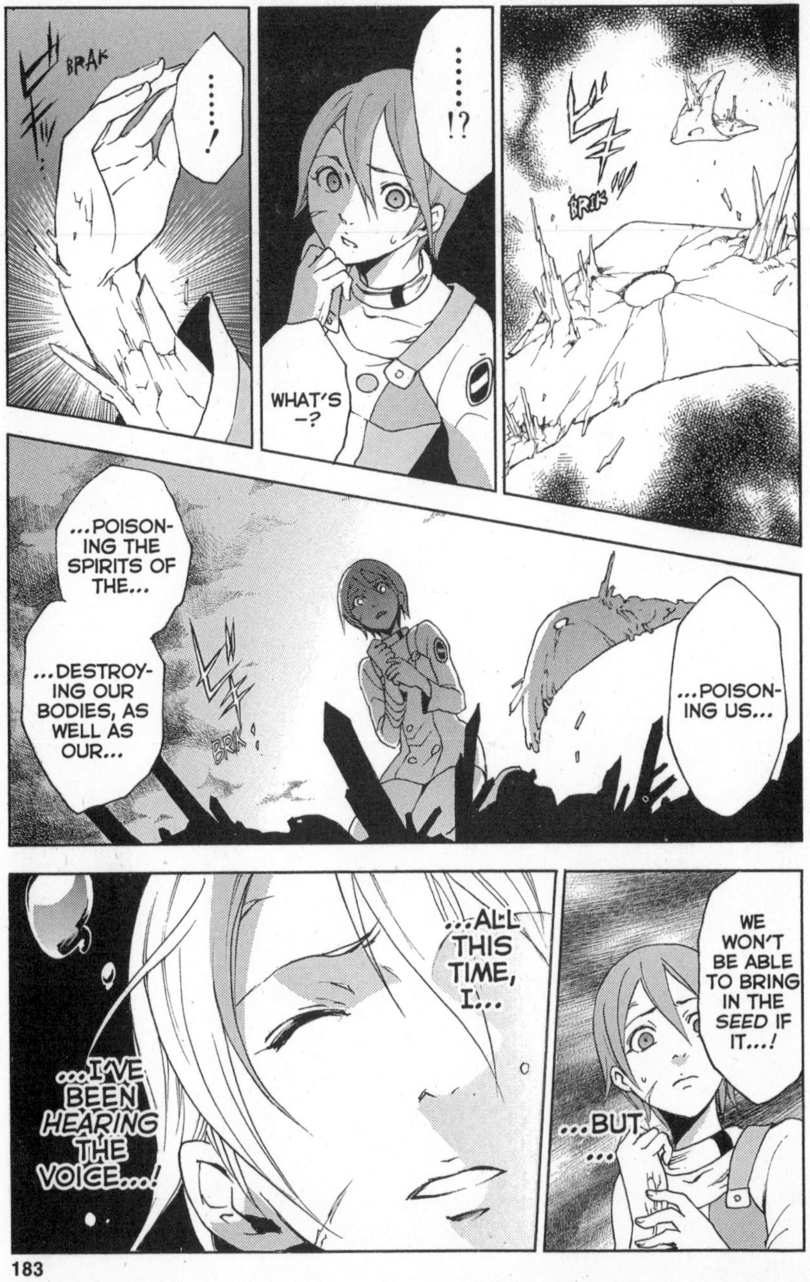
BRIK
……!?
WHAT'S—?
……!
BRAK
...POISONING US...
...POISONING THE SPIRITS OF THE...
...DESTROYING OUR BODIES, AS WELL AS OUR...
BRIK
WE WON'T BE ABLE TO BRING IN THE *SEED* IF IT...!
...BUT...
...ALL THIS TIME, I...
...I'VE BEEN *HEARING* THE VOICE...!

...HEARING *RENTON'S* VOICE...!

GLORBLE

......

!!

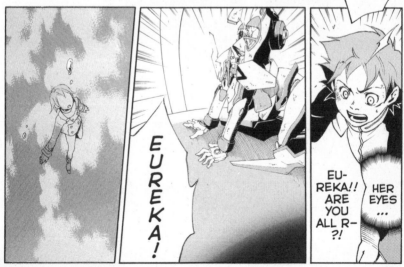

EUREKA!

EU-REKA!! ARE YOU ALL R–?!

HER EYES...

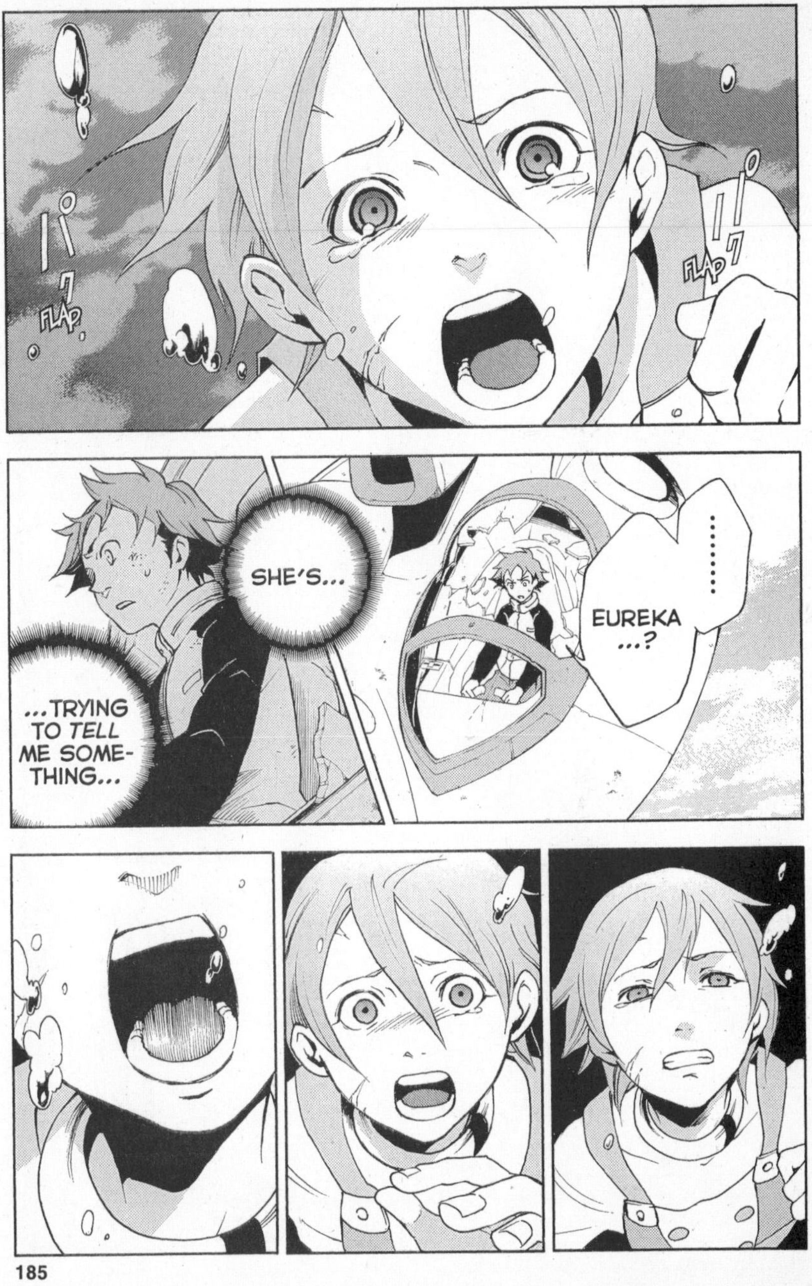
FLAP
FLAP
......
EUREKA ...?
SHE'S...
...TRYING TO *TELL* ME SOME-THING...

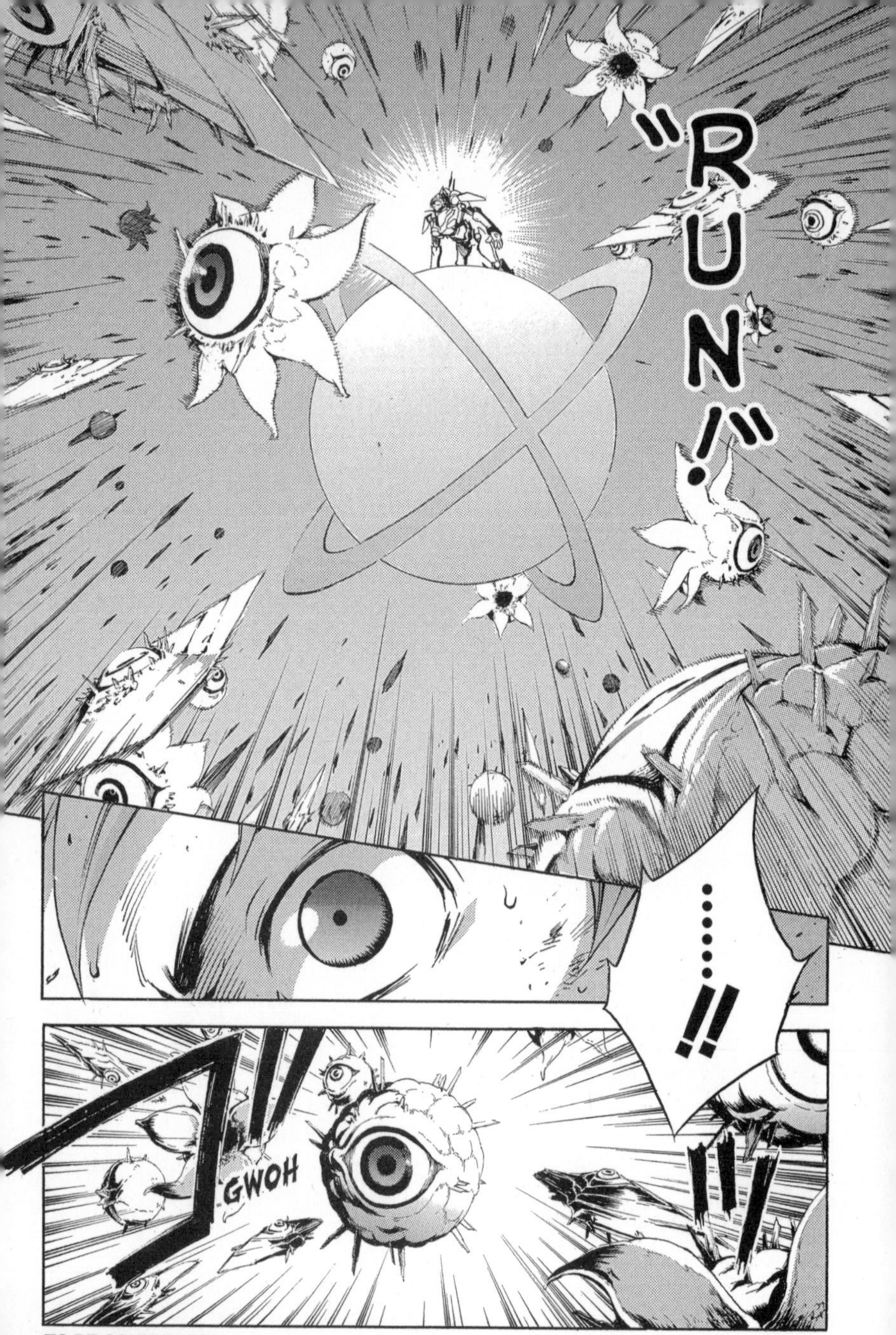
"RUN"
......!!
GWOH

TO BE CONTINUED...

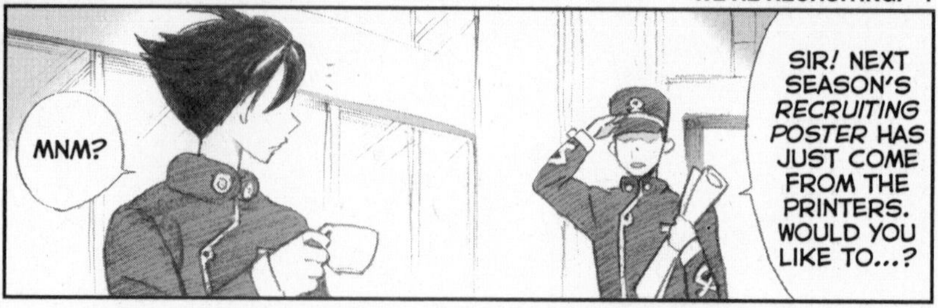
SIR! NEXT SEASON'S *RECRUITING POSTER* HAS JUST COME FROM THE PRINTERS. WOULD YOU LIKE TO...?
MNM?

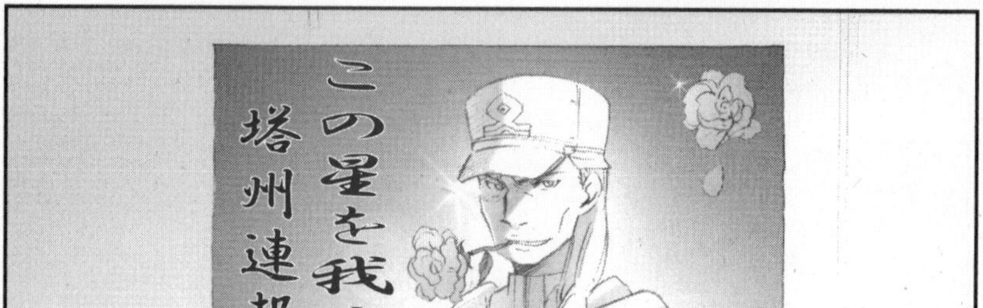
この星を我らが手に！
塔州連邦軍軍人募集
UFF Recruitment, Public Relations Division
FOR MORE INFORMATION, CONTACT A65-3354

*POSTER - **YOU'VE GOT THE WHOLE WORLD IN YOUR HANDS!** United Federation Forces Recruitment Agency

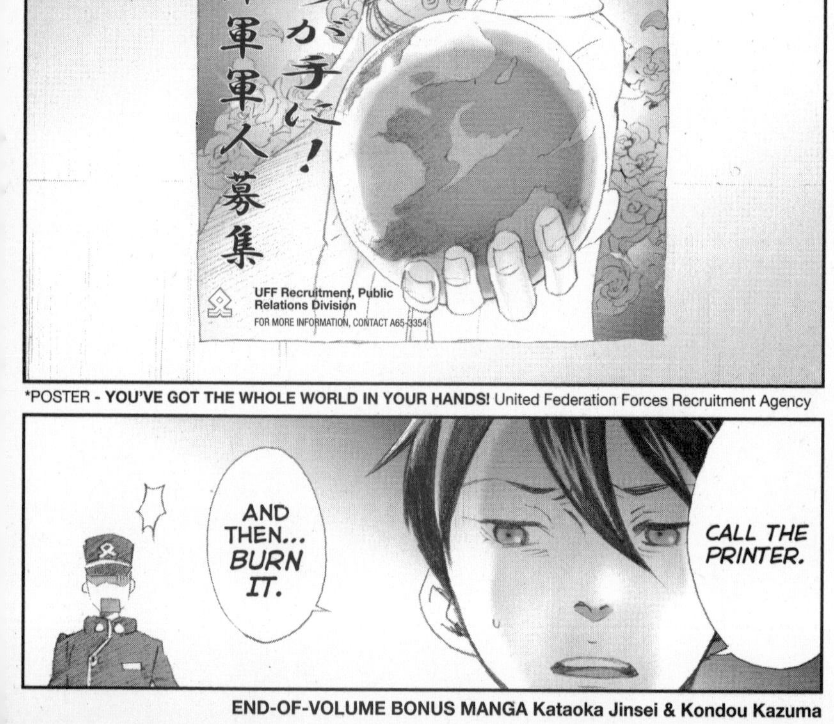
CALL THE PRINTER.
AND THEN... BURN IT.

END-OF-VOLUME BONUS MANGA Kataoka Jinsei & Kondou Kazuma

THE SUFFERING OF HAP

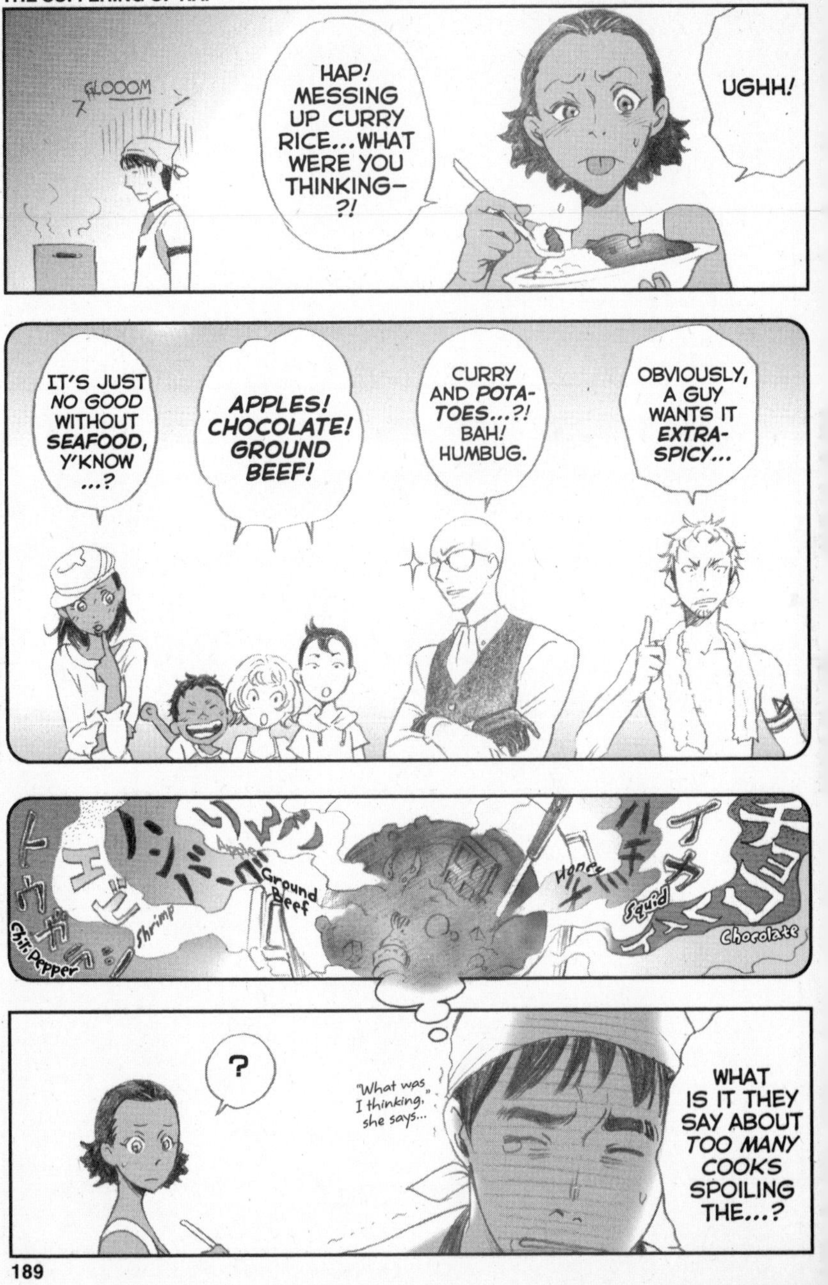

UGHH!
HAP! MESSING UP CURRY RICE...WHAT WERE YOU THINKING—?!
GLOOOM
OBVIOUSLY, A GUY WANTS IT *EXTRA-SPICY*...
CURRY AND *POTATOES*...?! BAH! HUMBUG.
APPLES! CHOCOLATE! GROUND BEEF!
IT'S JUST *NO GOOD* WITHOUT *SEAFOOD*, Y'KNOW ...?
Chocolate
Squid
Honey
Ground Beef
Apple
Shrimp
Chili Pepper
WHAT IS IT THEY SAY ABOUT *TOO MANY* COOKS SPOILING THE...?
"What was I thinking," she says...
?

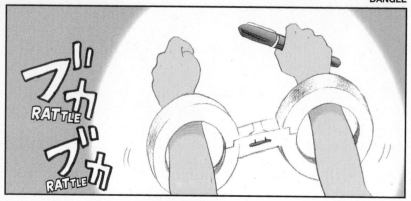

RATTLE

RATTLE

TA-DAH!

HOW'S THIS?

JUST A SEC...

Hey! Hey!

EHEH-HEH-HEH

WHOEVER THOUGHT THERE'D BE A NEED FOR *CHILD-SIZED*...?

MUCH BETTER.

DAN-N-NGLE

WE'RE RECRUITING! - 1

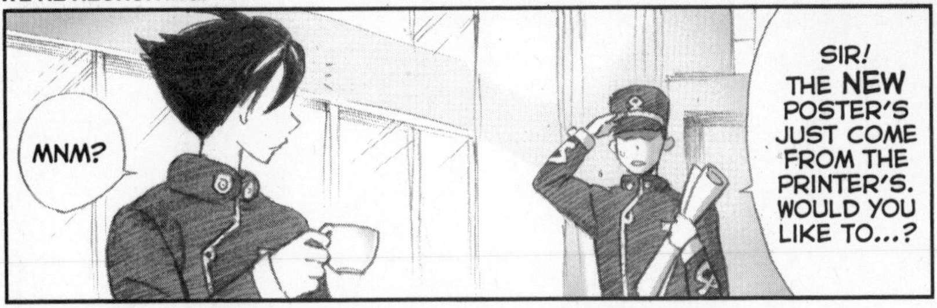
SIR! THE NEW POSTER'S JUST COME FROM THE PRINTER'S. WOULD YOU LIKE TO...?
MNM?

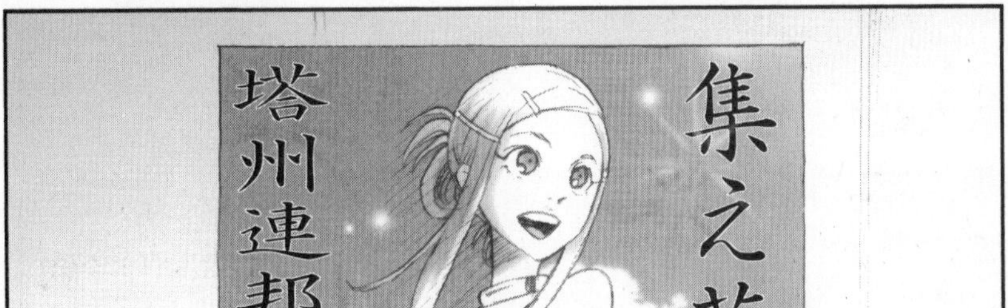
集え若人！
塔州連邦軍軍人募集
UFF Recruitment, Public Relations Division
FOR MORE INFORMATION, CONTACT A65-3354

*POSTER - **COME 'N' GET IT, BOYS!** United Federation Forces Recruitment Agency

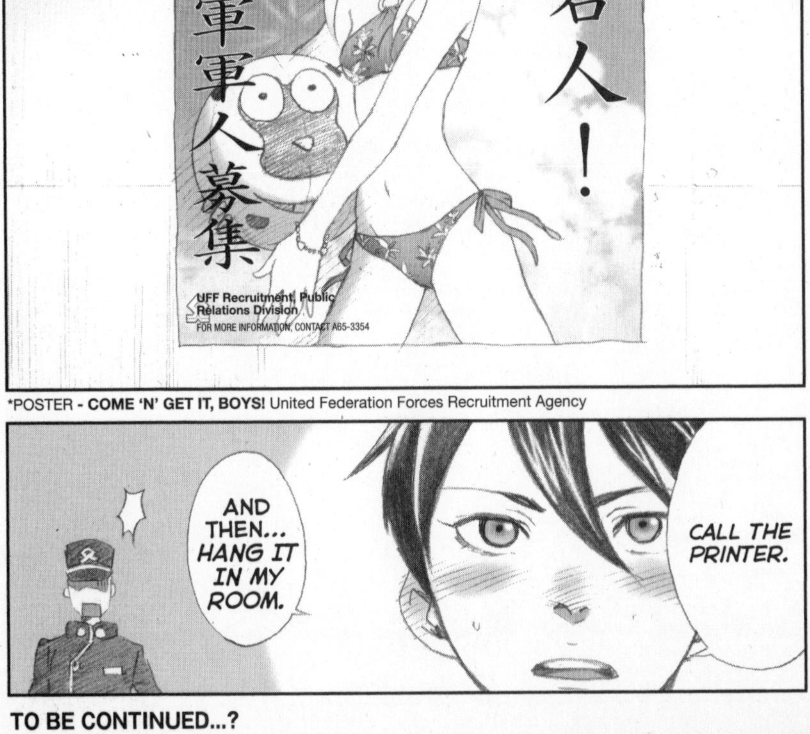
CALL THE PRINTER.
AND THEN... HANG IT IN MY ROOM.

TO BE CONTINUED...?

postscript

character&story

jinsei kataoka

robots&color&more

kazuma kondou

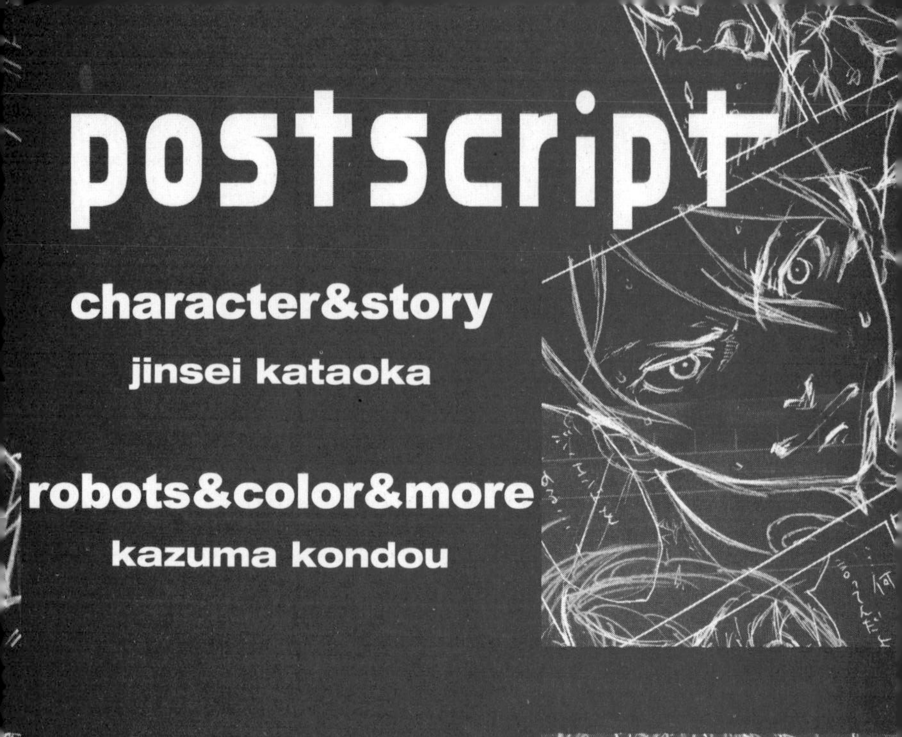

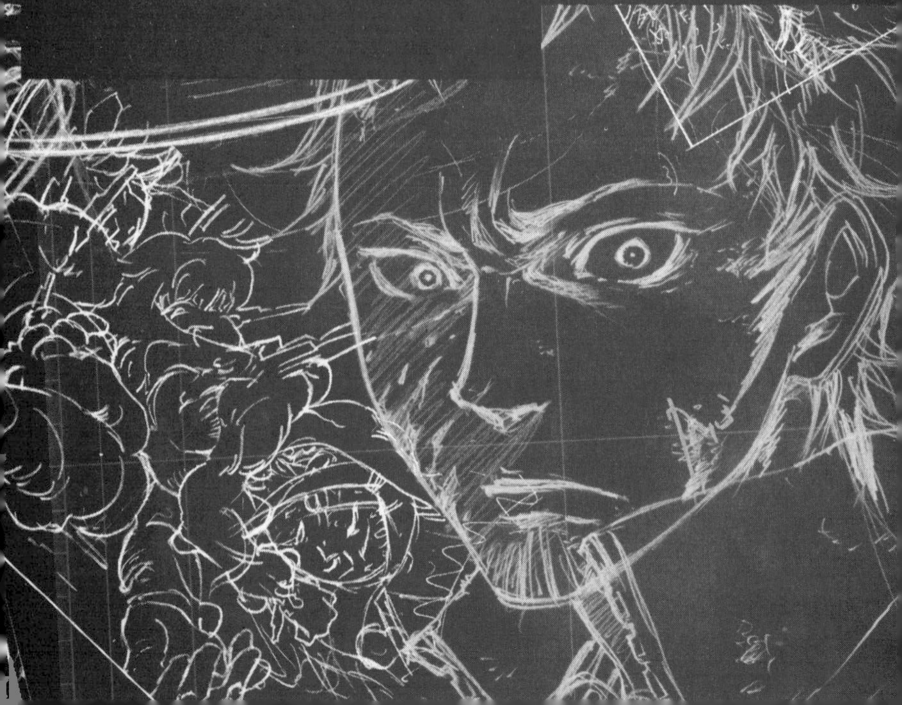

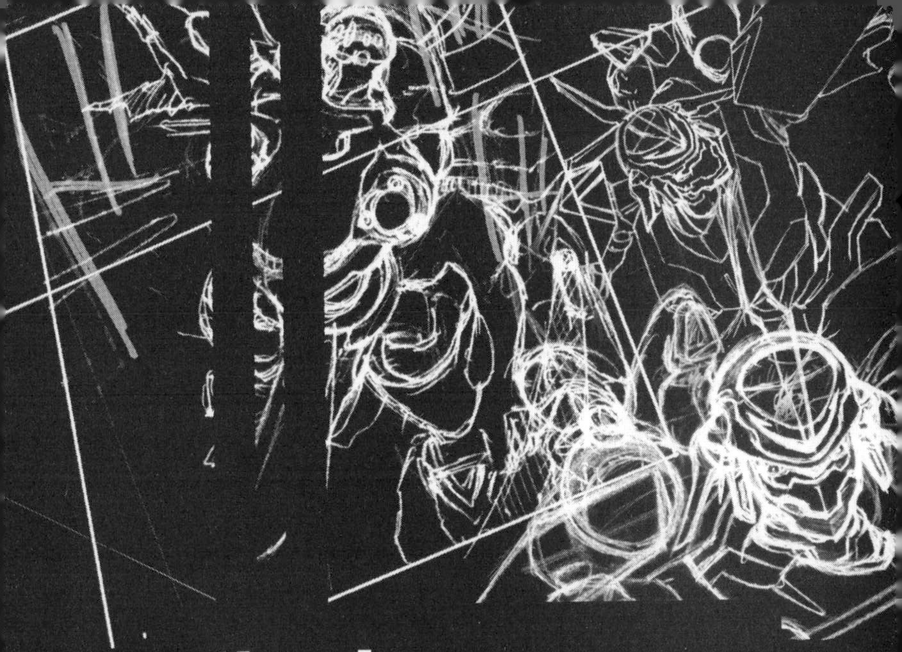

thanks

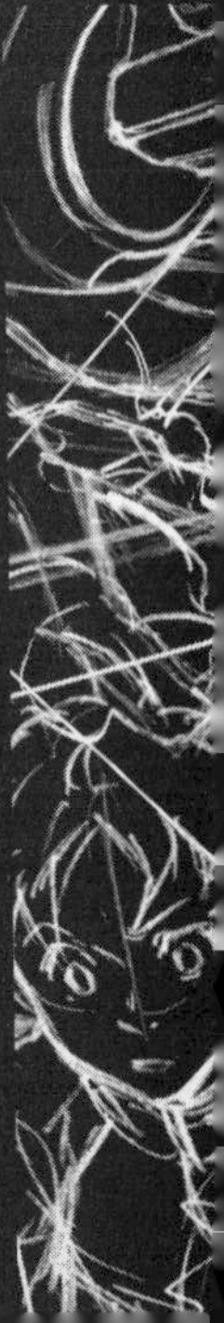

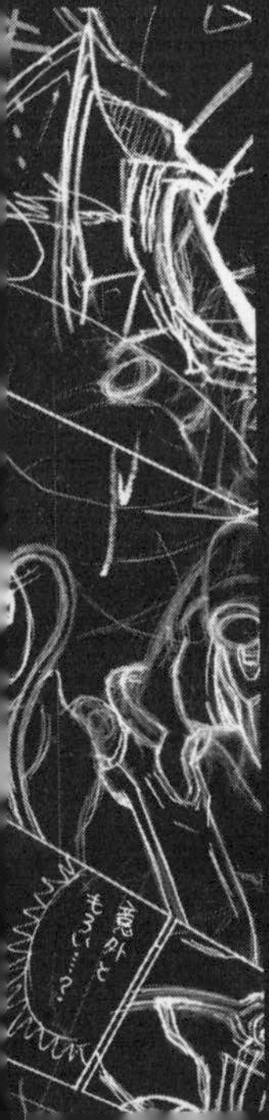

Kei Ishibashi
Keisuke Imade
Uta Ekaki
Hiroshi Katou
Ryouichi Saiyatani
Shou Nakata
Barusu Noda
Takako Nobe
Akihiko Higuchi
Nozomi Hirama
Wraith Benjamin

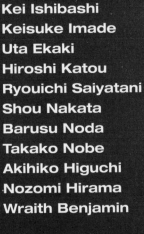

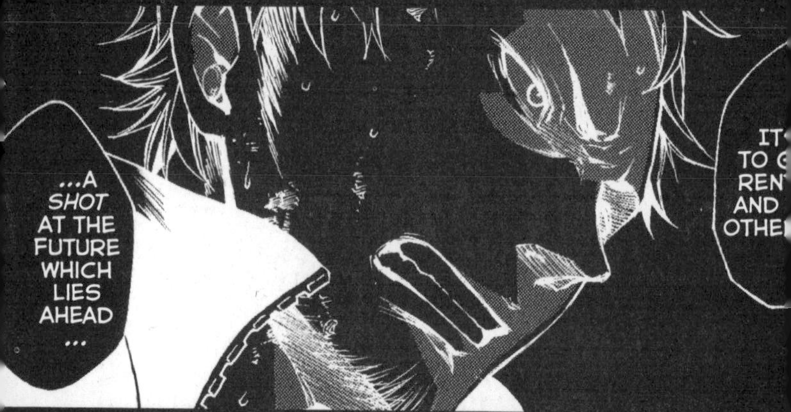

IT TO G REN AND OTHE
...A SHOT AT THE FUTURE WHICH LIES AHEAD ...

Emotions surge as a planet threatens collapse...

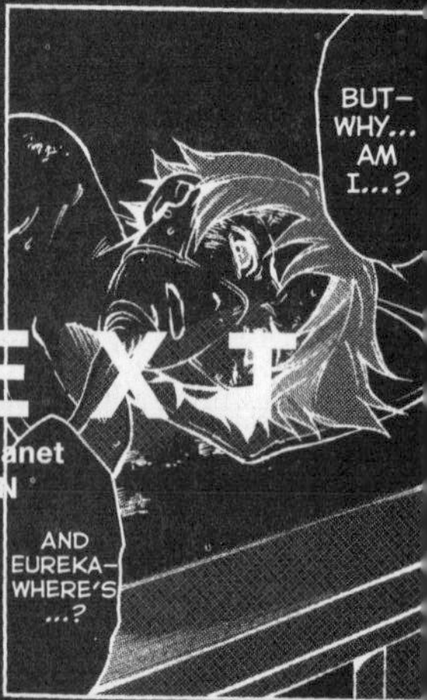

BUT— WHY... AM I...?
AND EUREKA— WHERE'S ...?

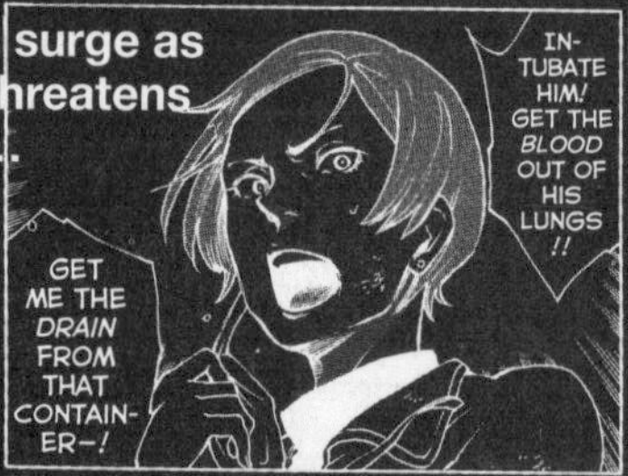

IN-TUBATE HIM! GET THE *BLOOD* OUT OF HIS LUNGS !!
GET ME THE *DRAIN* FROM THAT CONTAIN-ER—!

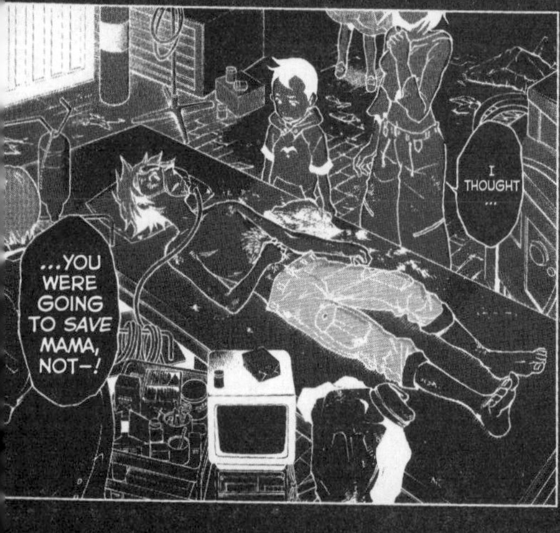

I THOUGHT ...
...YOU WERE GOING TO *SAVE* MAMA, NOT—!

NEXT

Psalms of Planet Eureka seveN

Heavily injured after the detonation of the self-destruct program, Renton manages to survive, thanks to the help of everyone aboard *Moonlight*. Reunited with Eureka at last within the center of the Coralian core—and with so many sacrifices having been made—what will be the "future" he chooses...?

Volume 6

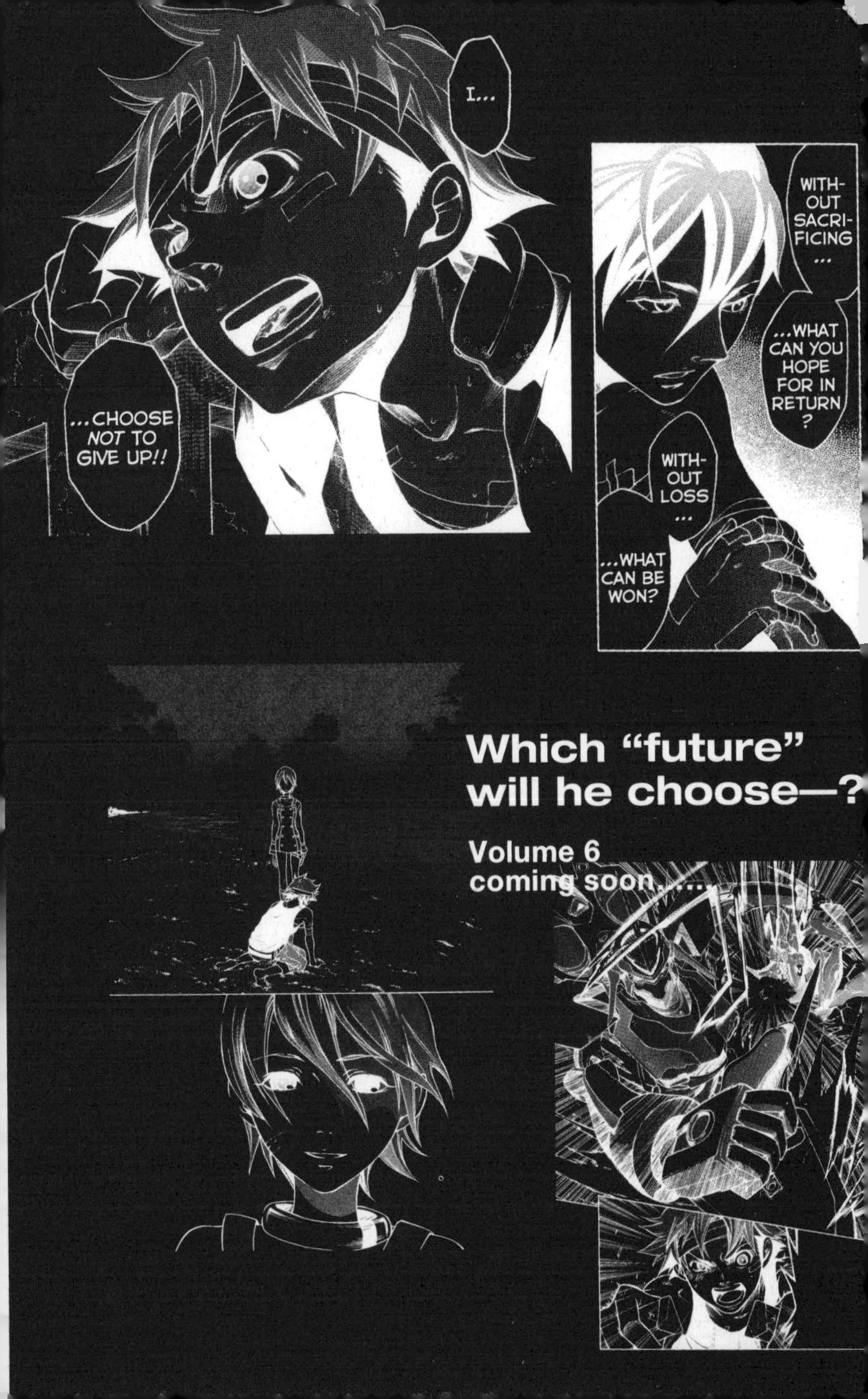
WITH-OUT SACRI-FICING ...
...WHAT CAN YOU HOPE FOR IN RETURN?
WITH-OUT LOSS ...
...WHAT CAN BE WON?
I...
...CHOOSE *NOT* TO GIVE UP!!
Which "future" will he choose—?
Volume 6 coming soon......

TO BE CONTINUED IN EUREKA SEVEN **VOL. 6**

ON SALE IN
**JULY
2007!**